Lecture Notes in Computer Science 3285

Commenced Publication in 1973
Founding and Former Series Editors:
Gerhard Goos, Juris Hartmanis, and Jan van Leeuwen

Editorial Board

David Hutchison
Lancaster University, UK

Takeo Kanade
Carnegie Mellon University, Pittsburgh, PA, USA

Josef Kittler
University of Surrey, Guildford, UK

Jon M. Kleinberg
Cornell University, Ithaca, NY, USA

Friedemann Mattern
ETH Zurich, Switzerland

John C. Mitchell
Stanford University, CA, USA

Moni Naor
Weizmann Institute of Science, Rehovot, Israel

Oscar Nierstrasz
University of Bern, Switzerland

C. Pandu Rangan
Indian Institute of Technology, Madras, India

Bernhard Steffen
University of Dortmund, Germany

Madhu Sudan
Massachusetts Institute of Technology, MA, USA

Demetri Terzopoulos
New York University, NY, USA

Doug Tygar
University of California, Berkeley, CA, USA

Moshe Y. Vardi
Rice University, Houston, TX, USA

Gerhard Weikum
Max-Planck Institute of Computer Science, Saarbruecken, Germany

Suresh Manandhar   Jim Austin
Uday Desai   Yoshio Oyanagi
Asoke Talukder (Eds.)

Applied Computing

Second Asian Applied Computing Conference,
AACC 2004
Kathmandu, Nepal, October 29-31, 2004
Proceedings

 Springer

Volume Editors

Suresh Manandhar
Jim Austin
University of York, Computer Science Department
York, YO10 5DD, UK
E-mail: {suresh, austin}@cs.york.ac.uk

Uday Desai
Indian Institute of Technology, Department of Electrical Engineering
Powai, Bombay 400076, India
E-mail: ubdesai@ee.iitb.ac.in

Yoshio Oyanagi
University of Tokyo, Department of Computer Science
7-3-1 Hongo, Bunkyo-ku, Tokyo 113-8654, Japan
E-mail: oyanagi@is.s.u-tokyo.ac.jp

Asoke Talukder
Indian Institute of Information Technology
Hosur Road, Bangalore 560 100, India
E-mail: akt@iiitb.ac.in

Library of Congress Control Number: 2004114271

CR Subject Classification (1998): C.2, C, D, F, H, I.2

ISSN 0302-9743
ISBN 3-540-23659-7 Springer Berlin Heidelberg New York

Springer is a part of Springer Science+Business Media

springeronline.com

© Springer-Verlag Berlin Heidelberg 2004
Printed in Germany

Typesetting: Camera-ready by author, data conversion by Olgun Computergrafik
Printed on acid-free paper   SPIN: 11333692   06/3142   5 4 3 2 1 0

Preface

The focus of the Asian Applied Computing Conference (AACC) is primarily to bring the research in computer science closer to practical applications. The conference is aimed primarily at topics that have immediate practical benefits. By hosting the conference in the developing nations in Asia we aim to provide a forum for engaging both the academic and the commercial sectors in that region. The first conference "Information Technology Prospects and Challenges" was held in May 2003 in Kathmandu, Nepal. This year the conference name was changed to "Asian Applied Computing Conference" to reflect both the regional- and the application-oriented nature of the conference.

AACC is planned to be a themed conference with a primary focus on a small set of topics although other relevant applied topics will be considered. The theme in AACC 2004 was on the following topics: *systems and architectures, mobile and ubiquitous computing, soft computing, man machine interfaces,* and *innovative applications for the developing world.*

AACC 2004 attracted 184 paper submissions from around the world, making the reviewing and the selection process tough and time consuming. The selected papers covered a wide range of topics: genetic algorithms and soft computing; scheduling, optimization and constraint solving; neural networks and support vector machines; natural language processing and information retrieval; speech and signal processing; networks and mobile computing; parallel, grid and high-performance computing; innovative applications for the developing world; cryptography and security; and machine learning. Papers were primarily judged on originality, presentation, relevance and quality of work. Papers that had clearly demonstrated results were given preference.

AACC 2004 not only consisted of the technical program covered in this proceedings but also included a workshop program, a tutorial program, and demo sessions. Special thanks are due to the general chair, Lalit Patnaik for the overall organization of the conference both in 2003 and 2004. Thanks are due to the tutorial chair Rajeev Kumar for looking after the tutorial program. The conference would not have been possible without the local organization efforts of Deepak Bhattarai and Sudan Jha. Thanks are due to Thimal Jayasooriya for help with the proofreading.

We would like to thank the program committee members for their efforts, and our reviewers for completing a big reviewing task in a short amount of time. Finally, we would like to thank all the authors who submitted papers to AACC 2004 and made possible a high-quality technical programme.

August, 2004

Suresh Manandhar
Jim Austin
Uday Desai
Asoke Talukder
Yoshio Oyanagi

Committee Chairs

General Chair	Lalit Patnaik (IISc, India)
Program Chair	Suresh Manandhar (University of York, UK)
Area Chairs	
Soft Computing	Jim Austin (University of York, UK)
Innovative Applications	
for the Developing World	Uday Desai (IIT, Bombay)
Man Machine Interfaces	Suresh Manandhar (University of York, UK)
Systems and Architectures	Yoshio Oyanagi (University of Tokyo)
Mobile and Ubiquitous Computing	Asoke Talukder (IIIT, Bangalore)
Local Organization	Sudan Jha (Nepal Engineering College)
Tutorials	Rajeev Kumar (IIT Kharagpur, India)
Publicity	
Southeast Asia	Prabhas Chongstitvatana
	(Chulalongkorn University, Thailand)
Europe & USA	Keshav Dahal
	(University of Bradford, UK)
Pacific	Andrew Simmonds
	(UTS, Sydney, Australia)
South Asia	Prabal Basu Roy
	(Lucent Technologies, India)

Local Organization

AACC 2004 was organized by the Nepal Engineering College, Kathmandu, Nepal.

Sponsoring Institutions

Ministry of Science and Technology, Nepal
WorldLink Communications, Nepal
Kathmandu Engineering College
Nepal College of Information Technology
IEEE Computer Society, India Council Chapter

Program Committee

Jay Bagga	Ball State University, USA
Michael Best	MIT Media Labs, USA
Shekhar Borgaonkar	HP Labs, India
Yiuming Cheung	Hong Kong Baptist University
Debabrata Das	IIIT Bangalore, India
Alistair Edwards	University of York, UK
Gita Gopal	HP Labs, USA
Hans-Gerhard Gross	Fraunhofer Institute, Germany
Puneet Gupta	Infosys Technologies, India
Frank van Harmelen	Vrije Universiteit, The Netherlands
Aynal Haque	BUET, Bangladesh
Visakan Kadirkamanathan	University of Sheffield, UK
Nik Kasabov	Auckland University of Technology, New Zealand
M.H. Kori	Bell Labs, India
Jinwen Ma	Peking University, China
Susil Meher	AIIMS, India
Arun Mehta	Consultant on ICT for Development, India
J.C. Mishra	IIT Kharagpur, India
Priyadarshi Nanda	University of Technology, Sydney, Australia
Mahesan Niranjan	University of Sheffield, UK
Paddy Nixon	University of Strathclyde, UK
Bhaskar Ramamurthy	IIT Madras, India
Partha Sarathi Roop	University of Auckland, New Zealand
Peter Thomas	University College London, UK
Jon Timmis	University of Kent, UK
Stefan Wermter	University of Sunderland, UK
Hujun Yin	UMIST, UK

Referees

R. Arvind	Arvind Keerthi	A.N. Rajagopalan
Chris Bailey	Chris Kimble	K. Rajan
Alan Black	Daniel Kudenko	Sumantra Dutta Roy
John Clark	Sunil Kumar	Pradip K. Sinha
Keshav Dahal	Bojian Liang	Bhabani Prasad Sinha
Andy Evans	Serge Massicotte	Purnendu Sinha
V.M. Gadre	S.N. Merchant	Nick Walton
Tom Hesseltine	Ian Miguel	Michael Weeks
Vicky Hodge	Simon O'Keefe	Richard Wilson
Thimal Jayasooriya	Nick Pears	Peter Young

Table of Contents

Machine Learning and Soft Computing

Scheduling, Optimisation and Constraint Solving

Neural Networks and SVMs

Natural Language Processing and Information Retrieval

Speech and Signal Processing

Networks and Mobile Computing

Parallel, Grid and High Performance Computing

Innovative Applications for the Developing World

Cryptography and Security

Effective Evolutionary Multimodal Optimization by Multiobjective Reformulation Without Explicit Niching/Sharing

Rajeev Kumar[1] and Peter Rockett[2]

[1] Department of Computer Science & Engineering
Indian Institute of Technology, Kharagpur 721 302, India
rkumar@cse.iitkgp.ernet.in
[2] Department of Electronic & Electrical Engineering
Mappin St, University of Sheffield, Sheffield S1 3JD, UK
p.rockett@sheffield.ac.uk

Abstract. In this paper, we revisit a general class of multimodal function optimizations using Evolutionary Algorithms (EAs) and, in particular, study a reformulation of multimodal optimization into a multiobjective framework. For both multimodal and multiobjective problems, most implementations need niching/sharing to promote diversity in order to obtain multiple (near-) optimal solutions. Such techniques work best when one has *a priori* knowledge of the problem - for most real problems, however, this is not the case. In this paper, we solve multimodal optimizations reformulated into multiobjective problems using a steady-state multiobjective genetic algorithm which preserves diversity without niching. We find diverse solutions in objective space for two multimodal functions and compare these with previously published work. The algorithm without any *explicit* diversity-preserving operator is found to produce diverse sampling of the Pareto-front with significantly lower computational effort.

1 Introduction

Evolutionary Algorithms (EAs) search a solution space from a set of points and are, therefore, attractive compared to traditional single-point based methods for those optimization domains which require multiple (near-) optimal solutions. Multimodal optimization (MMO) and multiobjective optimization (MOO) are two classes of optimizations belonging to this category. Having found multiple optimal or near-optimal solutions, a user selects a single solution or a subset of solutions based on some criterion. The problem solving strategy, therefore, should provide as many diverse solutions as possible.

In this context, niching/sharing techniques have been commonly employed to find a diverse set of solutions although such techniques work best when one has *a priori* knowledge of the problem. If the number of niches, a sharing function employing user-defined parameters computes the extent of sharing and may produce multiple (near-) optimal solutions. The technique has been employed by many researchers in the past, *e.g.*, [1-6] on many multimodal problems represented by analytic functions whose multimodality was known. However, in most real-world problems the analytical form is unknown, prior visualization of the solution set is not possible and the proper selection of niche formation parameters is problematic. Knowing the number of niches beforehand is a paradox since this implies one has *a priori* knowledge of the solution set. In actuality, most of the work related to multimodal optimization using

S. Manandhar et al. (Eds.): AACC 2004, LNCS 3285, pp. 1–8, 2004.

EAs has been done to *test* the efficacy of EAs in solving *known* problems rather than solving *unknown* problems. The niching/sharing strategy cannot be used reliably to solve multimodal problems where the solution is unknown due to the paradox mentioned above. Additionally, species formation in high-dimensional domains does not scale well and is a computationally-intensive task.

Much work has been done on locating multiple optimal values using niching algorithms – see Mahfoud [7] and Watson [8] for critical reviews of the approaches, testing functions and the performance measures and the relative merits/de-merits of each approach. Watson considered many test functions of varying complexity for a variety of performance measures and concluded that sharing-based GAs often perform *worse* than random search from the standpoint of the *sensitivity* of the user-selected sharing parameters. He further remarked that it is questionable whether niching-based GAs are really useful for identifying multiple fitness peaks of the MMOs.

The commonly used techniques for preventing genetic drift and promoting diversity are: sharing, mating restrictions, density count (crowding) and pre-selection operators. These approaches can be grouped into two classes: parameter-based sharing and parameter-less sharing. The pioneering sharing scheme of Goldberg and Richardson [1] needs a niching parameter, σ_{share} and is thus a parameter-based technique. Other sharing-based approaches, for example, the adaptive clustering algorithm [5] and the co-evolutionary sharing scheme [6] attempt to avoid σ_{share} directly; the clustering technique, is based on K-means clustering and requires an estimate of the initial number of clusters although the deterministic crowding [3] scheme does not need any niching parameters. Starting with the original work of Goldberg & Richardson [1], many other schemes have been proposed over the years and together with these, many studies have been done to measure the effectiveness and sensitivity of the values of the selected parameters on a wide-range of problems. For example, Watson [8] performed an extensive empirical analysis to find-out the effectiveness of niching-based GAs and remarked that it is debatable whether these are really very useful for identifying the multiple fitness peaks in MMOs. Many more studies, *e.g.*, [23-24] are available in literature.

In the absence of *a priori* knowledge of the multimodal function, some work has been done on parameter-less MMO. Mahfoud [3] developed a parameter-less method in the form of crowding which does not need *a priori* knowledge of the solution space. Hocaoglu & Sanderson [9] adopted a clustering technique to hypothesize-and-test the species formation for finding multiple paths for a mobile robot.

By analogy, finding multiple (near-) optimal solutions for a multimodal problem is identical to finding multiple (near-) optimal solutions for a multiobjective problem in the sense that in both types of problem-domain need to find all the possible diverse solutions which span the solution space. (For multimodal problems, the diversity of solutions is desired across the space of the variable(s) while for multiobjective problems diversity is required in objective space. In the multiobjective domain, the set of diverse solutions which are non-dominated form a (near-) optimal front known as (near-) Pareto-front.) For both problem domains, the most commonly used approach for preserving diversity is niching/sharing: see [8] for a review of the multimodal domain and [10-11] for reviews of multiobjective genetic optimization. Apart from the heuristic nature of sharing, the selection of the domain in which to perform sharing: variable (genotype) or objective (phenotype) is also open to debate. Some other recent studies have been done on combining convergence with diversity. Laumanns et al. [14] proposed an ε-dominance for getting ε-approximate Pareto-front for problems whose optimal Pareto set is *known*. Kumar & Rockett [15-16] proposed the use of rank-histograms for monitoring convergence of a Pareto front while maintaining diversity without any *explicit* diversity-preserving operator. Their algorithm was demonstrated to work for problems for which the solution was not known *a priori*. Secondly, assessing convergence does not need any prior knowledge for monitoring movement towards the Pareto front using rank-histograms. This approach has been found to significantly reduce computational effort.

Deb [17] retargeted single-variable multimodal problems into two-variable, two-objective problems and studied niching/sharing techniques for finding diverse solutions for some standard test functions [17]. While presenting his results, Deb observed that variable-space sharing is more effective than objective space sharing (p 19, [17]) however we believe that this interpretation cannot be generalized across all problem-domains. Interestingly, in a recent study, Purshouse & Fleming [18] studied the effect of sharing on a wide-range of MOO two-criteria benchmark problems using a range of performance measures and concluded that sharing can be beneficial, but can also prove surprisingly ineffective if the parameters are not properly tuned. They statistically observed that parameter-less sharing is more robust than parameter-based equivalents (including those with automatic fine-tuning during program execution).

In this context, we have revisited MMO using EAs and attempted to solve MMO problems without any problem-dependent parameters using the same reformulation of multimodal optimization into a multiobjective framework [17]. We have used PCGA [16], a steady-state algorithm [19] and we have used two benchmark problems which have been considered previously. The key result of this paper is that we demonstrate that diversity in objective space can be achieved without any *explicit diversity-preserving* operator.

2 Test Functions and Results

We have tested the PCGA algorithm on two multimodal functions which were considered by earlier researchers using multiobjective formulations. For fair comparison, we have used exactly the same formulation, coding, identifiers and parameters, as far as is known. We repeated the experiments many hundreds of times, each with a different initial population to check the consistency of the results. Typical results selected on the basis of their *average* performance are presented in the following subsections.

2.1 Function F1

First, we considered a bi-modal function $g(x_2)$ given by

$$g(x_2) = 2.0 - \exp\left\{-\left(\frac{x_2 - 0.2}{0.004}\right)^2\right\} - 0.8 \exp\left\{-\left(\frac{x_2 - 0.6}{0.4}\right)^2\right\}; \quad g(x_2) > 0$$

For, $(0 < x_2 < 1)$, $g(x_2)$ is a function with a broad local minima at $x_2 = 0.6$, and a spike-like global minima at $x_2 = 0.2$ (Figure 1). Retargeting this single-objective problem to a multiobjective one, the corresponding, two-objective problem having two variables x_1 (>0) and x_2 is:

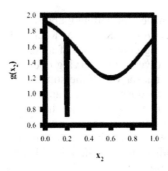

Fig. 1. Bi-modal function F1

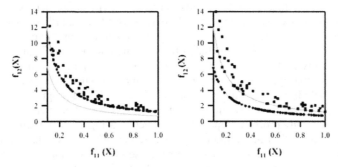

Fig. 2. Function **F1** – Two sets of population, one each converging to (a) local minima ($x_2 = 0.6$), and (b) global minima ($x_2 = 0.2$)

$$Minimize \quad f_{11}(x_1, x_2) = x_1$$

$$Minimize \quad f_{12}(x_1, x_2) = \frac{g(x_2)}{x_1}$$

For a fixed value of $g(x_2)$, each $f_{11} - f_{12}$ plot is a hyperbola. (See [17] for function characteristics and a related theorem.) For each local and global minimum solution we get one local and global Pareto front, respectively; each of the optimal-fronts are shown by gray-colored curves in Figures 2. We generated many hundreds of random initial populations and observed that, with a population size of 60, most of the individuals were close to the *local* Pareto front but barely one was close to the to the *global* Pareto front. For each of the many runs, we got the whole population of sixty individuals converged within a range of 12 to 41 epochs, with an average of 23.8 epochs per run. (We were able to stop further population evolution by monitoring the advancement of the population to the Pareto front using rank-histograms [16].) Results from two typical runs are shown in Figure 2. The initial population is shown with open squares and the final converged population with filled circles in Figure 2; Figure 2(a) shows the convergence to the local front while Figure 2(b) shows the global front. For some solutions, the population gets trapped in the local Pareto front. We were able to locate the global Pareto front in $36 - 44\%$ of the independently initialized runs, an observation identical to Deb's. The fact that we had a similar success rate to Deb's NSGA in finding the local-to-global Pareto front suggests that this ratio may be an intrinsic feature of the problem connected to a density-of-states-type argument in the objective space.

Deb [17] studied this problem using a niching-based genetic algorithm implementation and reported the results for 100 generations. The results in Figures 2 are superior to those of Deb (Fig. 5, Page 10 in [17]) in terms of the well-known metrics: (i) closeness to the true Pareto-optimal front, (ii) diversity across the front, and (iii) the visualization of the two-dimensional Pareto front. (For such a simple two-dimensional objective space both diversity and convergence can *trivially* be assessed directly from simple plots, thus we do not include any metrics.) Most importantly, the PCGA implementation without an *explicit* diversity preserving mechanism achieved better sampling at reduced computational cost.

2.2 Function F2

Next, we consider the function:

$$Minimize \ \ f_{21}(x_1) = 1 - \exp(-4x_1)sin^4(5\pi x_1); \ \ 0 \le x_1 \le 1$$

The function $f_{21}(x_1)$ is shown in Figure 3(a) by a gray-curve and has five minima for different values of x_1. Retargeting this to a two-objective function, the second objective [17] is:

$$Minimize \ \ f_{22}(x_1,x_2) = g(x_2) \times h(f_{21},g)$$

where,

$$h(f_{21},g) = \begin{cases} 1 - \left(\dfrac{f_{21}}{g} \right)^4, & if \ f_{21} \le g \\ 0, & otherwise \end{cases}$$

The functions f_{21} and $h(.)$ can have different settings for various complexity levels. We have taken the h function identical to that used in [17]. For g, we have modified the $g(x_2)$ function of the previous test problem (*F1*) to a single-modal function with a minimum value equal to unity. Moreover, it does not matter which $g(x_2)$ function is chosen since the Pareto front is formed for the particular value of x_2 which minimizes $g(x_2)$. The corresponding concave Pareto front is shown in Figure 3(b) with a gray-curve.

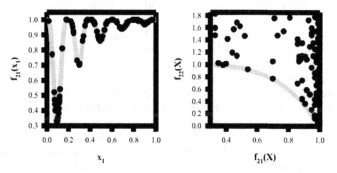

Fig. 3. Function F2 – Initial population shown in (a) f_{21}- x_1 and (b) f_{21}- f_{22} plots

We generated an initial population consisting of 100 individuals. The f_{21}- x_1 and f_{21}- f_{22} plots corresponding to the initial population are shown in Figures 3(a) and 3(b), respectively. This randomly assigned population is uniformly distributed as are the points x_1 on f_{21}-x_1 plot. (All the five minima of function f_{21} can be seen in the randomly generated population which is the case with most initial populations.) We stress that this sort of uniform population distribution along the x-axis of the f_{21}- x_1 plot is inherent to the random number generator and has little to do with the diversity-achieving ability of an algorithm. (Nonetheless, for such functions, this is the nature of the plot which is desired from a MMO algorithm.) We have shown this plot (Figure 3(a)) obtained from the zero epochs (*i.e.* the initial population) for comparison with the final plot (500 epochs) reported by Deb (Figure 14(a), page 18 in [17]). Both are almost identical and show the diversity of the solutions/populations across the variable-space.

Using PCGA, the population at epoch 100 is shown in Figure 4. The sampling of the Pareto front is superior to both the results reported in [17] after 500 generations using parameter- and objective-space niching. This result is wholly consistent with what we have observed with test function *F1* in the previous sub-section.

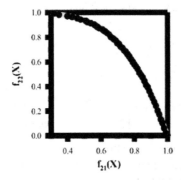

Fig. 4. Function F2 – Pareto-front and the population at epoch 100

3 Conclusions

We have demonstrated the application of a steady-state algorithm to the reformulation of two multimodal optimizations. The algorithm achieved diverse sampling of the Pareto front which is the key factor for a multiobjective optimization. This is facilitated mainly by: (i) the steady-state nature of the algorithm, (ii) no loss of any non-dominated solution during evolution, (iii) progressive advancement towards the Pareto front, and (iv) a reduced range of Pareto ranks at each iteration.

This paper has shown that we can effectively solve multimodal problems by recasting to the multiobjective domain *without an explicit niching/sharing*. This means that we do not need *a priori* knowledge of the function multimodality. Most of the real-world problems are of unknown nature, so it is a paradox to have prior knowledge of niches and their counts. Further, we need fewer epochs/generations to get multiple solutions, and this is partly attributed to monitoring of the advancement towards the Pareto-front using rank-histograms [15-16]. On comparing our results with those in previous work [17], the algorithm employed here provided superior sampling (in terms diversity and proximity to the true Pareto front) at reduced computational cost for both the multimodal functions investigated.

This type of diversity-preserving mechanism works for those multimodal problems which can be retargeted to the multiobjective domain and solved using multiobjective optimization techniques.

References

1. Goldberg, D. E., Richardson, J.: Genetic Algorithms with Sharing for Multimodal Function Optimization. Proc. 2nd Int. Conf. Genetic Algorithms (1987) 41-49
2. Deb, K., Goldberg, D. E.: An Investigation of Niche and Species Formation in Genetic Function Optimization. Proc. 3rd Int. Conf. Genetic Algorithms (1989), 42-50
3. Mahfoud, S. W.: Crowding and Preselection Revisited. Proc. Parallel Problem Solving from Nature (PPSN-2), 1992
4. Beasley, D., Bull, D. R., Martin, R. R.: A Sequential Niche Technique for Multimodal Function Optimization. Evolutionary Computation 1 (1993) 101-125
5. Yin, X., Germay, N.: A Fast Genetic Algorithm with Sharing Scheme using Cluster Analysis Methods in Multimodal Function Optimization. Proc. Int. Conf. Artificial Neural Nets and Genetic Algorithms (1993)
6. Goldberg, D. E., Wang, L.: Adaptive Niching via Coevolutionary Sharing. Genetic Algorithms and Evolutionary Strategies in Engineering and Computer Science (1998)
7. Mahfoud, S. W.: Niching Methods for Genetic Algorithms. IlliGAL Tech. Report 95001, Illinois Genetic Algorithm Laboratory, Univ. Illinois, Urbana, (1995)
8. Watson, J. P.: A Performance Assessment of Modern Niching Methods for Parameter Optimization Problems. Gecco-99 (1999)
9. Hocaoglu, C., Sanderson, A. C.: Multimodal Function Optimization Using Minimal Representation Size Clustering and Its Application to Planning Multipaths. Evolutionary Computation 5 (1997) 81-104
10. Deb, K.: Multiobjective Optimization Using Evolutionary Algorithms. Chichester, UK: Wiley, 2001
11. Coello C. A. C., Van Veldhuizen, D. A., Lamont, G. B.: Evolutionary Algorithms for Solving Multi-Objective Problems. Boston, MA: Kluwer, May 2002
12. Fonseca, C. M., Fleming, P. J.: Multiobjective optimization and multiple constraint handling with evolutionary algorithms-Part I: a unified formulation. IEEE Trans. Systems, Man and Cybernetics-Part A: Systems and Humans, 28(1): 26 - 37, 1998
13. Zitzler, E., Laumanns, M., Thiele, L.: SPEA2 – Improving the Strength Pareto Evolutionary Algorithm. EUROGEN (2001)
14. Laumanns, M., Thiele, L., Deo, K., Zitzler, E.: Combining Convergence and Diversity in Evolutionary Multiobjective Optimization. Evolutionary Computation 10: 263-182, 2002
15. Kumar, R., Rockett, P. I.: Assessing the Convergence of Rank-Based Multiobjective Genetic Algorithms. Proc. IEE/ IEEE 2nd Int. Conf. Genetic Algorithms in Engineering Systems: Innovations & Applications (1997) 19-23
16. Kumar, R., Rockett, P. I.: Improved Sampling of the Pareto-Front in Multiobjective Genetic Optimizations by Steady-State Evolution: A Pareto Converging Genetic Algorithm. Evolutionary Computation 10(3): 282-314, 2002
17. Deb, K.: Multiobjective Genetic Algorithms: Problem Difficulties and Construction of Test Problems. Evolutionary Computation 7 (1999) 1-26
18. Purshouse, R. C., Fleming, P. J.: Elitism, Sharing and Ranking Choices in Evolutionary Multi-criterion Optimization. Research Report No. 815, Dept. Automatic Control & Systems Engineering, University of Sheffield, Jan. 2002
19. Whitley, L. D.: The GENITOR Algorithm and Selection Pressure: Why Rank Based Allocation of Reproductive Trials is Best. Proc. 3rd Int. Conf. Genetic Algorithm (1989) 116-121

20. Davidor, Y.: A Naturally Occurring Niche and Species Phenomenon: the Model and First Results. Proc. 4th Int. Conf. Genetic Algorithm (1991) 257-262
21. Eshelman, L. J.: The CHC Adaptive Search Algorithm: How to have Safe Search when Engaging in Nontraditional Genetic Recombination. FOGA (1991) 265-283
22. De Jong K., Sarma, J.: Generation Gap Revisited. Foundations of Genetic Algorithms II (1993) 19-28
23. Mengshoel, O. J., Goldberg, D. E.: Probability Crowding: Deterministic Crowding with Probabilistic Replacement. Proc. GECCO (1999) 409-416
24. Li, J.-P., Balazs, M. E., Parks, G. T., Clarkson, P. J.: A Species Conserving Genetic Algorithm for Multimodal Function Optimization. Evolutionary Computation 10(3): 207-234, 2002

Development of Genetic Algorithm Embedded KNN for Fingerprint Recognition

H.R. Sudarshana Reddy[1] and N.V. Subba Reddy[2]

[1] University BDT College of Engg.
Davanagere-57704, India
hrsreddy@hotmail.com
[2] Manipal Institute of Technology,
Manipal, India
dr_nvsreddy@rediffmail.com

Abstract. A Kohonen self-organizing neural network embedded with genetic algorithm for fingerprint recognition is proposed in this paper. The genetic algorithm is embedded to initiate the Kohonen classifers. By the proposed approach, the neural network learning performance and accuracy are greatly enhanced. In addition, the genetic algorithm can successfully avoid the neural network from being trapped in a local minimum. The proposed method was tested for the recognition of fingerprints. The results were promising to applications.

Keywords: Fingerprint, KNN, Genetic Algorithm, Image enhancement.

1   Introduction

Fingerprints are imprints formed by friction ridges of the skin in the fingers and thumbs. They have long been used for identification because of their immutability and individuality. Immutability refers to the permanent and unchanging character of the pattern on each finger, from before birth until decomposition after death. Individuality refers to the uniqueness of ridge details across individuals, the probability that two fingerprints are alike is about 1 in 1.9 x 10^{15}. The use of computers in fingerprint recognition is highly desirable in many applications, such as forensic science, security clearance, and anthropological and medical studies. The scientific foundations of employment for personal identification were laid by F.Galton (1822-1916), H.Faulds (1843-1930), H.Wilder (1864-1928) and H.Poll (1877-1939). Many approaches to fingerprint identification have been presented in the literature. Yet, it is still an active research field.

In the unsupervised learning scheme, Kohonen self-organizing feature map is widely used. The self-organizing feature maps are neural networks that can nonlinearly map N-dimensional vectors to a two-dimensional array. The input data representing similar characteristics are mapped to the same clusters. This nonlinear projection makes the topological neighborhood relationship geometrically explicit in the low dimensional feature space.

With unsupervised KNN, an improper selection of initial weights may result in NN with isolated regions without forming adequate clusters. Because of the optimization tendency in each evolution/generation, the genetic algorithm is proposed to decide the initial weights intelligently. In such hybrid system, the genetic algorithm is served to

S. Manandhar et al. (Eds.): AACC 2004, LNCS 3285, pp. 9–16, 2004.

help coarse clustering. The competitive learning is then performed to fine tune the weight vectors.

In this paper, the genetic algorithm embedded Kohonen self-organizing feature map is proposed. By this new technique, the NN is used for the recognition of unconstrained fingerprints.

2 Paradigm of Genetic Algorithms

Genetic Algorithms (GAs) are global search and optimization methods simulating natural evolution and natural genetics [Holland, 1975; Goldberg, 1989]. GAs have been initially developed by John Holland, his colleagues, and his students at the University of Michigan.

GAs start with a whole randomly initialized population of feasible solutions. Each individual solution in the population is referred to as chromosomes. These chromosomes compute to reproduce offspring based on the Darwinian principle of survival of the fittest. In each generation "the best get more copier, the average stay even and worst die off" [Goldberg, 1989]. Hopefully, after a number of generations of evolutions, the chromosomes remaining in the group are the optimal solutions.

Genetic algorithms has become an efficient tool for search, optimization and machine learning. Even in the pre-genetic algorithms era, concepts of GAs had been applied in game playing (Bagley, 1967), pattern recognition (Cavicchio, 1972), biological cell simulation (Rosenberg, 1970) and complex function optimization (Hollsteen, 1971). GAs has been widely employed in many fields, including traveling salesman problem (Brady, 1985; Grefenstette, 1985; Suh and Van Gucht, 1987), VLSI circuit layout design (Davis and Smith, 1985; Fourman, 1985), optimization of gas pipeline layout (Goldberg, 1983), function optimization (De, Jong, 1975), genetic based machine learning system (Bickel et al. 1987), genetic based classifier system (Riolo, 1986, Zhou, 1985, Wilson, 1986), and many other instances.

3 Genetic Algorithm Embedded Kohonen Neural Networks

The genetic algorithm is used to intelligently decide the initial weights and the competitive learning for the further unsupervised training. The frame work of the proposed system is shown in Figure 1. After the initial populations are generated, an individual with high fitness will be selected to mate for evolution. The best individual will be kept in each generation. The chromosomes of the individual will be decoded to network weights. The competitive learning is then applied to train neural networks.

4 Feature Extraction and Database Generation

The proposed method consist of the processing steps of image enhancement, binarization, feature extraction and recognition.

4.1 Image Acquisition

In our work, we have collected 50 volunteers fingerprint, each of 10 resulting in 500 fingerprints. Special ink and paper is used for recording the fingerprints. The fingerprints obtained are then scanned by a regular computer flatbed scanner as gray level

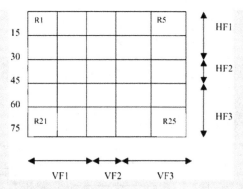

Feature Vector Calculation:
CF1= Sum of regions of R(3,7,8,9,11,12,13,14,15,17,18,19,23)
CF2= Sum of regions of R(3,4,5,6,7,9,10)
CF3= Sum of regions of R(8,12,14,18)
DF1= Sum of regions of R(1,6,7,11,12,13,16,17,18,19,21,22,23,24,25)
DF2= Sum of regions of R(5,9,10,13,14,15,16,17,18,19,20,21,22,23,24,25)
DF3= Sum of regions of R(1,2,3,4,5,6,7,8,9,11,12,13,16,17,21)
DF4= Sum of regions of R(1,2,34,5,7,8,9,10,13,14,15,18,19,20,25)
DF5= Sum of regions of R(1,2,5,6,7,8,11,12,13,17,18,19,20,24,25)
DF6= Sum of regions of R(4,5,7,8,9,10,12,13,14,16,17,18,19,21,22)

Fig. 1. Modified 15 Segement Encoder

images with 400 dpi. The performance of the classifier improves as the number of samples used to train the system increases. But it is very difficult to normally collect very large number of samples, we have developed an algorithm that uses a standard set of fingerprints and iterative process produces a large number of samples by distorting the original set of samples.

4.2 Fingerprint Enhancement and Binarization

The ridge structures in the digitized fingerprint images are not always well. Therefore, many methods have been proposed to enhance the raw fingerprint images. We have used fingerprint image enhancement by using orientation field, and also the binarization by the method proposed by Yuling He [10].

4.3 Feature Extraction

Feature extraction refers to the process of finding a mapping that reduces the dimensionality of the patterns. Feature extraction is an important step in achieving good performance of optical character recognition systems.

In this paper, we propose the modified feature extraction method which makes use of a 75x75 bit map as shown in the Fig. 2. The bitmap is divided into 3 horizontal bars (HF1, HF2, HF3), 3 vertical bars (VF1, VF2, VF3), 3 central bars (CF1, CF2, CF3), six diagonal bars (DF1, DF2, DF3, DF4, DF5, DF6). Using these 15 regions, 15 feature of the pattern are extracted. Computationally, the horizontal feature HF1 is defined as the number of marked bits in the region HF1 divided by the total number of bits in that region. Similarly, all other features are extracted.

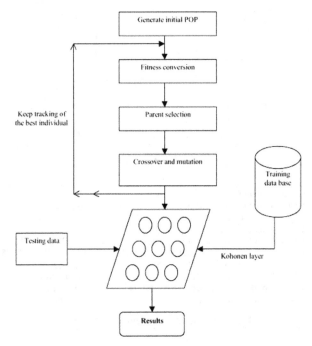

Fig. 2. Genetic algorithm embedded Kohonen neural network

5 GA-KNN Algorithm for Fingerprint Recognition

5.1 Modified Genetic Algorithm for the Initialization of Weights of Kohonen Layer

1. Define w_{ji} $(1 \le i \le m)$ to be the weight from input node i to the output node j at time t. Initialize the weight values to small random real numbers for all N x N neurons of KNN layer.
2. Draw the input sample x from the input space. Apply corresponding input vector $x_1(t)$, $x_2(t)$, …… $x_m(t)$ to the input layer at time t.
3. Fitness calculation:
   (a) *Euclidean Distance (ED):*
       Compute the ED between input vector x and weight vector w_{ij}, given by
       $$ED(j) = \sqrt{[x(t) - w_{ij}(t)]^2},$$
       for all j = 1, N x N, where N x N is the dimension of the Kohonon layer.
   (b) *Fitness Value (FV):*
       $$FV(j) = \frac{100 - ED(j)}{100}$$

   (c) Select the best fit N1 neurons and respective weights are the initial population.

4. Initialize the iteration count t = 0 read the all N1 neurons input weights and treat this as strings of the initial population, with fitness value FV.
5. Compute the average fitness (AF) given by

$$AF = \frac{\displaystyle\sum_{j=1}^{N1} FV(j)}{N1}$$

And individual Fitness (IF),

$$IF(j) = \frac{FV(j)}{AF}, \qquad j = 1, \ldots\ldots\ldots, N1$$

6. Select the best 'P' individuals according to Elitism selection method (where 'P' is the initial population number).
7. Do the random selection for forming the mating pool.
8. Do the one point cross over randomly. This results in new off-springs.
9. Here mutation is neglected, since the strings are real numbers (not binary strings).
10. After above process, new population is formed, increment the iteration t = t + 1, go to step 4, and stop the iteration process when required number of iterations are reached. Replace the old weights with new weights in KNN layer.
11. Continue the same procedure from step 2 to step 10 for different input vectors.
12. After completion of all the input vectors, now the weights of KNN are intelligently initialized for the further unsupervised training.

5.2 KNN Learning Algorithm

1. Initialization
Read the weight vector $w_{ji}(t)$ ($1 \le i < m$), computed from the modified genetic algorithm as the initial weight vector at time t. Set the initial radius of the neighborhood around node j, Nj(0) to be large.
    Choose the initial value for the learning rate parameter α_0.

2. Sampling
Draw the input sample x from the input space. Apply corresponding input vector $x_1(t)$, $x_2(t)$, ... $x_m(t)$ to be the input layer at time t.

3. Similarity Matching
Find the winner node by applying Euclidean minimum distance criterion.
    Distance calculation: Compute the distance dj between the input and each output node j given by

$$dj = \sqrt{[xi(t) - w_{ij}(t)]^2}$$

Select the minimum distance: Designate the output code with minimum distance dj to be j^*.

4. Weight updating

Update the weights for the winner node j^* and its neighbors, defined by the neighborhood size $Nj^*(t)$. New weights are

$$w_{ij}(t + 1) = w_{ij}(t) + \alpha(t) [x_i(t) - w_{ij}(t)]$$

For all j in $Nj^*(t)$, and $1 \leq i < m$. The learning rate $\alpha(t)$ has a value in the range (0, 1), given by

$$\alpha = \alpha_0(1 - t/T)$$

where α_0 = Initial value,

   t = The current training iteration,
   T = Total number of training iterations to be done.
   The α begins at a value α_0 and is decreased until it reaches a value closer to zero.

The neighborhood size $Nj^*(t)$ also decreases in size as time goes on, thus localizing the area of maximum activity.

5. Continue with step 2 until all patterns are presented.

5.3 Training Phase

The numerical data corresponding to the training set are self organized into a feature map. Final updated weights of the entire network are stored in one file and the winner nodes (centroids) of all the samples are stored in another file. The weights corresponding to the winner nodes are considered as prototypes of the input patterns. The Euclidean distance measure is applied to assign any pattern to its closest prototype.

   For a given pattern x, if

$$\left| x - w_{ji}^* \right| = \min \left| x - w_{ji} \right|$$

x is assigned to the prototype w_{ji}^*. In the feature map, the prototypes of the same class (or classes with similar feature characteristics) are close to one another. The labels corresponding to these prototypes are then used in classifying the unknown patterns present in the test set.

6 Recognition Algorithm

1. Read the test sample to be classified and identify the winner node after mapping the input to the classifier.
2. Find the Euclidean distance from the winner node to the centroids of all the classes as follows

$$ED (c, n) = \sqrt{[(c, n) - y]^2}$$

Where x is the centroid vector y is the winner node vector.

c – indicates for different classes c = 1, 2, ... ,10
n– Number of centroids in each class.

3. Compute the confidence value (CV) for each centroid

CV (c, n) = 100 – ED (c, n)

For all n and for all c

4. Compute the Average Confidence Value (ACV) for each class

$$ACV\ (c) = \frac{CV\ (c,\ n)}{n}$$

5. For each sample, an array of ten ACV values are obtained. Each value represents the extent to which the sample belongs to a particular class.

6. The test sample belongs to class which is having highest ACV.

7. Continue the above procedure until the entire test patterns are presented.

7 Experiments and Results

In the interest of investigating the performance of the fingerprint recognition that uses genetic algorithm embedded Kohonen neural network, the system is executed with 10 classes of fingerprints. Each class is a collection of four hundred fingerprints created by distorting a standard fingerprint of a volunteer. Four thousand samples, which are generated, are used. 2000 samples each are used for training and testing.

The population size used is 200, and the size of the Kohonen layer is 20 x 20. The probability of crossover (P_c) used is 0.9, in this algorithm the probability of mutation is zero. And the number of iterations performed is 20. Since the population size is very large, increase in the number of iterations increases the computation time. Always not necessarily all the 2000 training samples are used for initializing the weights using the genetic algorithm. It is appropriate to use the optimal number so that it reduces the computation time. We have observed that by decreasing the number of training samples is not going to affect its performance much.

KNN classifier uses 20 x 20 output units, and 15 input units. For each pattern, the extracted 15 feature values are used. The initial neighborhood size is 15. The value of learning rate (α) varies from 0 to 1, at various stages during the training process. The following conclusions are drawn with respect to the results tabulated in Table 1.

1. The average recognition rate of 92.75% is achieved by the modified genetic algorithm, but recognition rate is 94.40% with the KNN classifier.

2. With the use of Neuro-Genetic architecture its performance has been increased to 98.15%.

3. The rejection rate is zero in all the three methods indicates that, the system has classified all the given patterns of the test data.

4. The performance of the proposed systems compares favorably with the existing standard methods available in the literature.

Table 1. Comparison of three developed architectures for the recognition of 2000 fingerprints on Pentium IV processor

Sl. No.	Technique	Recognition rate (%)	Substitution rate (%)	Rejection rate (%)
1	Modified genetic algorithm	92.75%	7.25%	0%
2	KNN Classifier	94.40%	5.60%	0%
3	Genetic algorithm embedded KNN	98.15%	1.85%	0%

8   Conclusion

In this paper, we have presented a novel hybrid method for the recognition of unconstrained fingerprints. In the first phase genetic algorithm is used to initialize the weights of Kohonen layer, instead of random initialization of weights. In the second step the KNN classifier is used for the classification of fingerprints .The result demonstrates the performance enhancement by the aid of genetic algorithms. Note that there is some computation time required for the genetic algorithms in the proposed scheme. However, as the overall learning characteristic is improved, the total required time is significantly reduced. In the proposed method, a problem of learning stagnation due to the improper initial weights no longer exists. The proposed method reduces the computation time and also facilitates the good recognition rate.

References

1. Gader P.D. and M.A. Khabou, "Automatic feature generation for handwritten digit recognition", IEEE Transactions on Pattern analysis and Machine Intelligence. Vol. 18, No.12, pp. 1256-1261, Dec, 1996.
2. Galton. F. "Fingerprints", London: McMillan, 1982.
3. Goldberg D.E. "Genetic Algorithms in search, Optimization and Machine Learning", Addison Wesley, Pub, 1989.
4. Henry. E.R. "Classification and uses of Fingerprints", London: Routledge, 1990.
5. Jain A.K et al., "Feature selection evaluation, application and small sample performance", IEEE Transactions on Pattern Analysis and Machine Intelligence., Vol. 19, No. 2, pp. 153 – 158 Feb., 1997.
6. Kamijo. M. "Classifying Fingerprint Images using Neural Network: Deriving the Classification State", IEEE International Conference on Neural Network, Vol. 3, 1932-1937pp, 1993.
7. Kangas J.A., T. Kohonen and J.T. Laaksonen, "Variants of self-organizing Maps", IEEE Transactions on Neural Networks, 1(1), 93-99, March, 1990.
8. Kohenon T, "The self-organizing map", Proc. of IEEE, Vol. 78, No. 9, September, 1990.
9. Moayer. B. and Fu. K.S. "A Syntactic Approach to Fingerprint Pattern Recognition", Pattern Recognition, Vol. 7, 1-23pp, 1975.
10. Yulinang He., Jie Tian. "Image enhancement and minutiae matching in fingerprint verification", Pattern Recognition Letters Vol. 24, 1349-1360, 2003.

Genetic IMM_NN Based Tracking of Multiple Point Targets in Infrared Image Sequence

Mukesh A. Zaveri, S.N. Merchant, and Uday B. Desai

SPANN Lab, Electrical Engineering Dept., IIT Bombay – 400076
{mazaveri,merchant,ubdesai}@ee.iitb.ac.in

Abstract. Tracking of maneuvering and non-maneuvering targets simultaneously is a challenging task for multiple target tracking (MTT) system. Interacting multiple model (IMM) filtering has been used for tracking multiple targets successfully. IMM needs to evaluate model probability using an observation assigned to the track. We propose a tracking algorithm based on IMM which exploits the genetic algorithm for data association. Genetic algorithm performs nearest neighbor (NN) based data assignment. A mixture probability density function (pdf) for the likelihood of the observation is used for data assignment.

1 Introduction

In real world application, a target may be maneuvering or non maneuvering and there is no apriori knowledge about its movement. This makes the model selection for target tracking a difficult problem. Along with tracking an observation is to be assigned to the target for state update and prediction. Here data assignment plays a major role for maintaining true trajectory in the presence of dense clutter. The proposed scheme overcomes all these difficulties. A review of different tracking and data association methods is presented in [1]. IMM [2] approach includes different models for the target dynamics and hence, it is possible to track maneuvering and non-maneuvering targets simultaneously. IMM filtering needs an observation to be assigned to the track for calculation of model probability. For the data assignment, different methods IMM_NN and IMM_PDA have been proposed in [3]. IMM_PDA requires the evaluation of all possible events, consequently the complexity of the algorithm increases exponentially with increase in number of targets and observations. IMM_NN uses nearest neighbor based data association, but it requires determining an observation which gives minimum error measure *among all the models* used for tracking. Typically, Munkres' optimal data assignment algorithm is used for this purpose.

We propose a method based on IMM filtering, which exploits the genetic algorithm for data association. Genetic algorithm gives the best solution for observation-to-track pairing. It uses a mixture pdf for the likelihood of an observation. The mixture pdf takes care of model likelihood explicitly instead of finding a model which gives minimum error measure for a given observation. Genetic algorithm is widely used to solve complex optimization problem; unfortunately, there is no guarantee of obtaining the optimal assignment. But it does

S. Manandhar et al. (Eds.): AACC 2004, LNCS 3285, pp. 17–25, 2004.
© Springer-Verlag Berlin Heidelberg 2004

provide a set of potential solutions in the process of finding the best solution. In [4], the neural energy function is optimized for solving the data association problem. The drawback with the neural net based approach is that it requires large number of iterations and the selections of coefficients is by trial and error. In our approach, we do not use neural energy function as it is used in [4]. The proposed method avoids complex logic of Munkres' optimal algorithm.

2   Genetic IMM_NN Tracking Algorithm

In this section, the problem is described in multiple model framework for data association. We assume that there is no measurement (occlusion of the target) or only one measurement from the target at a given time. Multiple measurements from the same target is ruled out for infrared target detection and tracking application. With this assumption, we propose a method for data association using genetic algorithm [5], which provide robust alternative to Munkres' optimal data assignment algorithm [6] based on nearest neighbor method. Let N_t be the number of targets at time k, and it may vary with time. Φ_k represents concatenated combined state estimates for all targets $t = 1, \ldots, N_t$, i.e.

$$\Phi_k = (\Phi_{1,k}, \Phi_{2,k}, \ldots, \Phi_{N_t,k})^T$$

where $\Phi_{t,k}$ is combined state estimate at time instant k for target t. The state at time instant k by model m for target t is represented by $\phi_{t,k}^m$. Let the observation process $\mathbf{Y}_k$ and its realization at time instant k be denoted by a vector $\mathbf{y}_k = (y_{k,1}, y_{k,2}, \ldots, y_{k,N_k})^T$, where N_k denotes the number of measurements obtained at time k, N_k may also vary with time. To assign measurements to targets, an association process defined as $\mathbf{Z}_k$ is formed. It is used to represent the true but unknown origin of measurements. $\mathbf{z}_k$ is a realization of an association process at time instant k, and it is referred to as an association matrix.

For each model, a validation matrix or equivalently an association matrix is defined. For IMM, we represent $\mathbf{z}_k$ as combined (logically OR operation) realization of $\mathbf{Z}_k$ and is defined as,

$$\mathbf{z}_k = \mathbf{z}_{k,1} + \mathbf{z}_{k,2} + \ldots + \mathbf{z}_{k,M}$$

where $\mathbf{z}_{k,m}$ is the association matrix at time instant k for model m. Here M is the total number of models used in the IMM algorithm. Each $\mathbf{z}_{k,m}$ is $N_t \times N_k$ matrix, (t,i)-th element of association matrix $z_{km}(t,i)$ for $t = 1, \ldots, N_t$, $i = 1, \ldots, N_k$, is given by

$$z_{km}(t,i) = \begin{cases} 1 \text{ if observation } y_{k,i} \text{ originated from and} \\ \quad \text{falls in validation gate of target t} \\ 0 \text{ otherwise} \end{cases}$$

Validation gate is formed around the predicted position given by the combined target state prediction. Using this combined association matrix $\mathbf{z}_k$, a combined likelihood measure measure matrix $\mathcal{E}$ is formed, where each entry $\mathcal{E}(t,i)$ is given by

$$\mathcal{E}(t,i) = \begin{cases} p(y_{k,i}|\Phi_{t,k}) & \text{if } \mathbf{z}_k(t,i) = 1 \\ 0 & \text{if } \mathbf{z}_k(t,i) = 0 \end{cases} \tag{1}$$

where $p(y_{k,i}|\Phi_{t,k})$ represents the likelihood of the observation given a combined state estimate $\Phi_{t,(k|k-1)}$ for target t at time k, and it is treated as mixture probability. It is defined as

$$p(y_{k,i}|\Phi_{t,k}) = \sum_{m=1}^{M} p_m(y_{k,i}|\phi_{t,k}^m)\mu_k^m(t) \tag{2}$$

where $p_m(y_{k,i}|\phi_{t,k}^m)$ is the likelihood of observation given a state estimate $\phi_{t,k}^m$ for model m and target t at time instant k. Each pdf in a mixture is weighted by the model probability $\mu^m(t)$. Here, m $(1 \leq m \leq M)$ represents a model in IMM filter. Further, each entry $\mathcal{E}(t,i)$ is normalized, i.e.

$$\mathcal{E}(t,i) = \begin{cases} \dfrac{p(y_{k,i}|\Phi_{t,k})}{\sum_{j=1}^{N_k} p(y_{k,j}|\Phi_{t,k})} & \text{if } \mathbf{z}_k(t,i) = 1 \\ 0 & \text{if } \mathbf{z}_k(t,i) = 0 \end{cases} \tag{3}$$

The combined likelihood measure matrix $\mathcal{E}$, given by (3), is used by the genetic algorithm.

2.1 Genetic Nearest Neighbor Data Association

Genetic algorithm and its variants have been extensively used for solving complex non-linear optimization problems [5]. Genetic algorithm is based on salient operators like crossover, mutation and selection. Initially, a random set of population of elements that represents the candidate solutions is created. Crossover and mutation operations are applied on the set of population elements to generate a new set of offsprings which serve as new candidate solutions. Each element of the population of elements is assigned a fitness value (quality value) which is an indication of the performance measure.

In our formulation the likelihood measure $\mathcal{E}(t,i)$ is considered as a fitness value while designing the fitness function. In a given generation, out of the parents and the generated offsprings a set of elements are chosen based on a suitable selection mechanism. Each population of elements is represented by a string of either binary or real numbers. Each string is known as a chromosome. In our formulation, we form a string consisting of target number as a symbol and thus represents a solution for data association problem. It is called a tuple, and represents observation to track pairing. For example, with 4 measurements and 5 targets, a solution string (tuple) (2 1 4 3) indicates that observation number 1 is assigned to target 2, observation number 2 is assigned to target 1, observation number 3 is assigned to target 4, and so on. 0 in a string indicates that corresponding observation is not assigned to any target. It may be a false alarm or a new target. If tuple is indicated by symbol n then the quality of solution is represented by function $f(n)$, which is a fitness function. In our case, $f(n)$ is defined as, $f(n) = \sum_i \mathcal{E}(t, i)$ where i is the observation index and t represents target number from the given tuple n. Initial population is selected from the total population space, i.e. all possible tuples. We adopt the joint probabilistic data association (JPDA) approach which evaluates only feasible tuples, and hence the initial population consists of feasible solutions.

In our proposed method, the population size is determined dynamically. It is followed by crossover and mutation operation. These two operations are repeated for the specified number of generations or till terminating criterion is satisfied. For each generation, population set from the previous generation acts as an initial population set. The crossover operation is applied with a crossover probability. In crossover operation, two tuples are randomly chosen from the population. Then, two random indices are selected and all symbols between these two indices are swapped between two tuples selected for crossover operation. The swapping process may result in a tuple where more than one observations might be assigned to the same target and hence yields an inconsistent solution. In order to obtain a consistent solution we adopt the following crossover operation.

Let s_1 and s_2 be two tuples randomly chosen for crossover; next two indices p_1 and p_2 ($p_1 < p_2$) are randomly selected. Between these two indices, all symbols between tuples s_1 and s_2 are swapped. Say symbol A at index m ($p_1 \leq m \leq p_2$) from s_1 is to be swapped with corresponding symbol B in s_2. If symbol A appears in s_2 at any index other then m, say it appears at index r in s_2, then symbols at index m and r in s_2 are swapped. Subsequently, the symbol at m in s_1 is replaced by symbol at r in s_2. This process prevents the assignment of a track to multiple measurements. The above process is also applied to symbol B in s_2.

Mutation operation is applied to both new solutions (tuples) obtained from the parent tuples. The mutation operation is applied with a mutation probability. In mutation operation, a random index is chosen in a tuple and it is set to mutate. First an attempt is made to mutate the observation-to-track association to the track that is unassigned in this tuple. If there is none then, it is swapped with another target number (track number), which is chosen randomly in the same tuple. After each crossover and mutation operation, these tuples are marked to indicate that the tuples are visited. This helps in the selection of two other tuples for crossover and mutation operation. Thus, all tuples are visited, and new tuples are formed. The solutions or tuples for the next generation are selected from these old and new tuples. We define the best tuple is one that has the highest fitness value defined by function $f(n)$. It may happen that the best solution may be missed during this operation. To take care of this, the best fit tuple in a given generation is preserved for future use.

After a predefined number of generations, the best tuple corresponding to the optimal solution found among all best tuples is stored. It gives track to observation pairing. The advantage of genetic based data association method is that *it avoids the complex logic of Munkres' optimal data assignment algorithm.* Implementation of the proposed method is found simpler than that of Munkres' optimal algorithm.

In our approach, we have used adaption mechanism for crossover and mutation probabilities. Before each crossover and mutation operations, both probabilities are updated based on maximum and average quality value from the previous generation and quality values of the current tuples in process. These probabilities are compared with a uniform random number between zero and one; if the probability is greater than the random number we decide to carry out the respective operation on the selected tuples, otherwise we do not carry out the operation. This mechanism allows one to adapt the change in probabilities in the selection operation and helps in retaining good quality solutions, i.e solutions with good fitness or quality value, in the generation.

Using an observation-to-track pairing given by the best tuple, an assignment weight matrix $\mathcal{M}$ is formed. In this matrix, an entry $\mathcal{M}(t, i)$ corresponding to a pair in the best tuple is set to 1.0, and all the remaining entries are set to 0. This assignment weight matrix is used for target state update and prediction. For each model of the target, state vector and state covariance matrix are updated using the Gauss-Newton method. It is followed by model probability update and state prediction.

2.2   Proposed Tracking Algorithm

IMM filtering has mainly two steps: measurement update and time update. These steps are repeated for each target t $(1 \leq t \leq N_t)$.

1. Calculate the likelihood for each model m $(1 \leq m \leq M)$, which is used to update the model probability.

$$\mathcal{L}^m = \mathcal{N}[\tilde{z}^m; 0, S^m] \quad \text{where} \quad \tilde{z}^m = y_k^c(t) - h\hat{\phi}_{t,k|k-1}^m$$

and S^m is the innovation covariance. Here $y_k^c(t)$ is given by

$$y_k^c(t) = \frac{\sum_{i=1}^{N_k} \mathcal{E}(t, i) y_{k,i}}{\sum_{i=1}^{N_k} \mathcal{E}(t, i)} \tag{4}$$

2. Measurement Update: For each model m $(1 \leq m \leq M)$, Gauss-Newton method is used to update the model state vector $\hat{\phi}_k^m$.

$$\hat{\phi}^m(t) = \bar{\phi}^m + \triangle\phi$$

where $\triangle\phi = Fg$,

$$F^{-1} = P_{k|k-1}^{-1} + \sum_{i=1}^{N_k} \mathcal{M}(t, i) H^T R^{-1} H$$

and

$$g = \sum_{i=1}^{N_k} \mathcal{M}(t, i) H^T R^{-1} [y_{k,i} - h(\phi_k)]$$

H is the observation gradient $\nabla_\phi h(\phi_k)$ (in case of nonlinear observation model). The covariance of the state vector is updated using. An approximation

$$P_{k|k} \approx F \left[P_{k|k-1}^{-1} + \sum_{i=1}^{N_k} \mathcal{M}(t,i) H^T R^{-1} H \right] F^T \tag{5}$$

At the end of the above steps for each target and for each model, updated state $\hat{\phi}_{t,k|k}^m$ and updated covariance $P_{t,k|k}^m$ are obtained.

3. Mode probability update: For each model, $m = 1, \ldots, M$ calculate the mode probability

$$\mu_k^m = \frac{\mu_{k|k-1}^m \mathcal{L}^m}{\sum_i \mu_{k|k-1}^i \mathcal{L}^i}$$

4. Combined measurement update for state and covariance:

$$\hat{\Phi}_{k|k} = \sum_m \hat{\phi}_{k|k}^m \mu_k^m \quad and \quad P_{k|k} = \sum_m \left[P_{k|k}^m + (\hat{\Phi}_{k|k} - \hat{\phi}_{k|k}^m)(\hat{\Phi}_{k|k} - \hat{\phi}_{k|k}^m)^T \right] \mu_k^m$$

5. Time Update for the state vector and the covariance matrix:

$$\bar{\phi}^m = F_k^m \hat{\phi}^{0m} \quad and \quad \bar{P}^m = F_k^m P^{0m} (F_k^m)^T + Q_k^m$$

where $\hat{\phi}^{0m}$ and P^{0m} are the model-conditional initialization for the state vector and the covariance matrix.

$$\hat{\phi}^{0m} = \sum_i \hat{\phi}_{k|k}^i \mu^{i|m} \quad and \quad P^{0m} = \sum_i \left[P_{k|k}^i + (\hat{\phi}^{0m} - \hat{\phi}_{k|k}^i)(\hat{\phi}^{0m} - \hat{\phi}_{k|k}^i)^T \right] \mu^{i|m}$$

Here, $\mu_{k+1|k}^m = \sum_i \xi_{im} \mu_k^i$ and $\mu^{i|m} = \xi_{im} \mu_k^i / \mu_{k+1|k}^m$. ξ_{im} is the transition probability.

6. Overall Target Time Update for the state vector and the covariance matrix:

$$\hat{\Phi}_{k+1|k} = \sum_m \bar{\phi}^m \mu_{k+1|k}^m$$

$$P_{k+1|k} = \sum_m \left[[\bar{P}^m + (\hat{\Phi}_{k+1|k} - \bar{\phi}^m)(\hat{\phi}_{k+1|k} - \bar{\phi}^m)^T \right] \mu_{k+1|k}^m$$

3   Simulation Results

Synthetic IR images were generated using real time temperature data [7]. For simulation, the generated frame size is 1024×256 and very high target movement of ± 20 pixels per frame. Maneuvering trajectories are generated using the B-Spline function. It is important to note that these generated trajectories do not follow any specific model. In our simulations, we have used constant acceleration (CA) and Singers' maneuver model (SMM) for IMM. For the simulations, the number of generations is set to 20. By default, the number of solutions is set to 8. If the number of possible tuples (solutions) are less than the specified number, it is set to the minimum of these two numbers. The initial crossover and mutation probability are set to 0.650 and 0.010 respectively. In our simulations the crossover and mutation probabilities are modified adaptively based on maximum quality value and average quality value of the generation.

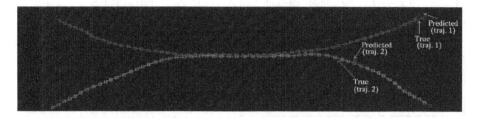

Fig. 1. Tracked trajectories at frame number 57 - ir44 clip (0.05% clutter).

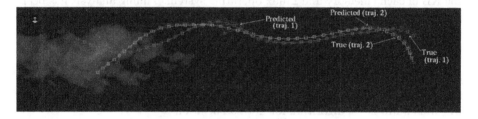

Fig. 2. Tracked trajectories at frame number 44 - ir50 clip (0.05% clutter).

Figure 1 depicts the result of tracking using the proposed algorithm for closely spaced two targets in ir44 clip with 0.05% clutter. For clip ir50 with 0.05% clutter, the tracked trajectories are shown in Figure 2. In Figures 1 and 2 the real trajectory is shown with a solid line, whereas predicted trajectory is shown using a dotted line with the same color. Using the proposed tracking algorithm, mean error in position is depicted in Table A for different trajectories without clutter and with clutter. The proposed method in this paper is compared with our earlier proposed algorithm, multiple filter bank (MFB) approach [8], which also performs data association based on nearest neighbor method using the genetic algorithm. The mean prediction error in position using MFB is depicted in Table B. We also compared our proposed method with the original IMM_NN algorithm [3]. The trajectory crossover occurs for a clip ir44 with the later one. Due to space limitation the mean prediction error in position and trajectory plots using the original IMM_NN algorithm are not depicted here.

For evaluating computational complexity of the proposed Genetic based IMM_NN algorithm the timing analysis is performed which is as follows. The proposed algorithm has been compared with original IMM_NN method which uses Munkres' algorithm for data association. The tracking algorithms have been executed on personal computer with Pentium III (847.435 MHz) processor with

Table A. Mean Error in Position using the proposed method.

Traj.	no clutter	with clutter		
		0.01%	0.03%	0.05%
ir44 clip				
1	1.7698	1.7685	1.8294	1.9805
2	2.6986	2.6835	2.6787	2.7783
ir49 clip				
1	2.1925	2.1913	2.1911	2.1869
2	2.4040	2.4011	2.4073	2.4075
ir50 clip				
1	2.7013	2.7014	2.6984	2.6925
2	2.4110	2.4110	2.4097	2.7045

Table B. Mean Error in Position Multipler Filter Bank approach.

Traj.	CA	Maneuver	CA	Maneuver
	0.01% clutter		0.03% clutter	
ir44 clip with clutter				
1	1.6796	1.4157	1.6293	1.4157
2	2.8360	2.4421	2.7810	2.5808
ir49 clip with clutter				
1	3.1629	2.3363	3.1629	2.3363
2	3.7539	2.4838	3.7539	2.4838
ir50 clip with clutter				
1	2.8566	3.0699	4.9067	3.0699
2	2.0185	2.4985	4.0521	3.1055

256 KB of cache memory and Linux operating system. Timing analysis has been performed using *gprof* utility available with Linux. *gprof* utility provides program profile and for this task the program is executed with debug option. The timing analysis for a particular clip "ir50" using the proposed tracking algorithm, namely, Genetic IMM_NN, and original IMM_NN algorithm has been depicted in Table C. From Table C it is clear that the overall execution time required by the proposed tracking algorithm is less compared to original IMM_NN algorithm which uses Munkres; algorithm for data association.

Table C. Computational Complexity – Timing analysis.

	Genetic IMM_NN	Original IMM_NN
ET_{total}	4.15	6.08
ET_{frame}	0.09	0.14
ET_{steps}	4.10	3.50

ET_{total} – Total execution time for given clip (in seconds)
ET_{frame} – Execution time per frame (in second)
ET_{steps} – Total execution time for tracking steps
(in percentage of total execution time)

4   Conclusion

From the simulations it is concluded that the proposed genetic based data association method provides an alternative to nearest neighbor based Munkres' optimal data assignment algorithm. Moreover, it is easy to implement compared to the original IMM_NN algorithm. Presently, the number of generation required by the genetic algorithm has been chosen based on large number of simulations and the proposed algorithm does not take care of an occlusion (i.e., no observation from the target). The choice of number of generations required by the genetic algorithm and the data association in the presence of occlusion need further research.

References

1. Chong, C.Y., Garren, D., Grayson, T.P.: Ground Target Tracking - a Historical Perspective. In: Proceedings of IEEE Aerospace Conference. Volume 3. (2000) 433–448
2. Li, X.R., Zhang, Y.: Numerically Roubst Implementation of Multiple-Model Algorithms. IEEE Transactions on Aerospace and Electronic Systems **36** (2000) 266–277
3. Kirubarajan, T., et al.: Comparison of IMMPDA and IMM-Assignment algorithms on real traffic surveillance data. In: Proc. of SPIE Signal and Data Processing of Small Targets. Volume 2759. (1996) 453–464
4. Jean-Yves Carrier, John Litva, Henry Leung, and Titus Lo: Genetic algorithm for multiple-target-tracking data association. In: Proceeding of SPIE, Acquisition, Tracking and Pointing X. Volume 2739. (1996) 180–190
5. David E. Goldberg: Genetic Algorithms in Search, Optimization, and Machine Learning. Addison-Wesley Publication (1989)
6. Samuel S. Blackman: Multiple-Target Tracking with Radar Applications. Artech House, Inc., Boston (1986)
7. More, S.T., et al.: Synthetic IR Scene Simulation of Air-borne Targets. In: Proceedings of 3rd Conference ICVGIP 2002, Ahmedabad, India (2002) 108–113
8. Mukesh A. Zaveri, S. N. Merchant, Uday B. Desai, P.K. Nanda: Genetic Algorithm Based Data Association and Tracking of Multiple Point Targets. In: Proceedings of 10th National Conference on Communications, Banglore, India (2004) 414–418

Finding the Natural Groupings in a Data Set
Using Genetic Algorithms

Nirmalya Chowdhury[1] and Premananda Jana[2]

[1] Department of Computer Science and Engineering, Jadavpur University, Kolkata-32, India
`nir63@vsnl.net`
[2] MCKV Institute of Engineering, 243, G.T Road (N), Liluah, Howrah-711 204, India
`prema_jana@yahoo.com`

Abstract. Genetic Algorithms (GAs) are generally portrayed as a search procedure which can optimize functions based on a limited sample of function values. In this paper, an objective function based on minimal spanning tree (MST) of data points is proposed for clustering and GAs have been used in an attempt to optimize the specified objective function in order to detect the natural grouping in a given data set. Several experiments on synthetic data set in $\Re^2$ show the utility of the proposed method. The method is also applicable to any higher dimensional data.

Keywords: Clustering, Genetic algorithms, Pattern recognition.

1 Introduction

A lot of scientific effort has already been dedicated to cluster analysis problems which attempts to extract the "natural grouping" present in a data set. The intuition behind the phrase "natural groups" is explained below in the context of data set in $\Re^2$.

For a data set $M = \{x_1, x_2, ..., x_m\} \subseteq \Re^2$, obtain the scatter diagram of M. By viewing the scatter diagram, what one perceives to be the groups present in M is termed as natural groups of M. For example, for the scatter diagram shown in Fig. 1(a), the groups that we perceive are shown in Fig. 1(b). Similarly for the scatter diagrams shown in Fig. 2(a) and Fig. 3(a), the natural groups are as shown in Fig. 2(b), and Fig. 3(b) respectively.

Clustering techniques [1, 7, 9, 14, 15] aim to extract such natural groups present in a given data set and each such group is termed as a cluster. So we shall use the term "cluster" or "group" interchangeably in this paper. The existing clustering techniques may not always find the natural grouping. In this paper, we have proposed an objective function for clustering based on MST of data points for each group and suggested a method using GAs that can detect the natural grouping in a given data set. The method for obtaining the natural groups in $\Re^2$ can also be extended to $\Re^p (p > 2)$.

We have applied this method on data sets in $\Re^2$ and obtained good results. Note that the perception of natural groups in a data set is not possible for higher dimensional data. But the concept used for detecting the groups in $\Re^2$ may also be applicable to higher dimensional data to obtain a "meaningful" grouping.

S. Manandhar et al. (Eds.): AACC 2004, LNCS 3285, pp. 26–33, 2004.

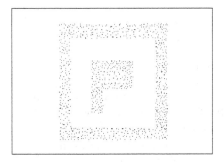

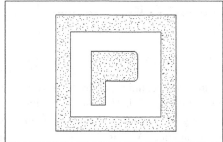

Fig. 1a. Scatter Diagram

Fig. 1b. Natural Grouping by proposed method

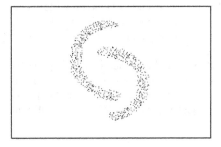

Fig. 2a. Scatter Diagram

Fig. 2b. Natural Grouping by proposed method

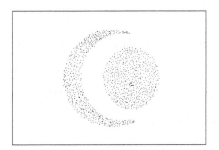

Fig. 3a. Scatter Diagram

Fig. 3b. Natural Grouping by proposed method

2 Description of the Problem

Clustering is an unsupervised technique used in discovering inherent structure present in the set of objects [1]. Clustering algorithms attempt to organize unlabeled pattern vectors into clusters or "natural groups" such that points within a cluster are more similar to each other than to points belonging to different clusters.

Let the set of patterns M be $\{x_1, x_2, \ldots\ldots\ldots, x_m\}$, where x_i is the i_{th} pattern vector. Let the number of clusters be K. If the clusters are represented by $C_1, C_2, \ldots\ldots, C_K$ then

P1. $C_i \neq \phi$, for $i = 1, 2, \ldots, K$

P2. $C_i \cap C_j = \phi$ for $i \neq j$ and

P3. $\cup_{i=1}^{K} C_i = M$ where ϕ represents null set.

Clustering techniques may broadly be divided into two categories: hierarchical and non-hierarchical [1]. The non-hierarchical or partitional clustering problem deals with obtaining an optimal partition of M into K subsets such that some clustering criterion is satisfied. Among the non-hierarchical clustering techniques, the K-means (or C-means or basic Isodata) algorithm has been one of the more widely used algorithms. This algorithm is based on the optimization of a specified objective function. It attempts to minimize the sum of squared Euclidean distances between patterns and their cluster centers. It was shown in [13] that this algorithm may converge to a local minimum solution. Moreover it may not always detect the natural grouping in a given data set, though it is useful in many applications.

There are several ways in which a given data set can be clustered. In this paper we have suggested an objective function for clustering that is based on MSTs of data points for all clusters, where each such MST corresponds to a cluster. And the principle used for clustering is to minimize the said objective function. Mathematically this principle is stated below.

1. Let $C_1, C_2, \ldots, C_k$ be a set of k clusters of M

2. Let $h_j = (\dfrac{l_j}{\#C_j})^{\frac{1}{p}}$ for $j = 1, 2, \ldots, k$

   where l_j is the sum of edge weights of MST for all the data points $x \in C_j$, p is the dimensionality of the data set and $\#C_j$ represents the number of data points in C_j. Euclidean interpoint distance is taken as the edge weight of the MST.

3. Let $f(C_1, C_2, \ldots, C_k) = \sum_{j=1}^{k} h_j$. We shall refer to $f(C_1, C_2, \ldots, C_k)$ as the objective function of the clustering $C_1, C_2, \ldots, C_k$.

4. Minimize $f(C_1, C_2, \ldots, C_k)$ over all $C_1, C_2, \ldots, C_k$ satisfying P1, P2 and P3 stated above.

   Note that h_j is a function of interpoint distances in C_j as well as the number of points in C_j. A similar such function is used in [10].

All possible clusterings of M are to be considered to get the optimal $C_1, C_2, \ldots, C_k$. So obtaining the exact solution of the problem is theoretically possible, yet not feasible in practice due to limitations of computer storage and time. One requires the evaluation of $S(m, k)$ partitions [1, 14] if exhaustive enumeration is used to solve the problem, where

$$S(m,k) = \frac{1}{k!} \sum_{j=1}^{k} (-1)^{k-j} \binom{k}{j} j^m.$$

This clearly indicates that exhaustive enumeration cannot lead to the required solution for most practical problems in reasonable computation time. Thus, approximate heuristic techniques seeking a compromise or looking for an acceptable solution have usually been adopted. In this paper, we have applied GAs in an attempt to get the optimal value of the function f for a given clustering problem. The next section describes the method in detail.

3 Clustering Using Genetic Algorithms

Genetic Algorithms (GAs) are stochastic search methods based on the principle of natural genetic systems [8, 12]. They perform a multi-dimensional search in order to provide an optimal value of an evaluation (fitness) function in an optimization problem. Unlike conventional search methods, GAs deal with multiple solutions simultaneously and compute the fitness function values for these solutions. GAs are theoretically and empirically found to provide global near-optimal solutions for various complex optimization problems in the field of operation research, VLSI design, Pattern Recognition, Image Processing, Machine Learning, etc. [2, 3, 4,5].

While solving an optimization problem using GAs, each solution is usually coded as a binary string (called chromosome) of finite length. Each string or chromosome is considered as an individual. A collection of P such individuals is called a population. GAs start with a randomly generated population of size P. In each iteration, a new population of the same size is generated from the current population using two basic operations on the individuals. These operators are Selection and Reproduction. Reproduction consists of crossover and mutation operations.

In GAs, the best string obtained so far is preserved in a separate location outside the population so that the algorithm may report the best value found, among all possible solutions inspected during the whole process. In the present work, we have used the elitist model (EGA) of selection of De Jong (1992), where the best string obtained in the previous iteration is copied into the current population.

The remaining part of this section describes in detail the genetic algorithm that we propose for clustering. First, the string representation and the initial population for the problem under consideration are discussed. Then the genetic operators and the way they are used are stated. The last part of this section deals with the stopping criteria for the GA.

3.1 String Representation and Initial Population

String representation: To solve partitioning problems with GAs, one must encode partitions in a way that allows manipulation by genetic operators. We consider an encoding method where a partition is encoded as a string of length m (where m is the number of data points in M). The i th element of the string denotes the group number assigned to point x_i. For example the partition $\{x_1,x_4\}$ $\{x_3,x_6\}$ $\{x_2,x_5\}$ $\{x_7\}$ is represented by the string (1 3 2 1 3 2 4). We have adopted this method, since it allows the use of the standard single-point crossover operation. The value of the i th element of a string denotes the cluster membership of the i th data point in M. Thus, each string represents a possible cluster configuration and the fitness function for each string is the sum of the edge weights of all the MSTs, where each MST corresponds to a cluster. So, here the fitness function is the objective function f described in Section 2.

Initial population: There exists no guidelines for choosing the 'appropriate' value of the size (P) of the initial population. An initial population of size P for a genetic algorithm is usually chosen at random. In this work, we have taken $P = 6$ and this value of P is kept fixed throughout the experiment. Several strings of length m are generated randomly where the value of each element of the string is allowed to lie between 1 and k. Only valid strings (that have at least one data point in each cluster) are considered to be included in the initial population to avoid wastage of processing time on invalid strings.

3.2 Genetic Operators

Selection: The 'Selection' operator mimics the 'survival of the fittest' concept of natural genetic systems. Here strings are selected from a population to create a mating pool. The probability of selection of a particular string is directly or inversely proportional to the fitness value depending on whether the problem is that of maximization or minimization. The present problem is a minimization problem and thus the probability of selecting a particular string in the population is inversely proportional to the fitness value. The size of the mating pool is taken to be same as that of population.

Crossover: Crossover exchanges information between two parent strings and generates two children for the next population. A pair of chromosomes

$$\beta = (\beta_m \beta_{m-1} \ldots \ldots \beta_2 \beta_1),$$

$$\gamma = (\gamma_m \gamma_{m-1} \ldots \ldots \gamma_2 \gamma_1)$$

is selected randomly from the mating pool. Then the crossover is performed with probability p (crossover probability) in the following way.

Generate randomly an integer position pos from the range of $[1, m-1]$. Then two chromosomes β and γ are replaced by a pair α and δ, where

$$\alpha = (\beta_m \beta_{m-1} \ldots \beta_{pos} \gamma_{pos+1} \ldots \gamma_2 \gamma_1),$$

$$\delta = (\gamma_m \gamma_{m-1} \ldots \gamma_{pos} \beta_{pos+1} \ldots \beta_2 \beta_1)_{.}$$

Crossover operation on the mating pool of size P (P is even) is performed in the following way:

- Select $P/2$ pairs of strings randomly from the mating pool so that every string in the mating pool belongs to exactly one pair of strings.
- For each pair of strings, generate a random number rnd from $[0,1]$. If $rnd \leq p$ then perform crossover; otherwise no crossover is performed.

Usually in GAs, p is chosen to have a value in the interval $[0.25,1]$. In the present work p is taken to be 0.8 and the population size P is taken to be 6 for all generations. The crossover operation between two strings, as stated above, is performed at one position. This is referred to as *single-point* crossover [12].

Mutation: Mutation is an occasional random alternation of a character. Every character β_i, $i = 1, 2, \ldots\ldots, m$, in each chromosome (generated after crossover) has equal chance to undergo mutation. Note that any string can be generated from any given string by mutation operation. The mutation introduces some extra variability into the population. Though it is usually performed with very low probability q, it has an important role in the generation process [11]. The mutation probability q is usually taken in the interval [0, 0.5]. The value of q is usually taken to be fixed. Sometimes it is varied with the number of iterations. For details, the reader is referred to [16]. We have considered varying the mutation probability for reasons explained in the next subsection.

Elitist strategy: The aim of the elitist strategy is to carry the best string from the previous iteration into the next. We have implemented this strategy in the following way:

(a) Copy the best string (say s_0) of the initial population in a separate location.
(b) Perform selection, crossover and mutation operations to obtain a new population (say Q_1).
(c) Compare the worst string in Q_1 (say s_1) with s_0 in terms of their fitness values. If s_1 is found to be worse than s_0, then replace s_1 by s_0.
(d) Find the best string in Q_1 (say s_2) and replace s_0 by s_2.

Note: Steps (b), (c) and (d) constitute one iteration of the proposed GA based method. These steps are repeated till the stopping criterion is satisfied. Observe that a string s_1 is said to be better than another string s_2, if the fitness value of s_1 is less than that of s_2, since the problem under consideration is a minimization problem.

3.3 Stopping Criterion

There exists no stopping criterion in the literature [6, 8, 12], which ensures the convergence of GAs to an optimal solution. Usually, two stopping criteria are used in genetic algorithms. In the first, the process is executed for a fixed number of iterations and the best string obtained is taken to be the optimal one. In the other, the algorithm is terminated if no further improvement in the fitness value of the best string is observed for a fixed number of iterations, and the best string obtained is taken to be the optimal one. We have used the first method in the experiment.

In order to obtain the optimal string, one needs to maintain the population diversity. This means that the mutation probability needs to be high. On the other hand, as the optimal string is being approached, fewer changes in the present strings are necessary to move in the desired direction. This implies that the mutation probability needs to be reduced as the number of iterations increases. In fact, we have started with a mutation probability value of $q = 0.5$. The q value is then varied as a step function of the number of iterations until it reaches a value of $\frac{1}{m}$. The minimum value of the mutation probability is taken to be $\frac{1}{m}$.

4 Experimental Results

This section provides the experimental results of the proposed method on various synthetic data set. Fig. 1(a) shows a data set of size 1200 where data points are generated from two clusters. One cluster is having the shape of a rectangle while the other is having the shape of the English letter 'P' enclosed within that rectangle. Here the maximum number of iterations is taken to be 14000. The minimum value of the objective function f obtained by the proposed method is 0.4317843 and the corresponding clustering is as shown in Fig. 1(b). It can be seen from Fig. 1(b) that the proposed method using GAs has indeed detected the two natural groups present in the given data set.

Fig. 2(a) shows a data distribution of size 800 where data points are generated from two clusters. Both the clusters are having the shape the English letter 'C'. Here the maximum number of iterations is taken to be 10000. The minimum value of the objective function f obtained by the proposed method is 0.1682312 and the corresponding clustering is as shown in Fig. 2(b). From Fig. 2(b) it is evident that the proposed method has successfully detected the two natural groups present in the given data set.

Fig. 3(a) shows a data set of size 1000 where data points are generated from two clusters. One cluster is having the shape of the English letter 'C' while the other is having the shape of a circular disk. Here the maximum number of iterations is taken to be 12000. The minimum value of the objective function f obtained by the proposed method is 0.3048672 and the corresponding clustering is as shown in Fig. 3(b). By viewing the grouping shown in Fig. 3(b) one can conclude that the proposed GAs based method is able to detect the two natural groups present in the given data set.

5 Conclusions and Discussion

The aim of this work is to observe whether minimizing the proposed objective function for clustering can lead to detection of natural grouping and also whether the proposed GAs based method can find the optimal value of the said objective function in order to detect the natural grouping. The proposed method has been found to provide good results for all the data sets considered for experimentation.

Observe that the population size P is taken to be 6 for all the experiments, although the sizes of the search spaces associated with each problem are not the same. But we have used different stopping times (maximum number of iterations of the GA-based method) depending upon the size of the search space. There probably exists a relationship between the stopping time and the population size for a given search space. The theoretical results available on this aspect of GAs are very little. For a higher value of P, probably, a smaller stopping time would provide similar results.

References

1. Anderberg, M.R.: Cluster Analysis for Application. Academic Press, Inc., NewYork (1973)
2. Ankerbrandt, C.A., B.P. Unckles and F.E. Petry.: Scene recognition using genetic algorithms with semantic nets. Pattern Recognition Letters. 11(1990) 285-293
3. Belew, R. and L. Booker, Eds.: Proceedings of the fourth int. conf. on genetic algorithms. Morgan Kaufmann, Los Altos, CA (1991)
4. Murthy, C.A. and Chowdhury N.: In search of optimal clusters using Genetic Algorithms. Pattern Recognition Letters, 17(8) (1996) 825-832
5. Bornholdt, S. and D. Graudenz.: Genetic asymptotic and neural networks and structure design by genetic algorithms, Neural Networks 5 (1992) 327-334
6. Davis, T.E. and C.J. Principe.: A simulated annealing like convergence theory for the simple genetic algorithm. In: (Belew and Booker, 1991), 174-181
7. Devijver, P.A. and J. Kittler.: Pattern Recognition: A statistical Approach. Prentice-Hall International. Hemel Hemstead, Hertfordshire, UK (1982)
8. Goldberg, D. E.: Genetic Algorithms: Search, Optimization and Machine Learning. Addison-Wesley, Reading, MA (1989)
9. Jain, A.K. and R.C. Dubes.: Algorithms for Clustering Data. Prentice-Hall, Englewood Cliffs, NJ (1988)
10. D. Chaudhuri, C. A. Murthy and B. B. Chaudhuri.: Finding a Subset of Representative Points in a Data Set." IEEE SMC, 24(9) (1994) 1416- 1424
11. Jones, D.R. and M.A. Beltramo.: Solving partitioning problems with genetic algorithms. In: (Belew and Booker, 1991), 442-449
12. Michalewicz, Z.: Genetic Algorithms + Data Structure = Evolution Programs. Springer, Berlin (1992)
13. Selim, S.Z. and M.A. Ismail.: K-means type algorithms: A generalized convergence theorem and characterization of local optimality. IEEE Trans. Pattern Anal. Mach. Intell. 6(1) (1984) 81-87
14. Spath, H.: Cluster Analysis Algorithms. Ellis Horwood, Chichester. UK (1980)
15. Tou, T.J. and C.R. Gonzalez.: Pattern Recognition Principles. Addison-Wesley, Reading, MA (1974)
16. Qi, Xiaofeng and F. Palmieri.: Theoretical analysis of evolutionary algorithms with an infinite population size in continuous space Part I: Basic properties of selection and mutation. IEEE Trans. Neural Networks 5 (1) (1994) 102-119

Volumetric Measurement of Heart Using PA and Lateral View of Chest Radiograph

I.C. Mehta, Z.J. Khan, and R.R. Khotpal

Rail Toly, Gondia, India
mehta_i_c@rediffmail.com

Abstract. Heart size is of fundamental importance in diagnosis and radiography is a reliable method of estimating size. Volume of the heart is computed by cardiac measurements in postero-anterior (PA) and lateral view of chest radiograph Determination of heart size is a major factor in the clinical evaluation of the healthy or failing heart. In this paper, we describe an automatic method for computing the approximate volume of the heart based on cardiac rectangle. The cardiac rectangle varies in size depending on the heart size. The chief measurement is made on the PA view. The measurement is also made in true lateral view. The first step in computer processing was to extract size, contour and shape of the heart from the standard PA and lateral chest radiograph using fuzzy c-means. An algorithm that constructs a cardiac rectangle around the heart is developed. The extent of rectangle is found from features present in horizontal and vertical profiles of the chest X ray. Once cardiac outline is obtained it is straightforward to obtain measurements characterizing the shape of the heart. Volume of the heart is computed from various features obtained from pa and lateral chest radiograph. The measurements have proved of most value in estimating alteration in size of the heart shadow due to physiological or toxic causes.

1 Introduction

Chest is described as the mirror of health and disease. An enormous amount of information about the condition of patient can be extracted from a chest film and therefore the routine chest radiograph should not be considered quite so routine. Chest radiographies provide the radiologist with information about several different organ systems: cardiovascular, respiratory and skeletal. The major challenge is the wide dynamic range of information between X-rays emerging from the heavily attenuated mediastinum (heart, spine, arota and other central features on the radiography) and those that have passed thought the air filled lungs [1]. Diagnosis of heart with the help of X-ray image has basically two directions heart abnormalities and congenital heart diseases. After the age of puberty the normal radiological heart shadow falls into one of three groups: the vertical heart, the oblique heart, and the transverse heart [2]. The most important fact in determining the shape appears to be the width of the chest. Thus in individual with a long and narrow chest, we see a small narrow heart, and in individuals with a wide chest we see the transverse type of heart [3].

Enlargement of the cardiac projection with elongation and greater rounding of left ventricular arch characterize miral insufficiency. Aortic stenosis is characterized by

S. Manandhar et al. (Eds.): AACC 2004, LNCS 3285, pp. 34–40, 2004.

elongation. Aortic insufficiency produces an overall cardiac enlargement that is greater than the enlargement caused by mitral stenosis. The average individual has an oblique heart. Since the heart shape is dependent to a large extent on the shape of chest, this coefficient is also fairly reliable guide to size. The cardiac rectangle varies in size depending on the heart size. Once heart measurements were obtained from cardiac rectangle this information can be used as basis for classifying the case normal or abnormal [4]. In the adult the heart lies in the center of the thorax, the outline projecting about one-third to the right and two-third to the left of spine. The proposed method is based on following assumption:

It is assumed that the figures supplied are adjusted such that the shadow of the heart should be clear cut and easily visible. The right dome usually lies about 1-3 cm higher than the left on full inspiration. If the airs adjacent to any intra thoracic structure say the heart or diaphragm is replaced by any structure of soft tissue density then outline of that part will not be separately visible, the two shadows merging into one homogeneous opacity and as a result the heart will become quite invisible. All cardiac measurements are normalized to obtain a ratio figure.

2 Method

Procedure for finding volume estimate consists of four different phases

1. Finding image features from horizontal and vertical signature of original chest X rays.
2. Finding fuzzy c-means on pa and lateral view of chest X ray.
3. Finding transverse, long diameter from pa view and horizontal depth of heart from lateral view.
4. Computing heart volume from all above phases.

2.1 Finding Image Features

Several image features determined from the horizontal and vertical signatures of the chest image are used to extract the thoracic cage as discussed by Xu X.W. and Doi K.[5]. Fig 1 show cardiac measurements in pa and lateral view respectively. The chief measurement is made on the PA view. The measurement is also made in true lateral view. The first step in computer processing was to extract size, contour and shape of the heart from the standard P.A. and lateral chest radiograph. Let. I [i,j] denote the intensity of pixel at (i,j), where $0 \leq i \leq N_r - 1$, $0 \leq j \leq N_c - 1$. N_r is the number of rows and N_c is the number of columns in the image.

The horizontal signature, denoted by F[j], is defined by.

$$F[j] = \sum_{i=0}^{N_r-1} I[i, j], j = 0, \ldots, N_c - 1. \tag{1}$$

To prevent the signature from having noisy peaks image is smoothed with a five point averaging operator: [11111]/5. One typical horizontal and vertical signature is shown in Fig. 2 with several feature points [6].

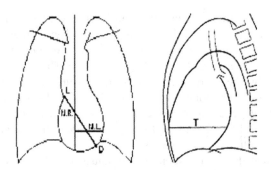

Fig. 1. Shows cardiac measurements in pa and lateral view

L_{min} : a minimum representing the right boundary of the thoracic cage,
L_{max} : a maximum representing the middle of the right lung,
M   : a minimum representing the center of the spinal column,
R_{max} : a maximum representing the middle of the left lung,
R_{min} : a minimum representing the left boundary of the thoracic cage.
L_s : location of the right edge of the spinal column,
R_s : location of the left edge of the spinal column,

The edge locations of the spinal column, L_s and R_s, are estimated from

$$L_s = M - (R_{min} - L_{min})/12 \tag{2}$$

$$R_s = M + (R_{min} - L_{min})/12 \tag{3}$$

The vertical signature, denoted by $g[i]$, is obtained from a vertical ribbon of width w centered column L_{max} where the ribs are most clearly seen.

$$g[I] = \sum_{i=L_{max}-w}^{L_{max}+w} I[i, j], I = 0, N_r - 1 \tag{4}$$

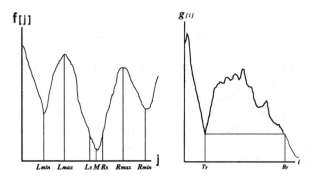

Fig. 2. Shows horizontal and vertical signature with several feature points

2.2   The Fuzzy C-Mean Algorithm

The structure of partition space for clustering algorithm is described by Benzek [7][8]. The fuzzy c-mean algorithm attempts to cluster feature vectors by searching for local minima of the objective function. The fuzzy c-mean has several advantages. 1) It is unsupervised, 2) it can be used with any number of features and any number of classes and 3) it distributes the membership values in a normalized fashion.

We have applied fuzzy c-means algorithm on original pa and lateral chest X ray. Fig 3 shows original chest X ray and Fig 4 shows fuzzy c means with cardiac measurement.

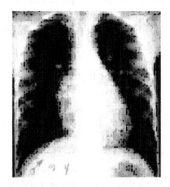

Fig. 3. Showing PA view original image

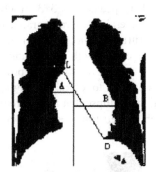

Fig. 4. Fuzzy c-means with cardiac measurements

2.3   X-Ray Measurement of the Cardio-Vascular Shadow

All the feature points obtained from original chest X ray are transferred on FCM computed image of pa view on one to one correspondence basis as both image size are same. Now M is point on FCM computed image, which represent the center of the spinal column, and vertical line is drawn from point M.

We have found image features from horizontal and vertical signature of original Chest X ray. We have applied FCM algorithms on pa and lateral image and now on this image we shall find out

1. Long diameter of heart (LD)
2. Transverse diameter of heart (TD)
3. Horizontal depth of heart (T).

2.3.1 Finding Long Diameter of Heart

First we shall find point L and then point D. Length of line between point L and D. This line is known as LD, the long diameter of the heart.

Finding the notch separating the right vascular auricular and right vascular shadows (point L): It has been observed that heart counter lies in the lower portion of chest X ray and point L approximately 50% of bottom. Point L of interest can easily be found as point nearest to the center of the spinal column starting from the bottom.

Finding left diaphragmatic shadow (point D): Starting from the bottom line finding point furthest away point from the center of the spinal column in the right direction gives us left diaphragmatic shadow point approximately.

2.3.2 Finding Transverse Diameter of Heart

Finding two widest points on each border and joining them at right angles to the central perpendicular line M obtain the transverse diameter of the heart. The sum of these two distances is the transverse diameter TD i.e. A+B as shown in Fig 4.

2.3.3 Measurement in Lateral View

Fig 5 shows image of chest radiograph in lateral view. We have applied Sobel's edge detector with kernel 3*3 on both direction with threshold of 0.25. Now we have applied morphological opening on this image, which smoothens the heart contour and eliminates small islands and sharp peaks with 3*3 structuring element. Fig 6 shows the images of FCM computed lateral chest radiograph, image with Sobel edge and ellipse found out using curve-fitting method. Lateral view shows the heart contour that can be approximated as the ellipse with certain angle of inclination with x-axis. The horizontal depth of heart can be found out approximately by calculating the chord (MN) of ellipse that is parallel to x-axis passing through the center of ellipse. We have found out the equation of ellipse that fits approximately to the heart contour [9][10]. We have used Matlab curve fitting toolbox to automatically fit the curve in the form of ellipse.

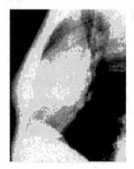

Fig. 5. Showing lateral view of original image

2.4 Estimate the Volume of Heart

Having found cardiac measurements from pa and lateral view it is convenient to find the volume of the heart.

Transverse diameter TD of Chest X ray from Fig 4 = A + B = 6.1 + 7.00 = 13.1
Long diameter of Chest X ray computer from Fig 4 = LD = 14.2
Horizontal depth of heart from lateral view of Chest X ray = T= 9.1
Volume = product of three diameter
         = TD * LD * T
         =13.1 *14.2 * 9.2
         = 1711.384 cm3

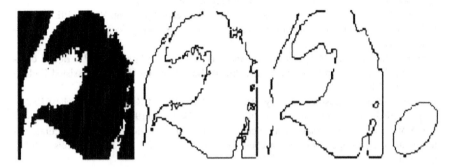

Fig. 6. Lateral Views of image after fuzzy c-means, image with Sobel edge, image with 3*3 structuring element on Sobel edge detected image, and Ellipse found out using curve-fitting method

3   Result and Discussion

It must-be emphasized that measurement of the radiological heart shadow are in no sense measurement of the real size heart. The average measured length of long diameter evaluated is 14 cm and it varied in normal between 11 and 15.5 cm depending on heart shadow. The average transverse diameter measurement is 12.2cm and it varies between 9.2 and 14.5 cm in adult male. All the measurement and image processing algorithms for finding various features has been in implemented using MATLAB Image Processing Toolbox and has been tested on number chest X rays. In addition, the in vivo beating heart displays a complicated series of motions in all dimensions in the thoracic cavity during the cardiac cycle. The method described in the present study, despite obvious limitations, may bring a unique value to the 2D evaluation of cardiac volume approximately. Calculation of the chord MN i.e. horizontal depth of heart is highly dependent on the sampled points, failure to collect data points from the entire heart contour will result in underestimation of the heart depth and in turn volume.

4   Conclusion

During full inspiration the heart decreases in size, during full expiration it increases in size. This effect is enhanced by the fact the heart rotates as the diaphragm descends and ascends and due to this alteration in shape of heart takes place. A physiological difference in heart size on films taken in systole and diastole can some times be seen, and this slight change must be recognized as non-significant. It must be emphasized that measurement of the radiological heart shadow are in no sense measurement of the real size of heart. The measurements have proved of most value in estimating alteration in size of the heart shadow due to physiological or toxic causes.

References

1. Hinshaw and Murray: Diseases of the chest. Prentice Hall (1985)
2. Sonka , M., Fitzpatrick , J.M., Editors: Hand book of medical imaging. Vol.II SPIE (2000)
3. Harlow,C.A.: On radiographics image analysis. Digital picture processing, Ed. A. Rosen-field. (1991)
4. Abe, K., Dei , K., MacMahon, H., etc.: Analysis of results in large clinical series of computer aided diagnosis in chest radiology. Proc.of Int. Symp. on Compute Assisted Radiology (1993) 600-605
5. Zhanjun Yue and Ardeshir Goshtaby: Automatic Detection of Rib Borders in chest Radiographs. IEEE Transaction on Medical Imaging, Vol.14. No.3 (1995) 525-536
6. Xu, X.W., and Doi, K.: Image feature analysis for computer-aided diagnosis: Accurate determination of ribcage boundary in chest radiographs. vol. 22. no. 5 Med. Phys., (1995) 617-626
7. Cannon R.L., Jdave and Bezdek, J.C.: Efficient implementation of the fuzzy c-means clustering algorithm. IEEE Trans on pattern Analysis and machine intelligence, vol-8 (1986) 248-255
8. Benzek, J.C., and Pal, S.K.: fuzzy models for pattern recognition. IEEE press, New York (1992)
9. Bak-Jensen, B., Bak-Jensen, J., Mikkelsen, S.D., Sorensen, J.T.: Curve-fitting method for transfer function determination. 9th IEEE Conference on Instrumentation and Measurement Technology (1992) 71 – 74
10. Miller, E.K.:Smart curve fitting .Potentials, IEEE, Volume.21. Issue.1(2002) 20-23

On the Optimization of Fuzzy Relation Equations with Continuous t-Norm and with Linear Objective Function

Dhaneshwar Pandey

Department of Mathematics, D.E.I. Dayalbagh, Agra-282005, India
dpdr@rediffmail.com

Abstract. According to [8,12,13,23], the optimization models with a linear objective function subject to fuzzy relation equations is decidable. Algorithms are developed to solve it. In this paper, a complementary problem for the original problem is defined. Due to the structure of the feasible domain and nature of the objective function, individual variable is restricted to become bi-valued. We propose a procedure for separating the decision variables into basic and non-basic variables. An algorithm is proposed to determine the optimal solution. Two examples are considered to explain the procedure.

Keywords: Fuzzy relation equations, feasible domain, linear function, continuous t-norms, basic and non-basic variables.

1 Introduction

We consider the following general fuzzy linear optimization problem:
minimize $Z = c_1 x_1 + \ldots + c_m x_m$

$$\text{subject to} \quad x \, O \, A = b$$
$$0 \leq x_i \leq 1 \tag{1}$$

where
$A = [a_{ij}]$, $0 \leq a_{ij} \leq 1$, be m×n-dimensional fuzzy matrix, $b = (b_j)$, $0 \leq b_j \leq 1$, $j \in J$, be n-dimensional vector,
$c = (c_1, \ldots, c_m) \in R^m$ be cost (or weight) vector, $x = (x_i)$, $i \in I$, be m-dimensional design vector,
$I = \{1, \ldots, m\}$ and $J = \{1, \ldots, n\}$ be the index sets and 'O' is Sup-T composition, T being a continuous t-norm. More literature on Sup-T composition can be found in [2,3]. The commonly used continuous t-norms are

(i) $T(u, v) = \min(u, v)$,   (2)
(ii) $T(u, v) = \text{product}(u, v) = u.v$,   (3)
(iii) $T(u, v) = \max(0, u + v - 1)$.   (4)

Let $X(A, b) = \{ x = (x_1, \ldots, x_m) \in R^m \mid x \, O \, A = b, x_i \in [0,1] \, \forall \, i \in I \}$ be the solution set.

We are interested in finding a solution vector $x = (x_1, \ldots, x_m) \in X(A, b)$ which satisfies the constraints

$$\underset{i \in I}{Sup} \text{-} T(x_i, a_{ij}) = b_j, \forall j \in J \tag{5}$$

and minimizes the objective function Z of (1).

S. Manandhar et al. (Eds.): AACC 2004, LNCS 3285, pp. 41–51, 2004.
© Springer-Verlag Berlin Heidelberg 2004

Now, we look at the structure of X(A, b). Let $x^1, x^2 \in$ X(A,b). $x^1 \leq x^2$ if and only if $x^1_i \leq x^2_i$, $\forall i \in$ I. Thus, $(X (A, b), \leq)$ becomes a lattice. Moreover, $\hat{x} \in$ X(A, b) is called maximum solution if $x \leq \hat{x}$ for all $x \in$ X(A, b). Also, $\check{x} \in$ X(A, b) is called a minimal solution, if $\check{x} \leq x$ implies $x = \check{x}$, $\forall x \in$ X(A,b). When X(A, b) is non-empty, it can be completely determined by a unique maximum and a finite number of minimal solutions [1,7,8,13].

The maximum solution can be obtained by applying the following operation:

$$\hat{x} = A \lozenge b = [\underset{j \in J}{Inf} (a_{ij} \lozenge b_j)]_{i \in I} \tag{6}$$

where $\lozenge$ is inverse operator of T. The inverse operators of (2), (3), (4) can be found in [22] as given below:

$$u_{ij} \lozenge v_j = \begin{cases} 1 & \text{if } u_{ij} \leq v_j \\ v_j & \text{if } u_{ij} \geq v_j \end{cases} \tag{7}$$

$$u_{ij} \lozenge v_j = \begin{cases} 1 & \text{if } u_{ij} \leq v_j \\ v_j / u_{ij} & \text{if } u_{ij} \geq v_j \end{cases} \tag{8}$$

$$u_{ij} \lozenge v_j = \begin{cases} 1 & \text{if } u_{ij} \leq v_j \\ 1 - u_{ij} + v_j & \text{if } u_{ij} > v_j \end{cases} \tag{9}$$

Let $\check{X}$ (A, b) be the set of all minimal solutions. Set X (A ,b) can be looked as X (A ,b) =

$$\bigcup_{\check{x} \in \check{X}(A,b)} \{x \in X \mid \check{x} \leq x \leq \hat{x} \}. \tag{10}$$

1.1 Corollary $\check{X}$ (A, b) $\subseteq$ X(A, b).
We list the following useful results established in [8,13].

1.2 Lemma. If $x \in$ X(A ,b), then for each $j \in$ J there exists $i_0 \in$ I such that $T(x_{i0}, a_{i0j}) = b_j$ and $T(x_i, a_{ij}) \leq b_j$ otherwise.

Proof: Since $x \ o \ A = b$, we have, $\underset{i \in I}{Sup} - T(x_i, a_{ij}) = b_j$ for $j \in$ J. This means for each $j \varepsilon$ J,/

$$T(x_i, a_{ij}) \leq b_j .$$

In order to satisfy the equality there exists at least one $i \in$ I, say i_0, such that $T(x_{i0}, a_{i0j}) = b_j$.

1.3 Proposition. Let T be the continuous t-norm and $a, b, x \in [0,1]$, then equation $T(x,a) = b$ has a solution if and only if $b \leq a$.

1.4 Definition. A constraint $j_0 \in$ J is called *scares or binding* constraint, if for $x \in$ X(A, b) and $i \in$ I, $T(x_i , a_{ij0}) = b_{j0}$.

1.5 Definition. For a solution $x \in$ X(A, b) and $i_0 \in$ I, x_{i0} is called *binding variable* if $T(x_{i0}, a_{i0j}) = b_j$ and $T(x_i, a_{ij}) \leq b_j$, for all $i \in$ I.

Let X $(A, b) \neq \varphi$. Define,

$$I_j = [\, i \in I \mid T(\widehat{x}_i, a_{ij}) = b_j, a_{ij} \geq b_j \,], \text{ for each } j \in J. \tag{11}$$

1.6 Lemma. If $X(A, b) \neq \varphi$, then $I_j \neq \varphi, \forall\, j \in J$.

Proof: Proof is consequence of lemma 1.□

1.7 Lemma. If $\| I_j \| = 1$, then $\widehat{x}_i = \breve{x}_i = a_{ij} \lozenge b_j$ for $i \in I_j$.

Proof: Since $x_i, i \in I_j$, is the only variable that satisfies the constraint j, it can take only one value equal to $\widehat{x}_i$, determined by (6) for $i \in I_j$ and hence the lemma.   □

1.8 Lemma. For i belonging to I_j and $I_{j'}$,

$$a_{ij} \lozenge b_j = a_{ij'} \lozenge b_{j'}.$$

Proof: Since x_i is the only variable that satisfies the constraints j and j',i.e. $T(x_i, a_{ij}) = b_j$ and $T(x_i, a_{ij'}) = b_{j'}$. Therefore, $x_i = a_{ij} \lozenge b_j = a_{ij'} \lozenge b_{j'}$.

Solving fuzzy relation equations is an interesting topic of research [1, 4–11, 13–21, 23–25]. Studies on fuzzy relation equations with max-T-norm composition or generalized connectives can be found in [18]. According to Gupta and Qi [10] performance of fuzzy controllers depends upon the choice of T-operators. Pedrycz [18] provided the existence conditions for max-T-norm composition. A guideline for selecting appropriate connector can be found in [24]. Extensive literatures on fuzzy relation equations with max-min composition [25] can be seen in [19]. Recently, Bourke and Fisher [4] studied a system of fuzzy relation equations with max-product composition. An efficient procedure for solving fuzzy relation equations with max-product can also be found in [13].

Fang and Li [8] made seminal study on fuzzy relation equations based on max-min composition with linear objective function. They have considered two sub problems of the original problem based on positive and negative costs coefficients. One sub problem with positive costs, after defining equivalent 0-1 integer programming problem, has been solved using branch-and-bound method with jump tracking technique. Related developments regarding this can be found in [12,15,23]. Wu.,et.al.[23] after rearranging (in increasing c and b) the structure of the linear optimization problem, have used upper bound technique in addition to backward jump-tracking branch– and –bound scheme for equivalent 0-1 integer programming problem.

Solving a system of fuzzy relation equations completely is a hard problem. The total number of minimal solutions has a combinatorial nature in terms of problem size. Further more, general branch-and-bound algorithm is NP-complete. Therefore, an efficient method is still required.

In this paper, we propose a procedure that takes care of the characteristics of feasible domain which shows that every variable is bounded between a minimal and the maximal values. According to definition(1.5), we can reduce the problem size by removing those constraints which bound the variables. Clearly, none of the variables gets increased over its maximum and gets decreased below zero. These boundary values can be assigned to any variable in order to improve the value of objective function and to satisfy the functional constraints.

In section 2, we shall make the solution analysis and shall describe an algorithm. In section 3, the step by step algorithm will be developed. In section 4, two numerical examples will be considered for illustration purpose.

Tabular computations of algorithm are presented. Conclusions are given in the last section 5.

2 Solution Analysis and Algorithm

Let $\hat{x} \in X(A, b) \neq \varphi$. Define

$$I_j = [\, i \in I \mid T(\hat{x}_i, a_{ij}) = b_j, \, a_{ij} \geq b_j \,], \quad \forall j \in J \tag{12}$$

$$J_i = \{j \in J \mid T(\hat{x}_i, a_{ij}) = b_j, \, a_{ij} \geq b_j \,\}, \quad \forall i \in I \tag{13}$$

Notice that the non-negative variables

$$x_i \leq \hat{x}_i, \quad \forall i \in I \tag{14}$$

have an upper bound.

We write (14) as

$$x_i = \hat{x}_i - y_i, \quad \forall i \in I \tag{15}$$

and refer x_i and y_i as complementary decision variables. Thus, whenever

(i) $x_i = 0$, then $y_i = \hat{x}_i$, and

(ii) $x_i = \hat{x}_i$, then $y_i = 0$.

Clearly, $0 \leq x_i \leq \hat{x}_i$ implies $0 \leq y_i \leq \hat{x}_i$

Rather than taking each variable $y_i \in [0, \hat{x}_i]$, we consider that the each of y_i's takes its values from the boundary values 0 (lower bound) and/or $\hat{x}_i$ (upper bound). This reduces the problem size, also. The original problem(1) can be defined, in terms of complementary variables y_i, as

$$\text{minimize } Z = Z_0 - \sum_{i=1}^{m} c_i y_i$$

subject to

$$\underset{i \in I_j}{Inf} -T(y_i, a_{ij}) = 0, \, \forall j \in J,$$

$$y_i \in \{0, \hat{x}_i\} \quad \forall i \in I. \text{ Where, } Z_0 = \sum_{i=1}^{m} c_i \hat{x}_i \tag{16}$$

2.1 Lemma. If $a_{ij} > 0$, some y_i have to become zero for solving (16).

Proof: T is continuous t-norm. $0 \leq y_i \leq \hat{x}_i$. For $i \in I_j$ and $j \in J_i$,

$$y_i = 0 \implies T(y_i, a_{ij}) = 0 \implies \underset{i \in I_j}{Inf} -T(y_i, a_{ij}) = 0.$$

Again, $\underset{i \in I_j}{Inf} -T(y_i, a_{ij})=0 \Rightarrow T(y_i, a_{ij})=0$, $\exists\ i \in I_j$.

Since $a_{ij} > 0$, therefore, $y_i = 0$ for some $i \in I_j$. $\square$

2.2 Lemma. If $c_i > 0$, selecting $y_i = \breve{x}_i$ improves the objective function in (16).

Proof: $Z_0 \geq Z_0 - \sum_{i=1}^{m} c_i y_i = Z \geq Z_0 - \sum_{i=1}^{m} c_i \breve{x}_i \geq min\ Z.$ $\square$

We call y_i, as leaving basic variable, if it takes the value $\breve{x}_i$ to improve Z_0 and we call it as entering non-basic variable, if it takes the value zero to satisfy the constraint(s). From (14), it is clear that the membership grade x_i of a fuzzy number can not exceed $\breve{x}_i$. Solution set (10) is a poset, Sanchez [21]. The objective of optimization problem is to find minimum value of Z. Intuitively, minimum Z can be achieved with maximally graded ($\hat{x}$) fuzzy numbers, if costs are negative, where as, at minimally graded ($\breve{x}$) fuzzy numbers, if costs are positive. So, the technique is to select complementary variables y_i from the boundaries 0 and $\breve{x}_i$ so as it either improves the initial value Z_0 or satisfies the constraint(s). Every complementary variable has to follow either of two rules:

(i)Rule for selecting entering non-basic variable, i.e.choose $y_i = 0$ in order to satisfy the constraints of J_j..(ii)Rule for selecting leaving basic variable, i.e. choose $y_i = \breve{x}_i$ in order to improve initial Z-value.

Procedure, adopted, is to find y_{NB}^E and y_B^L such that $y = (y_{NB}^E, y_B^L)$ and

$$y_i = \begin{cases} 0 & y_i \in y_{NB}^E \\ \breve{x}_i & y_i \in y_B^L \end{cases} \qquad \forall\ i \in I \qquad (17)$$

$y_{NB}^E = \{\ y_i \mid$ it satisfies the constraints of (16) for $j \in J_i\ )$ is the set of entering non-basic variables and $y_B^L = \{\ y_i \mid y_i \notin y_{NB}^E\ \}$ is the set of leaving basic variables.

Let c_{NB}^E and c_B^L denote the costs of variables y_{NB}^E and y_B^L respectively. Thus, cost vector $c = (c_{NB}^E, c_B^L)$.

To be practical, a $y_i \in y_{NB}^E$ is selected in such a way that it has least effect on Z-function and as well as satisfies the constraints I_j, $j \in J_j$. The following steps are involved in generating the set of entering non-basic variables.

2.3 Algorithm I

  (i) Compute the value set $V = \{\ V_i \mid V_i = c_i\ \breve{x}_i$ for each $i \in I\}$

  (ii) Generate index set $I' = \{k \mid V_k = min_{i \in I} (V_i)\}$

  (iii) Define $J_k = \{j \in J \mid k \in I_j\ \}$, $\forall k \in I'$.

(iv) Construct set $\qquad \{ y_k \,|\, k \in I' \} \subseteq y^E_{NB}$.

(v) Select the values for y_k, $\forall k \in I'$, according to (16) .

(vi) Remove the row(s) $k \in I'$ and   column(s) $j \in J_k$.

(vii) Define $\qquad\qquad\qquad \widehat{I} = I \setminus I'$ and $\widehat{J} = J \setminus \bigcup_k J_k$.

(viii) Set $I \leftarrow \widehat{I}$ and $J \leftarrow \widehat{J}$. Go to (i).

(ix) The generated $\qquad\qquad y^E_{NB} = \bigcup_k \{ y_k \mid y_k = 0 \}$.

Note: 1. Since $x_i + y_i = \widehat{x}_i$, $\forall i \in I$. Structure of I_j and J_i will remain unchanged

2. If $\overline{I} = \{ i \mid y_i = 0, i \in I \}$, then $\quad \| \overline{I} \| \leq \min(m,n)$.

This will help us in computing the complexity of the algorithm.
We give basic algorithm to obtain optimal solution of the problem (1).

3   The Basic Algorithm

Step 1: *Finding the maximum solution of system of FRE in* (1).
Consider the existence proposition 2 and compute $\widehat{x}$ according to (6).

Compute $\qquad\qquad\qquad \widehat{x} = A \lozenge b = [\, \underset{j \in J}{Inf} \, (a_{ij} \lozenge b_j)]_i \in {}_I$

Step 2: *Test the feasibility.* If $\widehat{x} O A = b$ then feasible. Else, infeasible and stop!

Step 3: *Compute index sets.* Compute

$$I_j = \{ i \in I \mid T(\widehat{x}_i, a_{ij}) = b_j \}, \ \forall \ j \in J \text{and} J_i = \{ j \in J \mid i \in I_j \}, \forall \ i \in I .$$

Step 4: *Problem transformation.* Transform the problem(1), given in variables x, into the problem(16)involving complementary variable y.

Step 5: *Generating entering non-basic variables.* Generate the set

$$y^E_{NB} = \bigcup_k \{ y_k \mid y_k = 0 \}, \text{ using algorithm I.}$$

Step 6: *Generating leaving basic variables.* Generate the set

$$y^L_B = \{ y_i \mid y_i \notin y^E_{NB} \}. \text{ Set } y_i = \widehat{x}_i, \ \forall \ y_i \in y^L_B.$$

Step 7: *Generating complementary variables.* Complementary decision vector,

$$y^* = (y^E_{NB}, y^L_B).$$

Step 8: *Generating the decision variables.* Compute the decision vector x*, according to (15).

i.e. $\qquad\qquad\qquad x^*_i = \widehat{x}_i - y^*_i \ \forall i \in I.$

Step 9: *Computing optimal value of objective function.*

$$Z^* = Z_0 - \sum c_B^L y_B^L$$

4 The Illustration

Following two examples are considered to illustrate the procedure.

Example 1. Solving problem (1) with t-norm (2) and inverse operator (7).
Let $m = 6$, $n = 4$, $c=(3,4,1,1,-1,5)$, $b=(0.85,0.6,0.5,0.1)$ and

$$A = \begin{bmatrix} 0.5 & 0.2 & 0.8 & 0.1 \\ 0.8 & 0.2 & 0.8 & 0.1 \\ 0.9 & 0.1 & 0.4 & 0.1 \\ 0.3 & 0.95 & 0.1 & 0.1 \\ 0.85 & 0.1 & 0.1 & 0.1 \\ 0.4 & 0.8 & 0.1 & 0.0 \end{bmatrix}$$

Step 1: Finding the maximum solution: $\hat{x} = (0.5, 0.5, 0.85, 0.6, 1.0, 0.6)$.

Step 2: $\hat{x} \circ A = b$. Solution is feasible.

Step 3: Index sets I_j's and J_i's are: $I_1=\{3,5\}, I_2=\{4,6\}, I_3=\{1,2\}, I_4=\{5\}; J_1=\{3\}, J_2 = \{3\}, J_3 = \{1\}, J_4 = \{2\}, J_5 = \{1,4\}, J_6 = \{2\}$.

Step 4: Transformed problem is min $Z = Z_0 - 3y_1 - 4y_2 - y_3 - y_4 + y_5 - 5y_6$, $Z_0 = 6.95$, subject to $\underset{i=1,\dots,6}{Inf}$ -min $(y_i, a_{ij}) = b_j$, $j=1,\dots,4$.

$y_1 \in \{0, 0.5\}, y_2 \in \{0, 0.5\}, y_3 \in \{0. 0.85\}, y_4 \in \{0, 0.6\}, y_5 \in \{0, 1.0\}, y_6 \in \{0, 0.6\}$.

Step 5: Generating the set y_{NB}^E. This is shown via table.

	I_1 ↓	I_2 ↓	I_3	I_4 ↓	V
J_1			1		1.5
J_2			2		2.0
J_3	3				0.85
J_4		4			0.6
J_5	5			5	-1.0←
J_6		6			3.0

Minimum (V) = -1.0 corresponds to y_5. Setting $y_5 = 0$, satisfies the constraints of J_5 = {1,4}. Remove row 5 and columns I_1, I_4 from the table. Since J_3 becomes empty, therefore row 3 will disappear. The next table is

	I_2 ↓	I_3	V
J_1		1	1.5
J_2		2	2.0
J_4	4		0.6←
J_6	6		3.0

Minimum (V) = 0.6 corresponds to y_4. Setting y_4 =0 satisfies the constraint of J_4 = {2}. Removing row 4 and column I_2 from the table. The reduced table is

	I_3 ↓	V
J_1	1	1.5←
J_2	2	2.0

Minimum (V) =1.5 corresponds to y_1. Setting y_1 = 0 satisfies the constraint of $J_1 = \{3\}$. The generated $y_{NB}^{E} = (y_1, y_4, y_5) = (0, 0, 0)$.

Step 6: Generating the set y_B^L. $y_B^L = (y_2, y_3, y_6) = (0.5, 0.85, 0.6)$

Step 7: $y^* = (0, 0.5, 0.85, 0, 0, 0.6)$

Step 8: $x^* = (0.5, 0, 0, 0.6, 1.0, 0)$

Step 9: $Z^* = 6.95 - 5.85 = 1.10$.

Example 2. Solving problem (1) with t-norm (3) and inverse operator (8). Let m = 10 and n = 8.
c = (-4, 3, 2, 3, 5, 2, 1, 2, 5, 6),b = (0.48, 0.56, 0.72, 0.56, 0.64, 0.72, 0.42, 0.64) and

$$A = \begin{bmatrix} 0.6 & 0.2 & 0.5 & 0.3 & 0.7 & 0.5 & 0.2 & 0.8 \\ 0.5 & 0.6 & 0.9 & 0.5 & 0.8 & 0.9 & 0.3 & 0.8 \\ 0.1 & 0.9 & 0.4 & 0.7 & 0.5 & 0.7 & 0.4 & 0.7 \\ 0.1 & 0.6 & 0.2 & 0.5 & 0.4 & 0.1 & 0.7 & 0.5 \\ 0.3 & 0.8 & 0.8 & 0.8 & 0.8 & 0.5 & 0.5 & 0.8 \\ 0.8 & 0.4 & 0.1 & 0.1 & 0.2 & 0.8 & 0.8 & 0.3 \\ 0.4 & 0.5 & 0.4 & 0.8 & 0.4 & 0.7 & 0.3 & 0.4 \\ 0.6 & 0.3 & 0.4 & 0.3 & 0.1 & 0.2 & 0.5 & 0.7 \\ 0.2 & 0.5 & 0.7 & 0.4 & 0.9 & 0.9 & 0.7 & 0.2 \\ 0.1 & 0.3 & 0.6 & 0.6 & 0.6 & 0.4 & 0.4 & 0.8 \end{bmatrix}$$

Step 1: Finding the maximum solution. $\hat{x} = (0.8, 0.8, 0.622, 0.6, 0.7, 0.525, 0.7, 0.8, 0.6, 0.8)$.

Step 2: $\hat{x} oA = b$. Solution is feasible.

Step3: Index sets I_j's and J_i's are: $I_1=\{1,8\}$, $I_2=\{3,5\}$, $I_3=\{2\}$, $I_4=\{5,7\}$, $I_5=\{2\}$, $I_6=\{2\}$, $I_7=\{4,6,9\}$, $I_8=\{1,2.10\}$

$J_1 = \{1, 8\}$, $J_2 = \{3, 5, 6, 8\}$, $J_3 = \{2\}$, $J_4 = \{7\}$, $J_5 = \{2, 4\}$, $J_6 = \{7\}$, $J_7 = \{4\}$, $J_8 = \{1\}$, $J_9 = \{7\}$, $J_{10} = \{8\}$.

Step 4: Problem (1) can be transformed to become

$$\min Z = Z_0 + 4y_1 - 3y_2 - 2y_3 - 3y_4 - 5y_5 - 2y_6 - y_7 - 2y_8 - 5y_9 - 6y_{10} \ , Z_0 = 16.894$$

subject to

$$\underset{i \in I}{Inf} - (y_i \cdot a_{ij}) = 0, \quad \forall \ j \in J$$

$y_1 \in \{0, 0.8\}$, $y_2 \in \{0, 0.8\}$, $y_3 \in \{0. 0.622\}$, $y_4 \in \{0, 0.6\}$, $y_5 \in \{0, 0.7\}$, $y_6 \in \{0, 0.525\}$, $y_7 \in \{0, 0.7\}$, $y_8 \in \{0, 0.8\}$, $y_9 \in \{0. 0.6\}$, $y_{10} \in \{0, 0.8\}$.

Step 5: Computing the set y_{NB}^E. The associated table given below, yields

	I_1 ↓	I_2	I_3	I_4	I_5	I_6	I_7	I_8 ↓	V
J_1	1							1	-3.2←
J_2		2			2	2		2	2.4
J_3		3							1.244
J_4							4		1.8
J_5		5		5					3.5
J_6							6		1.05
J_7				7					0.7
J_8	8								1.6
J_9							9		3.0
J_{10}								10	4.8

$$y_{NB}^E = (\ y_1, y_2, y_3, y_6, y_7\ ) = (0, 0, 0, 0, 0\ )$$

Step 6: $y_B^L = (y_4, y_5, y_8, y_9, y_{10}) = (0.6, 0.7, 0.8, 0.6, 0.8)$.

Step 7: $y^* = (\ 0, 0, 0, 0.6, 0.7, 0, 0, 0.8, 0.6, 0.8\ )$.

Step 8: $x^* = (0.8, 0.8, 0.622, 0, 0, 0.525, 0.7, 0, 0, 0\ )$.

Step 9: $Z^* = 16.894 - 14.700 = 2.194$.

5 Conclusions

This paper studies a linear optimization problem subject to a system of fuzzy relation equations and presents a procedure to find the optimal solution. Due to non-convexity of feasible domain, traditional methods, viz, simplex method etc. cannot be applied.

Procedure, adopted here, finds a way of separating the set of decision variables into basic and non-basic variables and evaluates their values. Since every binding variable is bounded and has discrete behavior, because of non-convexity, they can assume only boundary values of the interval in which they lie. In turn, we define the complementary variables and hence the complementary optimization problem. Algorithm is developed to solve this complementary problem.

Effectively, the whole procedure is presented in tabular form and it is found that time complexity is lesser. Procedure discussed may be economical in solving some related problems. An extension of this paper and, of course, comparison with other approaches will appear in next paper.

Acknowledgements

Author is thankful to anonymous referees for their valuable suggestions.

References

1. G.I. Adamopoulos, C.P. Pappis, Some results on the resolution of fuzzy relation equations, Fuzzy Sets and Systems 60(1993) 83-88.
2. B. De Baets, Analytical solution methods for fuzzy relational equations in D. Dubois, H.Prade (eds), Fundamentals of Fuzzy Sets, The Handbook of Fuzzy Sets Series, Kluwer Academic Publishers, Dordrecht, NL 2000.
3. B.De Baets, E.Kerre, A primer on solving fuzzy relational equations on the unit interval, Internal. J.Uncertain. Fuzziness Knowledge-Based Systems 2 (1994) 205-225
4. M. Bourke, D.G. Fisher, Solution algorithms for fuzzy relational equations with max- product composition, Fuzzy Sets and Systems 94(1998) 61-69.
5. L. Cheng, B. Peng, The fuzzy relation equation with union or intersection preserving operator, Fuzzy Sets and Systems 25(1988) 19-204.
6. F. Chung, T. Lee, A new look at solving a system of fuzzy relational equations, Fuzzy Sets and Systems 88(1997) 343-353.
7. E. Czogala, J. Drewniak, W. Pedrycz, fuzzy relation equations on a finite set, Fuzzy Sets and Systems 7(1982) 89-101
8. S.C. Fang, G. Li, Solving fuzzy relation equations with a linear objective function, Fuzzy Sets and Systems 103 (1999) 107-113.
9. S.Z. Guo, P.Z. Wang, A.Di Nola, S. Sessa, Further contributions to the study of finite relation equations, Fuzzy Sets and Systems 26(1988) 93-104.
10. M.M. Gupta, J.Qi, Design of fuzzy logic controllers based on generalized T-operators, Fuzzy Sets Syst., vol. 40 (1991) 473-489.
11. M. Higashi, G.J. Klir, Resolution of finite fuzzy relation equations, Fuzzy Sets and Systems 13(1984) 64-82.
12. J Loetamophong, S.C. Fang, An Efficient Solution Procedure for Fuzzy Relation Equations with Max-Product composition, IEEE Tarns. Fuzzy systems, vol.7 (1999), 441- 445.
13. J. Leotamonphong, S.C. Fang, Optimization of fuzzy relation equations with max-product composition, Fuzzy Sets and Systems 118(2001) 509-517.
14. G. Li, S.C. Fang, On the resolution of finite fuzzy relation equations, OR Report No.322, North Carolina State University, Raleigh, North Carolina, May 1996.
15. J.Lu, S.C. Fang, Solving nonlinear optimization problems with fuzzy relation equation constraints, Fuzzy Sets and Systems 119(2001) 1-20.
16. A.Di Nola, Relational equations in totally ordered lattices and their complete resolution, J. Math. Anal. Appl. 107(1985) 148-155.
17. A.Di Nola, S. Sessa, W. Pedrycz, E. Sanchez, Fuzzy Relation Equation and their Applications to Knowledge Engineering, Kluwer Academic Publisher, Dordrecht, 1989.

18. A.Di Nola, S. Sessa, W. Pedrycz, W.Pei-Zhuang, Fuzzy relation equations under a class of triangular norms: a survey and new results, Stochastica, vol. 8(1984) 99-145.
19. W.Pedrycz, An identification algorithm in fuzzy relation systems, Fuzzy Sets Syst.,vol. 13 (1984) 153-167.
20. M.Prevot, Algorithm for the solution of fuzzy relations, Fuzzy Sets and Systems 5 (1981) 319-322.
21. E. Sanchez, Resolution of composite fuzzy relation equations, Information and Control 30 (197 6) 38-48.
22. W. Wu, Fuzzy reasoning and fuzzy relational equations, Fuzzy Sets and Systems, 20(1986) 67-78.
23. Y.-K.Wu, S.-M.Guu,J. Y.-C.Liu, An Accelerated Approach for Solving Fuzzy Relation Equations With a Linear Objective Function, IEEE, Trans. Fuzzy Syst.V.10, No.4 (2002), 552-558.
24. R.R. Yager, Some procedures for selecting fuzzy set-theoretic operations, Int. J. General Syst, vol.8(1982) 235-242.
25. H.J. Zimmermann, Fuzzy set theory and its applications, Kluwer Academic Publishers, Boston, 1991.

Progressive Boosting for Classifier Committee Learning

Md. Waselul Haque Sadid, Md. Nazrul Islam Mondal, Md. Shamsul Alam,
Abu Sayeed Md. Sohail, and Boshir Ahmed

Department of CSE,
Rajshahi University of Engineering and Technology
Rajshahi 6204
{whsadid,nimbd,shamsulbd,boshirbd}@yahoo.com

Abstract. Most applications of artificial intelligence to tasks of practical importance are based on constructing a model of the knowledge used by a human expert. In a classification model, the connection between classes and properties
can be defined by something as simple as a flowchart or as complex and unstructured as a procedures manual. Classifier committee learning methods generate multiple classifiers to form a committee by repeated application of a single base learning algorithm. The committee members vote to decide the final
classification. Two such methods are bagging and boosting for improving the
predictive power of classifier learning systems. This paper studies a different
approach progressive boosting of decision trees. Instead of sampling the same
number of data points at each boosting iteration t, our progressive boosting algorithm draws n_t data according to the sampling schedule. an empirical evaluation of a variant of this method shows that the progressive boosting can significantly reduce the error rate of decision tree learning. On average this is more
accurate than bagging and boosting.

1 Introduction

Accuracy is a primary concern in all applications of learning and is easily measured.
There has recently been renewed interest in increasing accuracy by generating and
aggregating multiple classifiers. Although the idea of growing multiple trees is not
new, the justification for such methods is often empirical. In contrast, two new approaches for producing and using several classifiers are applicable to a wide variety of
learning systems and are based on theoretical analyses of the behavior of the composite classifier. The data for classifier learning systems consists of attribute-value vectors or instances. Both bootstrap aggregating or bagging and boosting manipulate the
training data in order to generate different classifiers.

Many existing data analysis algorithms require all the data to be resident in a main
memory, which is clearly untenable in many large databases nowadays. Even fast data
mining algorithms designed to run in a main memory with a linear asymptotic time
may be prohibitively slow, when data is stored on a disk, due to the many orders of
magnitude difference between main and secondary memory retrieval time.

Boosting sometimes leads to deterioration in generalization performance. Progressive sampling starts with a small sample in an initial iteration and uses progressively
larger ones in subsequent iterations until model accuracy no longer improves. As a
result, a near-optimal minimal size of the data set needed for efficient learning an
acceptably accurate model is identified. Instead of constructing a single predictor on
identified data set, our approach attempts to reuse the most accurate and sufficiently
diverse classifiers built in sampling iterations and to combine their predictions. In

S. Manandhar et al. (Eds.): AACC 2004, LNCS 3285, pp. 52–58, 2004.
© Springer-Verlag Berlin Heidelberg 2004

order to further improve achieved prediction accuracy, we propose a weighted sampling, based on a boosting technique [4], where the prediction models in subsequent iterations are built on those examples on which the previous predictor had poor performance. The sampling procedure is controlled not only by the accuracy of previous prediction models but also by considering spatially correlated data points. In our approach, the data points that are highly spatially correlated are not likely to be sampled together in the same sample, since they bear less useful data information than two non-correlated data points.

2   Related Works

We assume a given set of N instances, each belonging to one K classes and a learning system that constructs a classifier from a training set of instances. The number T of repetitions or trials will be treated as fixed, although this parameter could be determined automatically by cross-validation.

2.1   Bagging

For each trial $t = 1, 2, \ldots, T$, a training set of size N is sampled with replacement from the original instances. This training set is the same size as the original data, but some instances may not appear in it while others appear more than once. A classifier C^t is generated from the sample and final classifier C^* is formed by aggregating the T classifiers from these repetitions. The classifier learned on trial t will be denoted as C^t while C^* is the composite (bagged or boosted) classifier. To classify an instance x, a vote for class k is recorded by every classifier for which $C^t(x)=k$ and $C^*(x)$ is then the class with the most votes. Using a CART as the learning system, Breiman [2] reports results of bagging on seven moderate-sized datasets. With the number of replicates T set at 50, the average error of the bagged classifier C^* ranges from 0.57 to 0.94 of the corresponding error when a single classifier is learned. Breiman [2] introduces the concept of an order-correct classifier-learning system as one that, over many training sets, tends to predict the correct class of a test instance more frequently than any other class. An order correct learner may not produce optimal classifiers, but Breiman [2] shows that aggregating classifiers produced by an order correct learner results in an optimal classifier.

2.2   Boosting

The version of boosting investigated is AdaBoost.M1. Instead of drawing a succession of independent bootstrap samples from the original instances, boosting maintains a weight for each instance- the higher the weight, the more the instance influences the classifier learned. At each trial, the vector of weight is adjusted to reflect the performance of the corresponding classifier, with the result that the misclassified instances are increased. The final classifier also aggregates the learned classifiers by voting, but each classifiers vote is a function of its accuracy. Let w_x^t [1] denote the weight of instance x at trial t where, for every x, $w_x^1 =1/N$. at each trial $t=1, 2, \ldots, T$, a classifier C^t is constructed from the given instances under the distribution w^t. the error ε^t of this classifier is also measured with respect to the weights of the instances that it mis-classifies. If ε^t is greater than 0.5, the trials are terminated and T is altered to t-1. Conversely, if C^t correctly classifies all instances so that ε^t is zero, the trials terminate and T becomes t. Otherwise, the weight vector w^{t+1} for the next trial is generated by multiplying the weights of instances that C^t classifies correctly by the factor $\beta^t = \varepsilon^t / (1 - \varepsilon^t)$ and then renormalizing so that $\sum_x w_x^{t+1}$ equals 1. The boosted classifier C^* is obtained by summing the votes of the classifiers $C^1, C^2, ..., C^T$, where the vote for classifier C^t is worth $\log(1/\beta^t)$ units. The objective of boosting is to construct a classifier C^* that performs well on the training data even when its constituent classifiers C^t are weak. A simple alteration attempts to avoid overfitting by keeping T as small as possible without impacting this objective. AdaBoost.M1 stops when the error of any C^t drops to zero, but does not address the possibility that C^* might correctly classify all the training data even though no C^t does. Further trials in this situation would seem to offer no gain-they will increase the complexity of C^* but cannot improve its performance on the training data.

2.3 Progressive Sampling

Given a data set with N examples, its minimal size n_{min} is to be determined, for which a sufficiently accurate prediction model will be achieved. The modification of geometric progressive sampling is used in order to maximize accuracy of learned models. The central idea of the progressive sampling is to use a sampling schedule:

$$S = \{n_0, n_1, n_2, n_3, ..., n_k\}$$

where each n_i is an integer that specifies the size of a sample to be provided to a training algorithm at iteration i. Here, the n_i is defined as:

$$n_i = n_0 \cdot a^i ,$$

where a is a constant which defines how fast we increase the size of the sample presented to an induction algorithm during sampling iterations. The relationship between sample size and model accuracy is depicted by a learning curve. The horizontal axis represents n, the number of instances in a given training set that can vary between zero and the maximal number of instances N. The vertical axis represents the accuracy of the model produced by a training algorithm when given a training set with n instances. Learning curves typically have a steep slope portion early in the curve, a more gently sloping middle part, and a plateau late in the curve. The plateau occurs when adding additional data instances is not likely to significantly improve prediction. Depending on the data, the middle part and the plateau can be missing from the learning curve, when N is small. Conversely, the plateau region can constitute the majority of curves when N is very large. In a recent study of two large business data sets, Harris-Jones and Haines found that learning curves reach a plateau quickly for some algorithms, but small accuracy improvements continue up to N for other algorithms [3].

The progressive sampling [3] was designed to increase the speed of inductive learning by providing roughly the same accuracy and using significantly smaller data sets than available. We used this idea to further increase the speed of inductive learning for very large databases and also to attempt to improve the total prediction accuracy.

3   Progressive Boosting for Decision Tree

Samples often provide the same accuracy with less computational cost. We propose here an effective technique based on the idea of progressive sampling when progressively large larger samples are used for training as long as model accuracy improves.

3.1   Progressive Boosting

The proposed progressive boosting algorithm is based on an integration of Adaboost.M2 procedure [4] into the standard progressive sampling technique. The AdaBoost.M2 algorithm proceeds in a series of T rounds. In each round t, a weak learning algorithm is called and presented with a different distribution D_t that is altered by emphasizing particular training examples. The distribution is updated to give wrong classifications higher weights than correct classifications. The entire weighted training set is given to the weak learner to compute the weak hypothesis h_t. At the end, all weak hypotheses are combined into a single hypothesis h_{fn}.

Instead of sampling the same number of data points at each boosting iteration t, our progressive boosting algorithm (Fig. 1) draws n_t data points ($n_t = n_0 \cdot a^{t-1}$) according to the sampling schedule S. Therefore, we start with a small sample containing n_0 data points, and in each subsequent boosting round we increase the size of the sample used for learning a weak classifier L_t.

Each weak classifier produces a weak hypothesis h_t. At the end of each boosting round t all weak hypotheses are combined into a single hypotheses H_t. However, the distribution for drawing data samples in subsequent sampling iterations is still updated according to the performance of a single classifier constructed in the current sampling iteration.

➤   Given: Set S $\{(x_1, y_1), \ldots , (x_n, y_m)\}$ $x_i \in X$, with labels $y_i \in Y = \{1, \ldots, C\}$
➤   Let B = $\{(i, y): i = 1,\ldots,N, y \neq y_i\}$. Let $t = 0$.
➤   Initialize the distribution D_1 over the examples, such that $D_1(i) = 1/N$.
➤   *REPEAT*
1. $t = t + 1$
2. Draw a sample Q_t that contains $n_0 \cdot a^{t-1}$ data instances according to the distribution D_t.
3. Train a weak learner L_t using distribution D_t
4. Compute the pseudo-loss of hypothesis h_t:

$$\varepsilon_t = \frac{1}{2} \cdot \sum_{(i,y) \in B} D_t(i, y)(1 - h_t(x_i, y_i) + h_t(x_i, y))$$

5. Set $\beta_t = \varepsilon_t / (1 - \varepsilon_t)$ and $w_t = (1/2) \cdot (1 - h_t(x_i, y) + h_t(x_i, y_i))$
6. Update D_t: $D_{t+1}(i, y) = (D_t(i, y) / Z_t) \cdot \beta_t^{w_t}$
where Z_t is a normalization constant chosen such that D_{t+1} is a distribution.
7. Combine all weak hypotheses into a single hypothesis:

$$H_t = \arg\max_{y \in Y} \sum_{j=1}^{t} \left(\log \frac{1}{\beta_j} \right) \cdot h_j(x, y)$$

UNTIL (accuracy of H_t is not significantly larger than accuracy of H_{t-1})
8. – Sort the classifiers from ensemble according to their accuracy.
   – *REPEAT* removing classifiers with accuracy less than prespecified threshold
   UNTIL there is no longer improvement in prediction accuracy

---

Fig. 1. The progressive boosting algorithm

We always stop the progressive sampling procedure when the accuracy of the hypothesis H_t, obtained in the tth sampling iteration, lies in 95% confidence interval of the prediction accuracy of hypothesis H_{t-1} achieved in the $(t-1)$th sampling iteration:

$$acc(H_t) \in \left[acc(H_{t-1}), acc(H_{t-1}) + 1.645 \cdot \sqrt{\frac{acc(H_{t-1}) \cdot (1 - acc(H_{t-1}))}{N}} \right]$$

where $acc(H_j)$ represents classification accuracy achieved by hypothesis H_j constructed in jth sampling iteration on the entire training set. It is well known in machine learning theory that an ensemble of classifiers must be both diverse and accurate in order to improve the overall prediction accuracy. Diversity of classifiers is achieved by learning classifiers on different data sets obtained through weighted sampling in each sampling iteration. Nevertheless, some of the classifiers constructed in early sampling iterations may not be accurate enough due to insufficient number of data examples used for learning. Therefore, before combining the classifiers constructed in sampling iterations, we prune the classifier ensemble by removing all classifiers whose accuracy on a validation set is less than some prespecified threshold until the accuracy of the ensemble no longer improves. A validation set is determined before starting the sampling procedure as a 30% sample of the entire training data set. Assuming that the entire training set is much larger than the reduced data set used for learning, our choice of the validation sets should not introduce any significant unfair bias, since only the small fraction of data points from the reduced data set are included in the validation set. When the reduced data set is not significantly smaller than the entire training set, the unseen separated test and validation sets are used for estimating the accuracy of the proposed methods. Since our goal is to identify a nonredundant representative subset, the usual way of drawing samples with replacement used in the AdaBoost.M2 procedure cannot be employed here. Therefore, the reminder stochastic sampling without replacement [8] is used, where the data examples cannot be sampled more than once. Therefore, as a representative subset we obtain a set of distinct data examples with no duplicates.

3.2   Comparison Progressive Boosting with Boosting, Bagging and C4.5

Table 1 shows the error rates of the four algorithms. To facilitate the pairwise comparisons among these algorithms, error ratios are derived from these error rates and are included in Table 1. An error ratio, for example for Boost vs C4.5, presents a result for Boost divided by the corresponding result for C4.5 { a value less than 1 indicates an improvement due to Boost . To compare the error rates of two algorithms in a domain, a two-tailed pairwise t-test on the error rates of the 20 trials is carried out. The difference is considered as significant, if the significance level of the t-test is better than 0.05.

From Table 1, we have the following four observations. (1) All the three committee learning algorithms can significantly reduce the error rate of the base tree learning algorithm. The average error rate of C4.5 in the 40 domains is 19.18%. Boosting, Bagging, and Progressive Boosting reduce the average error rate to 15.97%, 16.35%, and 14.81% respectively. The average relative error reductions of these three committee learning algorithms over C4.5 in the 40 domains are 20%, 14%, and 24% respectively. A one-tailed pairwise sign-test shows that all these error reductions are significant at a level better than 0.0001. (2) Boosting is more accurate than Bagging on

Table 1. The error rates of the four algorithms.

Domain	Error rate				Error rate ratio				
	C4.5	Boost	Bagg	P_Boost	Boost	Bag	P.Boost	P. Boost vs	
					Vs C4.5			Boost	Bag
Anncaling	7.40	4.90	5.73	4.96	0.66	0.77	0.67	1.02	0.87
Andiology	21.39	15.41	18.29	16.04	0.72	0.86	0.75	1.04	0.88
Automobil	16.31	13.42	17.80	12.56	0.82	1.09	0.77	0.94	0.71
Breast(w)	5.08	3.22	3.37	3.05	0.63	0.66	0.60	0.95	0.91
Chess(kp)	0.72	0.36	0.59	0.48	0.50	0.82	0.66	1.32	0.81
Chess(kn)	8.89	3.54	7.80	5.42	0.40	0.88	0.61	1.52	0.69
Credit(a)	14.49	13.91	13.84	14.06	0.96	0.96	0.97	1.01	1.02
Credit(g)	29.40	25.45	24.95	24.40	0.87	0.85	0.83	0.95	0.98
ECG	37.80	36.24	33.57	36.67	0.96	0.89	0.97	1.01	1.09
Glass	33.62	21.09	27.38	21.85	0.63	0.81	0.65	1.03	0.80
Heart(c)	22.07	18.80	18.45	15.45	0.85	0.84	0.70	0.82	0.84
Heart(h)	21.09	21.25	20.38	17.72	1.01	0.97	0.84	0.83	0.87
Hepatitis	20.63	17.67	18.73	17.95	0.86	0.91	0.87	1.01	0.96
Colic	15.76	19.84	15.77	16.55	1.26	1.00	1.05	0.83	1.05
H votes 84	5.62	4.82	4.71	4.22	0.86	0.84	0.75	0.87	0.90
Hypo	0.46	0.32	0.45	0.36	0.70	0.98	0.79	1.13	0.80
H_thyroid	0.71	1.14	0.71	0.77	1.61	1.00	1.08	0.67	1.08
Image	2.97	1.58	2.62	1.75	0.53	0.88	0.59	1.11	0.67
Iris	4.33	5.67	5.00	4.63	1.31	1.15	1.07	0.82	0.93
Labor	23.67	10.83	14.50	13.73	0.46	0.61	0.58	1.26	0.95
LED24	36.50	32.75	31.00	25.55	0.90	0.85	0.70	0.79	0.82
Letter	12.16	2.95	5.93	3.28	0.24	0.49	0.27	1.12	0.55
L. disorder	35.36	28.88	27.43	29.35	0.82	0.78	0.83	1.01	1.07
L. cancer	57.50	53.75	42.50	43.70	0.93	0.74	0.76	0.82	1.03
Lympho	21.88	16.86	18.50	17.72	0.77	0.85	0.81	1.05	0.96
Nettalk(L)	25.88	22.14	22.98	19.67	0.86	0.89	0.76	0.88	0.86
Nettalk(P)	18.97	16.01	17.33	17.26	0.84	0.91	0.91	1.08	1.00
Nettalk(S)	17.25	11.91	14.97	12.08	0.69	0.87	0.70	1.01	0.81
Pima	23.97	26.57	23.37	22.29	1.11	0.97	0.93	0.84	0.95
P. operativ	29.44	38.89	30.00	28.85	1.32	1.02	0.98	0.74	0.96
P. tumor	59.59	55.75	55.46	48.86	0.94	0.93	0.82	0.87	0.88
Promoters	17.50	4.68	9.32	5.78	0.27	0.53	0.33	1.21	0.62
Sick	1.30	0.92	1.18	1.13	0.71	0.91	0.87	1.23	0.96
Solar flare	15.62	17.57	15.91	14.37	1.12	1.02	0.92	0.82	0.90
Sonar	26.43	14.64	21.12	15.07	0.55	0.80	0.57	1.03	0.71
Soyabean	8.49	6.22	6.80	5.01	0.73	0.80	0.59	0.81	0.74
S. junction	5.81	4.80	5.18	4.30	0.83	0.89	0.74	0.89	0.83
Vehicle	28.50	22.40	25.30	23.37	0.79	0.89	0.82	1.04	0.92
W.form-21	23.83	18.33	19.67	18.59	0.77	0.83	0.78	1.01	0.95
Wine	8.96	3.35	5.29	3.58	0.37	0.59	0.40	1.07	0.68
Average	19.18	15.97	16.35	14.81	0.80	0.86	0.76	0.98	0.88

average, but Bagging is more stable than Boosting in terms of less frequently obtaining significantly higher error rates than C4.5. This is consistent with previous findings [1, 7]. (3) On average, Progressive Boosting is more accurate than Boosting and Bagging. Progressive Boosting achieves 12% average relative error reduction over Bagging in the 40 do-mains. The former obtains significantly lower error rates than the latter in 9 out of the 40 domains, and significantly higher error rates in 3 domains. Progressive Boosting demonstrates its advantage over Bagging in terms of lower error rate, although a one-tailed sign-test fails to show that the frequency of the error reductions in the 40 domains is significant at a level of 0.05. The average error ratio of Progressive Boosting over Boosting is 0.98 in the 40 domains. It is noticed that the average accuracy ratio of Progressive Boosting against Boosting (the accuracy for Progressive Boosting divided by the corresponding accuracy for Boosting) is 1.02. That is, on average Progressive Boosting is slightly more accurate than Boosting. The one-tailed sign-test shows that the frequency of error decreases is not significant over the 40 domains at a level of 0.05. In addition, it is found that Progressive boosting is likely to outperform Boosting when Boosting cannot obtain large error reductions over C4.5, for example, when the reduction is less than or equal to 15%.

4 Conclusion

We have studied in this paper the progressive boosting with decision tree learning. This approach generates different trees by varying the set of attributes available for creating a test at each decision node, but keeping the distribution of the training set unchanged. Like bagging, progressive boosting is amenable to parallel and distributed processing while boosting is not. This gives progressive boosting an advantage over boosting for parallel machine learning and data mining. To improve model accuracy, an effective pruning technique for inaccurate models is employed in our method. We will work on that further. The spatial progressive boosting is a good research topic for future work, where spatial data represent a collection of attributes whose dependence is strongly related to a spatial location where observations close to each other are more likely to be similar than observations widely separated in space.

References

1. J.R.Quinlan, Bagging, Boosting, and C4.5, Programs for Machine Learning, Morgan Kaufmann San Mateo (1996)
2. Breiman, L., Friedman, J.H., Olshen, R.A., and Stone, C.J., Classification and regression trees, CA Wadsworth Belmont (1984)
3. Brodley, C. E., Addressing the selective superiority problem: automatic algorithm/model class selection. In Proceedings 10th International Conference on Machine Learning, Morgan Kaufmann San Francisc (1993) 17-24
4. Buntine, W. L.: Learning classi_cation trees. In Hand, D. J. (ed), Artificial Intelligence Frontiers in Statistics, Chapman & Hall London (1991) 182-201
5. Catlett, J.: Megainduction: a test ight. In Proceedings 8th International Workshop on Machine Learning, Morgan Kaufmann San Francisco (1991) 596-599
6. Chan, P. K. and Stolfo, S. J.: A comparative evaluation of voting and meta-learning on partitioned data. In Proceedings 12th International Conference on Machine Learning, Morgan Kaufmann San Francisco (1995) 90-98
7. Kohavi, R., and John, G. H.: Automatic parameter selection by minimizing estimated error. In Proceedings 12th International Conference on Machine Learning, Morgan Kaufmann San Francisco (1995) 304-311
8. Murphy, P. M., and Pazzani, M. J.: ID2-of-3: constructive induction of M-of-N concepts for discriminators in decision trees. In Proceedings 8th International Workshop on Machine Learning, Morgan Kaufmann San Francisco (1991) 183-187
9. Quinlan, J. R.: Inductive knowledge acquisition: a case study. In Quinlan, J. R. (ed), Applications of Expert Systems. Wokingham, UK: Addison Wesley (1987)
10. Quinlan, J. R. : C4.5: Programs for Machine Learning. Morgan Kaufmann San Mateo (1993)

Parallel SAT Solving with Microcontrollers

Tobias Schubert and Bernd Becker

Institute for Computer Science
Albert–Ludwigs–University of Freiburg, Germany
{schubert,becker}@informatik.uni-freiburg.de

Abstract. We present a parallel solver for the propositional satisfiability problem called PICHAFF. The algorithm is an adaption of the
state-of-the-art solver CHAFF optimised for a scalable, dynamically reconfigurable multiprocessor system based on Microchip PIC microcontrollers. PICHAFF includes lazy clause evaluation, conflict driven learning, non-chronological backtracking, clause deletion, and early conflict
detection, all of them adapted to the environment considered. For the
parallel execution Dynamic Search Space Partitioning is incorporated to
divide the search space into disjoint portions to be treated in parallel.
We demonstrate the feasibility of our approach by a set of experiments
on a multiprocessor system containing 9 Microchip PIC17C43 microcontrollers.

1 Introduction

The NP-complete problem of proving that a propositional Boolean formula is
satisfiable (SAT) is one of the fundamental problems in computer science. Many
problems can be transformed into a SAT problem in such a way that a solution
of the SAT problem is also a solution of the corresponding original problem. In
the last years a lot of developments in creating powerful SAT algorithms were
made: SATO [1], GRASP [2], or CHAFF [3] for example. These algorithms have
been successfully applied to real-world problems in the field of model checking,
equivalence checking, or timing analysis to name only a few.

Besides using faster CPUs parallel implementations seem to be a natural
way to speed up SAT algorithms. In the last decade powerful distributed SAT
procedures have been designed: on one hand implementations for network clusters of general purpose workstations [4,5] and on the other hand realisations for
special hardware architectures like transputersystems [6] or application specific
multiprocessing systems [7].

In this paper we propose a parallel version of a modern SAT solver for a multiprocessor system using Mircochip PIC17C43 microcontrollers. As the starting
point for this distributed SAT algorithm called PICHAFF we use one of the most
competitive prover for the Boolean satisfiability problem: CHAFF. Hereby, all
parts of the original implementation have been optimised for the limited resources of the Microchip microcontrollers. Furthermore, the parallelization is
adapted to the needs of the parallel system under consideration. We work out

S. Manandhar et al. (Eds.): AACC 2004, LNCS 3285, pp. 59–67, 2004.
© Springer-Verlag Berlin Heidelberg 2004

main points of this adaption and demonstrate the feasibility of our approach by a series of experiments. Hereby, a reconfigurable multiprocessor system developed at the Chair of Computer Architecture in Freiburg is used [8]. The experiments show a superlinear speedup on average for configurations with up to 9 Microchip PIC processors.

To summarize, the main aspects of our work are (1) adapting a complex algorithm to a *simple* microcontroller, (2) setting up a parallel version, and (3) evaluating the algorithm in an existing multiprocessor system.

The remainder of the paper is organised as follows: Section 2 gives a short overview of the satisfiability problem and the CHAFF algorithm. Our multiprocessor system is presented in Section 3. After that the implementation details of our approach are discussed. Finally the results of the performance measurements are reported in Section 5 followed by a conclusion.

2   Satisfiability Problem

For this section we assume that the reader is somewhat familiar with the propositional satisfiability problem, for a general introduction see e.g. [1]. An instance of a SAT problem corresponds to the question whether there exists an assignment for all variables in a given formula in *Conjunctive Normal Form* (CNF) such that the CNF formula evaluates to TRUE. Regarding the pseudo-code given in Figure 1 we provide a short explanation of modern SAT algorithms.

The function `decide_next_branch()` selects the next branching variable. After that `deduce()` propagates the effect of the assigned decision variable: some clauses may become unit clauses. All the unit clauses are assigned to TRUE and the assignments are propagated until no further unit clauses exist. If all variables are assigned, a model for the given problem is found and the formula is said to be satisfiable. Otherwise, if a conflict occurs the function `analyse_conflict()` is called: the reasons for the conflict are analysed and stored in a so-called *conflict clause*, and a backtrack level will be returned. The conflict clause is added to the clause set and contains all information about the actual conflict to prevent the algorithm from doing the same error again. The backtrack level indicates where the wrong decision was made and `back_track()` will undo all the wrong branches. If the backtrack level is zero the formula is unsatisfiable, because a conflict exists even without assigning at least one variable.

The main differences between the various modern SAT solvers stem from the fact that the functions mentioned above are realised in different ways. In CHAFF a so-called *1UIP learning scheme* is used for conflict analysis stopping the process when the first *Unique Implication Point* (UIP) was found [9]. Intuitively, a UIP is the single reason that implies the actual conflict and has to be flipped to avoid the conflict. For speeding up the `deduce()` function a lazy clause evaluation technique based on the notion of *watched literals* is used: depending on the value of these 2 watched literals it is easy to decide whether the clause is already solved (at least one literal defined correctly), a unit clause exists (one literal improperly defined), or a conflict occurs (both literals improperly defined). For further information the reader may refer to [3].

```
while(1) {
  if (decide_next_branch()) {
    while (deduce() == CONFLICT) {
      blevel = analyse_conflict();
      if (blevel == 0) return UNSAT
      else back_track(blevel);
    }
  }
  else return SAT;
}
```

Fig. 1. Pseudo-code of modern SAT solvers

3   Multiprocessor System

In this section we describe the most important hardware components of our *Multiprocessor System* called MPS. A picture of the layout is given in Figure 2. It mainly consists of three elements: the *Carrier Board* (CB), the *Processor Nodes* (PNs) and the *Communication Processor* (CP).

3.1   Carrier Board (CB)

A long PC ISA slot card serves as the CB. Besides the communication processor up to 9 processor nodes fit onto one board. The CB is the core of the multiprocessor system and is used for *communication switching* between the different processors. Hereby, the connection between the PNs is established by a so-called Field Programmable Interconnection Device (FPID) from I-CUBE realising a hardware crossbar switch. Furthermore, all target applications, i.e. the SAT solver is downloaded via the CB into the external memory of the PNs using the interface to the PC. A dual port RAM on the CB serves for connecting the local bus of the ISA card to the PC bus.

3.2   Processor Node (PN)

The PNs are the basic computing units and consist of the following main characteristics: Microchip PIC17C43 RISC type CPU, 32 MHz operating speed, 4 kByte local ROM, and 64 kWord external RAM.

The external RAM is reserved for the target applications of the PN, while the local ROM contains a simple operating system with basic functionality. The PNs are equipped with a serial communication channel, capable of transferring data at 5 Mbit/s. The serial ports of all PNs are connected to the FPID device on the CB to enable communication between the processors. In PICHAFF these channels are used to transfer subproblems between the PNs.

3.3   Communication Processor (CP)

The CP – located on a separate board in the middle of Figure 2 – serves for handling the requests for communication issued by the PNs and for controlling the channel switching FPID on the CB. Some of the features are: Motorola MC68340 CISC type CPU, 16.78 MHz operating speed, 256 kByte RAM, and 128 kByte ROM.

In our approach the CP also handles the overall communication to the PC like downloading applications, transferring results and so on. It is important to notice that the communication topology of the FPID can be reconfigured by the CP during runtime in less than 1 ms. Due to the fact that the crossbar switch provides real hardware connections between the PNs the exchange of information can be done very fast and without the influence of the CP.

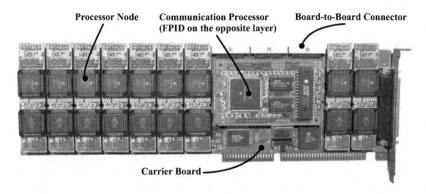

Fig. 2. Multiprocessor system

4   PICHAFF Implementation

In this section we discuss the realisation of PICHAFF for our multiprocessor system introduced in the section before. After giving general properties of the algorithm we will focus on some of the main points, i.e. the memory management, Dynamic Search Space Partitioning, and the overall application flow. Due to the limited resources of the Microchip PIC17C43 processors all these methods have been programmed completely in assembler.

4.1   General Properties

As mentioned before CHAFF is the starting point for our implementation and has been briefly introduced in Section 2. So we only describe the main differences between the two approaches in this section.

Instead of the *Variable State Independent Decaying Sum* branching heuristic (VSIDS) implemented in CHAFF a fixed variable order is used in our approach. The main reason is that the VSIDS heuristic is not suitable for smaller benchmarks analysed in the experiments: in these cases the overhead for choosing the next branching variable is greater than the advantage resulting from a decreased number of backtracks when selecting *better* branching variables.

In contrast to the CHAFF algorithm PICHAFF also employs a technique called *Partial Early Conflict Detection BCP* (ECDB) that has been introduced by the authors in [10]: when evaluating clauses during the BCP stage, the implication queue can become quite large. The larger it becomes, the more information about the current problem it contains and the better the probability of a conflict existing within the queue. The idea behind the ECDB procedure is (1) to utilize this information to detect conflicts sooner; and (2) to prevent the BCP procedure from processing many clauses that are not required because a conflict already exists in the implication queue.

4.2 Memory Management

A sketch of the data structures and the organisation of the 64 kWord external memory of the PNs is given in Figure 3. At the top of the figure the overall partition of the memory is outlined: only the block ranging from address \$1200 to \$FFFF is available for the PICHAFF procedure and the given benchmark problem. In our approach each PN holds a copy of the original clause set to be able to switch to any given subproblem. This also limits the maximum size of the problem instances to approximately 4000–5000 clauses per PIC processor. To handle instances near this upper bound an aggressive clause deletion mechanism has been integrated: if the number of clauses (initial ones and conflict clauses) exceed the available memory all conflict clauses that are currently *not active*[1] will be deleted. The reader should notice, that deleting non-active conflict clauses does not influence the correctness of the algorithm [11]. Nevertheless, in the worst case it could happen – even after the clause deletion process – that a memory overflow occurs. In this case the algorithm stops with a corresponding failure message.

All parameters like the values of the variables, the decision stack, the lists of watched literals, or the clauses are arranged in a linear list. As can be seen in the middle of Figure 3 pointers are used to access the first element of each memory block.

In PICHAFF, the clauses follow the data structure given at the bottom of the figure: a pointer to the first literal of each clause and a special element ("0") indicating the end of the clause. To avoid additional pointers and to have access in constant time the two watched literals for each clause are always located at the first two positions.

4.3 Dynamic Search Space Partitioning

For the parallel execution of PICHAFF the algorithm has to be extended by a mechanism to divide the overall search space of the given benchmark problem into disjoint portions. These parts of the search space than could be treated in parallel by the processors.

---

[1] In this sense an active clause currently forces an implication.

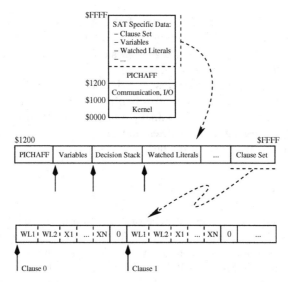

Fig. 3. Memory management

To do so we use a technique called *Dynamic Search Space Partitioning* (DSSP) based on *Guiding Paths* (GP) [4,5]. A guiding path is defined as a path in the search tree from the root to the current node, with additional information attached to the edges: (1) the literal l_d selected at level d, and (2) a flag indicating whether the algorithm is in the first or second branch, i.e. if backtracking might be needed at this point (Flag B) or not (Flag N).

Due to this definition it is clear, that every entry in a GP attached with Flag B is a potential candidate for a search space division, because the second branch has not been analysed yet. Thus the whole subtree rooted at the node of the search space corresponding to this entry in a GP can be examined by another processor.

An example for dividing the search space is given in the left part of Figure 4. Assume that the search process has reached the state indicated by the GP printed in black: $\{(x, B), (y, N), (z, B)\}$. A new task can be started by defining a second GP $\{(\overline{x}, N)\}$ (printed with dotted lines), as this part of the search space has not been examined so far. The original task will proceed the search after modifying its initial GP from $\{(x, B), (y, N), (z, B)\}$ into $\{(x, N), (y, N), (z, B)\}$ to guarantee that both processors work on different parts of the search space.

We have modified our PICHAFF algorithm to start at any arbitrary point in the search space by specifying an initial guiding path. This means that every time a PN gets idle during runtime, it contacts the CP by sending the corresponding signal. Then the CP opens a communication channel of the crossbar switch to an *active* processor, which is generating and encoding a *new* subproblem as a guiding path. In our design always the PN with the largest remaining portion of the search space (equal to the shortest GP) is contacted by the CP. Finally this GP is transferred directly to the idle PN via the FPID device. An illustration of the communication process is shown in the right part of Figure 4.

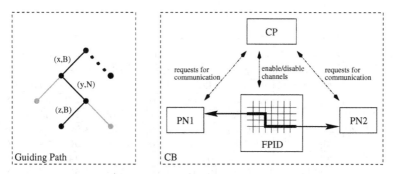

Fig. 4. Guiding path / Principle of the communication process

4.4   Application Flow

Besides the implementation of the distributed DP method several supporting routines have been developed for the CP and the PC according to the following application flow:

1. Besides the PICHAFF algorithm the given benchmark will also be encoded as an assembler file and compiled afterwards. In particular it contains the number of literals, the number of clauses, the clause set, and the initial lists of watched literals.
2. The received fragments of assembler code of the previous step will be used as the target applications and downloaded into the external memory of the PIC processors. After that only one PN gets started, while all other PNs remain idle. This directly leads to the next step.
3. If a PN gets idle during runtime the DSSP method is called until the search process is finished.

5   Experimental Results

For evaluating the performance of our implementation we made experiments using standard benchmarks available for download at http://www.satlib.org and http://www.lri.fr/~simon/satex. In columns 1 through 6 of Table 1 the main characteristics of the instances are given: the name of the benchmark set, the number of instances (#I), the number of satisfiable (#S), and the number of unsatisfiable benchmarks (#U). Also the number of variables (#V) and the number of clauses (#C) are listed. The results for the PICHAFF algorithm using 1, 3, 6, and 9 PNs are presented in the right part of Table 1. The CPU times given are always the sum of the CPU times needed to solve all the instances of the corresponding benchmark class, while SU represents the received speedup.

As can be seen, the obtained speedup ranges on average from 3.41 (3 PNs) to 9.13 (9 PNs) demonstrating that our methods work very well on a wide range of satisfiable and unsatisfiable benchmark problems. One reason for the super-linear behaviour in some cases might be, that the PNs explore different parts

Table 1. Experimental results

Benchmark Set						1 PN	3 PN		6 PN		9 PN	
Name	#I	#S	#U	#V	#C	CPU [s]	CPU [s]	SU	CPU [s]	SU	CPU [s]	SU
hfo3l	40	20	20	120	510	302.70	93.36	**3.24**	59.62	**5.08**	35.96	**8.42**
hfo4l	40	20	20	48	487	416.01	112.00	**3.71**	57.38	**7.25**	40.01	**10.40**
hfo5l	40	20	20	29	621	317.48	99.19	**3.20**	50.60	**6.27**	36.05	**8.81**
hfo6l	40	20	20	21	924	245.32	84.32	**2.91**	48.13	**5.10**	33.44	**7.34**
hfo7l	40	20	20	16	1460	200.52	72.02	**2.78**	43.97	**4.56**	30.92	**6.49**
hfo8l	40	20	20	13	2325	232.94	86.18	**2.70**	46.96	**4.96**	38.16	**6.10**
hfokl	40	20	20	55	1087	179.81	65.47	**2.75**	40.51	**4.44**	29.94	**6.01**
uf125	100	100	0	125	538	500.16	157.01	**3.19**	90.42	**5.53**	57.48	**8.70**
uuf125	100	0	100	125	538	1583.94	441.89	**3.58**	231.52	**6.84**	161.47	**9.81**
uf150	100	100	0	150	645	2050.20	426.50	**4.81**	244.79	**8.38**	167.69	**12.23**
uuf150	100	0	100	150	645	8340.99	1817.27	**4.59**	812.63	**10.26**	516.96	**16.13**
								ø 3.41		**ø 6.24**		**ø 9.13**

of the search space and by this usually generate different conflict clauses. These recorded clauses will not be deleted when a PN switches to a new subproblem. It obviously turns out that this obtained information is useful not only in the subproblem where the corresponding clauses have been created but also in the whole search space. And secondly, the total number of clauses every processor has to deal with is smaller than the number of clauses one PN has to analyse in the sequential case resulting in a decreased number of clause deletion operations and an improved performance of the *Boolean Constraint Propagation* procedure.

6   Conclusion

In this paper we demonstrated how a complex SAT procedure like CHAFF could be implemented using simple microcontrollers. The PICHAFF algorithm has been developed in less than 2500 lines of assembler code. All features of modern backtrack search algorithms like lazy clause evaluation, conflict-driven learning, non-chronological backtracking, and clause deletion have been integrated and optimised for the limited resources of the Microchip PIC17C43 processors. For the parallel execution we enhanced PICHAFF by an efficient technique for dividing the search space using the FPID device of our multiprocessor system. The experimental results point out the efficiency of the implemented methods.

References

1. Zhang, H.: SATO: An efficient propositional prover. In: International Conference on Automated Deduction. (1997)
2. Marques-Silva, J., Sakallah, K.: GRASP - a new search algorithm for satisfiability. In: International Conference on CAD. (1996)
3. Moskewicz, M., Madigan, C., Zhao, Y., Zhang, L., Malik, S.: Chaff: Engineering an efficient SAT solver. In: Design Automation Conference. (2001)

4. Blochinger, W., Sinz, C., Küchlin, W.: Parallel propositional satisfiability checking with distributed dynamic learning. In: Parallel Computing. (2003)
5. Zhang, H., Bonacina, M., Hsiang, J.: PSATO: a distributed propositional prover and its application to quasigroup problems. In: Journal of Symbolic Computation. (1996)
6. Böhm, M., Speckenmeyer, E.: A fast parallel SAT-solver - efficient workload balancing. In: Annals of Mathematics and Artificial Intelligence. (1996)
7. Zhao, Y., Malik, S., Moskewicz, M., Madigan, C.: Accelerating Boolean satisfiability through application specific processing. In: 14th International Symposium on System Synthesis. (2001)
8. Drechsler, R., Drechsler, N., Mackensen, E., Schubert, T., Becker, B.: Design reuse by modularity: A scalable dynamical (re)configurable multiprocessor system. In: 26th Euromicro Conference. (2000)
9. Zhang, L., Madigan, C., Moskewicz, M., Malik, S.: Efficient conflict driven learning in a Boolean satisfiability solver. In: International Conference on CAD. (2001)
10. Lewis, M., Schubert, T., Becker, B.: Early conflict detection based SAT solving. In: 7th International Conference on Theory and Applications of Satisfiability Testing (SAT2004). (2004)
11. Zhang, L., Malik, S.: Validating SAT solvers using an independent resolution-based checker: Practical implementations and other applications. In: Design, Automation, and Test in Europe. (2003)

Flow Shop Scheduling with Late Work Criterion – Choosing the Best Solution Strategy

Jacek Blazewicz[1], Erwin Pesch[2], Malgorzata Sterna[1], and Frank Werner[3]

[1] Institute of Computing Science, Poznan University of Technology, Piotrowo 3A,
60-965 Poznan, Poland
blazewic@sol.put.poznan.pl
malgorzata.sterna@cs.put.poznan.pl

[2] Institute of Information Systems, FB 5 - Faculty of Economics, University of Siegen,
Hoelderlinstr. 3, 57068 Siegen, Germany
pesch@fb5.uni-siegen.de

[3] Faculty of Mathematics, Otto-von-Guericke-University, PSF 4120,
39016 Magdeburg, Germany
Frank.Werner@mathematik.uni-magdeburg.de

Abstract. In the paper, we analyze different solution methods for the two-machine flow shop scheduling problem with a common due date with the weighted late work criterion, i.e. $F2 \mid d_i = d \mid Y_w$, which is known to be NP-hard. In computational experiments, we compared the practical efficiency of a dynamic programming approach, an enumerative method and heuristic procedures. Test results showed that each solution method has its advantages and it cannot be rejected from the consideration a priori.

1 Introduction

The late work objective function is a due date involving criterion, which was proposed in the context of parallel machines [1], [2] and then applied to the one-machine scheduling problem [9], [10]. Recently, this performance measure has been analyzed for the shop environments [3], [4], [5], [6], [11]. Minimizing the amount of the late work finds many practical applications. For example, the late work based approach can be applied in control systems [1], where the amount of data not collected by the control process from sensing devices before the due date corresponds to the late work. Data exposed after the time required cannot be used by the control procedure, which must work out the decision based only on the measurements gathered in the feasible time interval. The late work criteria can be also analyzed in agriculture, especially in all cases concerning perishable goods, as for example harvesting [9] or field fertilizing [11]. Minimizing the total late work is equivalent to minimizing the amount of wasted crops or the decrease in the crop amount caused by not executed fertilizing procedures. The criterion under consideration can be also applied in the design of production execution plans within predefined time periods in manufacturing systems [11]. The processes described above, are usually complex and consist of a set of operations restricted with some precedence constraints, hence, they are often modeled as the flow shop environment. Summing up, the late work criteria apply to all those scheduling problems that concentrate on the amount of late work delayed after a given due date not on the duration of this delay.

S. Manandhar et al. (Eds.): AACC 2004, LNCS 3285, pp. 68–75, 2004.
© Springer-Verlag Berlin Heidelberg 2004

In the paper, we present a comparison of different solution methods for a non-preemptive scheduling problem with the total weighted late work criterion (Y_w) and a common due date ($d_i=d$) in the two-machine flow-shop environment (F2), $F2 \mid d_i =d \mid Y_w$.

In this problem, we have to find an optimal schedule for a set of jobs $J=\{J_1, ..., J_i, ..., J_n\}$ on two dedicated machines M_1, M_2. Each job $J_i \in J$ consists of two tasks T_{1i} and T_{2i}, executed on machines M_1, M_2, for p_{1i}, p_{2i} time units, respectively. Particular jobs have to be performed, without preemptions, first on M_1 then on M_2. Moreover, each job can be processed on at most one machine at the same time and each machine can perform at most one task at the same time. Solving the problem, we are looking for a schedule minimizing the total weighted late work in the system (Y_w), where the late work (Y_i) for a particular job $J_i \in J$ is determined as the sum of late parts of its tasks executed after a common due date d. Since, we minimize the late part of a task, the maximum late work for a particular activity cannot be bigger than its processing time (in case it is totally late). Denoting with C_{ki} the completion time of task T_{ki}, Y_i for job $J_i \in J$ equals to $\sum_{k=1,2} \min\{\max\{0, C_{ki} - d\}, p_{ki}\}$.

Within our earlier research, we have proved the binary NP-hardness of problem $F2 \mid d_i =d \mid Y_w$ proposing a dynamic programming approach [5] of $O(n^2d^4)$ complexity. In the presented paper, we compare the performance of three solution methods for this scheduling case: a dynamic programming approach (DP), an enumerative method (EM) and a heuristic one. Results of computational experiments summarized in the paper, made it possible to verify the correctness of DP and to validate the efficiency of particular approaches implemented.

2 Solution Methods

Problem $F2 \mid d_i =d \mid Y_w$, as a binary NP-hard case, can be solved optimally by a dynamic programming approach [5] in pseudo-polynomial time $O(n^2d^4)$. According to the special feature of the problem analyzed [5] all early jobs have to be scheduled, in an optimal solution, by Johnson's algorithm [7], designed for two machine flow shop problem with the makespan criterion, $F2 \mid \mid C_{max}$. Johnson's method divides the set of all jobs J_i into two subsets with $p_{1i} \leq p_{2i}$ and $p_{1i} > p_{2i}$, respectively. Then it schedules the first set of jobs in non-decreasing order of p_{1i} and the latter one in non-increasing order of p_{2i} on both machines, in $O(n \log n)$ time.

The implemented DP method determines the first late job in the system and, then, it divides the set of the remaining jobs into two subsets containing activities being totally early and partially or totally late. As we have mentioned all early jobs have to be processed in Johnson's order, while the sequence of totally late activities can be arbitrary. Moreover, maximizing the weighted early work is equivalent to minimizing the weighted late work in the system. Denoting with $\hat{J}_n$ the job selected as the first late job and numbering the remaining jobs $J\backslash\{\hat{J}_n\}$ from $\hat{J}_1$ to $\hat{J}_{n-1}$ in Johnson's order, the dynamic programming algorithm takes decisions based on an initial condition $f_n(A, B, t, a)$ and a recurrence function $f_k(A, B, t, a)$. The value of these functions denotes the maximum amount of early work of jobs $\hat{J}_k, \hat{J}_{k+1}, ..., \hat{J}_n$ assuming that $\hat{J}_n$ is the first late job, the first job among $\hat{J}_k, \hat{J}_{k+1}, ..., \hat{J}_n$ starts on machine M_1 exactly at time A and not earlier than at time B on M_2. Exactly t time units are reserved for executing jobs $\hat{J}_1$ to $\hat{J}_{k-1}$ after $\hat{J}_n$ on M_1 and before the common due date d. Moreover, it is assumed that no job (a=0) or exactly one job (a=1) among $\hat{J}_1$ to $\hat{J}_{k-1}$ is partially executed on machine M_1 after $\hat{J}_n$ before d. The total weighted early work corresponding to a certain selection of the first late job is represented by value $f_1(0, 0, 0, 0)$. To find an optimal schedule, each job is considered as the first late job in order to determine the best first late job ensuring the optimal criterion value.

To check the correctness of this quite complicated method, we have designed an enumerative approach too, which finds an optimal solution by systematic exploring the solution space. This algorithm checks all possible subsets of early jobs E, executing them in Johnson's order, and, then, it completes such partial schedules with the remaining jobs. The method considers each job besides E as the first late job J_x and it completes a partial schedule with other jobs from $J\backslash E$ sequenced according to the non-increasing weights. In consequence, not all possible permutations of jobs are explicitly checked by the method, which, despite this fact, is obviously an exponential one, and runs in $O(n2^n)$ time.

In practice, the methods mentioned above make it possible to find an optimal solution of the problem for small instances only. To obtain feasible solutions for bigger instances, heuristic algorithms have to be applied. Within our research, we compared the exact methods with Johnson's algorithm (JA) and a list scheduling method.

The list scheduling approach is a technique commonly used in the field, especially for practical applications. The constructive procedure proposed adds particular jobs, one by one, to a set of executed jobs (E). All jobs from this set are scheduled on machines in Johnson's order. At each step of the method, a new job is selected from the set of the remaining (available) jobs $A = J\backslash E$ according to a certain priority dispatching rule and it is added to E. Then, set E is rescheduled in Johnson's order. In consequence of adding a new job, the set of early jobs may change and the criterion value may be improved. The solution returned by the heuristic is the best solution obtained for particular sets of jobs E, for which the partial schedule length exceeds the common due date d. We have proposed 15 rules of selecting jobs from set A (cf. Table 1).

Some of them determine the sequence of adding the jobs to a schedule at the beginning of the algorithm (static rules), while others arrange jobs from set A at each step of the method with regard to the length of a partial schedule obtained so far (dynamic rules). For static rules the algorithm runs in $O(n^2 \log n)$ time, while for dynamic rules the complexity is bounded with $O(n^3 \log n)$.

Johnson's algorithm designed for problem $F2 \mid \mid C_{max}$ can be used as a fast heuristic for the problem under consideration ($O(n\log n)$), especially with regard to the fact

Table 1. The definitions of static (S) and dynamic (D) priority dispatching rules (PDR)

Notation	Priority dispatching rule
S1	$\max\{w_i\}$ for $J_i \in A$, where w_i denotes the job weight
S2	$\max\{w_i(p_{1i}+p_{2i})\}$ for $J_i \in A$
S3	$\min\{p_{1i}\}$ for $J_i \in A$
S4	$\max\{p_{1i}\}$ for $J_i \in A$
S5	$\min\{p_{1i}+p_{2i}\}$ for $J_i \in A$
S6	$\max\{w_i p_{1i}\}$ for $J_i \in A$
S7	$\max\{w_i p_{2i}\}$ for $J_i \in A$
S8	selecting jobs in Johnson's order
S9	selecting jobs randomly
D1	$\min\{x_i\}$ for $J_i \in A$, where $x_i = p_{1i}/(d-T_1) + p_{2i}/(d-T_2)$ and T_k denotes a partial schedule length on machine M_k
D2	$\min\{w_i x_i\}$ for $J_i \in A$
D3	$\max\{x_i\}$ for $J_i \in A$
D4	$\max\{w_i x_i\}$ for $J_i \in A$
D5	$\max\{z_i\}$ for $J_i \in A$, where $z_i = \max\{0, d-T_1-p_{1i}\} + \max\{0, d-T_2- p_{2i}\}$
D6	$\min\{z_i\}$ for $J_i \in A$

that early jobs are sequenced in Johnson's order in an optimal solution for $F2 \mid d_i = d \mid Y_w$. It is worth to be mentioned, that the schedule constructed by Johnson's method is not identical with the one built by the list algorithm with Johnson's rule (S8). The list algorithm constructs a solution in an iterative way, adding one job at a time. As the partial schedule length exceeds the due date, then an additional optimization step is performed: the newly added job is removed and the remaining jobs from the set of available jobs A are introduced one by one to the set of executed activities E, in order to create a new solution, and then removed before the next job is taken into consideration. In consequence, the list algorithm constructs more feasible solutions, which are different from (and possibly better than) Johnson's schedule.

3 Computational Experiments

Within computational experiments, we have checked the time efficiency of particular methods and the quality of heuristic solutions obtained. All algorithms proposed have been implemented in ANSI C++ and run on AMD Duron Morgan 1GHz PC [8]. The selected summarized results of the extended tests are presented below.

For small instances, with the number of jobs not exceeding 20, all implemented methods were analyzed (cf. Table 2, Columns 1-3). We have tested 25 instances of 5 different sizes for a number of jobs equal to 10, 12, 14, 16, 18. The task processing times were randomly generated from the interval [1, 10], while job weights were chosen from the interval [1, 5]. The common due date value was settled to 30% of the mean machine load (i.e. to 30% of a half of the total processing time of all jobs).

Obviously, the dynamic programming (DP) and enumerative (EM) methods gave the same optimal solutions, that practically confirmed the correctness of the DP algorithm [5]. The simplest method, Johnson's algorithm (JA), constructed solutions of the poorest quality: 69% of the optimum, on average (to simplify the analysis, we compare results based on the weighted early work, so JA found schedules with only 69% of the weighted early work obtained by DP and EM). The efficiency of the list algorithm strictly depended on a priority dispatching rule applied and fluctuated from about 73% to almost 98% of the optimum. The best rules are static rules preferring jobs with the biggest weight or the biggest weighted processing time on single or both machines. As one could predict, the efficient rules have to take into account job weights. Surprisingly, the dynamic selection rules do not dominate static ones – the additional computational effort does not result in the increase of the solution quality. Nevertheless, the dynamic selection rules ensured also quite good performance measure values (more than 80% of the optimum). Moreover, the most efficient rules appeared to be the most stable ones (with the smallest standard deviation of the solution quality).

The ranking of the priority dispatching rules for big instances, with the number of jobs $n \leq 250$, is similar (cf. Table 2, Columns 4-6). We analyzed 25 instances of 5 different sizes with 50, 100, 150, 200, 250 jobs, processing times and weights randomly chosen form the interval [1, 20], and the due dates specified as 50% of the mean machine load. In this case, the solution quality was compared to the best heuristic schedule, because the optimal one cannot be obtained due to the unacceptably long running times of the exact approaches.

Table 2. The ranking of priority dispatching rules based on the solution quality compared to the optimal criterion value for small instances (Columns 1-3) and to the best heuristic solution for big instances (Columns 4-6)

PDR ranking I	Average perform.[%]	Standard deviation	PDR ranking II	Average perform.[%]	Standard deviation
1	2	3	4	5	6
S1	97,66	0,028	S1	100,0	0,000
S2	92,40	0,054	S2	93,98	0,018
S6	91,55	0,058	S6	92,19	0,021
S7	91,03	0,051	S7	88,36	0,027
D4	85,15	0,067	D2	75,23	0,043
D2	83,25	0,081	D6	73,89	0,044
D1	83,23	0,077	D1	73,64	0,040
D6	81,85	0,081	D4	73,45	0,043
S5	81,64	0,081	D3	73,37	0,043
D5	81,25	0,088	S5	72,84	0,037
D3	80,44	0,068	D5	72,76	0,032
S4	78,68	0,091	S4	72,63	0,051
S9	78,41	0,068	S3	71,44	0,037
S3	76,17	0,083	S9	71,18	0,043
S8	73,87	0,069	S8	70,43	0,039
JA	69,57	0,084	JA	70,06	0,039

The running times of the dynamic programming (DP) and enumerative (EM) methods reflect their exponential complexities (cf. Table 3, Columns 2 and 3). John-son's algorithm (JA) required neglectedly short running time (cf. Table 3, Column 4) – from this point of view its solution quality (about 70% of the optimum) can be treated as a big advantage. On the other hand, a bit bigger time requirements of the list algorithm are compensated by the higher (nearly optimal) quality of schedules constructed. (In   Table 3, Columns 5 and 8, running times for the best selection rule, S1, are presented.)

To analyze the time efficiency of heuristic approaches more carefully, they were applied also for bigger problem instances (cf. Table 3, Columns 6-8). The running times of JA and S1 obviously increase with the number of jobs, reflecting methods' complexities, i.e. $O(n\log n)$ and $O(n^2\log n)$, respectively. The experiments confirmed that heuristic approaches are only possible solution methods for big instances of hard problems.

In the tests reported in Table 3 (Columns 1-3), the due date value was quite strict; it was settled to 30% of the half of the total processing time of all jobs. For such problem instances, DP appeared to be less efficient than the enumerative method, despite the much lower pseudo-polynomial complexity. The DP method is insensitive to problem data and its complexity strictly depends on two problem parameters – d and n. To investigate this issue more carefully, we tested both exact methods for the same job set changing only the due date value from 10% to 90% of the half of the total processing time of all jobs (cf. Table 4). Surprisingly, the enumerative method appeared to be more efficient than the pseudo-polynomial algorithm in general.

Table 3. The average running times for small (Columns 1-5) and big (Columns 6-8) instances for different numbers of jobs (n)

n	DP [µs]	EM [µs]	JA [µs]	S1 [µs]	n	JA [µs]	S1 [µs]
1	2	3	4	5	6	7	8
10	451 782	1 939	11	323	50	36	7331
12	1 081 864	20 357	11	448	100	72	29275
14	2 821 465	127 221	13	614	150	100	100422
16	4 101 604	7 928 479	14	758	200	132	180624
18	12 445 751	6 205 041	15	1039	250	165	289967

For strict due date values, the enumerative method cuts many partial solutions from the further analysis increasing its efficiency. On the other hand, for big due date values a set of early jobs, scheduled by Johnson's rule, is numerous. In consequence, checking all possible solutions can be done in relatively short time. This observation is confirmed by the results obtained for EM (cf. Table 4) – the running time increases with d to a certain maximum value and, then, it decreases. Moreover, the computa-tional experiments showed that taking into account problem constraints, the enumera-tive method constructs only a small part of all possible permutations for n jobs (the percentage of explicitly checked permutations is given in the last column of Table 4).

Similar experiments, with a variable due date value, were performed for the heuris-tic method as well. Changing d for a certain set of jobs does not influence the running time of the heuristic (whose complexity does not depend on d). However, one could notice the solution quality improvement with the increase of d. For the big value of d, almost all jobs are executed early and their order is strictly determined by Johnson's rule. For such instances, a heuristic solution cannot differ too much from the optimal one.

Table 4. The running times for different due date values d and the part of the solution space explored by EM

d [%]	DP [μs]	EM [μs]	Space checked [%]
10	31 580	63	0,001
20	238 335	138	0,005
30	648 829	547	0,029
40	1 791 391	3 654	0,200
50	3 490 018	7 289	0,380
60	5 512 625	8 845	0,444
70	8 790 002	9 311	0,440
80	14 079 739	4 841	0,196
90	20 049 948	1 991	0,059

4 Conclusions

In the paper, we have compared different solution methods for problem $F2 \mid d_i = d \mid Y_w$, which is known to be binary NP-hard. The computational experiments showed that the dynamic programming method, despite its pseudopolynomial time complexity, is less efficient than the enumerative one. It is important from the theoretical point of view, because its existence made it possible to classify the problem as binary NP-hard. But, for determining optimal solutions, the enumerative method is a better choice in this case. Moreover, we have proposed the list scheduling method with a few static and dynamic selection rules. The experiments showed that the heuristic constructs solutions of a good quality in the reasonable running time.

Within the future research, we are designing metaheuristic approaches for the problem $F2 \mid d_i = d \mid Y_w$. The exact methods presented in this work will be used for validating the quality of solutions, while the list heuristic can be applied as a method of generating initial schedules and a source of reference solutions for validating the meteheuristics performance for big problem instances.

Acknowledgment

We would like to express our appreciation to Krzysztof Kowalski for implementing methods proposed and performing computational experiments designed within the research.

References

1. Blazewicz, J.: Scheduling Preemptible Tasks on Parallel Processors with Information Loss. Recherche Technique et Science Informatiques 3/6 (1984) 415-420

2. Blazewicz, J., Finke, G.: Minimizing Mean Weighted Execution Time Loss on Identical and Uniform Processors. Information Processing Letters 24 (1987) 259-263
3. Blazewicz, J., Pesch, E., Sterna, M., Werner, F.: Total Late Work Criteria for Shop Scheduling Problems. In: Inderfurth, K., Schwoediauer, G., Domschke, W., Juhnke, F., Kleinschmidt, P., Waescher, G. (eds.): Operations Research Proceedings 1999. Springer-Verlag, Berlin (2000) 354-359
4. Blazewicz, J., Pesch, E., Sterna, M., Werner, F.: Open Shop Scheduling Problems with Late Work Criteria. Discrete Applied Mathematics 134 (2004) 1-24
5. Blazewicz, J., Pesch, E., Sterna, M., Werner, F.: The Two-Machine Flow-Shop Problem with Weighted Late Work Criterion and Common Due Date. European Journal of Operational Research (2004) to appear
6. Blazewicz, J., Pesch, E., Sterna, M., Werner, F.: Revenue Management in a Job-Shop: a Dynamic Programming Approach. Preprint Nr. 40/03, Otto-von-Guericke-University Magdeburg (2003)
7. Johnson, S.M.: Optimal Two- and Three-Stage Production Schedules. Naval Research Logistics Quarterly 1 (1954) 61-68
8. Kowalski, K.: Scheduling Algorithms for the Shop Scheduling Problems with the Late Work Criteria, Master Thesis, Poznan University of Technology, in Polish (2003)
9. Potts, C.N., van Wassenhove, L.N.: Single Machine Scheduling to Minimize Total Late Work. Operations Research 40/3 (1991) 586-595
10. Potts, C.N., van Wassenhove, L.N.: Approximation Algorithms for Scheduling a Single Machine to Minimize Total Late Work. Operations Research Letters 11 (1991) 261-266
11. Sterna, M.: Problems and Algorithms in Non-Classical Shop Scheduling. Scientific Publishers of the Polish Academy of Sciences, Poznan (2000)

GA-Based Multiple Route Selection
for Car Navigation

Basabi Chakraborty

Faculty of Software and Information Science
Iwate Prefectural University
152-52 Aza Sugo, Takizawamura, Iwate 020-0193, Japan
basabi@soft.iwate-pu.ac.jp

Abstract. Search for optimal route from source to destination is a well
known optimization problem and lot of good solutions like Dijkstra algorithm, Bellman-Ford algorithm etc. are available with practical applications. But simultaneous search for multiple semioptimal routes are
difficult with the above mentioned solutions as they produce the best
one at a time. Genetic Algorithm (GA) based solutions are currently
available for simultaneous search of multiple routes. But the problem in
finding multiple routes is that the selected routes resemble each other,i,e.,
partly overlap. In this paper a GA based algorithm with a novel fitness
function has been proposed for simultaneous search of multiple routes
for car navigation system avoiding overlapping. The simulation of the
proposed algorithm and other currently available algorithms have been
done by using a portion of real road map. The simulation results demonstrate the effectiveness of the proposed algorithm over other algorithms.

1   Introduction

Car navigation devices are widely used now as an information source for Intelligent Transportation Systems. One of the functionality of a car navigation
system is route planning. Given a set of origin-destination pair, there could be
many possible routes for a driver. A useful routing system for car navigation
should have the capability to support the driver effectively in deciding on an
optimum route to his preference. Search for optimal route from one point to
another on a weighted graph is a well known problem and has several solutions.
There are several search algorithms for the shortest path problem, breadth first
search, Dijkstra algorithm, Bellman-Ford algorithm to name a few. Though these
algorithms can produce stable solutions in polynomial time, they exhibit high
computational complexity specially in changing real time environment. Moreover in case of navigation systems like flight route selection or car navigation,
the shortest path may not be the best one from other considerations such as,
traffic congestion, environmental problem or simply user's satisfaction and some
of the parameters may vary with time. So for efficient car navigation in dynamic
environment, we need to specify multiple and separate good choices with rank
information. Simultaneous search for multiple short routes is difficult with the

S. Manandhar et al. (Eds.): AACC 2004, LNCS 3285, pp. 76–83, 2004.

above algorithms as they produce one solution (the shortest route) at a time and need to be rerun for alternate solutions which is computationally demanding and do not gurantee the successive shortest paths.

Genetic algorithms [1] are now widely used to solve search problems with applications in practical routing and optimization problems [2]. Some works [3–5] also have been reported for search of multiple routes for navigation systems using GA. But the problem in finding multiple semi optimal routes simultaneously is that the selected routes resemble each other i,e they partly overlap. Inagaki et.al [6] proposed an algorithm in which chromosomes are sequences of integers and each gene represents a node ID selected randomly from the set of nodes connected with the node corresponding to its locus number to minimize the effect of overlapping solutions. But the proposed algorithm requires a large solution space to attain high quality solution due to its inconsistent crossover mechanism. Inoue [7] proposed a method for finding out multiple different (non overlapping) short routes by dividing the road map in multiple areas and putting different weights in each of them so that the selected routes are through different areas of the map. But as their is no direct method for comparing the ovelapping of the selected paths this method is not guranteed to select minimally overlapped multiple shorter paths.

In this work a genetic algorithm has been developed for searching multiple non overlapping routes from starting point to destination point on a road map for use in car navigation system with the proposal of a new fitness function for ranking the probable solutions. The proposed algorithm has been evaluated against above mentioned algorithm using a real road map. In the next section a brief introduction to genetic algorithm and its use for multiple route selection is presented. The following section describes the proposed GA with new fitness function. Simulation experiments and results are presented in section 4. Section 5, the final section contains conclusion and discussion.

2   Genetic Algorithm

Genetic algorithms (GA) are adaptive and robust computational models inspired by genetics and evolution in biology. These algorithms encode a potential solution to a specific problem on a simple chromosome like data structure and apply recombination operators to produce new solutions. GA are executed iteratively on a set of coded solutions called population initially randomly drawn from the set of possible solutions with three basic operators namely, selection, crossover and mutation in such a way that better solutions are evolved in each iteration. The goodness of a solution is measured by a problem dependent objective function called fitness function, the design of which is very critical for the success of a GA based algorithm in finding out optimal solution. Genetic algorithms have been applied for shortest path routing, multicast routing or dynamic routing, bandwidth allocation and in several practical optimization problems.

2.1   Multiple Route Selection by GA

GA can be used effectively for searching multiple routes from a real road map with a rank order i.e., shortest, second shortest, 3rd shortest and so on (k short-est path problem). The road map is first converted into a connected graph, considering each road crossing as a node in the graph and all such nodes are numbered. The roads in map are represented by links in the graph. The distance between any two crossings is considered as the weight of the link between the corresponding nodes. The starting point and the destination on the map are defined as the starting node and goal node on the graph. Any possible path from start node to goal node or destination node via other nodes is a possible solution and coded as a chromosome by using node numbers. However looping in the path is generally avoided.

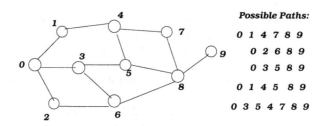

Fig. 1. Graphical Representation of road map and routes

Fig. 1 represents a simple graphical representation of a road map and the possible routes from source node 0 to the destination node 9. The general GA based algorithm for finding out m short routes simultaneously is described as follows [4, 7].

1. Coding the solution space: Population of chromosomes representing solution paths (routes) are generated by genetic coding. Chromosomes are equal length sequence of integers where each gene represents a node number. Genetic coding of the actual path through nodes has been done by changing the gene number in chromosome with the node number in the actual path sequence as shown in Fig. 2. Thus the integer 0 is changed by node number 3, 3 is changed by node number 5 and so on following the node sequence in the path $0 \rightarrow 3 \rightarrow 5 \rightarrow 4 \rightarrow 7 \rightarrow 8 \rightarrow 9$. The circles in the coding of the path is to be replaced by randomly taking from the connected nodes to the node represented by the integer, i,e first circle is replaced by 0 or 4, the nodes connected to the node number 1.

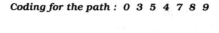

Fig. 2. Genetic Coding of the path

2. Setting fitness function: The fitness of any chromosome is measured by the following function:

$$fitness = \frac{1}{\sum_i^N rlength(i)} \qquad (1)$$

where $rlength(i)$ (the distance of the path between the crossings representing ith and $(i-1)$th nodes respectively) represents the weight of the link joining ith and $(i-1)$th nodes. N represents the total number of nodes in the path from start node to destination node.

3. Initialization of the population: A set of chromosomes are selected randomly from the pool of chromosomes for initial population. Genetic operations are carried out iteratively to generate better and better population until the termination condition is satisfied.

4. Genetic operation:
   (a) Selection: The fitness of individual chromosomes and the fitness of the population are evaluated respectively. Roulette wheel selection rule is used for selecting two parents.
   (b) Cross over and mutation with probability P_c and P_m are applied for generating new population from the selected parents.
   (c) Fitness evaluation :Fitness function is used to evaluate the new population.
   (d) The above steps are repeated until the preset number of iteration is achieved.

5. The individual chromosomes in the final population is evaluated and ranked. The best m chromosomes are taken as the best m solutions.

Now the selected routes by the above procedure may partly overlap. To avoid overlapping current method developed by others is to divide the road map into multiple areas and putting different weights in each of them so that the selected routes are through different areas of the map. To achieve this the fitness function has to be modified as follows.

$$fitness = \frac{1}{\sum_i^N rlength(i)\rho_i} \qquad (2)$$

$$\rho_i = \begin{cases} \rho & \text{if } route(i) \in A \\ 1 & \text{otherwise} \end{cases}$$

where $0 < \rho < 1$ is the weight associated to the $route(i)$, the path from node i to node $(i-1)$ passing through the selected area of the map. But as their is no direct method for comparing the overlapping of the selected paths, this method is not guranteed to select minimally overlapped multiple shorter paths.

In the next section the proposed method for selecting non overlapping multiple short paths for car navigation has been presented.

3   Proposed GA-Based Multiple Route Search

In the proposed algorithm for selecting m routes simultaneously group of m routes are considered to be one set of solution and a new fitness function incorporating direct measures for non overlappingness of the routes belonging to a group has designed. The algorithm is as follows:

1. Initial population is formed by a number of groups of m chromosomes representing m solution paths (routes), randomly drawn from the whole solution space. One group of routes is considered one solution.
2. The objective function is designed to calculate fitness of a group as a whole. The fitness $F_r(L_r)$ of any solution path L_r(group member) is calculated as follows:

$$F_r(L_r) = \sum_i^{N_r} rlength(i) \tag{3}$$

where N_r is the number of nodes in the path L_r including the start node and goal node and $rlength(i)$ is the weight of the link connecting i th and $(i-1)$th node in the path.

The fitness of the group is defined from three factors as

$$F(G) = F_1(G) + F_2(G) + F_3(G) \tag{4}$$

$F_1(G)$ is designed for ensuring non overlapping of the individual solution paths and is defined as:

$$F_1(G) = GF(L) + X \tag{5}$$

where GF(L) represents the average of the fitness of the individual paths belonging to the group i,e

$$GF(L) = \frac{1}{m} \sum_{r=1}^{m} F_r(L_r) \tag{6}$$

and $X = \sum_r \sum_i x_{ri}$ where x_{ri} represents the number of nodes with in a radius R of the ith node in the rth path of a group that is taken by any of the r th path of the same group. R is problem dependent and should be chosen by trial and error. The term X is a penalty term to ensure seperation of the individual path s in a group.

$$F_2(G) = GF(L) \times \frac{2z}{p_1} \tag{7}$$

$$F_3(G) = \begin{cases} GF(L) \times \frac{3z}{p_2} & \text{if } p_2 > C \\ \frac{GF(L)}{2} & \text{if } p_2 \leq C \end{cases} \tag{8}$$

where z represents the average number of nodes of m paths i,e $z = \sum_r N_r$, p_1 and p_2 represents the average of total number of nodes in any group of $\frac{m}{2}$ paths and total number of nodes in all the paths of the group respectively. C is a constant depending on the total number nodes on the graph and should be chosen by trial and error.

Equation. 7 and 8 represent the penalty terms due to the number of nodes shared by the routes in a group. Here the smaller value of the objective function corresponds to better fitness.

3. For crossover operation, the parent groups are selected according to Roulette wheel selection procedure using group fitness. Then the actual parents are selected, one each from two parent groups by the same procedure using individual fitness values. Then crossover position is selected randomly and crossover is done with a predefined probability of crossover P_c.
4. Mutation is done randomly with a probability P_m at a random position to generate different solution path inside a group.
5. The new groups are formed by changing the group members of the selected parent groups with a probability of P_g. The groups are evaluated by group evaluation function and better groups (ranked via evaluation function) are selected for next generation of population.
6. The process is repeated a pre-defined number of times to get the best solution group.

Now due to randomness in the process, there is a small possibility of generating non-existent solution paths. Those solution are discarded eventually as they do not contribute to the fitness function.

4   Simulation and Results

Simulation experiments have been done using a portion of the real road map Fig. 3 by applying Dijkstra's method, proposed algorithm and Inagaki's algorithm. In all the cases 4 alternate paths are selected. The road map is first converted into a graph with 130 nodes. The number of candidate paths from start(X) to destination node(Y) are found to be 100 (no looping is considered). First Dijkustra's method has been used to find out shortest, 2nd shortest, 3rd shortest and 4th shortest routes. Secondly Inagaki's method has been used to devide the road map into 4 parts and using different values of ρ of Eq. 2 for selecting 4 non overlapping paths from the different a reas of the map. Finally proposed algorithm has been used to select the optimal group of 4 short paths with minimum overlapping. The selected genetic parameters are represented in Table 1. In both the methods the parameters P_c and P_m have been changed to several values and the optimum values are noted in the table.

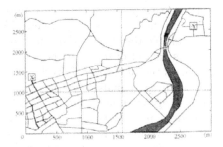

Fig. 3. A portion of road map used for simulation

Table 1. Setting of parameters of GA

Method	Population size	No. of iteration	P_c	P_m	P_g
Inagaki	100	40	0.9	0.5	
Proposed	150	40	0.8	0.6	0.2

Table 2. Comparative Performance of different Algorithms

Algorithm	Time taken	Number of overlapping nodes	Average weight of the path
Dijkstra	.014s	15	243
Inagaki	.182s	5	275
Proposed	.177s	2	257

4.1 Results and Discussion

Table 2. shows the comparative results of the different algorithms. The time taken is the average run time of the same computer used for simulation of the three algorithms. Average weight of the path in the 4th column is calculated from the weight of the links between nodes. The actual distance in the road map is converted to weight between nodes by taking 100m as 1 unit of weight. Lesser average weight represents shorter paths. Dijkstra algorithm takes much shorter time compared to other algorithms for finding out the shortest route and it also is able to find out better paths in terms of distance. But successive short routes are highly overlapped. Both Inagaki's method and the proposed algorithm take longer time than Dijkstra's algorithm but alternate routes can be found out simultaneously. The proposed GA is found to be better than Inagaki's method as only 2 nodes are shared by the individual paths in the alternate routes compared to 5 nodes shared in alternate routes selected by Inagaki's method. The average run time and the weight of the path in both the methods are nearly equal, proposed method being slightly better. The average weight of the selected path is also close to the average weight of the paths found out by Dijkustra algorithm. Fig. 4 and Fig. 5 represents the simulation results on the road map by Inagaki's method and the proposed method respectively.

5 Conclusion

In this work a Genetic Algorithm based solution technique for finding out m routes simultaneously has been proposed. Simultaneous multiple route selection is difficult by popular optimization technique like Dijkstra algorithm. Currently available GA based algorithm can produce multiple routes simultaneously but selected routes resemble each other. In this work a new GA based algorithm is developed for finding out multiple routes simultaneously with minimal overlapping by grouping m routes as one set of solution and designing fitness functions in such a way that it penalizes the function for overlapping. Simulation experiments on a piece of real road map demonstrates the efficiency of the algorithm over other algorithms in finding out nonoverlapping multiple routes. The usefulness of the proposed algorithm can be better understood in the problem of finding out multiple routes in dynamic environment. At present simulations are carried out for finding out multiple routes dynimically which I hope to report in near future.

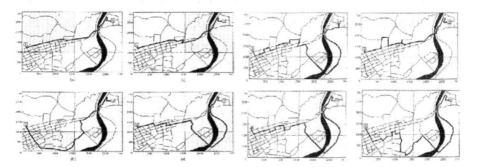

Fig. 4. Simulation by Inagaki's method   **Fig. 5.** Simulation by Proposed method

References

1. David E. Goldberg, "Genetic Algorithms in Search, Optimization, and Machine Learning". Addison-Wesley, 1989.
2. Chang, W. A., "A Genetic Algorithm for Shortest Path Routing Problem and the Sizing of Populations", IEEE Trans. on Evolutionary Computations, Vol. 6, no. 6,p p. 566-579, December 2002.
3. Kanoh, H. and Nakamura, T.,*Knowledge based Genetic Algorithm for Dynamic Route Selection*, in Proceedings of International Conference on Knowledge based Intelligent engineering Systems and Allied Technologies, pp. 616–619, 2000.
4. Inagaki, J. et, al., *A genetic algorithm for determining multiple routes and its applications* in Proc. IEEE Int. Symp. Circuits and Systems, pp. 137–14 0, 1999.
5. Tanaka, M. et,al., *A multi-Route Planning for Aircraft Using Genetic Algorithms* in Trans of IEICE, J85 D-I, No. 8, pp. 767–775, 2002. (in Japanese)
6. Inagaki, J. et, al.,*A method of Determining Various Solutions for Routing Application with a Genetic Algorithm*, in Trans of IEICE, J82-D-I, No.8. pp.11 02-1111, August 2002.(in Japanese)
7. Inoue, Y., *Exploration Method of Various Routes with Genetic Algorithm*, Master's Thesis, Information System Engineering, Kochi Institute of Technology, 2001.(in Japanese)

Genetic Algorithm for Airline Crew Scheduling Problem Using Cost-Based Uniform Crossover

Ketan Kotecha[1], Gopi Sanghani[2], and Nilesh Gambhava[1]

[1] Department of Information Technology, G H Patel College of Engg & Tech,
Vallabh Vidyanagar-388 120, India
{drketankotecha,nileshgambhava}@yahoo.com
www.gcet.ac.in
[2] Department of Computer Engineering, A D Patel Institute of Technology,
New Vallabh Vidyanagar-388 121, India
gopisanghani@yahoo.com

Abstract. Airline crew scheduling is a very visible and economically significant problem faced by airline industry. Set partitioning problem (SPP) is a role model to represent & solve airline crew scheduling problem. SPP itself is highly constrained combinatorial optimization problem so no algorithm solves it in polynomial time. In this paper we present a genetic algorithm (GA) using new Cost-based Uniform Crossover (CUC) for solving set partitioning problem efficiently. CUC uses cost of the column information for generating offspring. Performance of GA using CUC is evaluated using 28 real-world airline crew scheduling problems and results are compared with well-known IP optimal solutions & Levine's GA solutions [13].

1 Introduction

Scheduling and planning are the most crucial problems, which airline industry faces everyday because daily more than 25,000 flights are flying over the world. Crew cost in transportation is very high; approximately it costs 15-25% of total airline operational cost. In 1991, US airline industry had spent 1.3 billion for scheduling of the flights and may be the same amount of money was spent by other airline industry [15]. The problem is extremely difficult to solve when thousands of crewmembers are to be assigned and also it is subjected to time constraint, crew ability & availability and other constraints. Scheduling of aircrafts, pilots, and different crews are very much complex, so the entire problem is divided into several parts like construction of timetable, fleet assignment, crew pairing, crew assignment,etc... SPP is generally used to represent the airline crew scheduling problem mathematically. SPP is NP-complete problem so no algorithm exists which solves SPP in polynomial time.

Genetic Algorithm (GA) is heuristic search algorithm premised on the evolutionary ideas of natural selection and genetic [9][12]. The basic concept of GA is designed to simulate the processes in natural system necessary for evolution, specifically for those that follow the principle of survival of the fittest, first laid

S. Manandhar et al. (Eds.): AACC 2004, LNCS 3285, pp. 84–91, 2004.

down by Charles Darwin. GA represents an intelligent exploitation of a random search within a defined search space to solve a problem. GA is best suited for those problems, that do not have a precisely defined solving method and if it is, then by following that method, it will take too much time. So GA is best suited for NP-hard and optimization problems but also it can be applied to other wide category of problems [8][16].

2   The Set Partitioning Problem

The set partitioning problem is defined as

$$\text{Minimize } \sum_{j=1}^{n} c_j x_j$$

$$\text{subject to } \sum_{j=1}^{n} a_{ij} x_j = 1 \text{ for } i = 1, ..., m$$

$$x_j = 0 \text{ or } 1 \text{ for } j = 1, ...n$$

where $a_{ij} = 0$ or 1, $c_j > 0$, $i = 1, ..., m$ represents row indices, $j = 1, ..., n$ is set of column indices. x_j will be 1 if j^{th} column is in the solution set otherwise 0. A column can cover more than one row but one row must be covered by one and only one column. If one row is covered by more than one column then it is set covering problem and not a set partitioning problem [2].

In airline crew scheduling, each row $i = 1, ..., m$ represents a flight leg that must be flown. The columns $j = 1, ..., n$ represent legal round trip rotations that an airline crew might fly. Cost, c_j is associated with each assignment of a crew to a particular flight leg. The matrix elements a_{ij} are 1 if flight leg i is on rotation j otherwise 0. SPP can also be used for vehicle routing problem.

3   Related Work on SPP

SPP is widely used for many real world problems so many algorithms have been developed, which can be classified into two categories. Exact algorithms find the exact solution of SPP but it takes more time and whenever problem size is large, it is not possible to solve in feasible time. Heuristics can find better solution within less time but sometimes they fail to find global solutions [7].

Balas and Padberg [1] noted that cutting plane algorithms are moderately successful even with using general-purpose cuts and without taking advantage of any special knowledge of the SPP prototype. Tree search with branch and bound technique produces exact optimal solution by various bounding strategies. Harche and Thompson [10] developed an algorithm based on a new method, called column subtraction method, which is capable of solving large sparse instances of set covering, packing and partitioning problems. Hoffman and Padberg [11] presented an exact algorithm based on branch and cut and reported optimal solutions for a large set of real word SPP.

Levine used Parallel GA and hybrid GA to solve SPP during his doctoral work [13][14]. His algorithm was capable of finding optimal solutions for some problems, but in some test instances his algorithm is failed to find out even feasible solution. In [2],Besley and Chu have demonstrated better GA for constraint handling in SPP and results were compared with some linear programming implementation. Czech has shown that how parallel simulated annealing can be used to solve SPP [4].

4   Genetic Algorithm

GA is an optimization technique based on the natural evolution. It maintains a population of strings, called chromosomes that encode candidate solutions to a problem. The algorithm selects some parent chromosomes from the population set according to their fitness value [5], which is calculated using fitness function. The fittest chromosomes have more chances of getting selected for genetic operations in the next generation. Different types of genetic operators are applied to the selected parent chromosomes; possibly according to the probability of operator, and next generation population set is produced. In every generation, a new set of artificial creatures is created using bits and pieces of the fittest chromosomes of the old population.

4.1   Chromosome Encoding and Fitness Function

The first step to solve any problem using GA is to encode a solution as a chromosome such that crossover and mutation can be performed easily & effectively. Binary encoding & real value encoding are two choices for the SPP. Binary encoding is basically column representation in which length of the chromosome is equal to the number of columns and 1 at i^{th} bit implies that i^{th} column is in the solution. But it may be possible that chromosome is infeasible that means all the rows are not covered by the set of selected columns and genetic operators may change feasible solution to the infeasible. Another encoding is real value encoding which is basically row based encoding. In row based encoding chromosome length is equal to the number of rows, suppose i^{th} gene in the chromosome has some real value j, which means i^{th} row is covered by j^{th} column.

For evaluating infeasible chromosome, fitness function must have penalty term that penalizes infeasible chromosome with high value so there are less chances of infeasible chromosome to be selected by the selection method. But encoding of chromosome should be in such a way that it always produces feasible solution so GA is not misguided by infeasible solution. Better fitness value of infeasible chromosome should not rule over the feasible chromosome with poor fitness value [13]. So we have selected row based real value encoding and fitness function will be the total cost of selected columns, which covers all the rows. Moreover, real value encoding satisfies all the properties of encoding method [8].

$$\text{Fitness Value (F)} = \sum_{j=1}^{n} c_j x_j$$

4.2   Cost-Based Uniform Crossover

The primary objective of reproduction is to emphasize good solutions by making their multiple copies. Mutation is used rarely to avoid local minima. So crossover is the heart of GA. During crossover, two parent chromosomes are selected on the basis of fitness and they produce new offspring by genetic recombination. The sampling rate of crossover should be high so that good exploitation can be achieved using current solutions.

We have modified classical uniform crossover for the SPP, it is shown in Fig.1. CUC selects genes by cost instead of using mask for the selection. The gene that has less cost gets priority for selection in offspring provided that it does not make chromosome infeasible that means it should not cover a row by more than one column. If it makes chromosome infeasible then gene from other parent gets chance but with above said condition. If genes from both the parent fail to satisfy the condition then that gene position in offspring is kept blank which will be filled by the repair mechanism.

Select two parent chromosomes, $P1$ and $P2$, randomly for the crossover
for each gene position i, in the chromosome do
    $\mathcal{G} = \min(\text{cost}(P1_i), \text{cost}(P2_i))$;
    if(column $\mathcal{G}$ does not make chromosome infeasible)
        $G_i = \mathcal{G}$;
    else if(other $\mathcal{G}$ does not make chromosome infeasible)
        $G_i = \mathcal{G}$;
    else
        $G_i = 0$;
end

Fig. 1. Modified Crossover for SPP

4.3   Repair Mechanism and Mutation

The crossover often generates infeasible chromosomes because the SPP is highly constrained, i.e. some rows may be under-covered, which means that a row is not covered by any column. The heuristic repair operator is used to convert infeasible chromosomes into feasible ones. It identifies all under-covered rows and selects column one by one. If any column covers under-covered rows and does not make the solution infeasible then that column is added to the solution. If for any chromosome, it is not possible to generate the feasible set of columns then it is discarded and a new feasible chromosome is generated and inserted into the child population.

We do not perform mutation explicitly because it happens implicitly during the repair mechanism by two ways. First, whenever any chromosome becomes illegal, we discard it from the population and generate new feasible chromosome randomly. Whenever gene (column) at particular position from both the parents fail to satisfy the condition then some other column is selected to cover row so that chromosome becomes feasible, that is a kind of mutation. GA procedure is shown in Fig. 2.

```
begin
    t ← 0
    initialize P(t) randomly
    while (t < number_of_generation) do
        evaluate P(t) using fitness function
        elitism(best_found_so_far)
        reproduction(P(t))
        crossover(P(t))
        heuristic repair(P(t))
        t ← t + 1
    end while
    return best_found_so_far end
```

Fig. 2. GA Procedure for SPP

5   Computational Results

We have used well known instances of set partitioning problem from the OR-Library [3]. These data sets are real world problems and provided by an Air line industry. They are varying from small size to the large size.

We have used steady-state genetic algorithm because, by experiment we found that replacing a part of the population after each generation gives better result compared to replacing entire population. We set different parameters of GA as per below.

- Population Size N = 450
- Number of Generation = 200
- Probability of Crossover Pc = 1.0
- 70% worst chromosomes are replaced after each generation

Performance profile of three algorithms is shown in Fig. 3. It is incorporated in the analysis to avoid dominance of any one-test function on the final conclusions about the relative performance of the algorithms [6].

For considering solution cost as the performance metric, performance profiles can be generated as follows. Let $\mathcal{P}$ be the test set of examples, n_s be the number of algorithms and n_p be the number of examples. For each test function p and algorithm s, define

$$v_{p,s} = \text{Solution obtained on a test function } p \text{ by algorithms } s$$

The performance ratio for solution is calculated as

$$r_{p,s} = \frac{v_{p,s}}{\min\{v_{p,s} : 1 \leq s \leq n_s\}}$$

Table 1 compares performance of IP optimal [11], Levine's GA [13][14] and GA using CUC. Results of IP optimal is exact solutions achieved by Hoffman and Padberg [11]. So mainly we have compared performance of GA using CUC with

Levine's GA. In 17 test problems GA using CUC and Levine's GA give same results, in 9 test problems GA using CUC outperforms Levine's GA, whereas in only 2 cases Levine's GA gives better result compared to GA using CUC. Performance profile (Fig. 3) shows that GA using CUC gives exact solution in 82% cases. Fig. 3 also shows that GA using CUC gives better result compared to Levine's GA.

Table 1. Comparison of IP optimal, Levine's GA and GA using CUC

Problem Name	Row	Column	IP Optimal	Levine's GA	GA using CUC
nw41	17	197	11307	11307	11307
nw32	19	294	14877	14877	14877
nw40	19	404	10809	10848	10809
nw08	24	434	35894	37078	36068
nw21	25	577	7408	7408	7408
nw22	23	619	6984	7060	6984
nw12	27	626	14118	15110	14474
nw39	25	677	10080	10080	10080
nw20	22	685	16812	16965	16812
nw23	19	711	12534	12534	12534
nw37	19	770	10068	10068	10068
nw26	23	771	6796	6796	6804
nw10	24	853	68271	X	68271
nw34	20	899	10488	10488	10488
nw43	18	1072	8904	9146	8904
nw42	23	1079	7656	7656	7656
nw28	18	1210	8298	8298	8298
nw25	20	1217	5960	5960	5960
nw38	23	1220	5558	5558	5558
nw27	22	1355	9933	9933	9933
nw24	19	1366	6314	6314	6314
nw35	23	1709	7216	7216	7216
nw36	20	1783	7314	7336	7314
nw29	18	2540	4274	4378	4344
nw30	26	2653	3942	3942	3942
nw31	26	2662	8038	8038	8038
nw19	40	2879	10898	11060	11944
nw33	23	3068	6678	6678	6678

6   Conclusion

In this work, we have shown that GA works very well on a highly constrained combinatorial optimization like SPP. GA using CUC, gives exact IP optimal solution in more than 80% problems. In other problems, results are within 4% of the optimal solution. Moreover, CUC gives good result compared to Levine's

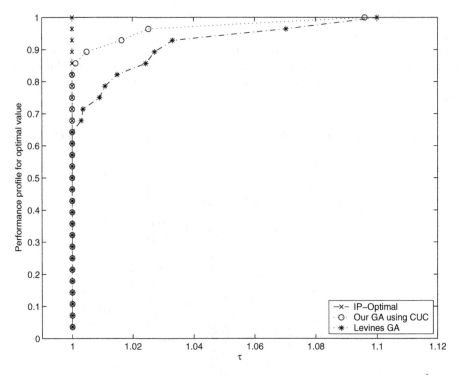

Fig. 3. Performance profile of IP-optimal, Levine's GA and GA using CUC[1]

GA due to two reasons, main reason is exploiting cost of the column information and another reason is only feasible chromosomes are allowed in the population. Our work supports the hypothesis that GA can be used effectively & efficiently for the real world problems, which are otherwise difficult to solve or too much time consuming.

References

1. E. Balas and M. Padberg. On the set-covering problem: II. an algorithm for set partitioning. *Operations Research*, 23:1152–1161, 1975.
2. J. Beasley and P. Chu. A genetic algorithm for the set partitioning problem. Technical report, Imperial College, The Management School, London, 1995.
3. J. E. Beasley. Or-library: distributing test problems by electronic mail. *Journal of the Operational Research Society*, 41(11):1069–1072, 1990.
4. Z. J. Czech. Parallel simulated annealing for the set-partitioning problem. In *Proc. of the 8th Euromicro Workshop on Parallel and Distributed Processing*, pages 343–350, Rhodos, Greece, January 2000.

---

[1] Higher the value of τ, worse the performance of the algorithm under the consideration. $\tau = 1$ represents the best performance of the algorithm.

5. D. R. Bull D. Beasley and R. R. Martin. An overview of genetic algorithms: Part 2, research topics. *University Computing*, 15(4):170–181, 1993.

6. E. D. Dolan and J. J. More. Benchmarking optimization software with performance profiles. *Mathematical Programming Online*, October 2001.

7. M. L. Fisher and P. Kedia. Optimal solutions of set covering/partitioning problems using dual heuristics. *Management Science*, 36:674–688, 1990.

8. M. Gen and R. Cheng. *Genetic Algorithms and Engineering Optimization*. Engineering Design and Automation. Wiley Interscience Publication, John Wiley & Sons. Inc., New York, 2000.

9. D. E. Goldberg. *Genetic Algorithms in Search, Optimization, and Machine Learning*. Addision-Wesley, 1989.

10. F. Harche and G. L. Thompson. The column substraction algorithm: An exact method for solving the weighted set covering problem. *Computers and Operations Research*, 21(6):689–705, 1994.

11. K. L. Hoffman and M. Padberg. Solving airline crew scheduling problems by branch and cut. *Management Science*, 39:657–682, 1993.

12. J. H. Holland. *Adaptation in Natural and Artificial Systems*. MIT Press, second edition, 1992.

13. D. Levine. A Parallel Genetic Algorithm for the Set Partitioning Problem. Technical Report ANL-94/23, May 1994.

14. D. Levine. Application of a hybrid genetic algorithm to airline crew scheduling. *Computers and Operations Research*, 23(6):547–558, 1996.

15. R. Tanga R. Anbil and E. L. Johnson. A global approach to crew-pairing optimization. *IBM Systems Journal*, 31(1):71–78, 1992.

16. D. Fogel T. Back, Z. Michalewicz and S. Pidgeon, editors. *Handbook of Evolutionary Computation*. Oxford University Press, 1997.

Neural Network and Wavelets
in Arrhythmia Classification

Vikas Jain and J.S. Sahambi

Dept. of Electronics and Comm. Engg.
Indian Institute of Technology Guwahati
jain_vikki@yahoo.com, jsahambi@iitg.ernet.in

Abstract. Cardiovascular diseases are a substantial cause of death in
the adult population. Changes in the normal rhythmicity of a human
heart may result in different cardiac arrhythmias, which may be immediately fatal or cause irreparable damage to the heart, when sustained over
long periods of time. In this paper two methods are proposed to efficiently
and accurately classify normal sinus rhythm and different arrhythmias
through a combination of wavelets and Artificial Neural Networks(ANN).
MIT-BIH ECG database has been used for training of ANN. The ability
of the wavelet transform to decompose signal at various resolutions allow
accurate extraction/detection of features from non-stationary signals like
ECG. In the first approach, a set of discrete wavelet transform (DWT)
coefficients which contain the maximum information about the arrhythmia is selected from the wavelet decomposition. In the second approach,
arrhythmia information is represented in terms of wavelet packet (WP)
coefficients. In addition to the information about RR interval, QRS duration, amplitude of R-peak and a set of DWT/WP coefficients are selected
from the wavelet decomposition. Multilayer feedforward ANNs employ
error backpropagation (EBP) learning algorithm (with hyperbolic tan-
gential activation function), were trained and tested using the extracted
parameters. The overall accuracy of classification for 47 patient records
in DWT approach (for 13 beats) is 98.02% and in WP approach (for 15
beats) is 99.06%.

1 Introduction

Heart diseases are caused due to abnormal propagation of impulses through the
specialized cardiac conduction system (cardiac arrhythmias. Cardiac arrhythmias are alterations of cardiac rhythm that disturb the normal synchronized
contraction sequence of the heart and reduce pumping efficiency. Several algorithms have been developed for classification of ECG beats. These techniques
extract some features, which are either temporal or transformed representation
of the ECG waveforms. On the basis of these features, classification has been
performed by Hidden Markov models [1] and the neural networks [2], [3,4,6,7].
There are several shortcomings with the above mentioned cardiac arrhythmia
classifiers. A common problem of ECG signal classifier is that structure complexity grows as the size of the training parameters increases, moreover, performance

S. Manandhar et al. (Eds.): AACC 2004, LNCS 3285, pp. 92–99, 2004.

of the classifier is poor in recognizing a specific type of ECG, which occurs rarely in a certain patient's ECG record. However, these classical methods have their limitations. These techniques are not always adaptable to cardiovascular signals, because the techniques assume the signals to be linear and stationary.

In the present work, two approach are used to extract features from the non-stationary ECG signal. Good time-frequency localization can be achieved by using wavelets. The wavelet transform (WT) is a tool that decomposes data or function or operators into different frequency components, and then studies each component with a resolution matched to its scale. Therefore wavelets are used to extract the significant information from the ECG signal. A supervised artificial neural network (ANN) is developed to recognize and classify the nonlinear morphologies. ANN trained with error back propagation algorithm, classifies the applied input ECG beat to appropriate class. Supervised learning requires standard data while training, hence ECG recordings from the MIT-BIH arrhythmia database [5] are employed in this work.

2   Methodology

The present work classifies the different types of beats present in the ECG. The block diagram of the proposed ECG classifier shown in the Fig. 1.

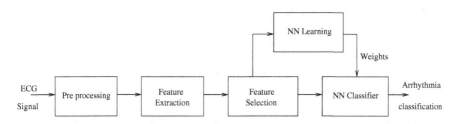

Fig. 1. Block diagram of the ECG classifier

2.1   Preprocessing

In order to reduce the classifier complexity few samples are selected around the R wave for processing. In all arrhythmias QRS complex has the dominant feature. Therefore data window containing the QRS complexes are isolated for each beat using the ECG samples in the range 110 ms before and 140 ms after reference point. Unwanted 0 Hz DC signal is removed from the signal.

2.2   Feature Extraction and Selection

A set of analyzing wavelets is used to decompose the ECG signal into a set of co-efficients that describe the signal's frequency content at given times. For achieving good time-frequency localization the preprocessed ECG signal is decomposed by using the DWT/WP up to the fourth level (using the bio-orthogonal Spline wavelet). We have taken two RR intervals RR_1 (RR interval between the processing beat and the previous beat) and RR_2 (RR interval between the processing beat and next beat), QRS interval, amplitude of R-peak and few wavelet coefficients as elements of the feature vector. Selecting few wavelet coefficients as a feature from the DWT/WP is the most important task.

Discrete wavelet transform. Subband coding is a method for calculating the DWT. The two level dyadic trees provide the octave frequency band split, and a multiresolution decomposition at each node (Fig. 2). Most of the energy of the ECG signal lies between 0.5 Hz and 40 Hz [11]. This energy of the decomposed coefficients is concentrated in the lower sub-bands A_4, D_4, D_3 (Fig.2). The detail information of levels 1 and 2 (sub-bands D_2,D_1) are discarded, as the frequencies covered by these levels were higher than frequency content of the ECG (Table 1).

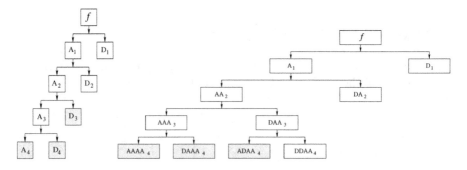

Fig. 2. 4 level DWT and WP decomposition

Wavelet packet. Unlike DWT is a fixed octaveband filter banks, the two channel filter bank can be iterated in an arbitrary fashion (binary tree) (Fig.2). Such arbitrary tree structures were recently introduced as a family of orthonormal bases for discrete time signals and are known under the name of wavelet packets. The promising wavelet packet transform provides a rich menu of orthonormal bases, from which the fittest one can be chosen. The bands $AAAA_4$, $DAAA_4$, $ADAA_4$ and $DDAA_4$ (Table:1) has good frequency resolution and contains the ECG frequency range.

QRS onset and offset detection. After the detection of R peak, the onset and offset of the QRS complex are also detected The onset of the QRS complex is defined as the beginning of the Q wave (or R wave when Q wave is not present), and the offset of the QRS complex is defined as the ending of the S wave (or R wave when the S wave is not present). Ordinarily, the Q and S waves are high frequency and low amplitude waves and their energies are mainly at small scale (2^1). The reason for detecting the beginning and ending at scale 2^1, rather than original signal, is to avoid the effect of baseline drift[10].

Table 1. Frequency Bands of 4-level DWT and WP Decomposition

DWT		WP	
Band	**Frequency range**	**Band**	**Frequency range**
A_4	0 - 11.25 Hz	$AAAA_4$	0 - 11.25 Hz
D_4	11.25 - 22.5 Hz	$DAAA_4$	11.25 - 22.5 Hz
D_3	22.5 - 45 Hz	$ADAA_4$	22.5 - 33.75 Hz
D_2	45 - 90 Hz	$DDAA_4$	33.75-45 Hz
D_1	90 - 180 Hz	DA_2	45-90 Hz
		D_1	90-180 Hz

2.3   Neural Network

In the present application, EBP algorithm with momentum is used for training the neural network (Fig.3). Classifying arrhythmias is a complicated problem, to solve this two hidden layer are taken. The input neurons are equal to the input vector size, and output neurons are equal to number of arrhythmias are going to classify. The configuration of the neural network is given in Table 2

Table 2. Nerual network configurations for DWT and WP approaches

Number of Neurons	DWT	WP
Neurons in Input nodes	27	28
Neurons in First Hidden Layer	25	25
Neurons in Second Hidden Layer	13	13
Neurons in Output Layer	13	15

During training phase, each output unit compares its computed activation y with its target value d to determine the associated error $E = \Sigma(d_k - y_k)^2$ for the pattern with that unit. The ANN weights and biases are adjusted to minimize the least-square error. The minimization problem is solved by gradient descent technique. Convergence is sometimes faster if a momentum term is added to the weight update formula. The weight update formulae for backpropagation with momentum are

$$W_{kj}(t+1) = W_{kj}(t) + \alpha\delta_k ZZ_j + \mu[W_{kj}(t) - W_{kj}(t-1)]$$
$$V_{ji}(t+1) = V_{ji}(t) + \alpha\delta_j Z_i + \mu[V_{ji}(t) - V_{ji}(t-1)] \tag{1}$$
$$U_{ih}(t+1) = U_{ih}(t) + \alpha\delta_i X_h + \mu[U_{ih}(t) - U_{ih}(t-1)]$$

where,

$$\delta_k = (d_k - Y_k)(f'(Y_{ink}))$$
$$\delta_j = \Sigma\delta_k W_{kj}(f'(ZZ_{inj})) \tag{2}$$
$$\delta_i = \Sigma\delta_j V_{ji}(f'(Z_{ini}))$$

In this work all neurons uses hyperbolic tangent activation function $f(y_{in}) = a\tanh(b \times y_{in})$ (nonlinear activation function). Here a and b are constants, given

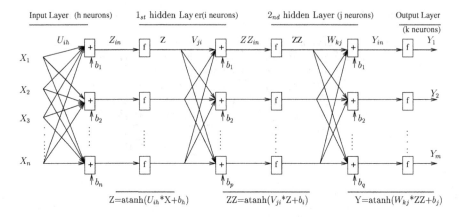

Fig. 3. Backpropagation neural network with two hidden layer

by $a=1$, $b=2/3$. The initial weights to be used in supervised learning has a strong influence in the learning speed and in the quality of the solution obtained after convergence. According to Rumelhart [9], initial weights of exactly zero cannot be used, and random weights (and biases) are initialized in between ±Th1 and ±Th2. Learning factor (α) and momentum parameter (μ) is constrained to be in the range from 0 to 1, excluding the end points. The weights and biases are updated in each iteration (called an epoch) until the net has settled down to a minimum.

3   Results and Discussions

In the present work forty-seven ECG records with a sampling frequency of 360 Hz are chosen for classification. The ECG records has a duration of 30 minutes and includes two leads. The studies proposed herein focus on the one-lead monitoring, MLII leads signal for processing. The Accuracy of an ECG classifier is given as:

$$Accuracy = \frac{\text{Total number of beats correctly classified}}{\text{Total number of beats tested}} \qquad (3)$$

DWT approach. The performance of the DWT approach is tested with thirteen different types of beats (normal beat(NB), Left bundle branch block (LBBB), Right bundle branch block (RBBB), Abberated atrial premature beat (AAPB), Premature ventricula contraction (PVC), Fusion of ventricular and normal beat (FVNB), Nodal (junctional) premature beat (NPB), Atrial premature beat (APB), Ventricular escape beat (VEB), Nodal (junctional) escape beat (NEB), Paced beat (PB), Ventricular flutter wave (VFW), Fusion of paced and normal beat (FPNB)). The number of selected training beats are tabulated in Table:3 (second column).

Table 3. Performance of DWT approach in training and testing phase

Beat	Number of Beats		Correctly Classified Beats number		Accuracy in %	
	Training	Testing	Training	Testing	Training	Testing
NB	36343	36343	36337	36293	99.98	99.86
LBBB	4034	4034	4026	2597	99.80	64.38
RBBB	3625	3625	3625	3622	100.00	99.92
AAPB	75	75	71	60	94.67	80.00
PVB	3509	3509	3504	3507	99.86	99.94
FVNB	401	401	401	401	100.00	100.00
NPB	42	41	42	37	100.00	90.24
APB	1271	1270	1271	1266	100.00	99.69
VEB	53	53	53	50	100.00	94.34
NEB	115	114	115	109	100.00	95.61
PB	3510	3510	3510	2880	100.00	82.05
VFW	236	236	236	235	100.00	99.58
FPNB	491	491	490	489	99.79	99.59
Total	53705	53702	53681	51546	99.96 %	95.99 %

Performance of the DWT approach. The trained network has been tested in the retrieval mode, in which the testing vectors are not taking part in training process. The efficiency of recognition in the testing mode is 95.99% while the efficiency of recognition in the training mode is 99.96%. Close analysis of misclassification results has revealed that all errors are of the same type and due to wrong neuron being fired. Few arrhythmias doesn't have sufficient data for training, this causes misclassification in the testing phase. Totally 1,07,407 number of different beats(with forty seven records) have been considered, and the overall classification rate is 98.02% (Table:5,column two).

WP approach. The performance of the WP approach is tested with fifteen different types of beats (including Unclassified beat (UC), Atrial escape beat (AEB)). The number of selected training beats are tabulated in Table:4 (second column).

Performance of the WP approach. The efficiency of recognition in the testing mode is 98% while the efficiency of recognition in the training mode is 99.97%. Totally 1,07,456 number of different beats have been considered, and the overall classification rate is 99.06% (Table:5,column three).

The overall classification rate of DWT approach is slightly less compared with WP approach, because with the wavelet packets gives good frequency localization than DWT. Proposed method is implemented on dual CPU with clock speed of 1 GHz and RAM of 256MB using Matlab Version 6.

4   Conclusions

A high quality of feature set is undoubtedly the first important factor for good performance of ECG classifiers. Wavelet analysis decomposes the signal into

Table 4. Performance of WP approach in training and testing phase

Beat Type	Number of Beats		Correctly Classified Beats		Accuracy in %	
	Training	Testing	Training	Testing	Training	Testing
NB	36343	36343	36335	36322	99.98	99.94
LBBB	4034	4034	4034	3107	100.00	77.02
RBBB	3625	3625	3624	3624	99.97	99.97
AAPB	75	75	75	68	100.00	90.67
PVB	3509	3509	3509	3508	100.00	99.97
FVNB	401	401	396	398	98.75	99.25
NPB	42	41	42	40	100.00	97.56
APB	1271	1270	1271	1269	100.00	99.92
VEB	53	53	53	48	100.00	90.57
NEB	115	114	115	114	100.00	100.00
PB	3510	3510	3509	3415	99.97	97.29
UC	17	16	16	12	94.12	75.00
VFW	236	236	235	235	99.58	99.58
AEB	8	8	8	6	100.00	75.00
FPNB	491	491	491	489	100.00	99.59
Total	53730	53726	53713	52655	99.97 %	98.01 %

Table 5. Individual record wise Performance of proposed method

Records	Accuracy %		Records	Accuracy %	
	DWT Approach	WP Approach		DWT Approach	WP Approach
100	100.000	100.000	202	99.953	99.9531
101	100.000	100.000	203	98.184	98.9590
102	100.000	100.000	205	100.000	100.000
103	100.000	100.000	207	40.258	63.2189
104	99.955	99.8653	208	99.966	100.000
105	99.961	99.9222	209	100.000	100.000
106	100.000	100.000	210	99.660	99.8112
107	99.859	100.000	212	100.000	100.000
108	99.943	100.000	213	100.000	99.9384
109	99.921	100.000	214	99.734	99.9557
111	99.906	99.9057	215	100.000	100.000
112	100.000	100.000	217	71.487	95.6029
113	100.000	100.000	219	99.954	99.9535
114	100.000	99.8934	220	100.000	100.000
115	100.000	100.000	221	100.000	100.000
117	100.000	100.000	222	99.718	100.000
118	100.000	99.9561	223	100.000	99.8847
119	100.000	100.000	228	99.951	100.000
121	100.000	100.000	230	100.000	100.000
122	100.000	100.000	231	99.873	100.000
123	100.000	100.000	232	99.775	99.9438
124	100.000	100.000	233	100.000	99.9350
200	99.962	99.9615	234	99.855	99.9636
201	99.541	99.9490	Total	98.0159 %	99.0564 %

different time-frequency regions, thus giving better localization of signal features. The bio-orthogonal Spline wavelet takes care of the discontinuities at the edges. The overall classification accuracy from DWT and WP approach is found to be 98.02% and 99.06%. This system can be very useful for clinical environment.

References

1. D. A. Coast, R. M. Stern, G. G. Cano, and S. A. Briller, "An approach to cardiac arrhythmia analysis using hidden markov models," IEEE Trans. Biomed. Eng., vol. 37, pp. 826-836, Sep 1990.
2. S.Osowsaki and T. H. Linh, "ECG beat recognition using fuzzy hybrid neural network," IEEE Trans. Biomed. Eng., vol. 48, pp.1265-1271, Nov 2001.
3. Y. Sun, "Arrhythmia Recognition from Electrocardiogram using Nonlinear Analysis and Unsupervised Clustering Techniques," PhDthesis, Nanyang Technological University, 2001.
4. K. Ichiro Minami, H. Nakajima, and T. Toyoshima, "Real-time discrimination of ventricular tachyarrhythmia with fourier-transform neural network," IEEE Trans. Biomed. Eng., vol. 46, Feb 1999.
5. MIT-BIH Arrhythmia Database,"http://ecg.mit.edu".
6. Y. H. Hu, S. Palreddy, and W. Tompkins, "A patient adaptable ECG beat classifier using a mixture of experts approach," IEEE Trans. Biomed. Eng., vol. 44, pp. 891-900, Sept 1997.
7. M. Lagerholm, C. Peterson, G. Braccini, L. Edenbrandt, and L. Sornmo, "Clustering ECG complexes using hermite functions and self-organizing maps," IEEE Trans. Biomed. Eng., 1998.
8. I. Daubechies, "Ten Lectures on Wavelets," Philadelphia, SIAM, 1992
9. D. E. Rumelhart, G. E. Hinton, and R. J. Williams, "Learning representations by back-propagating errors," Nature, 1986.
10. Cuiwei Li, Chongxun Zheng, and Changfeng Tai "Detection of ECG characteristic point using wavelet transforms," IEEE Trans. Biomed. Eng., vol. 42, No. 1, January 1995.
11. N. V. Thakor, J. G. Webster, and W. J. Tompkins, "Estimation of QRS complex power spectra for design of a QRS filter," IEEE Trans. Biomed. Eng.,1984.
12. Jacek M. Zurada, "Introduction to Artificial Neural System," 3rd edition, West publision, 1999.

ECG Arrhythmia Analysis
by Multicategory Support Vector Machine

Mahesh S. Khadtare and J.S. Sahambi

Dept. of Electronics & Comm. Engg.
Indian Institute of Technology, Guwahati, Assam, India
maheshkha@hotmail.com, jsahambi@iitg.ernet.in

Abstract. Heart diseases are caused by a multitude of reasons including abnormal propagation of pacing impulses through the specialized
cardiac conduction system. Such abnormalities where cardiac rhythm de-
viates from normal sinus rhythm are termed as arrhythmia. The present
contribution concentrates on the application of Multicategory support
vector machines (MC-SVMs) for arrhythmia classification. This system
of classification comprises of several units including signal preprocessing, wavelet transform (WT) for feature extraction and support vector
machine with Gaussian kernel approximation of each arrhythmia class.
Training and testing has been done on standard MIT-BIH Arrhythmia
database. A systematic and comprehensive evaluation of this algorithm
has been conducted where 25 features are being extracted from each
arrhythmia beat by wavelet transform, for multi-category classification.
Upon implementing MC-SVM techniques one-versus-one, DAGSVM was
found to be the most suitable algorithm in this domain. The overall
accuracy of classification of the proposed method is 98.50%. This system
is flexible, and implements a prototype graphical user interface (GUI)
based on MATLAB. The results shown in this paper prove that the
method can classify arrhythmia from given ECG data.

1 Introduction

A major problem faced by commercial automated ECG analysis machine is the
presence of unpredictable variations in the morphology of the ECG waveforms
for different subjects. Such an inconsistency in performance is a major hurdle,
preventing highly reliable, fully automated ECG processing systems to be widely
used clinically. Preprocessing that can recognize the predefined feature set of each
arrhythmia recordings. Various features are extracted with wavelet transform.
This tool implements an idea of supervised learning from examples by using
support vector machines [1],[2]. Arrhythmia detection research is going on for
accurate prediction of abnormality with neural networks [3], or by the other
recognition system [4],[5]. Standard MIT-BIH arrhythmia database [6] is used
for training and classification. We implemented prototype GUI based system
for arrhythmia classification by MC-SVMs one-vs-one (OVO)(gaussian compact
kernel) [9], DAGSVM (Directed Acyclic Graph SVM) [10] algorithm.

S. Manandhar et al. (Eds.): AACC 2004, LNCS 3285, pp. 100–107, 2004.

2 Methods and Materials

2.1 Support Vector Machine

Support Vector Machines (SVMs) [2] are arguably the single most important development in supervised classification of recent years. Moreover, several efficient, high quality, and user-friendly implementations of SVM algorithms [11] facilitate application of these techniques in practice. Moreover, all other things being equal, multicategory classification is significantly harder than binary classification [12]. Fortunately, several algorithms have emerged during the last few years that allow multicategory classification with SVMs. The preliminary experimental evidence currently available suggests that some multicategory SVMs (MC-SVMs) perform well in isolated class. In this subsection we outline the principles behind MC-SVM algorithms used in the study. Given a labelled training data

$$\mathcal{D} = \{(\mathbf{x}_i, y_i)\}_{i=1}^{\ell}, \quad \mathbf{x}_i \in \mathbf{X} \subset \mathbb{R}^d, \quad y_i \in \mathbf{Y} = \{-1, +1\} \tag{1}$$

where $\mathbf{x}_i$ is the input pattern for the i-th example and y_i is the corresponding desired response (target output). Constructs a maximal margin linear classifier in a high dimensional feature space, $\Phi(\mathbf{x})$, defined by a positive definite kernel function, $k(\mathbf{x}, \mathbf{x}')$, inner product in the feature space

$$\Phi(\mathbf{x}).\Phi(\mathbf{x}') = k(\mathbf{x}, \mathbf{x}') \tag{2}$$

A common kernel is the Gaussian radial basis function (RBF),

$$k(\mathbf{x}, \mathbf{x}') = e^{-||\mathbf{x}-\mathbf{x}'||^2/2\sigma^2} \tag{3}$$

The function implemented by a support vector machine is given by

$$f(\mathbf{x}) = \left\{ \sum_{i=1}^{\ell} \alpha_i y_i k(\mathbf{x}_i, \mathbf{x}) + b \right\} \tag{4}$$

To find the optimal coefficients, α, of this expansion it is sufficient to maximize the functional

$$W(\alpha) = \sum_{i=1}^{\ell} \alpha_i - \frac{1}{2} \sum_{i,j=1}^{\ell} y_i y_j \alpha_i \alpha_j k(\mathbf{x}_i, \mathbf{x}_j) \tag{5}$$

in the non-negative quadrant

$$0 \leq \alpha_i \leq C, \quad i = 1, \ldots, \ell \tag{6}$$

subject to the constraint

$$\sum_{i=1}^{\ell} \alpha_i y_i = 0 \tag{7}$$

where C is a regularization parameter. For a full exposition of the support vector method, refer[1],[13].

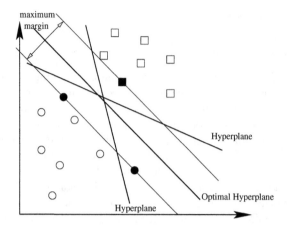

Fig. 1. Binary linear SVMs applied to two class

2.2 Multicategory Support Vector Machine (MC-SVM)

All formulations of multi-class SVM methods described below adopt the following notation: $\mathbf{x}_i \in \mathbb{R}^m$, are m-dimensional training instances and $y_i \in \{1, 2, 3, \ldots, k\}(i = 1, 2, \ldots, n)$, are corresponding class labels.

One-Vs-One (OVO). This technique involves construction of the standard binary classifiers for all pairs of classes [9]. In other words, for every pair of classes, $\frac{k(k-1)}{2}$ times a binary SVM problem is solved (with the underlying optimization problem to maximize the margin between two classes). The decision function assigns an instance to a class which has the largest number of votes (so-called "Max Wins" strategy [14]). If ties still occur, a sample will be assigned based on the classification provided by the furthest hyperplane.

DAGSVM. The training phase of this algorithm is similar to the OVO approach using multiple binary SVM classifiers; however the testing phase of

Table 1. Three binary OVO classifier are applied to arrhythmia classification problem

Regions	Decision of the Classifier			Resulting Class
	A Vs C	B Vs C	A Vs B	
1	**C**	**C**	A	C
2	**C**	**C**	B	C
3	C	**B**	**B**	B
4	A	**B**	**B**	B
5	**A**	C	**A**	A
6	**A**	B	**A**	A
7	A	C	B	Tie

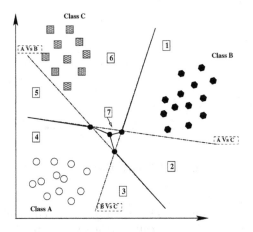

Fig. 2. OVO MC-SVM is applied to three class

DAGSVM requires construction of a rooted binary decision DAG (DDAG) using $\frac{k(k-1)}{2}$ classifiers [10]. Each node of this tree is a binary SVM for a pair of classes, say (p, q). On the topologically lowest level there are k leaves corresponding to k classification decisions. Every non-leaf node (p, q) has two edges the left edge corresponds to decision "not p" and the right one corresponds to "not q". The choice of the class order in the DDAG list can be arbitrary [10].

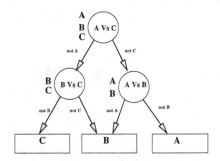

Fig. 3. DAGSVM algorithm

2.3   Data Set

The studies proposed herein focus on the MLII ECG records with different types of beats, shown in Fig. 4 i.e., the NB-normal beat, LBBB, RBBB, APB are filtered and sampled at 360 Hz. In all of the arrhythmias RR interval is one of the important feature [8]. In premature beats RR interval between the processing beat and the previous beat (RR_1) is shorter than normal, and the RR interval between the current beat and next beat (RR_2) is longer than normal. Most of the energy of the ECG signal lies between 0.5 Hz and 40 Hz. Totally 23 WT

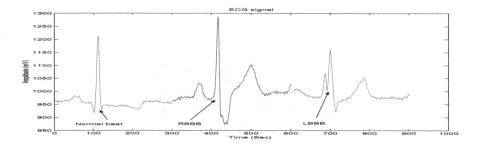

Fig. 4. ECG arrhythmia signal

coefficients are selected from A_4, D_4, D_3 sub-bands. RR_1 and RR_2 along with the selected 23 WT coefficients is called as feature vector for each arrhythmia type.

2.4   Discrimination

All data are parameterized by using the support vector approximation with gaussian kernels [15]. We calculated Lagrangian multipliers, α and bias for optimal separating hyperplane. The SVM training gives SVs, the non-zero α_i and the offset b.

For MC-SVM we discuss above one-vs-one classifier as every pair of classes refer Fig. 5. The number of SVs, OSH for classification depends on complexity. In the multi class classifier to compute a *confusion matrix*, which is used to

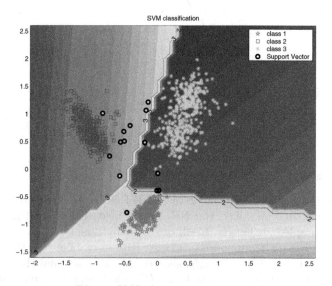

Fig. 5. OVO class in pattern space

reduce the number and complexity of two-class SVMs. That are built in the second stage using the one-vs-one approach. The rows show actual classes and the columns show predicted classes. The matrix clearly shows that different classes have different degrees of confusion with other classes. MATLAB based

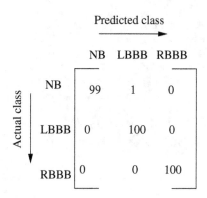

Fig. 6. Confusion Matrix

Prototype GUI system Fig. 7 to accurately analysis of arrhythmia but it is restricted to classify among three arrhythmias.

3   Results and Discussions

In present work few ECG beats are taken for training and testing binary SVM classifier. The beats are divided into 3 classes corresponding to normal sinus beats and 2 classes of pathological shapes from 2 focal ventricular contractions, probably LBBB and RBBB as shown in Fig. 4. Learning set consists of 1200 ECG samples. The actual class and predicted class is shown by confusion matrix Fig. 6. The test results for 32498 ECG beat samples are listed in Table 2. We observed that training vectors have good accuracy of classification compared with testing data

Table 2. Classification and Accuracy for test data set

Observations	Normal beat	LBBB beat	RBBB beat	Total
Total number of beats	28266	263	3988	32517
Correctly classified	27944	248	3840	32032
Misclassified beats	155	7	49	211
Unclassified beats	167	8	99	274
% Accuracy	98.86	94.29	96.28	98.50

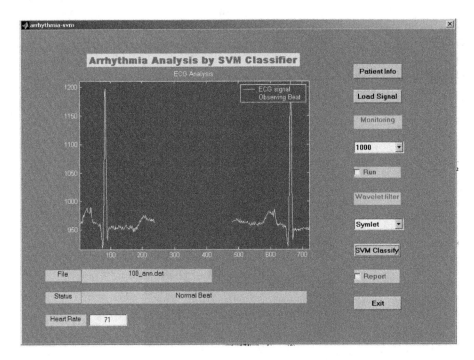

Fig. 7. Prototype GUI arrhythmia classifier

4   Conclusion

More accurate classifications are achieved with just a few support vectors, with consequent benefit in computational cost. A subset of WT coefficients carrying the important information about QRS complex are given as input to SVM. MC-SVMs with OVO have been trained to accurately classify the arrhythmia class. Accuracy is found to be 98.50 %. A user friendly GUI has also been developed and could be useful in the clinical environment.

References

1. N. Cristianini and J. Shawe-Taylor, *An Introduction to Support Vector Machines (and other kernel-based learning methods).* Cambridge, U.K.: Cambridge University Press, 2000.
2. V. N. Vapnik, *The Nature of Statistical Learning Theory.* New York: Springer-Verlag, 1995.
3. Y. H. Hu, S. Palreddy, and W. Tompkins, "A patient adaptable ecg beat classifier using a mixture of experts approach," *IEEE Trans. Biomed. Eng.*, vol. 44, pp. 891–900, Sept 1997.
4. J Millet-Roig, et al , "Study of frequency and time domain parameters extracted by means of wavelet transform applied to ecg to distinguish vf and other arrhythmias," *Proc. of. Computers in Cardiology*, 1998.

5. D. J. Strauss, "Adapted filter bank in machine learning applications in biomedical signal processing," *Proc. of. Computers in Cardiology*, 2002.
6. "MIT- BIH arrhythmia database," http://ecg.mit.edu.
7. Keiichiro Minami and Hiroshi Nakajima and Takeshi Toyoshima, "Real-time discrimination of ventricular tachyarrhythmia with fourier-transform neural network," *IEEE Trans. Biomed. Eng.*, vol. 46, Feb 1999.
8. I. Daubechies, "The wavelet transform, time-frequency localization and signal analysis," *IEEE Trans. Inform. Theory*, vol. 36, pp. 961–1005, Sept 1990.
9. Kressel U., "Pairwise classification and support vector machines," in *Advances in Kernel Methods - Support Vector Learning* (B. Schölkopf, C. J. C. Burges, and A. J. Smola, eds.), Cambridge, Massachusetts: MIT Press, 1999.
10. J. C. Platt, "Fast training of support vector machines using sequential minimal optimization," in *Advances in Kernel Methods - Support Vector Learning* (B. Schölkopf, C. J. C. Burges, and A. J. Smola, eds.), ch. 12, pp. 185–208, Cambridge, Massachusetts: MIT Press, 1999.
11. C.-C. Chang and C.-J. Lin, "Libsvm a library for support vector machines," http://www.csie.ntu.edu.tw/ cjlin/libsvm.
12. Mukherjee S., "Classifying microarray data using support vector machines," in *Understanding And Using Microarray Analysis Techniques: A Practical Guide*, Boston: Kluwer Academic Publishers, 2003.
13. V. N. Vapnik, *Statistical Learning Theory*. Wiley Series on Adaptive and Learning Systems for Signal Processing, Communications and Control, New York: Wiley, 1998.
14. Friedman, J., "Another approach to polychotomous classification," tech. rep., Stanford Univeristy, 1996.
15. J. Millet-Roig, "Support vector machine for arrhythmia discrimination with wavelet transform feature selection," *Proc. of. Computers in Cardiology*, 2000.

Approximation of Multi-pattern to Single-Pattern Functions by Combining FeedForward Neural Networks and Support Vector Machines

Vijayanarasimha Hindupur Pakka

Department of Electrical Engineering, Indian Institute of Science,
Bangalore 560 012, India
`vijay@ee.iisc.ernet.in`, `hpvijaynarasimha@hotmail.com`

Abstract. In many fields there are situations encountered, where a function has to be estimated to determine its output under new conditions. Some functions have one output corresponding to differing input patterns. Such types of functions are difficult to map using a function approximation technique such as that employed by the Multilayer Perceptron Network. Hence to reduce this functional mapping to Single Pattern-to-Single Pattern type of condition, and then effectively estimate the function, we employ classification techniques such as the Support Vector Machines. This paper describes in detail such a combined technique, which shows excellent results for practical applications.

1 Introduction

Function approximation (FA) or function estimation is typically the estimation of the output of an unknown function for a new input pattern, provided the function estimator is given sufficient training sets such that the unknown parameters defining the function are estimated through a learning strategy. FA is more commonly known as regression in statistical theory. This function is usually a model of a practical system. The training sets are obtained usually by simulation of the system in real time. If a training set is given by,

$$\left\{ \left(\overline{x_1}, \overline{y_1} \right), \left(\overline{x_2}, \overline{y_2} \right), \left(\overline{x_3}, \overline{y_3} \right), \ldots\ldots \left(\overline{x_N}, \overline{y_N} \right) \right\} \tag{1}$$

$\overline{x}$ = input pattern vector, $\overline{y}$ = target vector, N = number of patterns.

Then we need to estimate the functional relation between $\overline{x}$ and $\overline{y}$ i.e.,

$$\overline{y} = c_i f \left(\overline{x}; t_i \right) \tag{2}$$

c_i = constants in the function, t_i = parameters of the function, $f : S \rightarrow \mathbb{R}$, where

$S = \left\{ x \in \mathbb{R}^n \mid a_i \leq x_i \leq b_i, 1 \leq i \leq n \right\}$ is a closed bounded region.

FA by multilayer perceptron networks like the FeedForward Neural Networks (FFNNs) is proven to be very efficient [2], [3], considering various learning strategies like the simple Back Propagation or the robust Levenberg Marquardt and Conjugate Gradient approaches. Assume $f(x_1, x_2, \ldots\ldots, x_{m_0})$ is the approximate function with m_0 variables. Now if the true function is $F(\cdot)$, then the FFNN equates this to

S. Manandhar et al. (Eds.): AACC 2004, LNCS 3285, pp. 108–114, 2004.

$$\sum_{i=1}^{m_1} \alpha_i \, \phi\left(\sum_{j=1}^{m_0} w_{ij} \overline{x_{ij}} + b_i \right). \tag{3}$$

Now the objective is to find the parameter values of m_1 and values of all w_{ij}'s, b_i's and α_i's, such that $\left| F(\cdot) - f(\cdot) \right| < \varepsilon$, for all $\overline{x_1}, \overline{x_2}, \ldots\ldots, \overline{x_{m_0}}$.

2 Multi-pattern to Single-Pattern Functions

Let us look at the problem of FA as a mapping problem, where, by one-to-one mapping we mean that each input vector has a corresponding and unique target vector. These mappings are simple to model by FFNNs.

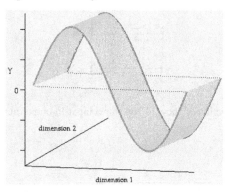

Fig. 1a. Sine wave characteristics of a sample system. Forward sine represents cycle 'a' and backward sine represents cycle 'b'

But, this is not the case in many fields. For example, let us study the case of a sine function. Assume that a system has the characteristic shown in figure 1a, which has to be estimated. The data sets that are available for training of the FFNN are the data corresponding to the two cycles a and b. For convenience, figure 1a is redrawn as figure 1b. Inputs X_{ai} and X_{bi} have same output Y_i. This value is *stored* by the FFNN in the form of a straight line. For both the inputs running through one cycle, we have a set of such straight lines with varying amplitudes (figure 2). Let us name this type of mapping as *Two-way mapping* or *Multi-Pattern to Single-Pattern mapping* in general, because, estimation of the actual function is the first FA problem, and estimation of the shapes of the lines in figure 2 is the second FA problem, i.e., two different input patterns X_{ai} and X_{bi} correspond to a single output pattern Y_i.

Now suppose there exists an intermediate sine cycle (p) between cycles a and b. If p has similar shape and size as of a and b, then, we can estimate its Y throughout the cycle just by noting the Y values at corresponding intermediate point X_p in figure 2. This estimation of Y turns out to be equal to that at X_a or X_b. Now instead of p being similar to a or b, suppose it to be of different size as shown in figure 3. Then, if Y's are estimated at $X=X_p$, the results would not match with that of the true function represented by p. This is due to the fact that the curves joining the two sets of vertical points in figure 2 are still straight lines, though in reality they are of the shape of curves with amplitudes (Y's) at X_p different from that at X_a or X_b.

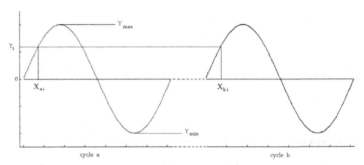

Fig. 1b. Simpler representation of figure 1a

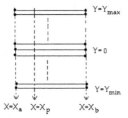

Fig. 2. Graphical depiction of "how FFNN stores input-to-output functional relationship"

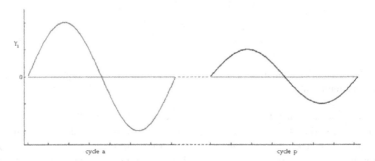

Fig. 3. Different characteristics of the same system

The misestimation of p is mainly due to insufficient data (cycles) between a and b. Even if there were data between a and b, this would have called for a *strain* on the FFNN to learn the entire input space [4]. This is because it has to learn in both directions, one in the direction of the sine propagation and the other in the direction of the vectors joining a and b. To relieve the FFNN of this burden, datasets are labeled and correspondingly classified using Support Vector Classifiers (SVCs) [5], which are then combined suitably with FFNNs so as to give effective approximation to the overall true function.

3 Function Approximation by Combined FFNNs and SVCs

I have described in detail, what I mean by the term *Multi-Pattern to Single-Pattern Functional Mappings*. These types of characteristics are often encountered in the modeling of practical systems. Hence their detailed analysis is of good relevance. To describe and apply the proposed approach to a practical system, I shall consider a live topic in the field of power engineering. I shall briefly describe here, the fault location problem in distribution systems. Consider a practical 11 KV, 19 node Distribution Feeder shown in figure 4. Each node is a distribution transformer with a specified load. The feeder line has a resistance (R) and reactance (X) of 0.0086 and 0.0037 p.u/km respectively. As R/X ratio is fixed, let me consider X as the only variable.

For fault location, we need to consider various practical aspects involved in the day-to-day operation of a distribution system. In a single day there are various loading patterns, which have to be simulated, and also we need to consider various types of faults that occur in a realistic scenario. During fault conditions, if three-phase voltage and current measurements at the substation (node 1) are considered as the input elements, the fault location can be predicted by the output of the function estimator. This output is the reactance of the line, which in turn is the length of the faulty part of the line measured from node 1. This is a *single-pattern-to-single-pattern* type of functional mapping, as each measurement vector produces a corresponding and unique output pattern.

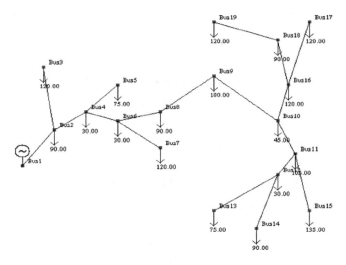

Fig. 4. A practical 19-node (Bus) 11KV distribution system feeder

The other practical factors mentioned before, lead to *Multi-Pattern to Single-Pattern Functional Mapping*, which has to be mapped to estimate the fault location in real time. For generating the data sets for training, following procedure is adopted:

- Fault is simulated with a particular type of fault (Line-Ground, Line-Line, Line-Line-Ground, Symmetrical 3phase) at a particular node, and at a particular Source Short Circuit (SSC) level (this is to simulate the loading patterns of the system).
- Measurements are noted at the substation. The 6x1 input pattern is reduced to 3x1 using Principal Component Analysis (useful in viewing the dataset).
- Now the SSC level, fault type, and the fault nodes are varied throughout their range, individually, and the data set is built up. The SSC range is from 20MVA to 50 MVA in steps of 5MVA.

We see from figure 5 that estimating this complex function is quite difficult for an individual FFNN with any architecture. Hence, the first *Function Breakup* is by labeling the data according to their fault types and then classifying them by a SVC. In real time, this SVC block classifies the type of fault of an input pattern and the function estimator corresponding to this fault type does the remaining job. This is seen from figure 6, where the function looks less complex and can be modeled with less difficulty. This dataset can be further reduced to a single curve (solid curves in figure 6) that corresponds to a dataset of each SSC level. This reduction is possible by considering each SSC level as a class, and by doing multiclass classification on the dataset in figure 6. As there are 7 SSC levels, 6 binary classifiers are present in each of the SSC level classifier 'SVM a' to 'SVM d'. Classifier 1 classifies faults of 20 MVA and 25 MVA, and so on. 'SVM a' in figure 7 refers to SSC level classifier that is trained with Line to Ground faults, 'SVM b' refers to Line to Line faults and so on.

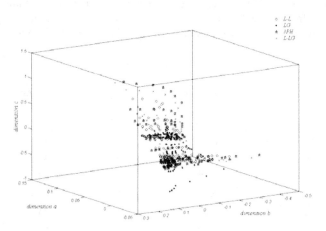

Fig. 5. Dataset of the complete function approximation problem

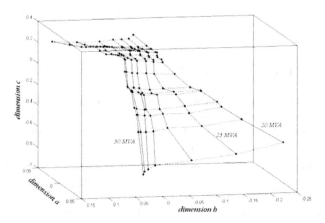

Fig. 6. Dataset corresponding to LG fault. Each dot represents fault on a node, the solid curves represent variation of fault positions, and the dotted curves represent variation along the SSC level

The value of f(x) in eqn (7) points to the class the pattern belongs to i.e., each SVC outputs the pattern as a positive or negative function value, which is indicative of it belonging to either class. Table 1 describes the classification of 32 MVA and 33 MVA source level faults as that of 30 MVA and 35 MVA source levels respectively. The f(x) value of the 32 MVA fault changes sign at classifier nos. 2, 3 (in third column of table 2 - the value of f(x) changes from −2.4922 to +1.0156) and the common class between these two classifiers being 30 MVA, we classify this fault as one that occurred in the group of 30 MVA. Similarly the 33 MVA fault is categorized as belonging to 35 MVA class. Now the work of the FFNNs is cut down to estimation of the solid curves, i.e., data relating to one fault type and one SSC level. Thus, a complex function is broken down into simpler functions and are then efficiently approximated.

Table 1. Classifying 3-Phase Symmetrical Faults of Two SSC Levels

Classifier No	Classes (MVA)	32 MVA	33 MVA
1	20 – 25	-3.3638	-3.8435
2	25 – 30	**-2.4922**	-3.3665
3	30 – 35	**1.0156**	**-0.5925**
4	35 – 40	3.8867	**2.4713**
5	40 – 45	7.1996	5.8708
6	45 – 50	8.6052	6.9059

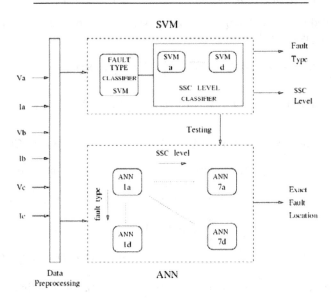

Fig. 7. Block Description of the proposed approach

References

1. Sprecher, D. A.: On the structure of continuous functions of several variables. In: Transactions of mathematical Society, Vol. 115. (1964) 340–355.

2. Blum, E. K., Li, L. K.: Approximation theory and feedforward networks. In: Neural Networks, Vol. 4. (1991) 511–515.
3. Hornik, K.: Multilayer FeedForward networks are universal approximators. In: Neural Networks, Vol. 2. (1986) 359–366.
4. Hornik, K.: Approximation capabilities of multilayer feedforward networks. In: Neural Networks, Vol. 4. (1991) 251–257.
5. Bredensteiner, E. J., Bennett, K. P.: Multi category classification by support vector machines. In: Computational Optimizations and Applications (1999).
6. Kaufmann, L.: Solving the quadratic programming problem arising in support vector classification. In: Adv in Kernel Methods: Support Vector Machines, Schölkopf B, Burges C, and Smola A, Eds. Cambridge, MA: MIT Press (1998).
7. Fletcher, R.: Practical Methods of Optimization, Wiley, New York (2000).

Appendix

If i, j are the two classes, then the following binary classification problem

$$\min_{w^{ij},b^{ij},\xi^{ij}} \frac{1}{2}(w^{ij})^T w^{ij} + C\sum_t \xi_t^{ij}$$

$$(w^{ij})^T \phi(x_t) + b^{ij} \geq 1 - \xi_t^{ij}, \quad if \ y_t = i,$$

$$(w^{ij})^T \phi(x_t) + b^{ij} \leq -1 + \xi_t^{ij}, \quad if \ y_t = j, \quad i.e.,$$ (4)

$$y_t[(w^{ij})^T \phi(x_t) + b^{ij}] \geq 1 - \xi_t^{ij}, \ t = 1,\ldots,k, \text{(pattern no)}$$

has to be solved [5]. Substituting the optimum weights and bias terms in the Lagrangian for (4) we get its dual [7]:

$$\max L = q(\alpha) = \sum_{i=1}^{N} \alpha_i - \frac{1}{2}\sum_{i=1}^{N}\sum_{i=1}^{N} y_i y_j K(x_i, x_j)\alpha_i\alpha_j$$

$$\text{subject to } \sum_{i=1}^{N} y_i\alpha_i = 0, \ 0 \leq \alpha_i \leq C \ 0 \leq i \leq N$$ (5)

The kernel function $K(x_i, x_j)$ used is: $e^{-\|x_i-x_j\|^2/2\sigma^2}$ for SSC Level Classification and, $(x_i x_j + 1)^2$ for Fault Type Classification. The conditions for optimality are [6]:

$$\alpha_i = 0 \Rightarrow y_i f(x_i) \geq 1, \quad 0 < \alpha_i < C \Rightarrow y_i f(x_i) = 1, \quad \alpha_i = C \Rightarrow y_i f(x_i) \leq 1 \quad (6)$$

$$f(x) = \sum_{i \in S} \alpha_i y_i K(x_i, x) - b$$

$$S = \{i : \alpha_i > 0\} \ \& \ b = y_j - \sum_{i \in S} \alpha_i y_i K(x_i, x_j) \text{ for some j such that } 0 < \alpha_j < C.$$ (7)

Patterns corresponding to nonzero α are the support vectors, which define the separating hyperplane.

Comparison of Numerical Integration Algorithms in Raster CNN Simulation

V. Murgesh[1] and K. Murugesan[2]

[1] Department of Computer Science & Engineering, National Institute of Technology,
Tiruchirappalli – 620 015, Tamil Nadu, India
murugesh@nitt.edu
[2] Department of Mathematics, National Institute of Technology,
Tiruchirappalli – 620 015, Tamil Nadu, India
murugu@nitt.edu

Abstract. An efficient simulator for Cellular Neural Networks (CNNs) is presented in this paper. The simulator is capable of performing Raster Simulation for any size of input image, thus a powerful tool for researchers investigating potential applications of CNN. This paper reports an efficient algorithm exploiting the latency properties of Cellular Neural Networks along with popular numerical integration algorithms; simulation results and comparison are also presented.

1 Introduction

Cellular Neural Networks (CNNs) are analog, time-continuous, nonlinear dynamical systems and formally belong to the class of recurrent neural networks. Since their introduction in 1988 (by Chua and Yang [5, 6]), they have been the subjects of intense research. Initial applications include image processing, signal processing, pattern recognition and solving partial differential equations etc.

Runge-Kutta (RK) methods have become very popular, both as computational techniques as well as subject for research, which were discussed by Butcher [3, 4]. This method was derived by Runge around the year 1894 and extended by Kutta a few years later. They developed algorithms to solve differential equations efficiently and yet are the equivalent of approximating the exact solutions by matching 'n' terms of the Taylor series expansion.

Butcher [3] derived the best RK pair along with an error estimate and by all statistical measures it appeared as the RK-Butcher algorithms. This RK-Butcher algorithm is nominally considered sixth order since it requires six functions evaluation, but in actual practice the "working order" is closer to five (fifth order).

Morris Bader [1, 2] introduced the RK-Butcher algorithm for finding the truncation error estimates and intrinsic accuracies and the early detection of stiffness in coupled differential equations that arises in theoretical chemistry problems. Recently Murugesan et al [8] used the RK-Butcher algorithm for finding the numerical solution of an industrial robot arm control problem. Oliveria [10] introduced the popular RK-Gill algorithm for evaluation of effectiveness factor of immobilized enzymes.

Chi-Chien Lee and Jose Pineda de Gyvez [7] introduced Euler, Improved Euler Predictor-Corrector and Fourth-Order (quartic) Runge-Kutta algorithms in Raster CNN simulation. In this article, we consider the same problem (discussed by Chi-Chien Lee and Jose Pineda de Gyvez [7]) but presenting a different approach using the algorithms such as Euler, RK-Gill and RK-Butcher with more accuracy.

S. Manandhar et al. (Eds.): AACC 2004, LNCS 3285, pp. 115–122, 2004.

2 Cellular Neural Networks

Cellular Neural Networks (CNNs) are analog, time-continuous, nonlinear dynamical systems and formally belong to the class of recurrent neural networks. Since their introduction in 1988 (by Chua and Yang [5, 6]), they have been the subjects of intense research. Initial applications include image processing, signal processing, pattern recognition and solving partial differential equations etc.

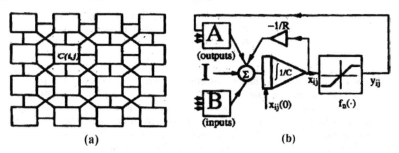

(a)   (b)

Fig. 1. CNN Structure and block diagram

The basic circuit unit (fig. 1) of CNN is called a cell [1]. It contains linear and non-linear circuit elements. Any cell, $C(i, j)$, is connected only to its neighbor cells i.e. adjacent cells interact directly with each other. This intuitive concept is called neighborhood and is denoted as $N(i, j)$. Cells not in the immediate neighborhood have indirect effect because of the propagation effects of the dynamics of the network. Each cell has a state x, input u, and output y. The state of each cell is bounded for all time $t > 0$ and, after the transient has settled down, a cellular neural network always approaches one of its stable equilibrium points. This last fact is relevant because it implies that the circuit will not oscillate. The dynamics of a CNN has both output feedback (A) and input control (B) mechanisms. The first order nonlinear differential equation defining the dynamics of a cellular neural network cell can be written as follows

$$C \frac{dx_{ij}}{dt} = -\frac{1}{R}x_{ij}(t) + \sum_{C(k,l) \in N(i,j)} A(i, j; k, l) y_{kl}(t) +$$

$$\sum_{C(k,l) \in N(i,j)} B(i, j; k, l) u_{kl} + I \tag{1}$$

$$y_{ij}(t) = \frac{1}{2}\left(\left|x_{ij}(t) + 1\right| - \left|x_{ij}(t) - 1\right|\right)$$

where x_{ij} is the state of cell $C(i, j)$, $x_{ij}(0)$ is the initial condition of the cell, C is a linear capacitor, R is a linear resistor, I is an independent current source, $A(i, j; k, l) y_{kl}$ and $B(i, j; k, l) u_{kl}$ are voltage controlled current sources for all cells $C(k, l)$ in the neighborhood $N(i, j)$ of cell $C(i, j)$, and y_{ij} represents the output equation.

Notice from the summation operators that each cell is affected by its neighbor cells. $A(.)$ acts on the output of neighboring cells and is referred to as the feedback operator. $B(.)$ in turn affects the input control and is referred to as the control operator. Specific entry values of matrices $A(.)$ and $B(.)$ are application dependent, are space invariant and are called cloning templates. A current bias I and the cloning templates determine the transient behavior of the cellular nonlinear network. The equivalent block diagram of a continuous-time cell implementation is shown in Fig. 1 (b).

3 Raster CNN Simulations

Raster CNN simulation is an image scanning-processing procedure for solving the system of difference equations of CNN. In this approach the templates A and B are applied to a square subimage area centred at (x, y), whose size is the same as that of the templates. The centre of the templates are then moved left to right pixel by pixel from the top left corner to the bottom right corner applying the A and B templates at each location (x, y) to solve the system of difference equations. This full scanning of the image is repeated for each time-step which is defined as iteration. The processing is stopped when the states of all CNN cells have converged to the steady-state values.

A simplified algorithm is presented below for this approach. The part where the integration is involved is explained in the Numerical Integration Algorithms section.
Algorithm: (Raster CNN simulation)

Obtain the input image, initial conditions and templates from user;
```
/*  M,N = # of rows/columns of the image */
while (converged_cells < total # of cells)
  {
for (i=1; i<=M; i++)
          for (j=1; j<=N; j++) {
               if (convergence_flag [i] [j])
                       continue; /* currnet cell already
              converged */
          /* calculation of the next state */
```

$$x_{ij}(t_{n+1}) = x_{ij}(t_n) + \int_{t_n}^{t_{n+1}} f(x(t_n)) dt$$

```
          /* convergence criteria */
```
if $\left(\dfrac{dx_{ij}(t_n)}{dt} = 0\right)$ and $y_{kl} = \pm 1$, $\forall C(k,l) \in N_r(i,j)$

```
          {
               convergence_flag[i][j]=1;
               converged_cells++;
          } /* end for */
          /*update the state values of the whole image*/
          for (i=1; i <= M; i++)
                  for (j=1; j <= N; j++)
                       { if (convergence_flag [i][j])
                         continue;
```
$$x_{ij}(t_n) = x_{ij}(t_n + 1) ; \}$$
```
               #_of_iteration++;
} / * end while */
```

The raster approach implies that each pixel is mapped onto a CNN processor. That is, we have an image processing function in the spatial domain that can be expressed as:

$$g(x, y) = T(f(x, y))$$

(2)

where $f(.)$ is the input image, $g(.)$ the processed image, and T is an operator on $f(.)$ defined over the neighborhood of (x,y).

4   Numerical Integration Methods

The CNN is described by a system of nonlinear differential equations. Therefore, it is necessary to discretize the differential equation for performing simulations. For computational purpose, a normalized time differential equations describing CNN is used by Nossek et al [9].

$$f'(x(\pi\tau)) := \frac{dx_{ij}(\pi\tau)}{dt} = -x_{ij}(\pi\tau) + \sum_{C(k,l)\in N_r(i,j)} A(i,j;k,l) y_{kl}(\pi\tau)$$

$$+ \sum_{C(k,l)\in N_r(i,j)} B(i,j;k,l) u_{kl} + I$$

(3)

$$y_{ij}(\pi\tau) = \frac{1}{2}(|x_{ij}(\pi\tau) + 1| - |x_{ij}(\pi\tau) - 1|)$$

Where τ is the normalized time. For the purpose of solving the initial-value problem, well established numerical integration techniques are used. These methods can be derived using the definition of the definite integral

$$x_{ij}((n+1)\tau) - x_{ij}(\pi\tau) = \int_{\tau_n}^{\tau_{n+1}} f'(x(\pi\tau)) d(\pi\tau)$$

(4)

Three of the most widely used Numerical Integration Algorithms are used in CNN Raster Simulation described here. They are the Euler's Algorithm, RK-Gill Algorithm discussed by Oliveria [10] and the RK-Butcher Algorithm discussed by Morris Badder [1, 2] and Murugesan et al [8].

4.1   Euler Algorithm

Euler's method is the simplest of all algorithms for solving ODEs. It is explicit formula which uses the Taylor-series expansion to calculate the approximation.

$$x_{ij}((n+1)\tau) = x_{ij}(\pi\tau) + \tau f'(x(\pi\tau))$$

(5)

4.2   RK-Gill Algorithm

The RK-Gill algorithm discussed by Oliveria [10] is an explicit method requiring the computation of four derivatives per time step. The increase of the state variable x^{ij} is stored in the constant $k^{ij}{}_1$. This result is used in the next iteration for evaluating $k^{ij}{}_2$. The same must be done for $k^{ij}{}_3$ and $k^{ij}{}_4$.

$$k^{ij}{}_1 = f'\left(x_{ij}(\pi\tau)\right)$$

$$k^{ij}{}_2 = f'\left(x_{ij}(\pi\tau) + \frac{1}{2}k^{ij}{}_1\right)$$

$$k^{ij}{}_3 = f'\left(x_{ij}(\pi\tau) + \left(\frac{1}{\sqrt{2}} - \frac{1}{2}\right)k^{ij}{}_1 + \left(1 - \frac{1}{\sqrt{2}}\right)k^{ij}{}_2\right) \quad (6)$$

$$k^{ij}{}_4 = f'\left(x_{ij}(\pi\tau) - \frac{1}{\sqrt{2}}k^{ij}{}_2 + \left(1 + \frac{1}{\sqrt{2}}\right)k^{ij}{}_3\right)$$

The final integration is a weighted sum of the four calculated derivatives:

$$x_{ij}((n+1)\tau) = x_{ij} + \frac{1}{6}\left[k^{ij}{}_1 + \left(2 - \sqrt{2}\right)k^{ij}{}_2 + \left(2 + \sqrt{2}\right)k^{ij}{}_3 + k^{ij}{}_4\right] \quad (7)$$

4.3 RK-Butcher Algorithm

The RK-Butcher algorithm discussed by Morris Badder [1, 2] and Murugesan et al [8], is an explicit method. It starts with a simple Euler step. The increase of the state variable x^{ij} is stored in the constant $k^{ij}{}_1$. This result is used in the next iteration for evaluating $k^{ij}{}_2$. The same must be done for $k^{ij}{}_3$, $k^{ij}{}_4$, $k^{ij}{}_5$ and $k^{ij}{}_6$.

$$k^{ij}{}_1 = \tau f'\left(x_{ij}(\pi\tau)\right)$$

$$k^{ij}{}_2 = \tau f'\left(x_{ij}(\pi\tau) + \frac{1}{4}k^{ij}{}_1\right)$$

$$k^{ij}{}_3 = \tau f'\left(x_{ij}(\pi\tau) + \frac{1}{8}k^{ij}{}_1 + \frac{1}{8}k^{ij}{}_2\right)$$

$$k^{ij}{}_4 = \tau f'\left(x_{ij}(\pi\tau) - \frac{1}{2}k^{ij}{}_2 + k^{ij}{}_3\right) \quad (8)$$

$$k^{ij}{}_5 = \tau f'\left(x_{ij}(\pi\tau) + \frac{3}{16}k^{ij}{}_1 + \frac{9}{16}k^{ij}{}_4\right)$$

$$k^{ij}{}_6 = \Delta t f\left(x_{ij}(\pi\tau) - \frac{3}{7}k^{ij}{}_1 + \frac{2}{7}k^{ij}{}_2 + \frac{12}{7}k^{ij}{}_3 - \frac{12}{7}k^{ij}{}_4 + \frac{8}{7}k^{ij}{}_5\right)$$

The final integration is a weighted sum of the five calculated derivatives:

$$x_{ij}((n+1)\tau) = \frac{1}{90}\left(7k^{ij}{}_1 + 32k^{ij}{}_3 + 12k^{ij}{}_4 + 32k^{ij}{}_5 + 7k^{ij}{}_6\right) \quad (9)$$

where $f(.)$ is computed according to (1). There are many methods available to us for this purpose. Among all the methods, RK-Butcher algorithm is a very efficient for solving this problem.

5 Simulation Results and Comparisons

All the simulation reported here are performed using a SUN BLADE 1500 work-station, and the simulation time used for comparisons is the actual CPU time used. The input image format is the X windows bitmap format (xbm), which is commonly available and easily convertible from popular image formats like GIF or JPEG.

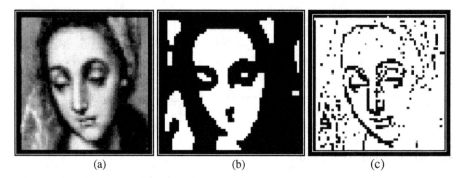

(a)   (b)   (c)

Fig. 2. Image Processing (a) Original Image (b) After Averaging Template (c) After Averaging and Edge Detection Templates

Fig. 2 shows results of the raster simulator obtained from a complex image of 1,25,600 pixels. For this example an Averaging template followed by an Edge Detection template were applied to the original image to yield the images displayed in Figures 3(b) and 3(c), respectively.

Since speed is one of the main concerns in the simulation, finding the maximum step size that still yields convergence for a template can be helpful in speeding up the system. The speed-up can be achieved by selecting an appropriate Δt for that particular template. Even though the maximum step size may slightly vary from one image to another, the values in Fig 3 still serve as good references. These results were obtained by trial and error over more than 100 simulations on a diamond figure. If the step size is chosen is too small, it might take many iterations, hence longer time, to achieve convergence. On the other hand, if the step size taken is too large, it might not converge at all or it would be converges to erroneous steady state values; the latter remark can be observed for the Euler algorithm.

The results of fig. 4 were obtained by simulating a small image of size 16 X 16 (256 pixels) using Averaging template on a diamond figure.

6 Conclusion

As researchers are coming up with more and more CNN applications, an efficient and powerful simulator is needed. The simulator hereby presented meets the need in three ways: (1) Depending on the accuracy required for the simulation, the user can choose

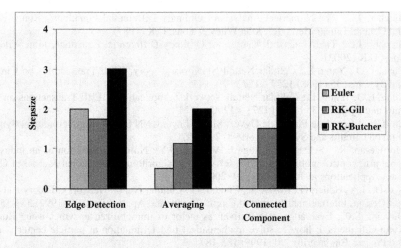

Fig. 3 Maximum step size still yields convergence for three different templates

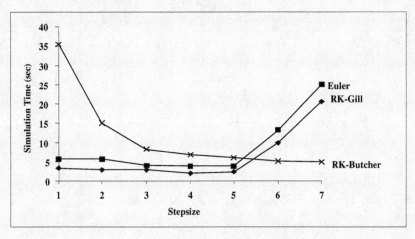

Fig. 4 Simulation time comparison of the three methods using the Averaging template

from three numerical integration methods (2) The input image format is the X-Windows bitmap (xbm), which is commonly available and (3) The input image can be of any size, allowing simulation of images available in common practices.

References

1. Bader, M.: A comparative study of new truncation error estimates and intrinsic accuracies of some higher order Runge-Kutta algorithms", Computers & Chemistry, 11 (1987) 121-124
2. Bader, M.: A new technique for the early detection of stiffness in coupled differential equations and application to standard Runge-Kutta algorithms, Theoretical Chemistry Accounts, 99 (1988) 215-219

3. Butcher, J.C.: The Numerical Analysis of Ordinary Differential Equations: Runge-Kutta and General Linear Methods", John Wiley & Sons, U.K (1987)
4. Butcher, J.C.: The Numerical Analysis of Ordinary Differential Equations, John Wiley & Sons, U.K (2003)
5. Chua, L.O., Yang, L.: Cellular Neural Networks: Theory, IEEE Transactions on Circuits and Systems, 35 (1988) 1257 – 1272
6. Chua, L.O., Yang, L.: Cellular Neural Networks: Applications, IEEE Transactions on Circuits and Systems, 35 (1988) 1273 – 1290
7. Chi-Chien Lee, Jose Pineda de Gyvez: Single-Layer CNN Simulator, International Symposium on Circuits and Systems, 6 (1994) 217 – 220
8. Murugesan, K., Sekar, S., Murugesh, V., Park, J.Y.: Numerical solution of an industrial robot arm control problem using the RK-Butcher algorithm, International Journal of Computer Applications in Technology, 19 (2004) 132-138
9. Nossek, J.A., Seiler, G., Roska, T., Chua, L.O.: Cellular Neural Networks: Theory and Circuit Design, International Journal of Circuit Theory and Applications, 20 (1992) 533-553
10. Oliveira, S.C.: Evaluation of effectiveness factor of immobilized enzymes using Runge-Kutta-Gill method: how to solve mathematical undetermination at particle center point?, Bio Process Engineering, 20 (1999) 185-187

Morphological Analyzer for Manipuri: Design and Implementation

Sirajul Islam Choudhury, Leihaorambam Sarbajit Singh,
Samir Borgohain, and Pradip Kumar Das

RCILTS, Department of Computer Science & Engineering, IIT Guwahati,
Assam, 781039, India
{si_chow,sarbajit,samir,pkdas}@iitg.ernet.in

Abstract. This paper presents the design of a morphological analyzer for Manipuri language. This language falls under agglutinating and Subject-Object-
Verb (SOV) type. The morphological analysis determines the syntactic properties of Manipuri words and it comprises of the following three major functions:
Morphographemics, Morphotactics and Feature Combination. We propose a
model to treat orthographic variations, sequential and non-sequential morpho-
tactic constrains and combination of morphosyntactic features. The morphological processing is based on the grammatical rules and the dictionaries: root
and affix dictionary. A model tagger is used to tag the analyzed word. The tagger tags the lexical category of the root and the grammatical category of the affixes. We show the design and implementation of the full morphosyntactic
analysis procedure for words in unrestricted Manipuri text.

1 Introduction

Morphological analysis of words is a basic tool for automatic language processing
and indispensable when dealing with highly agglutinating language like Basque [1].
Morphological analysis of words for agglutinating languages is a complex problem.
This is an endeavor to design a morphological analyzer to analyze the morphological
structures of Manipuri (Meiteiron) words automatically. Morphological structures of
unknown words contain the essential information of their syntactic and semantic
characteristics. In particular, morphological analysis is a primary step for predicting
the syntactic and semantic categories of out-of-vocabulary (unknown) words [2].
Manipuri words have complex agglutinative structures. Manipuri makes use of a
large number of suffixes and quite a few prefixes however the existence of infix is
not seen. The use of these affixes is almost exclusively associated with the inflectional system [3]. Only affixation: prefixing, suffixing or compounding takes the role
of formation of new words in this language. Due to the fact that new words are easily
formed in Manipuri, the number of unknown words is relatively large. Our approach
follows the Freges' Principle [2], which states that: the meanings of morphemes are
supposed to make up the meanings of the words. This principle has a restriction and
bound only to those words that has the property of semantic transparency. The words
come under idioms, compound words and proper nouns cannot be analyzed by using
this principle because these words do not have meaning transparency. We have con-

S. Manandhar et al. (Eds.): AACC 2004, LNCS 3285, pp. 123–129, 2004.
© Springer-Verlag Berlin Heidelberg 2004

centrated mainly on the derivational and inflectional morphology of nouns and verbs. It takes an unknown word as input and produces the morphological structure of the word. The strategy is described in detail in section 2. In section 3, the maneuver of implementation is summarized and in the final section we evaluate the results found.

2 The Morphological Analyzer

The framework we proposed for Morphological treatment is shown in Figure 1. The Morphological Analyzer is composed mainly of three modules: Segmentation, Morphosyntactic Analyzer and Tagging. The morphological analyzer takes the input and refers to segmentation module, which divides the input into root and affixes (prefix or suffix). After the segmentation is done, the root and affixes are supplied to the next module for checking the morphosyntactic features or rules. The tagging module performs the identification of morpheme meaning or category of each morpheme. The output text comes only after the tagging is completed.

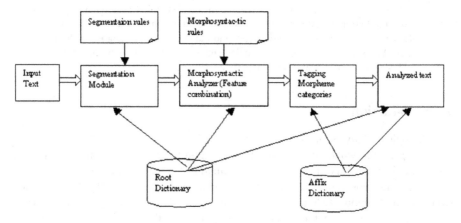

Fig. 1. Architecture of Manipuri Morphological Analyzer

2.1 Development of Dictionaries

The development of root dictionary and affix dictionary is the first action done. The root dictionary contains 3000 root entries as a model. All the possible affixes (the basic prefixes and suffixes, not the combination) have been identified. Morpheme, morpheme category, affix level (first level derivational, second level derivational, third level derivational, inflectional suffix, derivational prefix or an enclitics), are entered into the affix dictionary. There are 31 non-category changing derivational suffixes and 2 category changing derivational suffixes [4]. The non-category changing derivational suffixes may be divided into 8 first-level, 16 second-level, and 7 third-level. There are 8 inflectional suffixes and 23 enclitics. There are 5 derivational prefixes out of which 2–category changing and 3– non-category changing.

2.2 Segmentation

The goal of this process is to segment the input word into a sequence of morphemes and to find out the root form of the word. The left-to-right longest matching method is applied first. The segmentation module identifies the longest root contained in the input word and segment the word into two parts: the root and the subpart. The subpart may be prefix or suffix. The morphemes in the subpart are identified and recorded. If the root is not found in the root dictionary, the segmentation module uses right-to-left suffix stripping method. Special morphographemic rules are adopted when a consonant conjunct, which is formed due to the final consonant of a root and the initial consonant of a suffix, is found. There are 108 possible conjuncts in Manipuri using Bengali/Assamese scripts out of which 22 involves in suffixation [5].

2.3 Morphosyntactic Analyzer

The analysis of morphosyntactic structure is handled in two levels. The first level directly deals with word structure rules for noun as well as verb [4] and can be expressed in the following way.

N : Infl ; N : Infl : Encl ; N : 1 : Infl ; N : 1 : 2 ~ 10 : Infl ;

The rules are separated by a ';'. The first rule states that a noun root (N) can be followed by an inflectional suffix (Infl). The second rule states that a noun root can be followed by an inflectional suffix and an enclitic (Encl). The third rule says that a noun root can be followed by a first level derivational suffix and an inflectional suffix. The fourth rule says that a noun root can be followed by a first level derivational suffix, second level derivational suffixes (there may be up to 10th level derivational suffixes in sequence), and an inflectional suffix. In the same manner the other first level rules are written.

The second level morphosyntactic rules are developed to handle the morpheme sequence within the same level derivational suffixes as well as among the different level derivational suffixes. In some cases, particular suffix can follow a distinct morpheme. The rules related to allomorphs are also included in this level. The rules can be expressed in the form of a finite state automaton. Let us take an example.

0: bə,1|#; kʰaj,2; tʰət,3; tʰək,4; hat,5; sin,6; tʰok,7; tʰə,8; kʰət,9!

1: si, 10|#; du,#; nə,#; bu,#; tə,#; təgi,#; nə,#; gə,#; gi,#; ni,#; rə,#; di,#; mək,#; ne,#!

The first entry in the line is an arbitrary number designating the state that the automaton must be in when it scans the line. This state number is separated from the other entries by a colon. Any number of entries may follow the 'stateno'. A semicolon terminates each entry. An entry consists of two fields: the morpheme and the state number that the automaton will transit into if the morpheme is present. A comma separates these two fields. On encountering a morpheme, from a current state, the automaton can transit into multiple states. In that case, the multiple states are separated by a pipe '|'. The end state is represented by a hash '#' and the end of a line is represented by an exclamation '!'. In the example given above, initially, the automaton is at state 0. For instance, when /-bə/ is encountered after a root (Verb) the next state is 1 or the final state, when /-kʰaj / is found the next state is 2, and so on. The first level rules as well as the second level rules for nouns and verbs are written in different text files.

2.4 Tagging

This module provides the part-of-speech category for each morpheme (root as well as affixes). We discuss the morphemes into two different domains in the matter of parts-of-speech tagging: roots – lexical category and affixes – grammatical category. It is necessary to assign each morpheme with appropriate categories. Since the part-of-speech of the morphemes is context sensitive, we cannot apply n-gram like language models to resolve the part-of-speech ambiguity of morphemes [6, 7].

A] শুপাগবা /tʰugaj.bə/ = শু /tʰu/ + গাগ /gaj/ + বা /bə/ "to break"
                                                                                <verb><total affect><nominalizer>

C] গাৎ না /jəŋ.nə/ = গাৎ /jəŋ/ + না /nə/ "fast"
                                        <verb> <adverbial>

D] ফজনিদা /pʰəjənidə/ = ফজ /pʰəjə/ + নি /ni/ + দা /də/ "(It) will be nice."
                                                        <verb><copulative><contrary to expectation>

E] ঈশিংদগীনি /isiŋ.dəgini/ = ঈশিং /isiŋ/ + দগী /dəgi/ + নি /ni/ "(It) is from water."
                                           <noun> <ablative><copulative>

F] অঙগিনি /əŋaŋ.gini/ = অঙাং /əŋaŋ/ + গী /gi/ + নি /ni/ "(It) is for child."
                                      <noun><genitive/ benefactive ><copulative>

Fig. 2. Tagged output of some input words

While analyzing an input, the morphosyntactic rules, which were found true, were recorded to be used by the tagging module. The tagging module uses those rules and consults the root and the affix dictionary to tag the input word. A single affix may have multiple categories according to its syntactic position. The category of an affix can be identified if the level of the affix is known. However in the same level, the same affix may take the role of different functions depending on the root, and thereby, possessing different categories. For example, the second level suffix, /-lə/ may function as a proximal or a prospective aspect. This is a semantic problem and depends on the meaning of the root. It means that, to assign a particular morpheme category to an ambiguous morpheme, not only the information related to the syntax of the morpheme but also the semantics is necessary. Our morphological analyzer is restricted to syntax level only. The problem is tackled by combining all the possible categories separated by a slash '/' and assigning the same as the category of the morpheme. This is up to the user to understand the actual category of the affix. Tagged output of some analyzed input word shown in figure 2.

3 Implementation Details

A technique known as stemming is used to strip off the affixes from an input word in Manipuri Morphological Analyzer. Stemming is defined as a "procedure to reduce all words with the same stem to a common form, usually stripping each word of its derivational and inflectional suffixes". The segmentation of the unknown input word into stem and affixes is the first and foremost step in analysis of the word. The stemming technique is much simple and easy to implement as compared to Finite-state Transducers [3, 8, 9]. The analysis of an input text proceeds as follows: First, the input text will be accepted and then breaks it into strings or words. Each unknown word is searched into the root dictionary and if it is not found then the segmentation module is called for segmenting the input word into morphemes. The segmentation module returns the root, affixes detected (may be a prefix or a suffix), and the grammatical information of the root if the subpart of the input word is found in the root dictionary.

If a match is not found then right-to-left suffix stripping method is used to find out the consonant conjuncts present in the input word. If a conjunct is found then deletion-addition method is used to find out the root. There are 22 separate rules for each conjunct which take part in suffixation. Each rule defines the string to be deleted from the intermediate string, string to be added to the intermediate string and also gives the suffix. The newly formed string is checked for root in the root dictionary and if it is matched then the string is considered as the root of the input. Since the suffixes may contain more than one morpheme it is necessary to separate each morpheme distinctly. This is not necessary in case of prefixes because Manipuri prefixes are made up of a single morpheme by nature.

After getting the root and the morphemes of an unknown input word, the next task is to check the morphosyntactic features of the word. It goes through first level rules and second level rules. The second level rules are checked only when the input is accepted by one of the first level rules. When the first as well as the second level rules are found true the procedure calls the tagging module to tag the lexical category of the root and the grammatical category of each affixes. The overall flowchart of the process is given in Figure 3. Flat files are used for storing the data. Perl is used for writing the software. This is an interactive system. Perl/Tk is used for graphical user interface to make the system user-friendly. The modules are available in the form of APIs (Application Program Interfaces). Hence it can be used easily for other language processing works like spell checking, machine translation, etc.

4 Evaluations and Discussions

In the segmentation of words, we tested two methods: (i) First morpheme isolation, then detection of root and (ii) First detection of root, then isolation of morphemes. In the former case there is overhead due to repeated access to the root dictionary. On the other hand, the later approach needs a single pass in the root dictionary. The first approach handles the orthographic complexity well and the second strategy is much faster in comparison with the former. Therefore, we adopt the mixed strategy, which makes the process much better. It is not an easy task to collect all the morphological rules, as there are numerous rules, which are not commonly available. So far, the

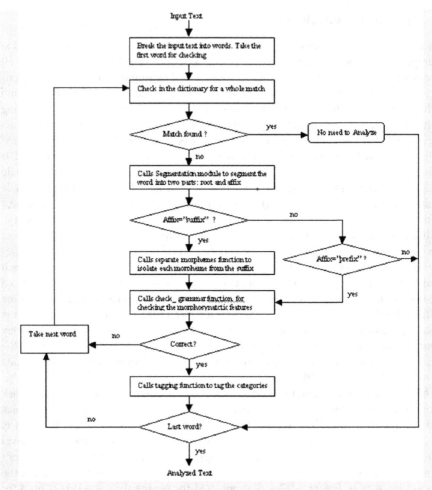

Fig. 3. Flowchart of Manipuri Morphological Analyzer

common rules are implemented. The common rules mostly dealt with feature combination of various suffixes. We tackle this orthographic problem by the morphographemic rules mentioned earlier. As per the evaluation by linguists, these common rules cover almost 80% of the complete morphology. However, it is hard to evaluate the accuracy of the morphological analyzer automatically, so we compare the results generated by the morphological analyzer with results generated by human experts, which are made out of their language intuition. Even though, it has been mentioned by the linguists that the accuracy of this morphological analyzer is about 75% and it can be increased to a much better accuracy by adding more specific rules and by increasing the number of entries in the root dictionary. The morphemes, which do not follow the usual rules, are yet to be studied and integrated to the analyzer. For the words with no meaning transparency and compound words need more extensive research.

Acknowledgements

We wish to evince our acknowledgements to the Ministry of Information Technology, Government of India, for the funding made available for work, as also to all the investigators and personnel involved in this project.

References

1. Aduriz, I., Agirre, E., Aldezabal, I., Alegria, I., Arregi, X., Arriola, J.M., Artora, X., Gojenola, K., Maritxalar, A.., Sarasola, K., Urkia, M.: A word-grammar based morphological analyzer for agglutinating languages. Proceedings of the 18th International Conference on Computational Linguistics Volume 1, COLING- 2000, Saarbrücken, Germany (2000)1- 7
2. Tseng, H., Chen, K.: Design of Chinese Morphological Analyzer. Proceedings of the 19th International Conference on Computational Linguistics, Howard International House and Academia Sinica, Taipei, Taiwan (2002)
3. Bhat, D. N. S., Ningomba, M. S.: Manipuri Grammar. Munchen, New Castle, Lincom Europa, (1997)
4. Chelliah, S.L.: A Study of Manipuri Grammar. Berlin, Mouton de Gruyter, (1994)
5. Gopendro Singh, N.: Manipuri Spelling. On Compilation of An Advanced Learner's Manipuri Dictionary, Language Cell, Directorate of Education(s), Government of Manipur, India, Working Paper Series-2, August, (1998) 18-19
6. Jurafsky, D., Martin James, H.: Speech and Language Processing. Pearson Education, Delhi, (2000)
7. Albro, D. M.: POSCLASS-An Automated Morphological Analyzer. (Unpublished paper), UCLA, Depart-ment of Linguistics, Los Angeles, (1996)
8. Beesley, K. R.: Arabic Finite-State Morphological Analysis. Proceedings of COLING '96, Copenhagen, (1996)
9. Beesley, K. R.: Finite-State Morphological Analysis and Generation for Aymara. www.aymara.org/biblio/aymaramorph.ps (online)

Using Selectional Restrictions
for Real Word Error Correction

R.S.D. Wahida Banu and R. Sathish Kumar

Department of Computer Science,
Government College of Engineering, Salem, India
rsdwb@yahoo.com
mail2shathish@mail.com

Abstract. Spell Checking is an integral part of modern word-processing applications. Current spellcheckers can only detect and correct non-word errors. They cannot effectively deal with real-word errors; misspelled words that result in valid English words. Current techniques for detecting real-word errors require huge volume of training corpus and the learned knowledge is represented by opaque set of features that are not apparent. This paper proposes a new method for dealing with real-word errors using selectional preferences of predicates for arguments in a case slot. The method requires very little in terms of resources and can use existing lexicons slightly modified to suit the above task.

1 Introduction

Spell checking is an integral part of current word-processing applications. Conventional spell checkers can only deal with non-word errors that is, a word that is not correctly spelled (E.g. *blagk* instead of *blank*). The main technique for non-word error detection is dictionary or lexicon lookup. Each word in the text is looked up in a lexicon and if not found, considered to be an error. Potential replacement candidates are generated by the Minimum Edit Distance technique [1] which selects words in the dictionary that require fewer number of basic operations such as insertion, deletion, substitution or transposition of characters to get the misspelled word. The above example would produce suggestions like: *black*, *blank*, *balk* and *blake*.

But current spell checkers cannot deal with real word errors that is, a misspelled word that accidentally result in an actual English word. (E.g. land instead of lend). Current spell checkers would not flag a spelling error, as the misspelled word would also be found in the lexicon. This paper proposes a new method based on Selectional Restrictions for detecting and correcting real word errors that requires very little in terms of resources. The natural question arises regarding the urgency for detecting such real-word errors. Studies [2] have shown that real-word errors account for 25 % to 50 % of word based errors in text. This justifies the urgency for dealing with real-word errors.

2 Previous Approaches

A pioneer approach to real-word spelling correction was the one using word and part-of-speech n-grams [3],[4],[5]. These word trigram methods require huge body of text for training the n-grams model and suffer from the data sparseness problem. Machine

S. Manandhar et al. (Eds.): AACC 2004, LNCS 3285, pp. 130–136, 2004.

Learning approaches to spelling correction include Bayesian Classifiers [6], Winnow–based method [7] and TriBayes – Bayesian Classifier + Tagger [8]. The Transformation Based Learning approach adopted by Eric and Mangu [9] appears promising, the learned knowledge being captured in a small easily understood set of rules as opposed to huge tables of n-grams or large opaque set of features and weights of Winnow based methods. Recent approaches based on semantic similarity of words include Lexical Chains [10],[11]. The semantic relatedness of words is measured using a semantic hierarchy like WordNet. Semantically related words in the input text form lexical chains. Any word that stands aloof of the lexical chains is a probable real-word error.

3 Selectional Restriction Based Approach

Selectional Restrictions is the preferences of the predicates for the semantic class of the arguments filling a particular role. For E.g. the verb *fly* prefers as its subject argument words from the semantic class *BIRD* as in

> The *swallow* flew over the nest
> *Swallow* ∈ BIRD

This type of preferences also exist for other case slots such as head noun-noun, adjective-noun etc. It is however customary to use selectional preferences rather than selectional restrictions because of the anomalies that exist due to metaphor.

> For E.g.
>> The *acid* ate the *metal*
>> acid ∈ NON-LIVING
>> metal ∈ NON-FOOD

The subject of eat here is NON-LIVING and object is NON-FOOD as opposed to the customary subject – ANIMATE-BEING and object – FOOD.

Selectional preferences of the verbs provide a very concise procedure for detecting real-word errors. In a given sentence if the selectional preferences are violated at any particular case slot then it is a good indication that a real-word error has occurred at the particular case slot.

> For E.g.
>> The cook served the *dessert*
>> * The cook served the *desert*

The selectional preferences of the verb serve for the object slot belong to the class FOOD. But in the second sentence above the object *desert* belongs to class GEOGRAPHICAL-LOCATION thus indicating a possible real-word error. Thus a concise method for real-word spell checking exists. This can be extended to other predicate argument relations also.

But the main shortcoming of this method is that selectional preferences are not explicitly encoded in machine readable dictionaries and whatever SR that exists are inadequate or too general to be of utility. For example the verb frames in WordNet are too general to be useful for the above task. However once machine-readable dictionaries encode SRs very systematically then full fledged commercial products using the above method is feasible.

3.1 Methodology

The method to detect and correct real-word errors is presented below: First check the subject slot of the verb for SR violation. If it occurs then it's an indication of a real-word error. This is the detection phase. Now generate all possible replacements for the subject word and check for SR violation at the same slot. If there is no SR violation for some replacement word then the real-word correction has been achieved.

If there is SR violation after considering all replacement subject words then revert back to the original word and generate all possible replacements for the predicate verb and find the verb for which there is no SR violation which eventually is the corrected word. Repeat the same for the object slot.

> For E.g.
> * The aid warned the secretary

The SR for subject slot is violated as the subject of *warned* should be LIVING-THING. Here *aid* belongs to the class ACTIVITY. So generate replacement candidates. One replacement *aide* satisfies the SR and hence correction has been achieved In case of multiple replacement candidates satisfying the SR, like *maid* in the above example then all possible replacements can be displayed permitting the user to make the correct choice.

3.2 Induction of Selectional Restrictions

As mentioned previously the selectional restrictions encoded in Machine Readable dictionaries are too general to be of use. Many techniques exist for automatically learning selectional preferences from examples in a corpus. These techniques combine knowledge from a pre-defined semantic hierarchy with statistics about word occurrence in a corpus. The learned SRs are probability distributions over entire semantic classes as opposed to individual words.

Resnik [12] initiated the technique of induction of selectional preferences from training corpus and a class hierarchy such as WordNet [13]. His method finds the KL Divergence between $p(C)$ and $p(C|v)$ where C is a semantic class and $p(C|v)$ is the conditional probability of C occurring as argument of v at some argument position and $P(C)$ is the marginal probability of C.From this, two quantities the *Selectional Preference Strength* (SPS) and S*electional Association* (SA) are determined.

$$SPS = \Sigma_{\text{c in C}} \, p(c|v) \, \log \, (\, p(c|v) \, / \, p(c) \,) \qquad (1)$$

$$SA = \, (p(c|v)\log(p(c|v)/p(c) \,)) \, / \, SPS \qquad (2)$$

Selectional Association is the degree of preference or dispreference of the class as the argument for the verb. To account for sense ambiguity of arguments, the counts for ambiguous words are divided equally among the possible classes for the word.

Li and Abe [14] used the Minimum Description length (MDL) to infer the correct class preferred by the verb. They modeled the preferences as a *Cut* in the semantic hierarchy and a probability distribution over the elements of the *Cut*. Clark and Weir [15] describe another method for inferring the cut, the problem framed as hypothesis testing; a χ^2 test is performed to determine the optimal semantic classes preferred by the predicate.

Abney and Light [16] use Hidden Markov Models (HMM) to model preferences of verbs. The main disadvantage of their approach is that parameter estimation proves elusive.

Ciarmita and Johnson [17] use the Bayesian Belief Network framework to infer, for each class in the network, the probability that the verb of interest v, selects for the class c.

The selectional restrictions mentioned in this paper were inferred using Li and Abe's Tree Cut Model, which is elaborated, in next section.

3.3 Tree Cut Model

Selectional preference induction is concerned with inferring the set of semantic classes preferred by the predicate at its argument position. The inferred semantic classes should not be too specific or too general. For E.g. For the arguments *swallow, crow, eagle, lark* of the verb *fly* the inferred class should not be ENTITY since it is too general. The optimally inferred class should be BIRD.

The Tree Cut Model of Li and Abe [14] addresses this problem using the Minimum Description Length Principle [18]. The MDL states that in order to model the data optimally the data description and parameter description should be optimal. That is the best probability model for given data is that which requires least number of bits to encode the model as well as the data. This permits effective transmission of data across a communication channel due to efficient data compression. The number of bits encoding the model is called the '*the model description length*' and that of the data is called '*the data description length*'. MDL strives to find a model that minimizes both.

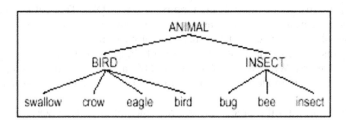

Fig. 1. An example Thesaurus Tree

The Tree cut model finds a partition or cut in the thesaurus tree or semantic hierarchy. The thesaurus tree is one in which each leaf node stands for a noun while each internal node represents a noun class. A cut in a tree is any set of nodes in the tree that defines a partition of the leaf nodes, where each node represents the set of all leaf nodes it dominates.

For example, for the thesaurus tree for subjects of fly in Figure 1. [15] there are five cuts: [ANIMAL],[BIRD,INSECT],[BIRD,bug,bee,insect],[swallow,crow,eagle, bird,INSECT][swallow,crow,eagle,bird,bug,bee,insect]. The first cut [ANIMAL] is a model near the root and is simpler having lesser number of parameters but tends to have a poorer fit to the data. The last cut, a model near the leaves of the tree fits data better but is complex having many numbers of parameters. MDL achieves a trade-off between these competing needs by minimizing both the data description length and the model description length.

For a tree cut model M and data S, the total description length is given by L(M).

L(M) = Model description Length+ Data description Length
Model description Length = Lmod(M)+Lpar(M)
Lmod(M) = log |G| where G is the set of cuts in the tree

The parameter description length Lpar(M) = [K/2] x log |S| where K is the number of parameters in the model.

The data description length

$$Ldat(M) = -\Sigma \log p(n|v) \tag{3}$$

Where $n \in S$ and $p(n|v)$ being calculated using Maximum Likelihood Estimator MLE. Since Lmod(M) is constant for all cuts we need only calculate L'(M) = Lpar(M)+Ldat(M). The problem reduces to one of finding a cut with minimum L'(M).

Since calculating every possible tree cut is computationally intractable Li and Abe proposes a top down procedure that iteratively finds the optimal MDL model for each child sub tree of a given node and appends all optimal models of these sub trees, collapsing them into a single node if description length is reduced and returns it.

4   Implementation and Evaluation

Triples of the form *subject-verb-object* were extracted using MINIPAR a broad coverage parser developed by Dekang Lin[19]. WordNet 2.0 was used as the thesaurus, with minor modifications made to the topology of WordNet. Tree cut model requires the noun senses be modeled by leaf nodes in the hierarchy, while the inner nodes model more abstract concepts. To ensure this for each inner node an additional node that represents the sense of those words which belong to the synset corresponding to that node is created. WordNet is not a pure tree but a DAG. The top down processing of nodes by Tree Cut model algorithm automatically resolves its DAG structure into a tree.

The module to infer the Tree cut from frequency of arguments was written in Perl making liberal use of the Perl Module WordNet::QueryData 1.31 developed by Jason Rennie [20]. The module to check for SR violation of input sentence was also developed in Perl.

For evaluating the method, the real words are modeled as confusion sets, a set of words that can be potential real word alternatives for the intended word including the intended word. Examples of confusion sets are {*warmed, warned*}, {*lend, lead*}. Triples of the verbs occurring in the confusion set were extracted from the ACL DCI corpus. Conditional probabilities $p(n|v)$ was computed and the appropriate tree cut for the words in the confusion set was inferred. The inferred SRs was checked on test data, data set aside from training data (10% of the training data for each verb in the confusion set). Artificial real word errors were created, by substituting randomly a word in confusion set by its alternative word. For E.g. Word *warmed* is substituted by *warned* and vice-versa randomly.

A contingency table of the results was created as follows:

	Warmed is Correct	Warned is Correct
Warmed inferred	A	B
Warned inferred	C	C

Fig. 2. Contigency table for the confusion set {warmed, warned}. A is the number of sentences where word *warmed* was correctly inferred as *warmed*

The evaluation measures are:

$$\text{Accuracy} = (A+B)/(A+B+C+D)$$
$$\text{Precision} = A/(A+B)$$
$$\text{Recall} = A/(A+C)$$
$$\text{Fallout} = B/(B+D)$$

To evaluate all the confusion sets *macro-averaging* was done. For all confusion sets, contingency table for each confusion set was constructed independently and the average of the evaluation measures over all confusion sets obtained. The confusion sets used where: [feel, fill] [warmed, warned] [lead, lend] [lay, lie] [pedal, peddle].

Precision was 10% while Recall was 19%. These figures do not provide for a practically efficient implementation. The moderate performance of the system may be partly due to the selectional preferences inferred by the Tree Cut model which are too abstract for semantic discrimination. A good method for inferring SRs or an explicitly SR encoded lexicon is the need of the hour. Once they are available the proposed method can be used in conjunction with other methods for efficient real word error correction.

5   Conclusion

This paper presented a new method for dealing with real word errors based on selectional preferences. A algorithmic method of Li and Abe for inferring semantic classes preferred by verbs is discussed. Evaluation measures has been proposed and the implemented system evaluated. The proposed method can be implemented as a full fledged commercial product once SRs are explicitly encoded in machine readable dictionaries such as WordNet.

References

1. Wagner, R.A.: Order–n correction for regular languages, Communications of ACM, Vol. 17(5). (1974) 265-268
2. Kukich, K.: Techniques for automatically correcting words in text. ACM Computing Surveys, Vol. 24(4). (1992) 377-439
3. Atwell, E., and Elliott, S.: Dealing with ill formed English text. In: The Computational Analysis of English: A Corpus–Based approach R.Garside, G.Leach, G.Sampson, (eds.) Longman, Inc. New York. (1987)
4. Church, K.W., and Gale, W.A.: Probability scoring for spelling correction. In: Stat. Comp, Vol.1. (1991) 93-103
5. Mays, E., Damerau, F.J, and Mercer,R.L.: Context based spelling correction . Information Processing and Management, Vol. 27(5). (1991) 517-522

6. Golding, A.: A Bayesian hybrid method for context-sensitive spelling correction. In: Proceedings of Third Workshop on Very Large Corpora, Boston, MA. (1995) 39-53
7. Golding, A., and Roth, D.: Applying Winnow to Context-Sensitive Spelling Correction. In: Machine Learning:Proceedings of the 13th International Conference, San Fransico. (1996) 182-190
8. Golding, A., and Schabes, Y.: Combining Trigram-based and Feature-based Methods for context-Sensitive Spelling Correction. In: Proceedings of the 34th Annual Meeting of the Association for Computational Linguistics, Santa Cruz, CA. (1996) 71-78
9. Eric Brill and Lidia Mangu.: Automatic Rule Acquisition for Spelling Correction. In: Proceedings of the 14th International Conference on Machine Learning (ICML-97), Nashville, TN, Morgan Kaufmann. (1997) 187-194
10. Alexander Budanitsky.: Lexical semantic Relatedness and its Applications in NLP. TR CSRG –390, Department of Computer Science, University of Toronto. (1999)
11. Graeme Hirst and David St. Onge.: Lexical Chains as representations of context for detection and correction of malapropism. In: Fellbaum. (1998) 305-332
12. Resnik, P.: Selectional preferences and Sense disambiguation. In: Proceedings of ANLP-97 workshop: tagging text with lexical semantics,Washington.DC. (1997) 52-56
13. Miller, G.: WordNet: An online lexical database. International Journal of Lexicography, Vol. 3(4). (1990)
14. Li, H., and Abe, N.: Generalizing case frames using a thesaurus and the MDL principle. Computational Linguistics, Vol. 24(2). (1998) 217-244
15. Clark, S., and Weir, D.: An iterative approach to estimating frequencies over a semantic hierarchy, In: Proceedings of 1999 Joint SIGDAT Conference on EMNLP and very large corpora. (1999)
16. Abney, S., and Light, M.: Hiding a semantic hierarchy in a Markov model. In: Proceedings of the ACL Workshop on Unsupervised Learning in Natural Language Processing. (1999)
17. Ciaramita, M., and Johnson, M.: Explaining away ambiguity: Learning verb selectional preferences with Bayesian Networks. In: Proceedings of the 18th International Conference on Computational Linguistics (COLING 2000) (2000)
18. Rissanen, J.: Modeling by shortest data description. Automatic, Vol. 14. (1978) 37-38
19. Dekang Lin.: MINIPAR – a broad coverage parser for English, Nalante Inc., Alberta, Canada. (1998)
20. Jason Rennie.: WordNet::QueryData: a Perl module for accessing the WordNet database. http://www.ai.mit.edu/people/jrennie/WordNet. (2000)

Mining Top − k Ranked Webpages Using Simulated Annealing and Genetic Algorithms

P. Deepa Shenoy[1], K.G. Srinivasa[1], A.O. Thomas,
K.R. Venugopal[1], and L.M. Patnaik[2]

[1] Department of Computer Science and Engineering
University Visvesvaraya College of Engineering, Bangalore – 560001
shenoypd@yahoo.com, kgsrinivas@msrit.edu, achint@ieee.org
[2] Microprocessor Applications Laboratory, Indian Institute of Science, Bangalore
lalit@micro.iisc.ernet.in

Abstract. Searching on the Internet has grown in importance over the last few years, as huge amount of information is invariably accumulated on the Web. The problem involves locating the desired information and corresponding URLs on the WWW. With billions of webpages in existence today, it is important to develop efficient means of locating the relevant webpages on a given topic. A single topic may have thousands of relevant pages of varying popularity. Top - k document retrieval systems identifies the top - k ranked webpages pertaining to a given topic. In this paper, we propose an efficient top-k document retrieval method (*TkRSAGA*), that works on the existing search engines using the combination of Simulated Annealing and Genetic Algorithms. The Simulated Annealing is used as an optimized search technique in locating the top-k relevant webpages, while Genetic Algorithms helps in faster convergence via parallelism. Simulations were conducted on real datasets and the results indicate that *TkRSAGA* outperforms the existing algorithms.

1 Introduction

Data mining and web mining are emerging areas of immense interest for the research community. These two fields deal with knowledge discovery on the Internet. Extensive work is being carried out to improve the efficiency of existing algorithms and to devise new and innovative methods of mining the Web. Such efforts have direct consequences on e-commerce and Internet business models.

The Internet can be considered as a huge database of documents, which is dynamic in nature and results in an ever-changing chaotic structure. Search engines are the only available interface between the user and the web. It allows the user to locate the relevant documents in the WWW. A huge number of webpages may exist on any given topic in the order of 10^4 to 10^6. It becomes tedious for the user to sift through all the web pages found by the search engine to locate the documents of interest to the user.

S. Manandhar et al. (Eds.): AACC 2004, LNCS 3285, pp. 137–144, 2004.

The problem of page ranking is common to many web-related activities. The basic goal of ranking is, providing relevant documents on a given search topic. Top - k selection queries are being increasingly used for ranking. In top - k querying, the user specifies target values for certain attributes and does not expect exact matches to these values in return. Instead a ranked list of top - k objects that best match the attribute values are returned [5].

Simulated Annealing (SA) is a powerful stochastic search method applicable to problems for which little prior knowledge is available. It can produce high quality solutions for hard optimization problems. The basic concept of SA comes from condensed matter physics. In this technique, the system (solid) is first heated to a high temperature and then cooled slowly. The system will settle in a minimum energy state if the cooling point of the system is sufficiently slow. This process can be simulated on a computer. At each step of the simulation, a new state of the system is generated from the current state giving a random displacement to a randomly selected particle. The new generated state will be accepted as the current state, if the energy of the new state is not greater than that of the current state. If not, it will be accepted with the probability, $e^{(-(E_{new-state}-E_{current-state})/T)}$, where E is the energy of the system and T is the temperature. This step can be repeated with a slow decrease of temperature to find a minimum energy state [1][3][4].

Another tested soft computing approach is Genetic Algorithms (GA), which works on the concept of evolution. Every species evolves in a direction suited for its environment. The knowledge they gain in this evolution is embedded in their chromosomal structure. The changes in chromosomes will cause changes in the next generation. The changes occur due to mutation and crossover. Crossover means the exchange of parts of genetic information between parents to produce the new generation. Mutation makes it possible for chromosomes to get a structure which is more suitable for the environment.

A combination of SA and GA is appropriate to the problems that place a premium on efficiency of execution, i.e., faster runtimes. This is an important consideration in any web-based problem as speed is of the utmost importance. The SA and GA techniques can be combined in various forms. GA can be applied before or after or even during the annealing process of the system under consideration [2].

Any page ranking algorithm has to be applied online and should be fast and accurate. The existing page ranking algorithms, though they give complete results, returns an enormous number of webpages resulting in lower efficiency. The use of soft computing approaches can give near optimal solutions, which are better than existing algorithms. In this paper, we combine Simulated Annealing with Genetic Algorithms to devise an efficient search technique. The Simulated Annealing is used because of its ability to handle complex functions and Genetic Algorithms is used to choose between the set of points in the intermediate states of Simulated Annealing, so as to eliminate the points that do not satisfy the fitness function. We thus achieve more accurate results with fewer runs of SA.

2   Problem Definition

Given a query to a search engine, returns a large number of web documents in terms of URLs (Uniform Resource Locators). Each webpage is characterized by the number of hits(the number of times a URL has been accessed by past users), number of referrer pages(incoming links), number of referred pages(out going links) and the number of occurances of the specified keywords of the given query. Let E be the dataset containing the set of URLs and their corresponding characterstics, i.e. $E = \{U_m, S_m\}$, where $1 \leq m \leq n$ and n is the total number of URLs returned. The function $S_m = N_m + I_m + O_m + D_m$, where, N_m is the number of hits, I_m is the number of incoming links, O_m is the out going links and D_m is the number of occurances of query keywords for the corresponding m^{th} URL. Our objective is to find the top - k relevant web documents from the dataset E using combination of Simulated Annealing and Genetic Algorithms.

3   System Architecture

This section deals with the various modules involved in the system. The first step is to submit a query to a commonly used search engine. The query is a string or collection of strings that represent a set of keywords for a particular topic in which the search is being performed. Each string in the query is separated by a space or a special symbol. The query is represented as a set, $S = \{s_1, s_2, s_3, ...s_n\}$, s_k is the kth string in the query. The query is submitted to the search engine. Once the search engine completes the search process, it will return a set of n unique web documents (URLs). It can be represented as the set, $E = \{U_m, S_m\}$ where $1 \leq m \leq n$. U_m is the actual address of mth URL in the result and S_m is the function on URL U_m. The resulting URLs are categorized by their characterstic function S_m to ease the retrieval process. Once the search engine returns n URLs, an objective function over S will be generated using harmonic analysis. The algorithm *TkRSAGA* is executed on the objective function $f(x)$ and outputs the top - k ranked URLs.

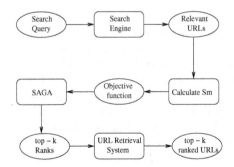

Fig. 1. The System Architecture

4   Algorithm *TkRSAGA*

Top – k Document Retrieval using Simulated Annealing and Genetic Algorithms:
Step 1: Preprocessing: Submit a query to an existing search engine like
Google. The search engine returns a list of n URLs (webpages) of relevance to the
topic. Each entry E, in the list of returned URLs must be composed of two entries
{U,S}. Thus E = {U, S}, where U is the actual URL and S is the function over
the corresponding to URL U and is denoted as $\{(U_1, S_1), (U_2, S_2), ...(U_n, S_n)\}$.

Step 2: Harmonic Analysis: Let the output of Step 1 be denoted as $\{(n_1, s_1),$
$(n_2, s_2), ...(n_n, s_n)\}$, where n_m is the mth URL and s_m is the function over m^{th}
URL and the objective function over these n points can be generated using the
formula $f(x) = a_0 + a_k cos(k\pi) + b_k sin(k\pi)$, where $1 \leq k \leq n$.

Step 3: Performing Search: The combination of Simulated Annealing and
Genetic Algorithms can be applied over the objective function *f(x)* as given
below,

Algorithm: Generate initial states $\alpha_0, \alpha_1, ...\alpha_{n-1}$ at random.
    Generate initial temperature T_0.
    loop
        for each α_i in $\{\alpha_0, \alpha_1, ...\alpha_{n-1}\}$
        loop
           β_i = generate_state(α_i, T_j);
        until point α_i satisfies $\{curve \pm \epsilon\}$, where ϵ is the error,
        if accept_state(α_i, β_i, T_j), then $\alpha_i = \beta_i$,
        next α_i,
           for each i, $\{0 \leq i \leq n - 2\}$
              crossover_pairs(α_i, α_{i+1})
              α_i = calculate_fitness(α_i, α_{i+1})
        next i,
        T_{j+1} = update_state(T_j),
        $j = j + 1$;
    until k states remain.
End
Let the initial states $\alpha_0, \alpha_1, ...\alpha_{n-1}$ be a randomly chosen set of points from
the objective function $f(\alpha)$, where $0 \leq \alpha_i \leq 2\pi$. The points α_i are chosen
on the x - axis at evenly spaced intervals. However, the actual initial states
are computed usng the objective function *f(x)*. The Simulated Annealing technique cools the system uniformly and slowly from a higher initial temperature
T_0 to a lower final temperature $T_k(T_0 > T_k)$. In the next iteration, a random
state is generated by the function generate_state(α_i, T_j) and is determined by
the probability $G_{\alpha\beta}(T_j)$ of generating a new state β_i from an existing state
α_i at temperature T_j. The generation function is defined as $g_i(Z) = 2 * (|$
$Z | +1/ln(1/T_j)) * ln(1 + ln(1/T_j))$. The generation probability is given by
$G_j(Z) = \frac{1}{2} + (\Sigma z * ln(1+ | z | ln(1/T_j)))/2 * ln(1 + ln(1/T_j))$.
    The newly generated state β_i is checked for acceptance by the function
accept_state(α_i, β_i, T_j) and is determined by the probability $A_{\alpha\beta}(T_j)$ of accepting

state β_i after it has been generated at temperature T_j. The acceptance proba-
bility $A_{\alpha\beta}(T_j)$ is given by, $A_{\alpha\beta}(T_j) = min\{1, exp(-(f(\beta) - f(\alpha))/T_j)\}$, where
$f(\alpha)$ is the objective function considered for optimization. The new state β_i is
accepted only if it has lower energy state than the pervious state α_i.

The rate of cooling in the Simulated Annealing technique(Annealing Schedule) is represented by ρ. It is a control parameter used to change the system
temperature as the time progresses. The annealing schedule used in the algorithm is of the form, $T_k = T_0/e^{e^k}$, where k represents the kth iteration. For
practical considerations, the annealing schedule is set to $T_{n+1} = \rho T_n$. The function update_state(T_j) updates the temperature with respect to the annealing
schedule. The function crossover_pairs(α_i, α_{i+1}) performs the genetic crossover
operation on states α_i and α_{i+1}. The random one-point crossover is performed
on two states i and j.

Finally, the function calculate_fitness(α_i, α_{i+1}) performs the fitness calculation that is used to select the two states which are allowed to propagate to the
next generation. The fitness function calculates the Euclidean distances of points
α_i and α_{i+1} to the objective function $f(x)$ and returns the closer point. Thus,
the algorithm starts with an initial number of states and terminates with k final
states.

Step 4: Once the algorithm returns k final states, they represent the points on
the global minima over the objective function $f(x)$. These points can be mapped
to the corresponding URLs and these URLs represent the top - k ranked URLs.

5   Performance Analysis

The algorithm *TkRSAGA* works in two basic phases. The first phase involves
the generation of the Fourier coefficients to determine the objective function $f(x)$
and is linear with respect to the number of URLs supplied. The second phase is
the application of combined SA and GA on the objective function $f(x)$ to obtain
the top - k ranked URLs. The convergence of the second phase depends on
the number of initial states, the annealing schedule and the initial temperature.
Keeping these parameters constant for the test runs, we see that the performance
curve for *TkRSAGA* tends to be linear. The execution tme is higher for smaller
number of URLs and relatively lower for larger URLs. The graph of execution
time versus the number of URLs for the algorithms *TkRSAGA* and HITS is
shown in Figure 2(a). It shows that the algorithm *TkRSAGA* works better for
larger databases.

The Figure 2(b), shows the graph of execution time versus the number of
initial states and the performance curve is roughly logarithmic. As the number
of initial number of states increases by a factor x, the execution time increases
by a factor of $log(2x)$. This is obvious since, the initial states only influence the
number of iterations made by GAs. After every crossover operation, exactly half
the new generation is retained for future propagation. The graph in Figure 3(a),
shows the execution time versus the desired top - k ranks. The graph is plotted for
varying number of URLs and varying k. Since the number of iterations increases
for lower values of k, the curve is logarithmic.

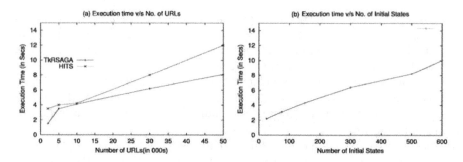

Fig. 2. 2(a): The graph of execution time versus number of URLs (Number of initial states = 128); 2(b): The graph of execution time versus number of initial states (Number of URLs = 10,000); for, Annealing schedule (ρ) = 0.95, k = 4

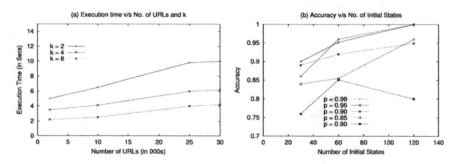

Fig. 3. 3(a): The graph of execution time versus varying number of URLs and k (Number of initial states = 128 and Annealing schedule (ρ) = 0.95); 3(b): The graph of Accuracy versus number of initial states (Number of URLs = 10,000 and k = 4)

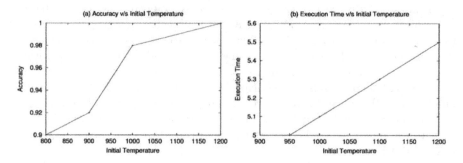

Fig. 4. 4(a): The graph of accuracy versus initial temperature; 4(b): The graph of execution time versus initial temperature; for, (Number of initial states = 128, Annealing schedule (ρ) = 0.95, Number of URLs = 10,000 and k = 4)

Figure 3(b), shows the graph of accuracy of the retrieved top - k documents versus varying annealing scheduling (ρ) and the initial number of states. The accuracy parameter defines the ratio of the number of top - k ranks returned by the *TkRSAGA* to the desired top - k. The accuracy increases with the number of iterations. For higher values of initial states, better results are obtained. This is because the GAs produce the generations satisfying the fitness function. Similarly, for higher annealing schedules, the accuracy increases as SA performs more number of iterations in search of global optima.

The initial temperature T_0 determines the temperature of the system as it starts cooling. The higher the temperature, the more time it takes the system to reach the lower equilibrium state, i.e., the algorithm performs more number of iterations and takes longer time to reach the final k states. However, the number of iterations is directly proportional to the number of intermediate states being generated. Therefore, more the number of intermediate states, higher the accuracy and hence generates accurate k final states. Thus, there exists a tradeoff between execution time and accuracy of results obtained, based on the initial temperature T_0. Figure 4(a), depicts the graph of initial temperature versus accuracy. Therefore, as the initial temperature increases, accuracy increases, in turn increasing the execution time. Figure 4(b), shows the linear relationship between the initial temperature and the execution time.

Experiments on real datasets: The datasets of university link files from cs.wlv.ac.uk are used for our experiments. A set of n webpages and corresponding number of hits are available. The number of hits is used to compute the harmonics for the objective function *f(x)*. The output of TkRSAGA is a set of k values representing the top - k relevant webpages. These values are mapped to the URLs to obtain the actual addresses. The HITS [5] algorithm is executed on the same database and the results of *TkRSAGA* and HITS algorithm are compared. The Table 1 shows the list of URLs and their corresponding number of hits. Table 2 shows the outputs of both *TkRSAGA* and HITS. The outputs

Table 1. Sample URLs taken from *cs.wlv.ac.uk*

URL(U_m)	No. of hits(N_m)
www.canberra.edu.au/UCsite.html	25482
www.canberra.edu.au/secretariat/council/minutes.html	1501
www.canberra.edu.au/Staff.html	199950
www.canberra.edu.au/Student.html	218511
www.canberra.edu.au/crs/index.html	178822
www.canberra.edu.au/uc/privacy.html	15446
www.canberra.edu.au	258862
www.canberra.edu.au/uc/convocation/index.html	16702
www.canberra.edu.au/uc/staffnotes/search.html	38475
www.canberra.edu.au/uc/search/top.html	190852
www.canberra.edu.au/uc/help/index.html	156008
www.canberra.edu.au/uc/directories/index.html	6547
www.canberra.edu.au/uc/future/body.html	25006
www.canberra.edu.au/uc/timetable/timetables.html	257899
www.canberra.edu.au/uc/hb/handbook/search.html	54962

Table 2. The output of *TkRSAGA* and HITS for ($T_0 = 1200$, No. of Initial States = 256, (ρ) = 0.95, $k = 4$)

RANK	*TkRSAGA*	HITS
1	www.canberra.edu.au	www.canberra.edu.au/uc/timetable/timetables.html
2	www.canberra.edu.au/uc/timetable/timetables.html	www.canberra.edu.au
3	www.canberra.edu.au/Student.html	www.canberra.edu.au/Student.html
4	www.canberra.edu.au/Staff.html	www.canberra.edu.au/Staff.html

of both the algorithms are same and our algorithm *TkRSAGA* executes much faster than HITS algorithm. From Table 2, we can conclude that *TkRSAGA* outperforms the HITS in execution time without compromising with the accuracy of the results obtained.

6   Conclusions

In this paper, we have proposed an efficient algorithm *TkRSAGA*, for mining top - k ranked web documents using the combination of Simulated Annealing and Genetic Algorithms. The ability of SA to solve harder problems and the combination of GA to reduce the number of iterations of SA and the inherent parallelism has made the algorithm efficient and effective.

References

1. Xin Yao, "Simulated Annealing with Extended Neighbourhood", International Journal of Computer Mathematics, 40:169 - 189, 1991.
2. Xin Yao, "Optimization by Genetic Annealing", Proc. Second Australian Conference on Neural Networks, pp. 94 - 97, 1991.
3. H.H. Szu and R.L. Hartley, "Fast Simulated Annealing", Physics Letters, 122:157 - 162, 1982.
4. L. Ingber, "Very Fast Simulated Re-Annealing", Mathl. Comput. Modelling, 12(8):967 - 973, 1989.
5. J.M. Kleinberg, "Authoritative Sources in a Hyperlinked Environment", Proc. ACM - SIAM Symp. on Discrete Algorithms, 1998.

Using Document Dimensions
for Enhanced Information Retrieval

Thimal Jayasooriya and Suresh Manandhar

Department of Computer Science, University of York, UK
{thimal,suresh}@cs.york.ac.uk

Abstract. Conventional document search techniques are constrained by attempting to match individual keywords or phrases to source documents. Thus, these techniques miss out documents that contain *semantically* similar terms, thereby achieving a relatively low degree of *recall*. At the same time, processing capabilities and tools for syntactic and semantic analysis of language have advanced to the point where an index-time linguistic analysis of source documents is both feasible and realistic. In this paper, we introduce *document dimensions*, a means of classifying or grouping terms discovered in documents. Using an enhanced version of Jakarta Lucene[1], we demonstrate that supplementing keyword analysis with some syntactic and semantic information can indeed enhance the quality of information retrieval results.

1   Introduction

Information retrieval has been attracting research attention since the 1940s[2]. Although the amount of information searchable electronically has climbed at a near exponential rate, the techniques employed for document search have not enjoyed similar advances. In commercial attempts at searching the World Wide Web, keyword based approaches still hold sway.

The process for search is generally as follows: A set of terms are extracted from a source document and stored within an inverted index[2]. Each term has an individual rank or weight within the index, which allows the document(s) associated with that particular term to be presented in order of relevance. A common means of weighing search terms discovered within source documents is the *tf-idf* scheme[3]. *tf-idf* maps the *frequency of terms* discovered within source documents to the *inverse document frequency*. Another commercial attempt is the Google search engine[4] which also exploits *backlinks*[1] or a graph structure of hypertext pages to determine relevance.

Our focus within this paper is to introduce *document dimensions*, a means of categorizing discovered terms into distinct semantically determined classes. Categorization experiments conducted within this paper employ various implementations of *semantic distance* algorithms as described by Brookes[5] and later evaluated in depth by Budanitsky and Hirst[6].

---

[1] Hypertext references to a particular document

S. Manandhar et al. (Eds.): AACC 2004, LNCS 3285, pp. 145–152, 2004.
© Springer-Verlag Berlin Heidelberg 2004

As noted by Dixon[7], van Rijke[8] and Yang[9] among many others, we have a need for more sophisticated means of searching for information. A closer look at relevance and linguistic nuances of written text seems to be a promising approach in this respect. For instance, a keyword search including the term *'train'* would return hits which correspond to the senses *'a series of connected railroad cars pulled or pushed by one or more locomotives'* as well as *'to coach in or accustom to a mode of behavior or performance'*. The context in which the term is used, either as a noun or as a verb, cannot be easily discerned using keyword indexing techniques. Semantic and syntactic analysis; more specifically part of speech tagging (POS) of source text can help distinguish between different usages of terms. Yet another problem which affects search *recall* is that of synonymy. For instance, if a source document used a common synonym *'coach'* in place of *'train'*, a pure keyword analysis would fail to return that document. However, our implementation of dimensions seek to classify related terms using *semantic distance*. In the case of synonyms, the semantic distance between terms would be a single *hop* or unit of distance, thereby such terms would be grouped together.

We also introduce an extensible framework for semantic and syntactic analysis of documents. Based on (*and extending*) the functionality provided by the open source Jakarta Lucene search API[1], we allow individual developers to use their own natural language processing tools to do source document analysis. Currently, this framework allows the inclusion of any Part of Speech tagger, Entity recognizer or Coreference resolver conforming to a standard API. Several open source and/or freely available natural language processing tools were incorporated into this framework for our experiments with dimensions.

2   Conventional Text Indexing and Its Limitations

Conventional web search based techniques have long been seen as inadequate for dealing with the glut of information, leading to research in many fields, for instance see the MoMInIS[10] initiative, Lawrence et al[11][12], Hu et al[13], Etzioni et al[14] among many others. While the approaches used for overcoming these inadequacies differ, there is general agreement on some of the issues that plague conventional search engines.

Context awareness: Current search tools have little ability to distinguish between contexts. For instance: *mouse* in the context of a small furry mammal and *mouse* in the context of a hand-held, buttoned input device attached to a computer.

Synonymy and other relations: Search engines are overly dependent on exactly matching indexed terms to search terms. Where the term *"Head of State"* is used to describe a politician, and where a search term would look for *"prime minister"* or *"president"*, a conventional search tool would be incapable of making a connection.

Relevant references: Another underdeveloped aspect of search engines is the capability to find related items or references concerning a particular search topic. Different projects solve this problem using different techniques. For instance, MoMinIS[10] uses both *focused crawlers*[2] and *webgraph*[3] techniques to determine other relevant terms for a particular search. WebFoun-tain[15], a research project launched by IBM, uses both *webgraph* and a mixture of *"probability, statistics and natural language processing"* techniques.

3   Semantic and Syntactic Analysis

As expressed previously, it is our belief that syntactic and semantic analysis of source documents can improve the *recall* and *precision* of document retrieval results. However, due to the unstructured and complex nature of freeform text documents available for search, a variety of processing tasks must take place before actual analysis can commence. These processing tasks can broadly be divided into three categories.

Cleansing and tokenization tasks: Formatting and tokenizing documents into a format required by other processes.
- Stripping markup and presentation tags from the source data[4]
- Sentence boundary detection - Some Part of Speech taggers require that only complete sentences be input for accuracy. Thus, the source document data must be tokenized into individual sentences before being fed into a POS tagger.
- Stop-word removal - removing common stop-words such as "a", "an", "it" and so on from sentences prior to indexing

Analysis and classification tasks: Performing analysis at the sentence and term levels
- Part of Speech tagging - to identify the speech component (noun, verb, adjective and so on) of an input sentence. Performing POS tagging allows better identification of the context in which a particular word is used.
- Morphological analysis and stemming - to normalize different morphological forms into a single term (for instance, *"runs"*, *"running"*, *"ran"* are all forms of the verb *"run"*.)
- Named entity recognition - Identification of names, places and organizations, ie: proper nouns which occur within sentences.
- Coreference resolution - Identification of entities associated with coreference words, such as *they, it, he* and so on.

A few of these tasks must be performed in sequence. For instance, sentence boundary detection is required as a prerequisite for our POS tagging tools. We also performed stop-word removal just prior to terms being categorized into dimensions. This preserved the sentence structures within source documents and prevented errors in the entity recognition and coreference resolution phases. Thus, the simplified sequence of events is as follows.

---

[2] Crawlers which only search and index documents related to specific topics
[3] Mapping hypertext documents as a directed graph of resources
[4] The test corpus was based on TREC-11, around 20,000 news articles from New York Times, Xinhua and AFP agencies, marked up in XML form

4   Integration: A First Look at Document Dimensions

The concept of *dimensions* are not new, see for instance the work of Eder and Koncilia[16]. In datawarehousing terminology, a *dimension* can be defined as a '*a structure that categorizes data in order to enable end users to answer questions*'. Further, the concept of organizing document content into a multi dimensional space is not new. For instance, see Brookes' comments[5] and even earlier, van Rijsbergen[2]. However, the means by which documents contents are organized into dimensional space has differed widely. For instance, Roelleke et al.[17] defined a document in terms of its *accessibility dimension*, a combination of metrics which associate *terms, document frequency* and the document components such as paragraphs.

Another look at dimensions was made by Mothé ([18], [19]). In the use of document dimensions[18], the results concentrated on vector space model analysis of common metadata found within documents. However, neither Roelleke nor Mothé attempted a categorization of dimensions according to semantic similarity.

Table 1. Comparison of Mothé's *dimensions* and our own use of the concept

	Mothé's work	Our work
Contents of dimensions	Primarily metadata (author, title and date) and a single *content* dimension	All textual content within the document identifiable as *terms*
Categorization criteria	SVD[5] techniques such as (LSI) *Latent Semantic Indexing*	Semantic distance metrics as evaluated by Budanitsky and Hirst[6]
Representation	Graphically represented using a scatter graph, for analysis	Mapped to user queries and used to discover relatedness
Potential uses	Patterns in various documents submitted to conferences	Finding semantically related documents in response to a search, clustering

Therefore, our contribution can be summarized as follows. Other work in dimensions has concentrated on document features (such as paragraphs) or significant metadata (author, title, date of publication etc). Our work attempts to perform an analysis of the body text and sort the individual sentences, phrases and even words into discrete dimensions. Thus, a level of syntactic and semantic analysis which has been previously unseen is used as a basis for collating candidate terms for dimensions. Once a candidate list of terms has been compiled, we apply various semantic distance algorithms (see [6],[5], and [20]) to categorize these terms into dimensions.

5   Experiments

An instructive example of a commercial grade crawler can be found in Haydn's work[21]. This has led to derivative works such as Nutch[6] and more pertinently in

---

[6] http://www.nutch.org

this case, to Mozdex, the open source search engine[7]. Our evaluations will seek to replicate the documented functionality of Mozdex, which uses Lucene internally. Using part of the TREC-11 collection as a baseline system, we compare and produce our results with our customized implementation of Lucene, which is supplemented with various natural language processing tools.

5.1 Profiling and Engineering Metrics

All experiments were performed on the full TREC-11 collection, 3396 locally available files of XML tagged news articles totalling 2.97GB of data. The figures shown below constitute the average values from 5 complete indexing runs.

Table 2. Performance benchmarks for indexing text

	Mozdex Lucene 1.3	Our framework Lucene 1.3 with NLP extensions
Memory usage	21.9mb (out of 150mb allocated)	80.3mb (out of 150mb allocated)
CPU usage	Peak 99%, Avg 14% Athlon XP 2400+	Peak 99% Avg 32% Athlon XP 2400+
Documents per minute	avg. 610 files per minute Total runtime avg. 5 min.	avg. 240 files per minute Total runtime avg. 14 minutes
Unique terms per minute	Not accessible in Lucene	avg. 7000 per minute Total unique terms about 550000

Although these processing activities constitute a significant amount of machine time and memory, it is clear from the metrics given by Mercator[21], that the task of crawling and indexing WWW pages consists primarily of I/O operations, such as disk read/write and HTTP GET and POSTs. This is further borne out by WEBFOUNTAIN[15] and MOMINIS[10], also by some unofficial Mozdex fetcher statistics[22].

5.2 Assessing Quality of Results

We evaluated several semantic distance learning algorithms, as described by Budanitsky and Hirst[6]. In each case, WordNet was used to compute the *distance* between two given terms and our methodology was as follows:

1. Select algorithm for measuring *relatedness.* In our experiments, we selected Jiang-Conrath, Lin, simple edge counting and Hirst-St Onge algorithms for evaluation
2. Run a test set of known synonyms, antonyms, hypernyms and hyponyms[8] to get base scores for relatedness. Based on these scores, we established a starting score for inclusion within a particular dimension. Our requirement was discovery of terms with the following heuristically established preferences:

---

[7] http:/www.mozdex.com

[8] We hope to expand on these experiments to include meronyms, holonyms and coordinate terms at levels higher than n = 2

  – closer to synonymy than antonymy (allows matches for "coach" when
    "train" is presented as a search term)
  – closer to hyponyms than hypernyms (allows more generic cases to be
    matched, "train" instead of "power-set")
3. With the test set for a particular algorithm, we selected a starting criteria
   score for inclusion of terms within a dimension. For instance, if our starting
   criteria score is 0.5, then all terms with a semantic distance score of larger
   than 0.5^9 would be included within a given dimension.
4. With these stated criteria scores, we process the input query terms[10] and
   return a list of member dimensions.
5. Each of the terms within the candidate dimensions yields a set of document
   references. They are placed within a list in the following order:
   – exact matches are placed first
   – intersecting documents are placed next (if a specific document reference
     is returned in response to multiple terms within a dimension)
   – document matches for a single term are placed last in the queue

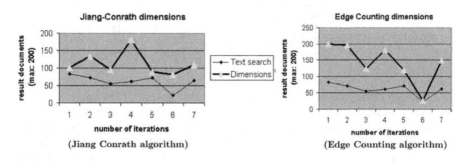

Fig. 1. Jiang-Conrath and edge-counting algorithms vs conventional text search

As can be seen from the results; the number of documents returned is higher
in absolute terms in both *Jiang-Conrath dimensions* and dimensions determined
by simple *edge counting*; sometimes by a factor of upto 3. This is consistent with
the position that simple synonymy leads to an explosion of the result document
set and consequently to a possible lower rate of precision.

However, the *recall* of these search results, the ratio of total relevant documents to retrieved documents was encouragingly improved over conventional
search techniques. In two cases, the recall was improved by as much as 10% over
a manually inspected *gold standard* for retrieved documents. [11]

---

[9] Some normalization of scores was required as different algorithms have different
   metrics and different criteria scores
[10] Unfortunately, we were forced to constrain ourselves to a maximum of 3 terms for
   the purposes of this experiment
[11] Test data and sample queries run are available at the author web site

5.3   Possible Enhancements and Alternative Techniques

Although our criteria for categorizing dimensions within this paper was the notion of *semantic distance*, it is a feature of our framework that other techniques can be easily incorporated for categorization. Therefore, we present a few candidate techniques which certainly merit attention in the future. Among them, we think that vector space techniques (LSI, CFA among others) are ideal for this categorization task. Resnik's technique for *semantic distance* incorporated machine learning, thus it is also an interesting choice for categorizing terms. Other potentially interesting techniques include thesaurus based approaches and lexical chaining.

An interesting aspect for consideration is the incorporation of real world data into semantic distance calculations. An implementation of this concept is found in Google Sets[12], which attempts to find related items in a "set" when the user enters a few sample items. A key weakness of our present semantic distance calculations is that the majority of methods rely heavily on WordNet for distance calculations. Obviously entities have limited representation within WordNet, therefore an alternate means of discovering the *Degrees of separation* between two persons, placenames or organizations is required.

References

1. Jakarta Lucene (http://jakarta.apache.org/lucene/docs/index.html)
2. van Rijsbergen, C.J.: Information Retrieval. 2nd edn. Butterworths (1980)
3. G. Salton, C.Y.: On the specification of term values in automatic indexing. Journal of Documentation **Vol. 29** (1973) pp351–372
4. Brin, S., Page, L.: Anatomy of a hypertextual web search engine. In: WWW7. (1998)
5. Brooks, T.: The semantic distance model of relevance assessment. Proceedings of the 61 st Annual Meeting of ASIS, Pittsburgh, PA, Information Access in the Global Information Economy, 35 (pp. 33-44). (1998)
6. Budanitsky, A.: Semantic distance in wordnet: An experimental, application-oriented evaluation of five measures. Workshop on WordNet and Other Lexical Resources, in NAACL-2000, Pittsburgh, PA, June 2001. (2000)
7. Dixon, M.: (An overview of document mining technology)
8. Rijke, M.V.: Beyond document retrieval. In: Trento, Nice. (2003)
9. Yang, K.: Combining Text-, Link-, and Classification-based Retrieval Methods to Enhance Information Discovery on the Web. PhD thesis, University of North Carolina (2002)
10. Modelling and mining of network information systems. (http://www.mathstat.dal.ca/~mominis/)
11. Lawrence, S., Giles, C.: Indexing and retrieval of scientific literature. In: Eighth International Conference on Information and Knowledge Management. (1999)
12. Lawrence, S.: Context in web search. In: IEEE Data Engineering Bulletin. (2000)
13. Hu, W.: An overview of world wide web search technologies. In: International Conference on Information Systems, Analysis and Synthesis. (2001)

---

[12] http://labs.google.com/sets

14. Etzioni, O.: On the instability of search engines. In: Content-Based Multimedia Information Access (RIAO), Paris, France. (2000)
15. WEBFOUNTAIN. (http://www.almaden.ibm.com/webfountain/)
16. Eder, J., Koncilia, C.: Evolution of dimension data in temporal datawarehouses. Springer Verlag (1998)
17. Roellke, T.: The accessibility dimension for structured document retrieval. In: Journal of Documentation. (1998)
18. Mothé, J.: Information mining: using document dimensions to analyse a document set interactively. In: European Colloquium on IR Research: ECIR. (2001) 66 – 77
19. Mothé, J.: Doccube: Multi-dimensional visualization and exploration of large document sets. In: JASIST (Journal of American Society for Information Science and Technology). (2003)
20. Tsang, V., Stevenson, S.: Calculating semantic distance between word sense probability distributions. In: Proceedings of CoNLL-2004, Boston, MA, USA (2004)
21. Heydon, A., Najork, M.: Mercator: A scalable, extensible web crawler. World Wide Web 2 (1999) 219–229
22. Mailing list archives of nutch.org. (http://sourceforge.net/mailarchive/forum.php?forum_id=13068&viewmonth=% 200404&viewday=26)

Effect of Phonetic Modeling
on Manipuri Digit Recognition Systems
Using CDHMMs

Sirajul Islam Choudhury and Pradip K. Das

RCILTS, Department of Computer Science and Engineering,
IIT Guwahati, Assam 781039, India
{si_chow,pkdas}@iitg.ernet.in

Abstract. This paper evaluates the phonetic modeling for continuous Manipuri speech recognition based on primitive speech units: monophones, diphones and triphones. The study is based on experiments conducted for recognition of Manipuri numerals using Manipuri phonetic structure. The results found after a series of experiments show that diphone and triphone units are more effective and less sensitive to the amount of training data than monophone units for speaker dependent continuous speech recognition for Manipuri.

1 Introduction

Real time continuous speech recognition is a demanding task, which tends to benefit from increasing available computing resources. The research on continuous speech recognition for the Manipuri Language is of recent interest. It is of great significance to study to what degree the modeling of context-dependent phonetic units, which has been demonstrated to be successful for English speech recognition [1], is efficacious for Manipuri speech recognition since the co-articulatory effect for continuous speech is stronger to an important degree than that for isolated utterances. The issue of modeling unit selection is particularly important for speaker-dependent recognition because the variability in the speech data is largely attributed to speakers as well as contextual factors.

A typical speech recognition system starts with a preprocessing stage, which takes a speech waveform as its input, and extract feature vectors or observations, which represent the information, required to perform recognition. The second stage is decoding, which is performed using a set of phone-level statistical models called Hidden Markov Models (HMM) [2, 3]. In most systems, several context-sensitive phone-level HMMs are used, in order to accommodate context-induced variation in the acoustic realization of the phone.

In this work, we report a systematic study on how the performance of a speaker dependent Manipuri continuous speech recognition is affected by the amount of contextual information utilized in the acoustic modeling. In particular, we will compare the recognition performance of the systems we developed which are based on the primitive speech units: monophones, diphones and triphones.

S. Manandhar et al. (Eds.): AACC 2004, LNCS 3285, pp. 153–160, 2004.
© Springer-Verlag Berlin Heidelberg 2004

2 Speech Recognition Theory

The most widespread and successful approach to speech recognition is based on the Hidden Markov Models (HMMs), whereby a probabilistic process models spoken utterances as the outputs of finite state machines [4]. The problem of speech recognition can be visualized as follows: Let us assume that an observation sequence $O=O_0$, $O_1, ..., O_{T-1}$, is given. Each O_t represents speech, which has been sampled at fixed intervals, and a number of potential models, each of which is a representation of a particular spoken utterance (e.g., word or sub-word unit). Our goal is to find the sequence of states that is most likely to have produced O. These models are based on HMMs.

A Markov Model is called n-state if it can be defined by a set of n states forming a finite state machine, and an n x n stochastic matrix defining transitions between states, whose elements a_{ij} = P (state j at time t | state i at time t-1); these are the transition probabilities. In a Hidden Markov model, the probability density function $b_j (O_t)$ is associated with each state additionally. The probability $b_j (O_t)$ known as observation probability determines that state j emits a particular observation O_t at time t. The model is called "hidden" because any state could have emitted the current observation. The probability density function can be continuous or discrete; accordingly the pre-processed speech data can be a multidimensional vector or a single quantised value. Such a model can only generate an observation sequence $O=O_0, O_1...,O_{T-1}$ via a state sequence of length T, as a state emits one observation at each time t. Viterbi decoding is used widely to find the state sequence which has the highest probability of producing the observation sequence O. Subject to having sufficient training data, the larger the number of HMMs, the greater the recognition accuracy of the system.

3 Manipuri Digit Recognition System Descriptions

The phonological system of Manipuri speech contains three major systems of sounds – vowels, consonants and tones. The balance of the phonological structure has to do with the inter-relationships of these elements and the ways in which they are combined to form syllables and pause groups. The sound system of Manipuri consists of 24 consonant phonemes classified as stops, fricatives, nasals, lateral/flap, trill and semivowels and 6 vowels [6, 7]. Among the stops the phonemes /p/, /ph/, /b/, /bh/ are bilabial; /t/, /th/, /d/, /dh/ are alveolar; /c/, /j/, /jh/ are palatal; /k/, /kh/, /g/, /gh/ are velar. The fricative /s/ is palatal and /h/ is glottal. The phonemes /m/, /n/, /ng/ are nasals of which /m/ is bilabial, /n/ is alveolar and /ng/ is velar. The phoneme /l/ is lateral/flap. The trill phoneme includes only /r/ and there are two semivowels /w/ and /y/ of which /w/ is bilabial and /y/ is palatal. The vowels include /ax/, /aa/, /e/, /i/, /o/, /u/. The vocabulary used for our experiments is shown in Table 1. The phonemes used by these words and their categories are shown in Table 2.

It is required to build a machine understandable phonetic dictionary (pronunciation dictionary) of all the words contain in the vocabulary. To build the pronunciation dictionary, we used the ARPAbet symbols [2] for each phoneme. ARPAbet is a phonetic alphabet, which was designed for American English and which uses ASCII symbols. Instead of designing a new set of ASCII symbols to represent Manipuri phonemes, we used ARPAbet because all the sounds used in Manipuri words can be represented by these symbols.

Table 1. Phonetic pronunciation of digits

Digit	Phonemes
Phun	/p^h/ /u/ /n/
Ama	/ax/ /m/ /ax/
Ani	/ax/ /n/ /i/
Ahum	/ax/ /h/ /u/ /m/
Mari	/m/ /ax/ /r/ /i/
Manga	/m/ /ax/ /ng/ /ax/
Taruk	/t/ /ax/ /r/ /u/ /k/
Taret	/t/ /ax/ /r/ /e/ /t/
Nipan	/n/ /i/ /p/ /aa/ /n/
Mapan	/m/ /aa/ /p/ /ax/ /n/
Tara	/t/ /ax/ /r/ /ax/

Table 2. Phonemes contained in the Manipuri digits

Category	Phonemes
Vowels	/ax/, /aa/, /e/, /i/, /u/
Stops	/p/, /p^h/, /k/, /t/
Fricatives	/s/, /h/
Nasals	/m/, /n/, /ng/
Trill	/r/

We have built two different recognizers for speaker dependent Manipuri digit recognition, and compared their respective performances. Each recognizer is associated with the use of a distinct set of speech units. The architectures of both the recognizers are same: both uses the Hidden Markov Models (HMMs) for acoustic modeling; Gaussian mixtures are employed as the state-conditioned output probability distributions; the HMM states are arranged in a left-to right, no-state-skipping topology; the segmental k-means algorithm is used for training and the Viterbi algorithm is used for decoding; and identical speech preprocessors are used to create inputs (MFCCs) to the recognizers. As a first step towards studying phonetic modeling for Manipuri speech recognition, we further limit ourselves at this time to consider only within-syllable co-articulations whenever context-dependent models are used. In this way we have simplified our decoding algorithm for search only at the syllable level.

The first recognizer uses monophones. There are 15 monophone models including short pause and silence. In this recognizer a five-state HMM is used for each of the phones identified for Manipuri. The second recognizer uses the generalized diphone and triphone models. Cloning of monophone models and subsequent clustering of states generates the diphone and triphone models. There are 17 diphones and 20 triphones in the Manipuri digits. In this case also, each of the generalized triphone is modeled by a five-state HMM. The middle state of the HMM is made to depend only on the center phone of the triphone context, while the leftmost or rightmost state depends only on the left or right contexts, respectively.

It is well known that the performance of a recognizer depends not only by the accuracy of the acoustic modeling but also by the number of free parameters in the recognition system (given a fixed amount of training data). Since our primary goal in this study is to examine the relative qualities of the two acoustic modeling approaches, we have attempted to keep the number of free parameters roughly the same in different systems by adjusting the number of Gaussian mixtures per state.

4   Speech Recognition Experiments

For this experiment we developed a small database consisting of 400 continuous speech sentences of digits. The speech material is recorded in a normal office environment. The training of acoustic and language models was performed using the HTK toolkit 3.2[5].

The speech signal feature vectors consist of log energy, 12 mel-cepstrum features and their derivatives and acceleration coefficients. The feature coefficients are computed every 10ms for a speech signal window of 25ms. The 12 MFCCs were calculated from the log of the Mel bank outputs using discrete cosine transform by taking 26 triangular filter blanks.

In the first step we trained the monophone models with continuous density output function (three mixtures Gaussian density functions), described with diagonal covariance matrices. Since the transcription of speech files is in the word level, we perform training procedures resulting in a monophone recognizer. Additional models for silence and short pauses are used. While developing triphones, diphones are automatically generated as contexts at word boundaries, which has only two phones. The diphones and triphones are developed in two steps: Firstly, the monophone transcriptions are converted to diphone and triphone transcriptions and a set of diphone and triphone models are created by copying the monophones and re-estimating. Secondly, similar acoustic states of these diphones and triphones are tied to ensure that all state distributions can be robustly estimated. Under the same conditions, the HMM diphone and triphone models are trained. We now discuss the results of the experiments.

The overall word correctness increases by 5.61% using HMM models trained by diphone/triphone phonetic units. In both recognizers, the vowel ending digits are more easily recognized than the stop or plosive ending digits. Let us discuss some special results found: the vowel ending digits /ama/, /manga/ found to be recognized as any one of these two in case of monophone model recognizer. In both words the last vowel is preceded by a nasal consonant. It is hard to detect the nasal sound that precedes the last vowel. Hence, the recognition of the word /manga/ is highly depend on the speaker whether he/she gives stress on the first nasal sound /m/ otherwise it is recognized as /ama/. It is seen that in case of monophone model recognizer, 9.76% of the spoken /ama/ words are recognized as /manga/ and 12% of /manga/ is recognized as /ama/. The confusion matrix of recognition in percentage for monophone and diphone/triphone based recognizers are as shown in Table 3 and Table 4 respectively. In case of words /phun/, /ahum/ the nasal sound at the last position is a bit difficult to recognize. The word /taruk/ is sometimes recognized as /phun/ or /ahum/. This happened because of the sudden change from the vowel /u/ to a stop or plosive depending on the accent of the speaker.

Table 3. Confusion matrix for recognition (%) using monophone models

Digit Spoken	Correct Recognition (%)										
	Phun	Ama	Ani	Ahum	Mari	Manga	Taruk	Taret	Nipan	Mapan	Tara
Phun	85.2			9.8			5				
Ama		85				9.76					5.24
Ani			86.2		13.8						
Ahum	9.45			84.05			6.5				
Mari			12.5		87.5						
Manga		12				84.65					2.35
Taruk	6.5			9.5			83				
Taret								94.25			4.75
Nipan									86.34	14.66	
Mapan									16.5	83.5	
Tara		9.3					6.7				84

The word /nipan/ and /mapan/ starts with a nasal sound and a vowel sound immediately following the nasal sound. If the speaker does not give stress on the vowel, the monophonic models are not easy to recognize the correct word. The word /tara/ and /taret/ are recognized well in both HMM models. The comparative recognition accuracy of monophone and diphone/triphone based recognizers are represented graphically as shown in Figure 1.

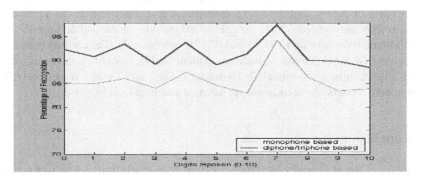

Fig. 1. Comparative recognition (%) of monophone and diphone/triphone based models

The Word Correctness (WC) and the Word Error Rate (WER) of the recognizers can be computed using the following formula:

$$WC = 100\% * [\ 1- (W_S+W_D) \ / \ N \ ]$$
$$WER = (W_S+ \ W_D+W_I) \ / \ N \ * \ 100\%$$

where WS, WD and WI are substituted, deleted and inserted words, while N is the number of words.

Table 4. Confusion matrix for recognition (%) using monophone models

Digit Spoken	Correct Recognition (%)										
	Phun	Ama	Ani	Ahum	Mari	Manga	Taruk	Taret	Nipan	Mapan	Tara
Phun	92.3			7.7			2				
Ama		90.7				6					3.3
Ani			93.4		7.6						
Ahum	4.79			89.21			5				
Mari			3.3		93.7						
Manga		8.21				89					2.79
Taruk	2			6.66			91.34				
Taret								97.5			3.5
Nipan									90.02	10.88	
Mapan									10.22	89.78	
Tara		6.5					3	2			88.5

The recognition rates for both monophone as well as diphone/triphone based recognizers are low. We increased the size of the speech database and repeated the process of training HMMs. We recorded 200 more continuous speech sentences of digits as before. Segmentation and training of acoustic signals are done using the original features. As a result, we could see significant improvement in the recognition process. An increase of 6.17% and 3.42% in monophone and diphone/triphone recognizers respectively was recorded. The recognizer based on monophone and diphone/triphone models could recognize up to 91.96 and 94.82% respectively. The confusion matrixes for recognition in percentage of both monophone and diphone/triphone based recognizers after retraining the models is shown in Table 5 and Table 6 respectively. The comparative recognition accuracy is represented graphically in Figure 2.

5   Conclusions

In this paper we presented a systematic performance evaluation of levels of acoustic modeling for Manipuri digit recognition system. We found in our experiments that

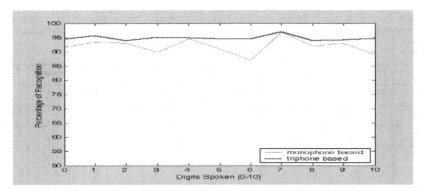

Fig. 2. Recognition rate(%) of monophone and diphone/triphone based models(600 sentences)

Table 5. Confusion matrix for recognition (%) using monophone models (after repetition)

Digit Spoken	Correct Recognition (%)										
	Phun	Ama	Ani	Ahum	Mari	Manga	Taruk	Taret	Nipan	Mapan	Tara
Phun	91.6			3.4			3			2	
Ama		93.5				2.5				1	2
Ani			93		5.3				1.7		
Ahum	5.23			89.87			2			1	
Mari			3.3		94.7				2		
Manga		7.51				91					3.49
Taruk	6			5.25			87	1.75			
Taret							1	96.9			2.1
Nipan			4.7						92	3.3	
Mapan	1.17								8.93	93	
Tara		2					6.5	2.5			89

the generalized diphone/triphone models are capable of providing better performance, especially when the amount of training data is small for single speakers. Another advantage of the triphone-based approach is its ability for robust acoustic modeling of context dependence and co-articulated syllables.

Acknowledgements

We acknowledge to the Ministry of Information Technology, Government of India, for funding the RCILTS project at IIT Guwahati and to all personnel of the project.

Table 6. Confusion matrix for recognition (%) using diphone/triphone models (after repetition)

Digit Spoken	Correct Recognition (%)										
	Phun	Ama	Ani	Ahum	Mari	Manga	Taruk	Taret	Nipan	Mapan	Tara
Phun	94.4			1.6			1		0.89	2.11	
Ama		95.6				2				1	1.4
Ani			94		2.57				3.43		
Ahum	3			95.16			1.84				
Mari			2.8		95				2.2		
Manga		3.41				94.59				1	1
Taruk	2			1.5			94.5	1			
Taret							2	97			1
Nipan			2						93.92	4.08	
Mapan									5.75	94.25	
Tara		2.45					2.87	3.13			94.6

References

1. Young, S.: Large Vocabulary Continuous Speech Recognition: A review. Proc. IEEE Workshop on Automatic Speech Recognition, Snowbird, Utah (1995) 3-28
2. Jurafsky, D., Martin James, H.: Speech and Language Processing: An Introduction to Natural Language Processing, Computational Linguistics, and Speech Processing. Pearson Education (2000) 235-279
3. Becchetti, C., and Ricotti, L.P.: Speech Recognition Theory and C++ Implementation. John Wiley and Sons, New York, USA (1999)
4. Rabiner, L. R.: A Tutorial on Hidden Markov models and selected applications in Speech Recognition. Proc. IEEE, 77, No. 2 (1989) 257-286
5. Young, S., Odell, J., Ollason, D., Vatchev, V., Woodland, P.: The HTK Book (3.2). Cambridge University Engineering Department, Cambridge, Great Britain (2002)
6. Yashawanta Ch., Singh: Manipuri Grammar. Rajesh Publications, New Delhi (2000) 4-20.
7. Shobhana L., Chelliah: A Grammar of Meithei. Monton de Gruyter, Berlin, New York (1997) 17-70

Building Language Models
for Tamil Speech Recognition System

S. Saraswathi and T.V. Geetha

Department of Computer Science & Engg., Anna University,
Chennai, India
swathimuk@yahoo.com, tvgeedir@cs.annauniv.edu

Abstract. An essential element of any speech recognition system is the language model. A language model attempts to identify and make use of the regularities in natural language to better define language syntax for easier recognition. One major obstacle in speech recognition is the variability and uncertainty of message content. This coupled with inherent noise distortion and losses that occur in speech emphasize the need for a good language model. This paper describes the work done in generation of language model for Tamil speech recognition system. From the study the performance of Morpheme based Language model is better compared to other models tried for Tamil speech recognizer.

1 Introduction

Building Language model for a continuous speech recognition system is a formidable task. The type of language model to be used is one of the first things that must be considered and their choice has a marked effect on the speech recognition system performance [1]. A language model must properly model the training corpus and it must also utilize a method for handling outliers (words not in training corpus). Methods that adjust the model parameters to account for outliers by shaping distributions are called smoothing. When a language model is created it is necessary to have some way of testing its quality. The most important method for doing this is to use the model in the application it was designed for and watch its impact on the overall performance. For language model designed for speech recognition system, the best way of testing its quality is to evaluate the word error rate (WER) obtained when the model is used in the system. This method is not very efficient, as it needs a lot of computer processing for reliably measuring the WER, which is time consuming [2]. Therefore alternative methods must be used instead. Perplexity is often used as a measure of the quality of the language model, as it tests the capability of a model for predicting an unseen text which is a text not used in the model training. Perplexity of a model relative to a text with n words is defined by the equation (1)

$$PP = 2^{LP}; \ LP = (1/n) \log P^1 (w_1, \ldots. w_n) \tag{1}$$

P^1 is the probability estimation of the sequence of n words given by the language model. Perplexity can be seen as the average size of the word set over which a word recognized by the system is chosen and therefore lower the value the better. During Speech recognition perplexity does not take into account acoustic similarity between words, which means that lower perplexity values may not result in lower WER. In this work the various language models were analyzed over Tamil language. For Language modeling purpose three text Corpuses one on "Health" of size 40K with 4500

S. Manandhar et al. (Eds.): AACC 2004, LNCS 3285, pp. 161–168, 2004.

words, corpus on "Thiyanam" of size 102K with 10000 words and corpus on "Politics" of size 500k with 50,000 words were collected. Text data has to go through several preprocessing stages in order to obtain clear and unambiguous data.

2   The Use of Language Models in Speech Recognition System

In speech recognition sequence of symbols generated by the acoustic component is compared with the set of words present in the lexicon to produce the optimal sequence of words to compose the systems final output. Rules are introduced during this stage that describe linguistic restrictions present in the language, which is accomplished by the use of a language model in the system. A language model comprises two main components, the vocabulary which is the set of words that can be recognized by the system and the grammar, which is the set of rules that regulate the way the words of the vocabulary are arranged to form sentences. Different statistical and linguistic based statistical language models are applied on the given two Tamil corpuses and the results are analyzed.

3   Statistical Language Model

A statistical language model is a probabilistic description of the constraints on word order found in a given language. Typical sequences of words are given high probabilities whereas atypical word sequences are given low probabilities. The quality of the language model is evaluated by measuring the probability of new test word sequences. In this work N-gram statistical language models is applied over the two Tamil corpuses.

3.1   N-Gram Model

The n-gram model uses the previous (n-1) words as the only information source to generate the model parameters. N-grams are easy to implement, easy to interface with and good predictors of short-term dependencies. Given any state (W_k, W_{k+1}), it is possible to proceed to state (W_{k+1}, W_{k+2}) with probability $P(W_{k+2} / W_{k+1} W_k \cdots W_{k-(n-3)})$. This approach can be mathematically viewed for some word sequence $W = W_1 W_2 W_3 \ldots W_n$ that satisfies the argument

$$P(W / Y) = \max P(W / Y) \tag{2}$$

From Baye's rule

$$W = \operatorname{argmax} P(W) . P(Y / W) \tag{3}$$

where W is any word string and Y is the string of acoustical observations [3] The acoustic model provides the probability P(Y/W). The language model provides apriori information of the training corpus, P(W) which is given by

$$P(W) = \prod_{I=1}^{N} P(W_i / W_1 W_2 \ldots W_{N-1}) \tag{4}$$

In case reliability becomes a problem, the search algorithm can use a back-off approach. The search procedure queries the language model for a certain probability of n-gram occurrence. If the score that is returned by the language model is not 'good' according to search procedure criteria or if the n-gram does not exist the search can then "back-off" from looking for match of length n to looking for suitable match of length n-1. This method can be applied until an acceptable score is returned or until unigrams are reached. The procedure is explained in Figure 1. The search starts looking for a suitable trigram. If it does not exist it searches for the corresponding bigram. If the bigram exists then the returned probability will be a product of the bigram back-off weight and conditional probability associated with the words three and two. And if the bigram does not exist the aforementioned conditional probability is returned. The back-off models provide an efficient method for increasing coverage and hence overall performance of the system.

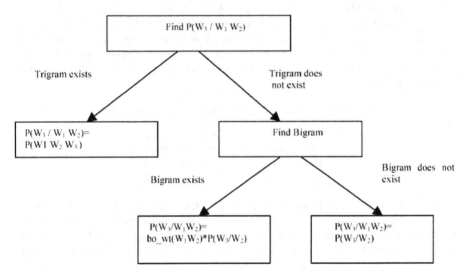

Fig. 1. Trigram example of back-off approach

Both bigram and trigam models with back-off smoothing effects where applied over the given corpus and the results (Table 1) were analyzed

Table 1. Results on Bigram and Trigram

Corpus	Bigram		Trigram	
	WER	Perplexity	WER	Perplexity
Health	68%	246	97%	1641
Thiyanam	57.8%	85	95%	2058
Politics	46.2%	45	92.1%	3258

The results show that the bigram language model produced the lowest WER and perplexity when compared to the trigram model.

4   Linguistic Based Statistical Language Model

Word-based n-gram models do not capture any linguistic constraints inherent in speech. In this work, Linguistic knowledge is incorporated with statistical language models to obtain improvements in perplexity results and recognition performance of the system.

4.1   Morpheme Based Language Models

Morpheme based models are suitable for highly inflectional languages. When building large vocabulary speech recognition system for these languages one major problem encountered is excessive vocabulary growth caused by great number of different word forms derived from one word. Using only a relatively small number of different words, an inflectional change of the word mostly affects word endings whereas stem remains constant. Therefore instead of considering derived words, a better alternative is to decompose words into stems and endings and treat these units/ morphemes separately as if they were independent words. Baseline Bigram and trigram models were trained on the given corpus. Decomposition of the text corpus into stems and endings is done using an existing Tamil morphological analyser. Examples of decomposition are given in Table 2.

Table 2. Example of decomposition into stem and ending

Words	Decomposition
மனிதனுடைய	மனிதன் உடைய
உண்மையான	உண்மை ய் ஆன
பொருத்தமட்டில்	பொருத்த மட்டில்

The size of the Morpheme vocabulary generated for the two Tamil corpus is shown in Table 3. Usage of this model, lead to significant reduction in the size of the language model vocabulary, and improvement of word accuracy in out of vocabulary words. The results that were analysed for Word error rate and perplexity of the given two Tamil corpuses are shown in Table 4.

Table 3. Size of Morpheme Vocabulary

Corpus	No. of Morpheme	No. of Stem	No. of Endings
Health	4068	3900	168
Thiyanam	8114	7829	285
Politics	40520	40,150	370

The result indicates that the morpheme based bigram models covers the test set far better than the word model and also gives reasonable perplexity even though they can generate an infinite number of distinct word form.

Table 4. Results on Morpheme based Bigram and Trigram

Corpus	Bigram		Trigram	
	WER	Perplexity	WER	Perplexity
Health	51%	132	84%	972
Thiyanam	46.2%	74	82.2%	1778
Politics	38.5%	35	79.2%	2780

4.2 Stochastic Context Free Grammars as Language Models

The SCFG consists of hand written context free rules. The non-terminals in the rules are very specific to the corpus. The rule probabilities are learned from 3000 sentences in Tamil corpus. The following ways of information provided by the SCFG were analysed

- Use mixture of SCFG and bigram probability directly to provide word transition probability on each frame.
- Use mixture of SCFG and Trigram probability directly to provide word transition probability on each frame.

SCFG is best at modelling long distance dependencies and hierarchical structure; the SCFG-bigram is best at local and lexical dependencies.[5]. Hence mixture of the two models on a frame-by-frame basis is tried out.

$$P(w_i / \text{prefix}) = 0.5 \, P(w_i / \text{prefix, SCFG}) + 0.5P(w_i / \text{prefix, Bigram}) \quad (5)$$

$$P(w_i / \text{prefix}) = 0.5 \, P(w_i / \text{prefix, SCFG}) + 0.5P(w_i / \text{prefix, Trigram}) \quad (6)$$

Using Bayes rule

$$P(w_I / \text{prefix}) = P(\text{SCFG} / \text{prefix}) \, P(w_i / \text{prefix, SCFG}) +$$
$$P(\text{bigram} / \text{prefix}) \, P(w_i / \text{prefix, bigram}) \quad (7)$$

$$P(w_i / \text{prefix}) = P(\text{SCFG} / \text{prefix}) \, P(w_i / \text{prefix, SCFG}) +$$
$$P(\text{trigram} / \text{prefix}) \, P(w_i / \text{prefix, trigram}) \quad (8)$$

The coupling system was tested on a test set of 150 sentences from "Health" using 300 sentences for training and on "Thiyanam" corpus with test set of 360 sentences using 700 sentences for training and "Politics" corpus with test set of 2670 sentences, using 4000 sentences for training. The results were analysed as shown in Table 5.

Table 5. Results on SCFG based Bigram and Trigram

Corpus	SCFG - Bigram		SCFG - Trigram	
	WER	Perplexity	WER	Perplexity
Health	67%	243	94%	1613
Thiyanam	56.2%	83	93.5%	1998
Politics	44.3%	41	91.2%	3167

The SCFG based bigram model produced better results than the SCFG based trigram model.

4.3 Class Based Language Model

Class based language models are very effective for rapid adaptation, training on small data sets and reduced memory requirements for real-time speech applications [6]. In this work classes for words that exhibit similar grammatical category (part of speech tag) is defined. For any given assignment of a word w_i to class c_i, there may be many-to many mappings, for example a word w_i may belong to more than one class and class c_i may contain more than one word. The n-gram model are computed based on the previous n-1 classes:

$$P(w_i / c_{i-n+1}....c_{i-1}) = P(w_i / c_i) \, P(c_i / c_{i-n+1}....c_{i-1}) \quad (9)$$

where $P(w_i / c_i)$ denotes the probability of word w_i given class c_i in the current position, and $P(c_i / c_{i-n+1}....c_{i-1})$ denotes the probability of class ci given the class history. In general the class trigram is expressed as equation (10).

$$P(W)= \sum_{c_i..c_n} \prod_I P(wi / ci) P(ci / ci\text{-}2,ci\text{-}1)$$

(10)

And the class bigram can be evaluated from equation (11).

$$P(w_i /w_{i-1})= P(w_i / c_{i-1}) = P(w_i / c_i) P(c_i / c_{i-1}) = C(w_i) C(c_{i-1} c_i) / C(c_i) C(c_{i-1})$$ (11)

The class based bigram and trigram models were applied on the corpuses Thiyanam and Health and the results are shown in Table 6.

Table 6. Results on Class based Bigram and Trigram

Corpus	Class based Bigram		Class based Trigram	
	WER	Perplexity	WER	Perplexity
Health	65%	235	89%	1331
Thiyanam	52%	79	91%	1788
Politics	42.1%	39	90.2%	3004

The class based bigram model produced better results than the class based trigram model.

5 Performance Analysis

Analysis were performed on the Tamil corpus Thiyanam and Health using WER and Perplexity. The health corpus had 4500 words and the first 3000 words were used for training. The Thiyanam corpus had 10000 words and the first 7000 words were used for training In Politics corpus first 35000 words were used for training and the remaining words were used for testing. The WER results obtained for the various language models in both the corpus is shown by the graph in Figure 2.

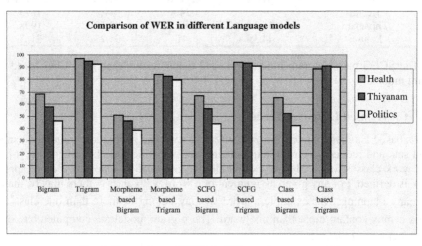

Fig. 2. Comparison of WER in different language models

The perplexity analysis on both the corpus using different language models is shown by the graph in Figure 3. From the results it is analysed that the morpheme based bigram models produced the lowest Word Error Rate and the perplexity value for both corpuses, irrespective of their sizes. Since Tamil is an inflectional language Morpheme based approach gave good results. From the study it was deduced that most recent word in the history alone predicts the probability of the next word more accurately in Tamil.

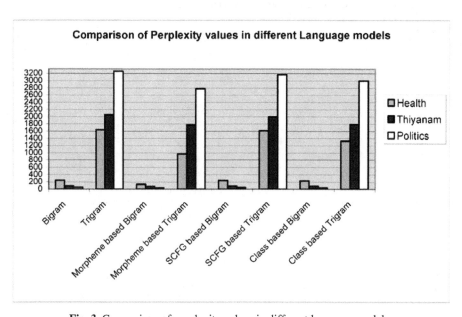

Fig. 3. Comparison of perplexity values in different language models.

6 Conclusion and Further Work

Eight language models were applied on two different Tamil corpuses. The Morpheme based bigram approach was found to be more suitable for Tamil speech recognition system. It produced the lowest WER and perplexity value when compared to the other models. The future scope of this work is to test this technique on large test sets from various domains to prove their robustness.

References

1. Goodman, "A bit of progress in language modelling", Computer Speech and Language 2001.
2. Picone.J, and Deshmukh.N, Methodologies for Language Modelling and search in Continuos Speech Recognition Institute for Signal and Information Processing, Mississippi State University, ECE Dept., 1998

3. Laferty.S, and Suhm B., Cluster Expansion and Iterative scaling of Maximum Entropy Language Models in 15th International workshop on maximum Entropy and Bayesian Methods, Kluwer Academic Publishers, 1995
4. M.Creutz and K.Lagus, "Unsupervised discovery of morphemes",Proceedings of the workshop on Morphological and phonological Learning of ACL 2002.
5. Jonathan Segal, "Precise n-gram probabilities from stochastic context free grammar", in proceedings of 32nd ACL 1994.
6. Jian Sun, Jianfeng Gao, Lei Zhang, Ming Zhou, Changning Huang, "Chinese Named Entity Identification using Class Based Language Model", 2002

Implementation of Tamil Speech Recognition System Using Neural Networks

S. Saraswathi and T.V. Geetha

[1] Department of Computer Science & Engg., Anna University, Chennai, India
swathimuk@yahoo.com, tvgeedir@cs.annauniv.edu

Abstract. This paper presents a neural network approach for speech recognition in Tamil language. In the present work the structure of a speaker-independent system for isolated word recognition, based on a neural network paradigm combined with a dynamic programming algorithm is applied. The experimental results demonstrate that a hybrid model leads to higher recognition rates than the classic technologies.

1 Introduction

Speech is a natural mode of communication for people. The human vocal tract and articulators are biological organs with nonlinear properties, whose operation are not just under conscious control but also affected by factors ranging from gender to emotional state. As a result, vocalizations can vary widely in terms of their accent, pronunciation, articulation, roughness, nasality, pitch, volume, and speed. All these sources of variability make speech recognition, a very complex task. People are so comfortable with speech and they like to interact with their computers via speech. Computers are still nowhere near the level of human performance at speech recognition, and it appears that further significant advances will require some new insights. Intriguingly, the human brain is wired differently than a conventional computer; in fact it operates under a radically different computational paradigm. While conventional computers use a very fast and complex central processor with explicit program instructions and locally addressable memory, by contrast the human brain uses a massively parallel collection of slow and simple processing elements (neurons), densely connected by weights (synapses) whose strengths are modified with experience, directly supporting the integration of multiple constraints, and providing a distributed form of associative memory. The brain's impressive superiority at a wide range of cognitive skills, including speech recognition, has motivated research into its novel computational paradigm since the 1940's, on the assumption that brain like models may ultimately lead to brain like performance on many complex tasks. This fascinating research area is known as connectionism, or the study of artificial neural networks. Neural networks have been used for many different tasks in several domains and they have proved to be very efficient for learning complex input-output mappings.[1] Neural algorithms offer alternatives to classical techniques and have an important potential for implementing discrimination, nonlinear feature extraction, or classification based on the distance to learned reference patterns. Neural networks

S. Manandhar et al. (Eds.): AACC 2004, LNCS 3285, pp. 169–176, 2004.

also play a major role in area of Tamil speech recognition, in classifying the feature vectors of the various Tamil phonemes.

1.1 An Overview of Speech Recognition System

Speech recognizers are normally divided into two stages, as shown in Figure 1. The Feature Extractor (FE) block generates a sequence of feature vectors, a trajectory in some feature space that represents the input speech signal. The FE block is the one designed to use the human vocal tract knowledge to compress the information contained by the utterance. It is based on *a priori* knowledge that is always true and it does not change with time. The Recognizer performs the trajectory recognition and generates the correct output word. This stage uses information about the specific way a user produce utterance and it must adapt to different users.

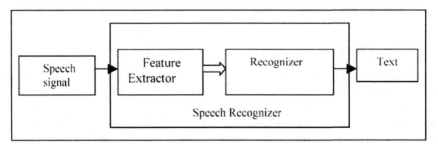

Fig. 1. Basic building blocks of a Speech Recognizer

This block transforms the incoming sound into an internal representation such that it is possible to reconstruct the original signal from it. We analyze the incoming information and classify it into the phonemes of the corresponding language. Once the FE block completes its work, the Recognizer module classifies its output. It integrates the sequences of phonemes into Tamil words. The process of correlating utterances to their symbolic expressions, translating spoken language into written language, is called speech recognition.

1.2 Features of Tamil Language

Tamil belongs to the Dravidian language family. Classical Tamil is considered the earliest Dravidian language, and more than eighty million people worldwide speak modern Tamil. Tamil is regarded as one of the four major literary languages of the Dravidian. There are thirty characters in the Tamil writing system. They are twelve vowels called as "uyire" and eighteen consonants called as "mei". The Tamil alphabet is syllabic, in that each letter denotes a syllable. A syllable may be formed by a vowel or by a consonant followed by a vowel. Vowel letters occur only in the initial position. When a vowel occurs after a consonant in the middle or at the end of a word, the vowel and consonant are expressed as one letter known as "uyire mei". The three dotted sign is called "aayudam" in Tamil and denotes that velar sound /x/ precedes a consonant. Some phonemes of Tamil have the same characteristics so that they can map to a single Tamil character. Linguistic and Tamil language specific rules are formed for mapping of the phonemes to the corresponding character.

2 Implementation

Speech recognition is the process of automatically recognizing the speech that has been delivered by the speaker on the basis of individual information included in speech waves. Speech Recognition enables us to convert the speech to text, which enhances the user interface to a broader one. The concept of speech to text enables the users interest in communicating with the computer by the speech. Figure 2 shows the Modules applied for Tamil speech recognition system, in this work. All the modules are implemented using MatLab, which is a high performance language for technical computing. It integrates Computation, Visualization and Programming in an easy to use environment where problems and solutions are expressed in mathematical notation.

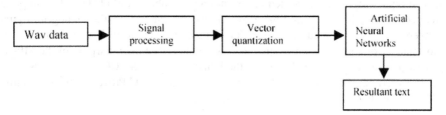

Fig. 2. Modules used in Tamil Speech Recognition System

The method of characterizing speech in terms of signals ensures easy extraction of information content by human and computers. The first module in Tamil speech recognition system is to extract the features from the speech.

2.1 Signal Processing

This module converts the speech waveform to parametric representation for further analysis and processing. The speech signal is a slow time varying signal. When examined over a sufficiently short period of time (between 5 and 100 msec), its characteristics are fairly stationary. However, over long period of time the signal characteristic change to reflect the different speech sounds being spoken. Therefore, *short-time spectral analysis* is the most common way to characterize the speech signal. A wide range of possibilities exists for parametrically representing the speech signal for the speaker recognition task, such as Linear Prediction Coding (LPC) and Mel-Frequency Cepstrum Coefficients (MFCC) [2]. MFCC is perhaps the best known and most popular, and it is used in this work. MFCC's are based on the known variation of the human ear's critical bandwidths with frequency, filters spaced linearly at low frequencies and logarithmically at high frequencies have been used to capture the phonetically important characteristics of speech. This is expressed in the *mel-frequency* scale, which is a linear frequency spacing below 1000 Hz and a logarithmic spacing above 1000 Hz. The speech waveform is passed as input to MFCC processor that generates the MFCC co-efficient of the speech signal.

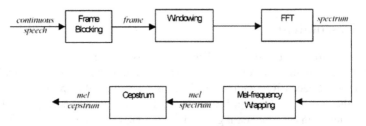

Fig. 3. Block diagram of the MFCC processor

2.1.1 Mel-Frequency Cepstrum Coefficients Processor

A block diagram of the structure of an MFCC processor is given in Figure.3 The speech input is typically recorded at a sampling rate above 10000 Hz. The sampling frequency was chosen to minimize the effects of *aliasing* in the analog-to-digital conversion. The sampled signals capture all frequencies up to 5 kHz, which cover most energy of sounds that are generated by humans. The main purpose of the MFCC processor is to mimic the behavior of the human ears and MFCC's are less suscepti-ble to variations. The following steps are involved in MFCC Processor for generating MFCC co-efficient.

Frame Blocking: In this step the continuous speech signal is blocked into frames of N samples, with adjacent frames being separated by M ($M < N$). The first frame consists of the first N samples. The second frame begins M samples after the first frame, and overlaps it by N - M samples. Similarly, the third frame begins $2M$ sam-ples after the first frame (or M samples after the second frame) and overlaps it by N - $2M$ samples. This process continues until all the speech is accounted for within one or more frames. Typical values for N and M are $N = 256$ (which is equivalent to ~ 30 msec windowing and facilitate the fast radix-2 FFT) and $M = 100$.

Windowing: The next step in the processing is to window each individual frame so as to minimize the signal discontinuities at the beginning and end of each frame. This minimizes the spectral distortion by using window to taper the signal to zero at the beginning and end of each frame. We define the window as $w(n), 0 \leq n \leq N-1$, where N is the number of samples in each frame. The result of windowing is the sig-nal

$$y_l(n) = x_l(n)w(n), \quad 0 \leq n \leq N-1$$

Typically the *Hamming* window is used, which has the form:

$$w(n) = 0.54 - 0.46\cos\left(\frac{2\pi n}{N-1}\right), \quad 0 \leq n \leq N-1$$

Fast Fourier Transform (FFT): The next processing step is the Fast Fourier Transform, which converts each frame of N samples from the time domain into the frequency domain. The FFT is a fast algorithm to implement the Discrete Fourier Transform (DFT) which is defined on the set of N samples $\{x_n\}$, as follow:

$$X_n = \sum_{k=0}^{N-1} x_k e^{-2\pi jkn/N}, \qquad n = 0,1,2,...,N-1$$

j denotes the imaginary unit, i.e. $j = \sqrt{-1}$, X_n's are complex numbers. The resulting sequence $\{X_n\}$ is interpreted as follow:

- the zero frequency corresponds to $n = 0$, positive frequencies $0 < f < F_s/2$ correspond to values $1 \le n \le N/2 - 1$
- negative frequencies $-F_s/2 < f < 0$ correspond to $N/2 + 1 \le n \le N - 1$.

F_s denote the sampling frequency. The result after this step is often referred to as *spectrum* or *periodogram*.

Mel-Frequency Wrapping: The human perception of the frequency contents of sounds for speech signals do not follow a linear scale. Thus for each tone with an actual frequency, f, measured in Hz, a subjective pitch is measured on a scale called the 'mel' scale. The *mel-frequency* scale is linear frequency spacing below 1000 Hz and a logarithmic spacing above 1000 Hz. As a reference point, the pitch of 1 kHz tone, 40 dB above the perceptual hearing threshold, is defined as 1000 mels. We use the following approximate formula to compute the mels for a given frequency f in Hz:

$$mel\ (f) = 2595\ *\log_{10}(1 + f/700)$$

Cepstrum: In this final step, we convert the log mel spectrum back to time. The result is called the mel frequency cepstrum coefficients (MFCC). The cepstral representation of the speech spectrum provides a good representation of the local spectral properties of the signal for the given frame analysis. As the mel spectrum coefficients are real numbers, we convert them to time domain using the Discrete Cosine Transform (DCT). $\tilde{S}_k, k = 1,2,...,K$, denotes those mel power spectrum coefficients, then the MFCC's, $\tilde{c}_n$, are calculated as follow:

$$\tilde{c}_n = \sum_{k=1}^{K} (\log \tilde{S}_k) \cos \left[n \left(k - \frac{1}{2} \right) \frac{\pi}{K} \right], \qquad n = 1,2,...,K$$

We exclude the first component, $\tilde{c}_0$, from the DCT since it represents the mean value of the input signal which carries little speaker specific information.

2.2 Vector Quantisation

After the enrolment session, the acoustic vectors extracted from input speech of a speaker provide a set of training vectors. The next important step is to build a speaker-specific VQ codebook for this speaker using those training vectors. There is a well-know algorithm, namely LBG algorithm [Linde, Buzo and Gray, 1980], for clustering a set of L training vectors into a set of M codebook vectors [3]. The algorithm is formally implemented by the following recursive procedure

1. Design a 1-vector codebook; this is the centroid of the entire set of training vectors (hence, no iteration is required here).
2. Double the size of the codebook by splitting each current codebook $\mathbf{y}_n$ according to the rule

$$\mathbf{y}_n^+ = \mathbf{y}_n(1+\varepsilon)$$
$$\mathbf{y}_n^- = \mathbf{y}_n(1-\varepsilon)$$

where n varies from 1 to the current size of the codebook, and ε is a splitting parameter (we choose $\varepsilon = 0.01$).

3. **Nearest-Neighbor Search:** For each training vector, find the codeword in the current codebook that is closest (in terms of similarity measurement), and assign that vector to the corresponding cell (associated with the closest codeword).
4. **Centroid Update:** Update the codeword in each cell using the centroid of the training vectors assigned to that cell.
5. Iteration 1: repeat steps 3 and 4 until the average distance falls below a preset threshold.
6. Iteration 2: repeat steps 2, 3 and 4 until a codebook size of M is designed.

Intuitively, the LBG algorithm designs an M-vector codebook in stages. It starts first by designing a 1-vector codebook, then uses a splitting technique on the codeword to initialize the search for a 2-vector codebook, and continues the splitting process until the desired M-vector codebook is obtained.

2.3 Neural Network

An artificial neural network consists of a potentially large number of simple processing elements (*neurons*), which influence each other's behavior via a network of excitatory or inhibitory weights [6]. Each unit simply computes a nonlinear weighted sum of its inputs, and broadcasts the result over its outgoing connections to other units. A training set consists of pattern of values that are assigned to designated input and/or output units. As patterns are presented from the training set, a learning rule modifies the strengths of the weights so that the network gradually learns the training set. Neural networks are usually used to perform static pattern recognition, that is, to statically map complex inputs to simple outputs, such as an N-ary classification of the input patterns. Moreover, the most common way to train a neural network for this task is via a procedure called *backpropagation* (Rumelhart et al, 1986) [5], whereby the network's weights are modified in proportion to their contribution to the observed error in the output unit activations (relative to desired outputs).

2.3.1 BackPropagation
Back propagation is the most widely used supervised training algorithm for neural networks [5]. The training was performed for uyire, uyire mei and mei characters of

Tamil language, which form the base for word generation in Tamil. We train a multi-layer feed forward network by gradient descent to approximate an unknown function, based on some training data consisting of pairs $(\mathbf{x}, \mathbf{t})$. The vector $\mathbf{x}$ represents a pattern of input to the network which are the feature vectors of the signals obtained from the codebook, and the vector $\mathbf{t}$ the corresponding target, the Tamil characters corresponding to the vector passed. The overall gradient with respect to the entire training set is just the sum of the gradients for each pattern. We number the units, and denote the weight from unit j to unit i by w_{ij}.

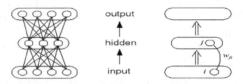

output

hidden

input

w_{ji}

Fig. 4. A feedforward neural network, highlighting the connection from unit i to j

The backpropagation algorithm is implemented as follows:

1. Initialize the input layer: $y_0 = x$
2. Propagate activity forward: for $l = 1, 2, ..., L$,
   $y_1 = f_1(w_1 y_{1-1} + b_1)$,   where b_1 is the vector of bias weights.
3. Calculate the error in the output layer: $\delta_L = t - y_L$
4. Backpropagate the error: for $l = L-1, L-2, ..., 1$,
   $$\delta_L = (w_{1+1}{}^T \delta_{l+1}). f_1{}^1 (net\ _1)$$
   where T is the matrix transposition operator.
5. Update the weights and biases: $\Delta W_1 = \delta_1 y_{1-1}{}^T$; $\Delta b_1 = \delta_1$

3 Experimental Results

The speaker independent isolated word recognition system on the 200 basic words in the Tamil corpus on sports is tested. Each word in the database is repeated ten times by each of the ten speakers in the database. For speech recognition, the acoustic observation vectors with 13 MFCC coefficients where extracted from a window of 20ms. 90% word recognition was reported when the words were tested with 10 speakers. The experimental results indicate that the, new approach developed for training the neural network's architecture proved to be simple and very efficient. It reduced considerably the amount of calculations needed for finding the correct set of parameters.

4 Performance Analysis

The result of the project is adversely affected by the environmental condition. The Environment should be noise free. The performance in case of normal circumstances is around 90%. In case of noisy environment, the performance will be around 80%.

The number of input and output neurons for each network trained for uyire, uyire mei and mei characters in Tamil is given below:

Class: Uyire	Class: Uyire-mei	Class: Mei
Input Neurons: 100	Input Neurons: 100	Input Neurons: 100
Output Neurons: 12	Output Neurons: 18	Output Neurons: 18

5   Conclusion and Further Work

The experiments made with dynamic programming and neural network learning process for distinguishing the exemplars in frequency and discriminatory template patterns for each word in the vocabulary, provided the basis for an effective Tamil speech recognition system. The future scope of the problem is to broaden to larger vocabularies continuous speech, and different speakers and to perform word recognition in noisy environment basically words uttered over the telephone network.

References

1. Tebelskis, "Speech Recognition Using Neural Networks," PhD Dissertation,Carnegie Mellon University, 1995.
2. L. Rabiner and B.H. Huang. *Fundamentals of Speech Recognition*. Prentice-Hall, Englewood Cliffs, NJ, 1993.
3. Xuedong Huang, Alex Acerd,Hsiao-Wuen Hon, "Spoken Language Processing", PH PTR 2001.
4. Chen. Audiovisual speech processing. *Signal Processing Magazine*, 18:9–21, January 2001.
5. Gasser, M., Eck, D., and Port, R. Meter as mechanism: A neural network model that learns metrical patterns. Connection Science, 11(2):187–216, 1999.
6. N.K.Bose and P.Liang, "Neural Network Fundamentals with Graphs, Algorithms, and Applications", McGraw-Hill 1996.

Introducing Pitch Modification in Residual Excited LPC Based Tamil Text-to-Speech Synthesis

M. Vinu Krithiga and T.V. Geetha

Department of Computer Science and Engineering, Anna University, Chennai-25, India
vinu_krithiga@yahoo.com, rctamil@annauniv.edu

Abstract. This paper describes the improvement of the quality of Tamil text to speech using LPC based diphone database and the modification of syllable pitch through time scale modification. Speech is generated by concatenative speech synthesizer. Syllable units need to be concatenated such that spectral discontinuities are lowered at unit boundaries without degrading their quality. Smoothing is done by inserting suitable diphone at the concatenation boundary and changing the syllable pitch by performing time scale modification. The suitable diphone is chosen based on LPC coefficient files and their corresponding residuals.

1 Introduction

In this paper, the aim is to improve the quality of Tamil text to speech system. One of the important issues in Text-to-Speech systems is the quality of smoothing. This paper describes two different methods to improve joint and individual smoothness of speech units. Smoothing when speech is synthesized using concatenation method has been dealt with many ways. Among the important methods are Frequency-Domain Pitch-Synchronous Overlap-Add algorithm (FD-PSOLA), Time-Domain Pitch-Synchronous Overlap-Add algorithm (TD-PSOLA), Multi-Band Re-synthesis Pitch-Synchronous Overlap-Add model (MBR-PSOLA), Multi-Band Re-synthesis Overlap-Add (MBROLA) [1], [4], [6], [10]. All the PSOLA methods can be applied only for voiced sounds and when applied to unvoiced signal parts it generates a tonal noise. Text-to-Speech using MBROLA technique gives better quality when compared to PSOLA. MBROLA technique is preferred for Tamil TTS. MBROLA, a speech synthesizer based on the concatenation of diphones. It takes a list of phonemes as input, together with prosodic information (duration of phonemes and a piecewise linear description of pitch), and produces speech samples with bit depth 16 bits (linear), at the sampling frequency of the diphone database used, However MBROLA does not accept raw text as input. While PSOLA used syllables as speech unit and MBROLA used only diphones as the speech unit.

The aim of this work is to further improve smoothness compared to MBROLA method and to accommodate raw text as input. In the system described in this work speech output is obtained by concatenation of syllables. Syllable is an intermediate unit which is the intermediate form between the phones and the word level. They need to be concatenated such that spectral discontinuities are lowered at unit boundaries without degrading their quality. The corresponding diphone is inserted between

S. Manandhar et al. (Eds.): AACC 2004, LNCS 3285, pp. 177–183, 2004.

syllable-syllable concatenations to remove the discontinuity at the concatenation point. The diphone is chosen and the end segments of the diphone are smoothened by the LPC coefficient and residue value. Syllables are used as speech unit and diphones are inserted between the syllables to smooth the output. Thus in this work smoothing across phoneme boundaries is performed by appropriate addition of diphone based on LPC coefficients and residues. To further improve the quality of speech, intra syllable smoothing through pitch modification required for adjusting duration is performed in this work using time scale modification.

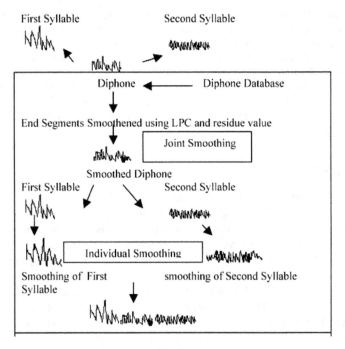

Fig. 1.

Figure 1 explains the steps followed to smooth the speech output of Tamil Text-to-Speech.

2 Linear Predictive Coding (LPC)

As already described smoothing at concatenation joints is performed using LPC. In general, LPC is used for representing the spectral envelope of a digital signal of speech using the information of a linear predictive model. It is one of the most powerful method for encoding good quality speech at a low bit rate and provides extremely accurate estimates of speech parameters [12].

LPC starts with the assumption that a speech signal is produced by a buzzer at the end of a tube. The glottis (the space between the vocal cords) produces the buzz, which is characterized by its intensity (loudness) and frequency (pitch). The vocal tract (the throat and mouth) forms the tube, which is characterized by its resonances, which are called formants. LPC analyzes the speech signal by estimating the formants and the intensity and frequency of the remaining buzz. The process of removing the formants is called inverse filtering, and the remaining signal is called the residue. The numbers which describe the formants and the residue can be stored. Because speech signals vary with time, this process is done on short chunks of the speech signal, which are called frames [12].

LPC is a very successful model used for smoothing and is mathematically efficient (IIR filters), remarkably accurate for voice (fits source-filter distinction) and satisfying physical interpretation (resonance). This model outputs a linear function of prior outputs and hence is called Linear Prediction [11]. Synthesis model splits the speech signal into LPC coefficients and residual signal. Since the LPC analysis is pitch synchronous, waveform interpolation could be used for the residual, but we found that the residual method is better due to the frame-to-frame variability of natural speech which would be lost if a series of residual frames were strictly interpolated [11]. Hence only the amplitude of the residual signal is scaled in order to smooth the energy of the output signal.

2.1 LPC Coefficient Representations

As mentioned earlier, LPC is used for transmitting spectral envelope information. Transmission of the filter coefficients directly is undesirable, since a very small error can distort the whole spectrum. Hence LPC values has to be represented as coefficients. More advanced representations of LPC values are log area ratios (LAR), line sprectrum pairs (LSP) decomposition and reflection coefficients. Of these, especially LSP decomposition has gained popularity, since it ensures stability of the predictor and localization of spectral errors for small coefficient deviations [12]. Hence in this work, LPC coefficients are represented using Line Spectrum Pairs (LSP) decomposition.

2.2 LPC in Tamil Text-to-Speech

This section describes how LPC is used to smooth the end segments of diphone in Tamil Text to Speech engine. Initially LPC coefficient and residue value of the end segments for each diphone corresponding to CV-CV combination are calculated from the recorded voice and maintained as an LPC database. The LPC and residue value is calculated using Matlab program. When input text is given in Tamil Text-to-Speech, Tamil text is split into syllables and diphone is chosen corresponding to Syllable-Syllable combination from the diphone database. The diphone is extracted depending on the first and the second syllable. In Tamil, if the first syllable is "ka" and the second syllable is "sa", the diphone "ka_s" is inserted between the concatenation point and the LPC value of the "ka_s" combination is calculated and the value is compared with the value of the already stored for "ka-sa" combination. The "ka_s" diphone is common if any one of the syllable "ka,kaa,ki,kee,ku,koo,ke,keq,kai,ko, koa,kov" comes first and the second syllable is "sa". Thus the diphones are grouped to reduce the database size. Tamil diphone database is built by storing the wave files corresponding to the syllable-syllable concatenation. A small end portion of the first syllable and a small start portion of the second syllable are extracted for each sylla-ble-syllable combination and the database is built. The diphone has been extracted for CV-CV combination, where C stands for consonant and V for vowel. A female speaker voice is recorded to develop diphone database. The speaker reads a set of carefully designed Tamil words, which have been constructed to elicit particular pho-netic effects. At present almost 1000 diphones have been created but around 3000 will probably be the final number of diphones.

LPC coefficient and residue value is calculated for end segments of the chosen diphone. This value is compared with the LPC value of already stored database. All coefficient values are compared to find the exact spectral features. If the LPC value of the syllable-syllable combination does not coincide with the LPC value of the stored segments, then the value is changed between the concatenation depending on the "CV-CV" combination to smooth the output.

The following Table 1 shows a sample of LPC coefficient values of the start segment for the diphones "ka_d", "kaa_r" and "ka_s".

Table 1. LPC coefficient values of the start segment for the diphones "ka_d", "kaa_r" and "ka_s"

Diphone	1	2	3	4	5
Ka_d	1.000000	-1.038448	-1.401614	-1.211756	-1.410790…
Kaa_r	1.000000	0.080596	-1.314152	-1.530058	-1.494284…
Ka_s	1.000000	-0.048233	-0.414213	0.008168	-0.088925…

The following Table 2 shows a sample of list of first syllable, second syllable and the corresponding diphone to be inserted between the syllable-syllable combination.

3   Time Scale Modification in Tamil Text-to-Speech

As mentioned earlier, to introduce individual smoothness for syllable in Tamil Text-to-Speech, time scale modification is carried out for each syllable. The pitch value for tamil syllable is changed by performing time scale modification. Duration value is calculated for each syllable using Praat software [10] and the value is maintained as database. A sample list is shown below. Syllable duration is calculated in milli seconds. The duration of a syllable affects the quality of sound produced. Duration, as a supra segmental feature, is a dependent feature as an element of intonation [3]. This feature operates in association with pitch pattern and accent. A pitch pattern has its own duration. Duration is one of the dimensions of intonation. It is counted at various segment levels, viz., syllable, word, utterance and pause [3]. It is also an effective factor as it exerts certain constraints over rhythm and tempo. The duration of sounds, syllables, words or phrases will have their share in the prosodic system of a language.

As per phase vocoder algorithm [13], pitch change is done by the following proce-dure. Let $y(n)$ be the segment (syllable) whose pitch has to be changed according to

Table 2. Shows the list of first syllable, second syllable and the corresponding diphone to be inserted between the syllable-syllable combination

First Syllable	Second Syllable	Diphone
Ka	Da	Ka_d
Ka	Sa	Ka_s
Ma	Za	Ma_z
Na	La	Na_l
Ta	Ma	Ta_m

some defined pitch profile information. Let $x(n)$ be each sub-segment and $x(n)$ has N number of sampling point and its period is T. Let the required period is T1. When T1 is greater than T, i.e., target pitch is lower than the original pitch, and then glottal period is extended by making a intermediate signal such that $x_{int}(n)$ is the concatenation of signals $x(n)$ and $\alpha x(n)$, where $0 < \alpha < 0.25$. Thus we will get a signal whose period is 2T having pitch half of the original and contains 2N numbers of sampling point. Now a window $W(n)$ is defined whose length is equal to the desired pitch period on the intermediate signal. Now concatenating those changed pitch periods generate the required segment. This procedure is adapted for Tamil syllables. One of the issues that were tackled was the fact that Tamil syllables in general were of variable duration.

Matlab program has been written to change the duration value. The following examples shows the duration value for some sample words.

Examples

Word 1 :	mozhi
Syllable	Duration
Mo	174
Zhi	458

Word 2 :	oli
Syllable	Duration
O_l	267
li	482

Word 3 :	inimai
Syllable	Duration
I_n	290
Ni	268
Mai	557

Word 4 :	namadhu
Syllable	Duration
Na	232
Ma	209
Dhu	435

4 Experimental Results

Speech output of Tamil text to speech based on simple concatenation technique is compared with the speech output of Tamil Text to Speech using residual excited LPC based synthesis. The quality is improved. The required diphone is inserted between CV-CV combinations and thus the spectral discontinuities are lowered at unit boundaries.

Example:
  An example comparison is done for the word "kadi"

  "kadi" Before smoothing

  "kadi" After smoothing

Fig. 2. Experimental result for word "kadi"

  It is seen from figure 2 that the preceding "ka" waveform takes on the characteristics of the succeeding "di" waveform.

5 Conclusion

The quality and smoothness of Tamil text to speech output has been improved. At present, 1000 diphones have been created. LPC based diphone selection improves the quality of Text to speech synthesis than simple concatenation of syllables. Efforts were taken to develop the complete diphone database and to create a table, which includes the duration value for all the syllable-syllable combination. The diphone database was developed for CV-CV combination and further improvement can be done by developing diphone database for CV, VC combination.

References

1. R. Muralishankar and A G Ramakrishnan (2000), *"Robust Pitch detection using DCT based Spectral Autocorrelation"*, Conference on Multimedia Processing, Chennai, Aug. 13-15, pp. 129-132.
2. R Muralishankar and A G Ramakrishnan (2001), *"Human Touch to Tamil Speech Synthesizer "*, Tamilnet 2001, Kuala Lumpur, Malaysia, pp. 103 - 109, 2001.

3. Soumen Chowdhury, A.K Datta, B.B.Chaudhuri (2001), *"Study of Intonation Patterns for text reading in standard colloquial Bengali"*, Proceedings of IWSMSP-2001.

4. A.Bandyopadhyay (2002), *"Some Important aspects of Bengali Speech Synthesis System"*, IEMCT JUNE ,Tata McGraw-Hill.

5. Aniruddha Sen (2001), *"Speech Synthesis in Indian Languages"*, Pre-Workshop Tutorial on Speech and Music Signal Processing IWSMSP-2001.

6. A. G. Ramakrishnan (2001), *"Issues in standardization for Text to Speech in Tamil"*, Tamilnet 2001, Kuala Lumpur, Malaysia.

7. Douglas O'Shaughnessy (2000), *"Speech Communication - Human and Machine"*, Second Edition, IEEE press.

8. G. L. Jayavardhana Rama, A. G. Ramakrishnan, V. Vijay Venkatesh, and R. Muralishankar, (2001) *"Thirukkural: a text-to-speech synthesis system"*, Proc. Tamil Internet 2001, Kuala Lumpur, pp. 92-97, August 26-28.

9. Min Tang, Chao Wang, Stephanie Seneff (2001), *"Voice Transformations: From Speech Synthesis to Mamalian Vocalizations"*, Conference on Speech Communication and Technology, Denmark.

10. R. Muralishankar, A. G. Ramakrishnan and Prathibha P (2002), *"Dynamic Pitch changes for concatenative synthesis"*, SPPRA, Greece, 2002.

11. S. Varho and P. Alku (1997), *A Linear Predictive Method Using Extrapolated Samples for Modelling of Voiced Speech*, Proceedings of IEEE Workshop on Applications of Signal Processing to Audio and Acoustics, New Paltz, NY, Session IV, pp. 13-16.

12. Susanna Varho (2001), *"New Linear Predictive Methods for Digital Speech Processing"*.

13. John Garas and Piet C.W.Sommen (1980), *"Time/Pitch Scaling Using The Constant-Q Phase Vocoder"*, Eindhoven University of Technology

14. "Issues in high quality {LPC} analysis and synthesis" Hunt, M. and Zwierynski D. and Carr R Eurospeech 89, Vol 2 pp 348-351, Paris, France

Separation Performance of ICA Algorithms on FECG and MECG Signals Contaminated by Noise

S.D. Parmar[1], H.K. Patel[1], and J.S. Sahambi[2]

[1] Shree U.V. Patel College of Engineering, Kherva 382711, India
sargam_parmar@yahoo.com
[2] IIT Guwahati, India
jssahambi@iitg.ernet.in

Abstract. This paper evaluates the performance of some major ICA algorithms like Bell and Sejnowski's infomax algorithm, Cardoso's Joint Approximate Diagonalization of Eigen matrices (JADE) and Comon's algorithm in a biomedical blind source separation problem. Independent signals representing Fetal ECG (FECG) and Maternal ECG (MECG) are generated and then mixed linearly in the presence of white or pink noise to simulate a recording of electrocardiogram. ICA has been used to extract FECG, but very less literature is available on the performance, i.e., how does it behave in clinical environment. So there is a used to evaluate performance of these algorithms in Biomedical. To quantify the performance of ICA algorithms, two scenarios, i.e., (a) different amplitude ratios of simulated maternal and fetal ECG, (b) different values of additive white gaussian noise or pink noise, were investigated. Higher order and Second order performances were measured by performance index and signal-to-error ratio respectively. The selected ICA algorithms separate the white and pink noises equally well. The performance of the Comon's algorithm is slightly less compared to the other two algorithms.

1 Introduction

The ECG of an adult describes the electrical activity of the heart. It is an important tool for the physician for identifying abnormalities in the heart activity. In the same way it is important to obtain the FECG and to trace problems in its heart activity. Most methods for acquiring the FECG are invasive which require placing an electrode on the fetal scalp. This procedure is available during delivery time only. It is important to try and find non-invasive techniques for earlier diagnosis. Obtaining FECG from recordings of electrodes on the mother's skin is fundamentally equivalent to the adult ECG but there are more difficulties that arise. The FECG is generated from a very small heart so the signal amplitude is low. Noise from electromyograpic activity affects the signal due to its low voltage. Another interesting source is the maternal ECG (MECG), which can be 5-1000 times higher in its intensity. The MECG shows in all the electrodes, thoracic and abdominal. There is no place to put an electrode on the mother's

S. Manandhar et al. (Eds.): AACC 2004, LNCS 3285, pp. 184–190, 2004.

skin and to receive just the fetal signal without the mother signal. In all cases where the FECG is observed, the MECG is higher in magnitude. So eliminating the MECG from the recorded signal is very important [1].

Technically, the above problem can be thought of as a set of desired and undesired signals linearly mixed to produce another set of body surface signals. It is assumed that these signals are non-gaussian (except the random noise signal) and independent. ICA decomposes the mixed signals into as statistically independent components as possible. ICA has been used to extract FECG [2,3], but very less literature is available on the performance, i.e., how does it behave in clinical environment. This needs an evaluation of its performance in clinical environment. Several ICA algorithms have been proposed. In this paper, we evaluates the performance of some major ICA algorithms like Bell & Sejnowski's infomax algorithm [4], Cardoso's Joint Approximate Diagonalization of Eigen matrices (JADE) [5] and Comon's algorithm [6] in a biomedical blind source separation problem. The signals, which is best suited for ICA, are designed to be biologically motivated for independent FECG and MECG. They are linearly mixed. The ICA separation produces independent FECG and MECG estimates.

2   Methodology

We consider the classical ICA model with instantaneous mixing

$$\mathbf{x} = \mathbf{As} + \mathbf{n} \tag{1}$$

where the sources $\mathbf{s} = [s_1, s_2, ..., s_n]^T$ are mutually independent random variables and $\mathbf{A}_{n \times n}$ is an unknown invertible mixing matrix and noise $\mathbf{n} = [n_1, n_2, ..., n_n]^T$. The goal is to find only from observations, $\mathbf{x}$, a matrix $\mathbf{W}$ such that the output

$$\mathbf{y} = \mathbf{Wx} \tag{2}$$

is an estimate of the possible scaled and permutated source vectors.

Jutten and Herault provided one of the first significant approaches to the problem of blind separation of instantaneous linear mixtures [7]. Since then, many different approaches have been attempted by numerous researches using neural networks, artificial learning, higher order statistics, minimization of mutual information, beam forming and adaptive noise cancellation, each claiming various degrees of success.

In this research, some major ICA algorithms like Bell & Sejnowski's infomax algorithm [4], Cardoso's Joint Approximate Diagonalization of Eigen matrices (JADE)[5] and Comon's algorithm [6] were used.

2.1   Signal Generation

The observed signals (Fig 1) at the electrodes were simulated by taking two different ECG signals from the MIT-BIH (Massachusetts Institute of Technology-Beth Israel Hospital Arrhythmia Laboratory) database [8]. These signals are sampled at 360 $\mathbf{H}_Z$. To simulate real conditions, the second signal (assumed as FECG) was 5 or 10 times less in amplitude and with double the number of QRS peaks compared to the first (assumed as MECG). Removing the mean of the original ECG signals and normalizing the two ECG signals to unity. Then the desired maternal to fetal amplitude ratio can be obtained by multiplying the signal with that constant.

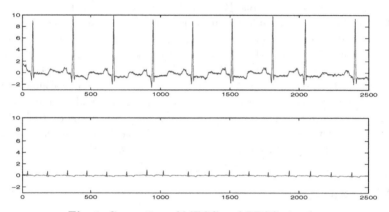

Fig. 1. Generation of MECG and FECG signals

2.2 Linear Mixing and Noise

We have set the mixing coefficient between the MECG and FECG signals to

$$\mathbf{A} = \begin{pmatrix} -0.1430 & -2.2008 \\ 0.9943 & -0.8061 \end{pmatrix}$$

The white noise was generated by MATLAB. In the body many electrical signals are time correlated and would be modelled better by colored noise instead of white noise [9]. The pink noise was created with a Fourier domain generator with the power spectrum given by

$$P_n(f)\alpha f^{-\beta}; \beta > 0 \tag{3}$$

and $\beta = 1$. These noise records(consider as $\mathbf{n}$ in Equation 1) were added to the mixed signals with a specified signal to noise ratio (SNR) (which is measured with respect to the mixed signals in the given channel). In this way, the SNR in both channels are the same, but the amplitudes are quite different. The results in our two channels are the simulated FECG and simulated MECG.

2.3 Performance Evaluation

To quantify the higher order performance of the demixing we use the performance index, *PI*. This is a measure on the global system matrix $\mathbf{P}=\mathbf{WA}$ suitable for the degeneracy conditions $\mathbf{W} = \mathbf{A}^{-1}$ and is calculated as

$$PI = \sum_{i=1}^{n} \{ (\sum_{k=1}^{n} \frac{|p_{ik}|^2}{max_j |p_{ij}|^2} - 1) + (\sum_{k=1}^{n} \frac{|p_{ki}|^2}{max_j |p_{ji}|^2} - 1) \} \qquad (4)$$

where p_{ij} is the $(i,j)^{th}$ element of the global system matrix $\mathbf{P} = \mathbf{WA}$ and $max_j p_{ij}$ represents the maximum value among the elements in the ith row vector of $\mathbf{P}$, $max_j p_{ji}$ does the maximum value among the elements in the ith column vector of $\mathbf{P}$. When perfect signal separation is carried out, the performance index PI is zero.

Since we are looking at the estimation of the FECG and MECG signals, we also consider the SER, which is a second order measure. The SER was obtained by using the following relation

$$SER = 10 \log_{10} (\frac{E|s(t)|^2}{E|e(t)|^2}) \qquad (5)$$

where $s(t)$ is the desired signal and $e(t) = \widehat{s(t)} - s(t)$ is the error (or noise to be more accurate). Here $\widehat{s(t)}$ is the estimated source signal and $\widehat{s(t)}$ and $s(t)$ should be at the same energy level and phase while calculating e(t).

3   Experimental Results and Discussion

The SER and Performance Index results from the ICA algorithms separation of our simulation are shown in Fig 2, 3, 4, and 5. ICA algorithms separate the white and pink noise equally well. By processing the data we clearly achieve a better second order estimate of the FECG independent of the noise color. In fact, the SER of the extracted FECG is equivalent to the SNR specified for the added noise up to 20 dB level,but different output SER between 20 to 30 dB. In this duration JADE perform well, which gives more output SER compare to Bell's and Comon's algorithms. All the algorithms are able to extract FECG considerably if the amount of input SNR is of the order of 10 dB or less. Even if the SNR approach 0 dB all the algorithms are still able to extract the R wave.

The performance index of the performance matrix $\mathbf{P=WA}$ indicates the same decay in higher order separation. As the noise contamination becomes dominant, the demixing performance is poorer between 0 to 5 dB. Performance index is zero means good separation. Again JADE have good performance index, which tends to zero when input SNR in dB increase. The performance of the Comon's algorithm is slightly less compared to the other two algorithms. JADE algorithm has the least computational cost and also no parameters to tune. The accuracy of Bell's algorithm is highly dependent upon the sweeps, or the iterations, to update the weights. This can give better results but with a higher computational cost and slower speed.

4   Conclusions

In this paper we have calculated the performance of the JADE, Bell and Comon's ICA algorithms in a simple electro physiologically motivated BSS problem to extract the FECG. Using simulated independent signals from the pregnant woman

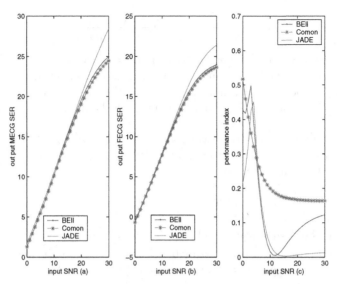

Fig. 2. MECG to FECG ratio 10:1 and Gaussian noise added. (a) And (b) Show Extracted output *SER* of MECG and FECG. (c) Shows Performance Index of three algorithms

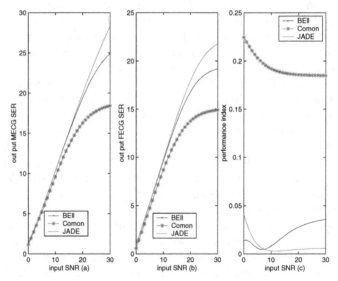

Fig. 3. MECG to FECG ratio 5:1 and Gaussian noise added. (a) And (b) Show Extracted output *SER* of MECG and FECG. (c) Shows Performance Index of three algorithms

skin (FECG and MECG), we observe that the BSS performance of the algorithms are unaffected by noise as long as the added noise does not exceed the

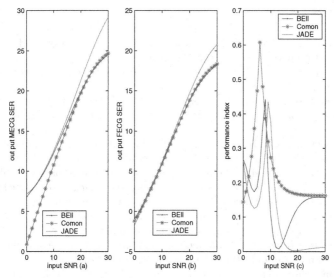

Fig. 4. MECG to FECG ratio 10:1 and Pink noise added. (a) And (b) Show Extracted output *SER* of MECG and FECG. (c) Shows Performance Index of three algorithms

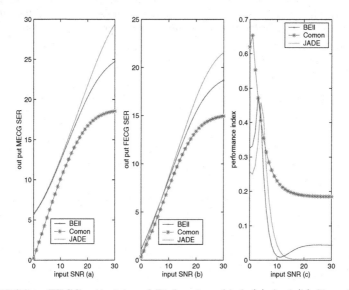

Fig. 5. MECG to FECG ratio 5:1 and Pink noise added. (a) And (b) Show Extracted output *SER* of MECG and FECG. (c) Shows Performance Index of three algorithms

corruption due to mixing. By processing the data we clearly achieve a better estimate of the FECG independent of the noise color. The performance of the JADE algorithm is slightly better compared to the other two algorithms.

References

1. Amit Kam and Arnon Cohen, "Maternal ECG ellimination and Foetal ECG detection-Comparision of several Algorithms," *Procee. of the 20th anual international conference of theIEEE Engineeing in Medicine and Biology Society.*, vol. 20, No.1, pp-174-177, 1998.
2. V.Zarzoso and A.Nandi, "Noninvasive fetal ECG extraction: Blind separation versus adaptive noise cancellation," *IEEE trans, Biomed Engg.*, vol 48, No1, pp. 12-18, 2001.
3. Seungjin choi, A.Chichocki, s.Amari, "flexible independent component analysis", *journal of VLSI Signal Processing, kluwer academic publishers.*, boston, 2000.
4. A. Bell and T.Sejnowski, "An information maximization approach to blind source separation and blind deconvolution," *Neural Computing.*, 7, pp. 1129-1159, 1995.
5. J.F. Cardoso and A. Souloumiac, "Blind beamforming for non-gaussian signals," *IEE Proceeding-F.*, vol.140, no. 6, pp. 362-370, Dec-1993.
6. P. Comon, " Independent component analysis, a new concept?," *Signal processing (Special Issue Higher Order Statistics)*, vol. 36, pp. 287-314, April 1994.
7. C.Jutten and J.Herault,"Blind separation of sources part I: An adaptive algorithm based on neuromimatic architecture," *Signal Processing.*, vol.24, pp. 1-10, July 1991.
8. MIT-BIH Database Distribution. [Online]. "Available: http://ecg.mit.edu".
9. M.Potter, N.Gadhok, and W.Kinsner, " Separation performance of ICA on simulated EEG and ECG signals contaminated by noise," *Proc. of the 2002 IEEE canadian conf. on Electrical and computing engg.*, pp.1099-1104, 2002.

Evaluation of BER/PER Performance
of a FLAMINGO Network

Satya Prasad Majumder and Sanjoy Dey

Department of Electrical and Electronics Engineering,
Bangladesh University of Engineering and Technology,
Dhaka-1000, Bangladesh
spmajumder@eee.buet.ac.bd, odhom@hotmail.com

Abstract. IP over WDM has been investigated in FLAMINGO – Flexible multiwavelength optical local access network supporting multimedia broadband services, a multidisciplinary project Involving Dutch research institutes and led by CTIT – University of Twente. Flamingo's focus on access networks comes from the tendency of the 80/20 rules, which says that 80% of the traffic is local and 20% is external. In this paper we evaluate the BER/PER performance of a FLAMINGO network. Here we consider the influence of receiver noise, photodetector shot noise, crosstalk and beat noise components carrying out of the beating of the signal with accumulated amplifiers spontaneous emission (ASE) and crosstalk developed at each access point or bridge. We carry out the performance evaluation at a bit rate of 10 Gbit/s which shows that the packet error rate (PER) and bit error rate (BER) both are limited by a signal spontaneous beat noise and crosstalk.

1 Introduction

The present E-world is facing a rapid growth in bandwidth demand due to the Internet explosion, which may only be satisfied by optical networks and particularly by using the wavelength division multiplexing (WDM) technology. WDM is a technology which can support more than a hundred of wavelength channels in a single optical fiber. So many researches have been carried out in the field of optical circuit switching and wavelength routing particularly for Metropolitan Area Network (MAN). FLAMINGO is a hybrid optoelectronic metropolitan ring network which was developed to support the group communication. It is based on packet switching technique. As in this network optical cells travel in a very high bit rate so they accumulate noise such as ASE noise, crosstalk and power losses. So the bit error rate (BER) and packet error rate (PER) performance evaluation of this network have become an important issue.

In this paper we evaluate the bit error rate (BER) and packet error rate (PER) of a FLAMINGO network in the presence of crosstalk and ASE noise.

2 Architecture of the Network

The basic architecture of FLAMINGO network is shown in Fig.1 [1]. FLAMINGO network [2] consists of time slotted interconnected city rings employing the multichannel nature of WDM. Each ring has N number of Access Points (APs) where N may be greater than the number of channels, W.

S. Manandhar et al. (Eds.): AACC 2004, LNCS 3285, pp. 191–197, 2004.
© Springer-Verlag Berlin Heidelberg 2004

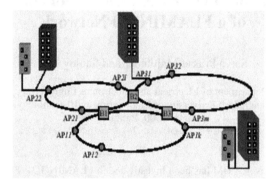

Fig. 1. Basic architecture of FLAMINGO (AP=access point, B=Intelligent Bridge) [1]

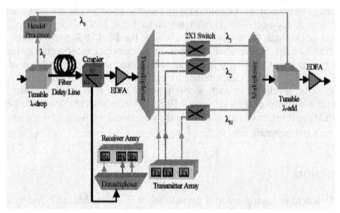

Fig. 2. Architecture of AP [1]

Access to time slots is made possible through the Access Points (APs) and one ring is connected with other rings via the bridges. Each AP is equipped with a fixed transmitter (FTx) and with array of receivers (ARxs). The W wavelength channels are used to carry payload information while a single extra wavelength channel is used to carry control information. The total bandwidth of all the channels is divided into fixed length time slots. The slots on the control channel are sent slightly ahead of their corresponding payload slots. The control slot informs the AP whether a corresponding payload slot on a wavelength is empty for transmitting data or not. An AP can transmit on only one wavelength and can receive on all wavelengths simultaneously. The APs are designed to support all-optical multicasting. To achieve this, a 90:10 optical power coupler is introduced between the fiber delay line (used to offer buffer at the AP) and the EDFA as in Fig.2 [1]. At the intelligent bridges optical buffers are used to transfer data from one ring to the other which includes large power losses and crosstalk. Here in this study the APs are considered with a single buffer as in uniform traffic a single buffer shows the same performance as the infinite buffer shows. Here we consider that the traffic is uniform that is all APs are equally active and generate a new packet at each slot with the same probability g. It is also assumed that the destination of packets generated at each AP is chosen uniformly among all APs in the network and independently in each slot.

3 BER/PER Performance

In this section we present an analysis to find the BER/PER in the presence of ASE and crosstalk. Here it is assumed that the tagged bit of a packet passes through n number of hops and collects cross-talk at the routing switches and ASE noise from the optical amplifiers. There is one EDFA located at the input of the AP for compensating the loss resulting from header-recognition tapping loss, alignment loss, add-drop coupler loss, fiber-loss and routing block loss. The EDFA has a power gain G which is constant for all input powers up to the saturation level. The ASE noise which is added at the output of each amplifier is an additive white Gaussian noise with spectral density $hv_0n_{sp}(G-1)$ where h is the Planck's constant, v_0 is the optical frequency with wavelength 1550 nm and n_{sp} is the spontaneous emission factor with value of 1.3. The amplifier's gain G is so chosen that it exactly compensate the per-hop loss. Thus G can be expressed as [3],

$$G = L_{hr}L_{al}L_{ad}L_{r}L_{f} \tag{1}$$

where L_{hr} is the header recognition loss with value of 1 dB, L_{al} is the alignment loss with value of 10 dB, L_{ad} is the add-drop coupler loss with value of 3 dB, L_r is the routing-block loss and $L_r = 3x (x=2$ for this network). L_f is the fiber-loss and $L_f = \alpha L$, where $\alpha = 0.25$ dB/km and L is the distance between two consecutive nodes in km. The accumulated ASE power density of the test bit while traveling from one hop to other hop can be written as [3],

$$N_{ase}(1) = hvn_{sp}(G-1) / (L_{hr}L_{al}L_{ad}) \tag{2}$$

Then the accumulated ASE power at the n-th hop can be expressed as [3],

$$N_{ase}(n) = nN_{ase}(1) \tag{3}$$

It is necessary for the newly injected packets to have the same power level as hopping packets. So the transmitter should satisfy the following equation,

$$P_{tx}L_{hr}L_{al} \leq P_{sat} \tag{4}$$

where P_{tx} is the transmitter power and P_{sat} is saturation output power. To achieve the maximum optical Signal-to-noise ratio (SNR), we set $P_{sat} = P_{tx}L_{hr}L_{al}$. The conditional bit-error-rate (BER) depends on the average number of hops, H. It is assumed that there is no polarization dependency for gains and losses. Using Personick's formula, the conditional BER can be expressed as [3],

$$\text{BER}(n) = Q\left(\frac{1}{\sqrt{\sigma_{s-xt}^2 + \sigma_{s-sp}^2 + \sigma_{sp-sp}^2} + \sqrt{\sigma_{sp-sp}^2}} \right) \tag{5}$$

$\sigma_{s-xt}^2, \sigma_{s-sp}^2, \sigma_{sp-sp}^2$ are the variances of noise with signal-crosstalk beat, signal-ASE beats and ASE-ASE beats correspondingly.

$$Q(y) = \frac{1}{\sqrt{2\pi}} \int_y^\infty e^{-t^2/2} \ dt$$

The variance of noise with signal-crosstalk beat can be expressed as [3],

$$\sigma_{s-xt}^2 = \frac{E[n_{xt}]}{2} \, a \, \eta(\rho) \tag{6}$$

Here a is switch crosstalk factor, $E[n_{xt}]$ is the average number of crosstalk and $E[n_{xt}]$ can be written as [3],

$$E[n_{xt}] = xn_d + u\{N_x - (xn_d)\} \tag{7}$$

where $n_d = [\max(n - H_{min}, 0) / C]$, H_{min} is value of the average number of hops at loads approaching zero, C is the number of hops added by each deflection, N_x is the number of points along the crosstalk arising path, u is the input slot utilization probability and u is given by[4],

$$u = \frac{[r^2 + g^2(1-r)^2]^{1/2} - r}{g(1-r)^2} \tag{8}$$

Here r can be obtained as $r = 1/H$ and g is the generation probability. In relation (6), $\eta(\rho)$ is the beat efficiency factor which can be expressed as [3],

$$\eta(\rho) = \frac{2}{\rho^2} [-3\gamma_e - 3\ln(\rho) + 3\mathrm{Ci}(\rho) + 2\rho\mathrm{Si}(\rho) - 1 + 2\cos(\rho) - \mathrm{sinc}(\rho/\pi)] \tag{9}$$

Here $\rho = 2\pi\Delta F/R$ where $\Delta F/R$ is the normalized sweep range and ΔF is the channel separation. $\gamma_e = 0.5772\ldots$ is Eular's gamma, $\mathrm{Si}(\rho)$ is the sine integral and $\mathrm{Ci}(\rho)$ is the cosine integral.

The variance of noise with signal-ASE beats can be expressed as [3],

$$\sigma_{s-sp}^2 \cong 2\frac{N_{ase}(1)}{P_{rx}} nR \tag{10}$$

Here P_{rx} is the received mark power and it is obtained as,

$$P_{rx} = \frac{P_{sat}}{G} \tag{11}$$

The variance of noise with ASE-ASE beats can be expressed as [3],

$$\sigma_{sp-sp}^2 \cong (4b-1)(\frac{\sigma_{s-sp}^2}{4})^2 \tag{12}$$

Here $b = B_0/R$ where B_0 is the optical bandwidth. Normally it is considered that the optical bandwidth is five times the bit rate.

The unconditional BER can be expressed as [4],

$$\text{BER} = \sum_{1}^{\infty} \text{BER}(n) P_h(n) \tag{13}$$

where $P_h(n)$ is the probability mass function of number of hops h [4].

The unconditional packet error rate (PER) is obtained [3] by conditioning on the number of hops n taken by a typical cell in the network.

$$\text{PER} = \sum_{n=1}^{\infty} [1 - (1 - BER(n))^{N_b}] P_h(n) \tag{14}$$

where N_b is the number of bits for each cell. For calculating PER it is assumed that errors are independent bit by bit.

4   Results and Discussion

To carry out the computation it is considered that each fiber ring is of 60 km long having 12 APs and there is no multicast receiver in the network. Results are evaluated at a bit rate of 10 Gbit/s. Plots of BER versus number of hops are shown in Fig. 3 for different values of switch crosstalk factors at $P_{tx} = -1$ dBm & g=1(which indicates the full load). It is noticed that there is a significant improvement in BER performance at a given number of hops with the decrease of switch cross-talk and at a given BER the number of hops that can be traveled by a cell is limited by switch crosstalk factor. For example, at a BER of 10^{-9} with a transmitter power of -1 dBm, the number of hops can be increased from ~6 hops to ~54 hops by decreasing the switch crosstalk factor from 14 dBm to 23 dBm.

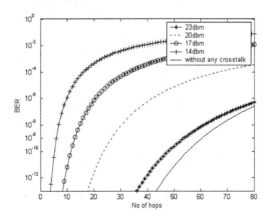

Fig. 3. BER versus number of hops with different switch crosstalk factors and with no crosstalk ($P_{tx} = -1$ dBm, $\Delta F/R = 4$, g =1)

In Fig.4 PER versus number of hops for different switch crosstalk factors are plotted (here $P_{tx} = -1$ dBm, cell size=1500 bytes, g=1). Like BER, PER also shows a tendency of improved performance at a lower switch crosstalk factor for a given number of hops. In Fig.5 PER versus number of hops for three different cell sizes, namely, 44, 552 and 1500 bytes are plotted. Because in the original FLAMINGO project it was found that the network shows a better performance with these three types of cell sizes, which travel in the ring one after another consecutively. The percentage of these three types of cells in the ring equaled 50%, 30% and 20%. From the figure it is found that the cell of size 44 bytes has the highest hop gain for the same PER level. For instance, at a PER of 10^{-9} with P_{tx}=-1 dBm the cell of 44 bytes has a hop gain of 41 hops where it is only 36 hops for the cells of 1500 bytes size.

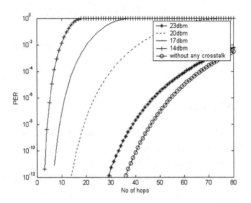

Fig. 4. PER versus number of hops with cell size=1500 byte, Δ *F/R* = 4, P_{tx}=-1 dBm, g=1

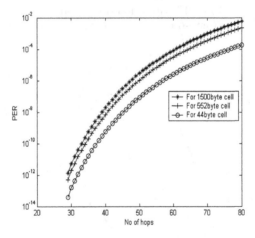

Fig. 5. PER versus No of hops for different cell size with Δ *F/R* = 4, P_{tx}=-1dBm at g=1

In Fig.6, PER versus number of hops are plotted for different sweep ranges where P_{tx}=-1 dbm, g=1 and cell size=1500 bytes. Here it is found that with an increase in the sweep range (that is increasing the channel separation), there is a noticeable improvement in the PER performance for a given number of hops. It is because of the reason that higher sweep range can reduce the dominant signal-crosstalk beats. Further it is found that the number of hops that can be traversed by a cell corresponding to given PER can be increased by increasing the sweep range.

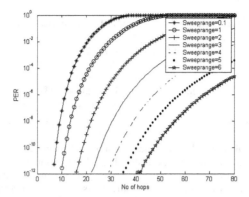

Fig. 6. PER versus number of hops for various sweep ranges with cell-size of 1500 bytes, P_{tx} = −1 dBm at g=1

5   Conclusion

We evaluate the BER / PER performance of a FLAMINGO network for different switch cross talk factors, different cell sizes and for different sweep ranges at a bit rate of 10 Gbit/s. It is found that the network shows a better BER/PER performance at higher sweep ranges, lower switch crosstalk and with small cell-size. Crosstalk and ASE noise limit the allowable number of hops at a given BER/PER.

References

1. D. Dey et al, "A Metropolitan Optical Network with support for Multicasting in the Optical domain", Proceedings 2001 IEEE/LEOS Symposium Benelux chapter.
2. D. Dey et al, "An All-Optical WDM Packet-Switched Network Architecture with Support for Group Communication". In Proc. of IEEE Int. Conf. on Networking (ICN), France, Jul-01.
3. Alberto Bononi,"Weakly versus strongly multihop space-division optical networks" IEEE J.lightwave Technology, 16 (1998) 4, pp 490-500.
4. A. Bononi,G.A Castanon,O.K Tonguz, "BER performance of multiwavelenth optical cross-connected networks with deflection routing" IEEE Proc.Comm, 144(1997) 2, pp 114-119.

Fault Tolerance Studies for Wormhole Routing in Multiconnected Double-Loop Networks

Ramesh Vasappanavara[1], Sasikiran Kandula[2], and Nimmagadda Chalamaiah[3]

[1] Dept. of CSE, GVPCOE, VIZAG-41
ramesh_vasappanavara@yahoo.com
[2] GVPCOE, VIZAG-41
[3] Dept. of CSE, JNTU, Kakinada-03
nchalm@yahoo.com

Abstract. MCDL networks are generally preferred owing to their grater reliability and less latency in packet transfer. Though routing in these networks can be done through different techniques, the wormhole routing algorithm is generally used because of its' low buffer requirements. However, wormhole routing does not guarantee deadlock or livelock free routing. Moreover, additional algorithms to deal with faults in the network need to be studied. We propose in this paper a simple fault tolerant algorithm that requires only local fault information and works well for small networks with few faults. A MCDL network has been simulated and the variance in the performance of the algorithm to changes in network configuration and network traffic is studied.

1 Introduction

A weighted double-loop network G $(n; h_1, h_2; w_1, w_2)$ is a directed graph with vertex set $Z_n = \{0, 1 \ldots n-1\}$ and edge at $E = E_1 \cup E_2$ where n, h_1, h_2 are positive integers and w_1, w_2 are positive real numbers denoting the weights of edges in E_1 and E_2 respectively.

$$E_1 = \{(u, u+h_1) \mid u \text{ belongs to } Z_n\} \tag{1}$$

$$E_1 = \{(u, u+h_1) \mid u \text{ belongs to } Z_n\} \tag{2}$$

In a double-loop network there are two types of links h_1 and h_2 where every link h_1 connects k^{th} node to node $(k\pm h_1)$ mod n and link h_2 connects node k to node $(k\pm h_2)$ mod n. If either h_1 or h_2 is equal to 1, then we have ring network with some additional links added homogenously to it. These networks are called Multi Connected Double-Loop Networks (MCDL) and are denoted as G (n; h, 1). In our study, we concentrate on algorithms to achieve fault tolerance in Multi Connected Double-Loop Networks.

The Wormhole routing technique is being widely used in recent multi computers. In this technique a packet is divided into a sequence of fixed-size units of data called 'flits'. If a communication channel transmits the first flit of a message, it must transmit all the remaining flits of the same message before transmitting flits of other messages. However, each flit can be forwarded independent of other flits i.e. flits can be transmitted in any order.

A deadlock can occur if more than one packet competes for the same channel, and some parts of packet, flits, get blocked in some channel. If the two messages mutually

S. Manandhar et al. (Eds.): AACC 2004, LNCS 3285, pp. 198–204, 2004.

block and none of them can forward to its destination, a 'routing deadlock' is said to have occurred. Congestion in the networks is another predominant problem in worm-hole routing. It generally results when any node is generating traffic much more traf-fic than what the network can handle. Moreover, the network should be made tolerant to faults. Achieving fault tolerance is much more difficult owing to the constraints inherent in the wormhole routing technique. One way out from these problems is to simulate multiple virtual channels on each physical channel and to enforce a pre–defined order in the allocation of the virtual channel to the messages. Since worm-hole technique has been found to achieve high throughput, low latency message de-livery, avoidance of deadlocks and starvation and ability to perform well under all traffic patterns, it is highly preferred.

Fault-Tolerance Studies
An extensive amount of study has been done in the area of fault-tolerance [3] and algorithms to overcome faults have been proposed. The algorithms vary on the basis of how the fault information is available in the network. This information of faults can be global Information i.e every processor has the faulty node information and local knowledge i.e only nodes adjacent to the faulty node have the faulty node informa-tion.

In local fault information, since the adjacent node knows that the next node to which the packet is to be forward is faulty, it can use an alternate path or link to route the packet to its destination. If we are using global knowledge of faults, the fault in-formation is used at the packet's source processor to determine its shortest path. We try to bypass a faulty node or link and use an alternate path without adversely affect-ing the length of the path.

2   Background and Related Studies

A fault can be either a node fault or a link fault. Boppana et al. in [3] deal with fault tolerance algorithms in mesh networks using wormhole routing. The algorithms used four virtual channels and are deadlock and livelock free. However the shape of the f-rings was restricted to rectangle. Later algorithms have been proposed that need only three virtual channels. Park, Youn and Bose in [4] extend the study by relaxing the restriction on the shape of the f-rings. [4] proposes algorithms using four virtual channels and can work on more relaxed f-rings. They have also proposed algorithm that works with three virtual for more restricted f-rings. In this paper, concepts of convex, concave and plain nodes have been introduced.

Based on the number of faulty links incident on it, a node can be classified into the following:
a) Convex node – no faulty link is incident
b) Concave node – exactly two faulty links are incident
c) Plain node – only one faulty link is incident.

In a 2D mesh, a node in column a and row b is represented as (a, b) and a link con-necting node (a, b) and (c, d) is represented as (a, b) $\leftrightarrow$ (c, d). If $l1 = (x_a, y_b)$ $\leftrightarrow$ (x_a, y_{b+1}) and $l2 = (x_c, y_d)$ $\leftrightarrow$ (x_c, y_{d+1}) are any two faulty links from inside the f-ring, then every node between $l1$ and $l2$ is faulty if $x_a = x_c$.

For all nodes in a portion of the f-ring, if their y value does not decrease (respec-tively increase) as x value increases, the portion is called monotonically increasing (respectively monotonically decreasing). If a side is monotonically increasing first and then monotonically decreasing then it is called a convex edge. Similarly, if an edge is decreasing first and then monotonically increasing then it is called a concave edge. It the edge consists of any combination of monotonically increasing portions and monotonically decreasing portions than it is called a zigzag side.

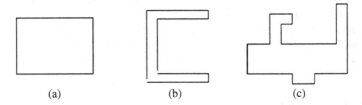

(a)   (b)   (c)

In the above figures, figure (a) is an example of a convex ring, figure (b) a concave ring and figure (c) a zigzag ring. Algorithms proposed in [3] deal with f-rings of only type (a) whereas that of [4] can handle both (a) and (b). Figure (c) cannot be handled by either of the algorithms.

3   Methodology

In our study we have tried to simulate routing in the presence of faults both with global and local fault information. The algorithms used are discussed in [2]. In global fault information, we tried to maintain a central table containing all the faulty node information. Whenever any node generates a packet, it has to access the table for faulty node information and then compute the shortest path for the packet, bypassing all the faulty nodes with minimum increase in the path. But maintaining a central table led to a bottleneck and the performance was found to deteriorate with increase in network size and network traffic. We attempted to maintain a separate table at each of the nodes. But even in this case, at regular intervals all the tables need to be updated, thus creating greater overhead. Some other problems have also been observed, namely,

1. If the faulty information had to be updated dynamically, then the behaviour of the system during the transient period was not predictable and resulted in mis-routing of packets.
2. The shortest path was computed at the source node, before transmitting the packet. However, if one of the nodes in the packet's computed path turned faulty, after a certain instance of time, the packet was blocked. To prevent such blocking, we can verify and recompute the path (if necessary) of the packet after every updation. But verifying all the packets after every updation can cause large delays and is far from optimal. Hence global fault information is not preferred.

In fault tolerance using local fault information, each node has information about whether, any of its' adjacent nodes is faulty. It is assumed that all faulty nodes are known and that there is no change in the status of the node during the simulation. The path of the packet is computed and placed in the packet's header at the packet's source. At each intermediate node, the header is read and the link by which the packet should be routed out is decided. If this link is found to be faulty or if the next node in the path was found to be faulty, then the node can decide an alternate path to forward the packet. The process continues either until the packet reaches its' destination or until the packet reaches a node adjacent to the destination and finds that its destination is faulty. In the latter case, the packet is killed and removed from the network by the node adjacent to the faulty destination. Let us assume that the packet has reached a node d, one of whose adjacent nodes is faulty. The remaining number of [+h] and [+1] links (w_{i-d}, y_{i-d}) are in the header of the packet. Algorithm [2] is used to decide the outgoing link:

Algorithm
1. Let node (d + h) be faulty.
   If $y_{i-d} > 0$, the [+1] link is chosen to avoid the faulty node.
   If $y_{i-d} = 0$, choose a path segment consisting of the following series of links [+1], [+h], [+h], [-1]. This avoids the faulty node and reaches the node (d+2h). However the path length increases by 2 links.

2. Let node (d+1) be faulty
   If $w_{i-d} > 0$, choose [+h] link
   If $w_{i-d} = 0$, choose the series [+h], [+1], [+1], [-h]. Path length increases by 2 links.

Similarly, faults at nodes (d – h) and (d-1) can be explained. The algorithm considers only [+h, +1] link combination, but it can be easily extended to the other link combinations. For this algorithm, if more than one node is faulty, then the algorithm does not offer a path. For example if both (d + h) and (d+1) are faulty, the algorithm cannot work. In our implementation we have extended the algorithm to work for cases where two adjacent nodes can be faulty. We call this the Double Fault condition.

Modified Algorithm
1. Let node (d + h) be faulty.
   If $y_{i-d} > 0$,
   a) If (d+1) is not faulty, the [+1] link is chosen to avoid the faulty node.
   b) Else, choose [-1] link.
   If $y_{i-d} = 0$,
   a) If (d+1) is not faulty, choose a path segment consisting of the following series of links [+1], [+h], [+h], [-1].
   b) Else, the path segment consisting of the following series of links [-1], [+h], [+h], [+1].
   In both cases, the faulty node is avoided and the node (d+2h) is reached. However the path length increases atleast by 2.

2. Let node (d+1) be faulty
   If $w_{i-d} > 0$,
   a) If (d+h) is not faulty, the [+h] link is chosen to avoid the faulty node.
   b) Else, choose [-h] link.
   If $w_{i-d} = 0$,
   a) If (d+h) is not faulty, choose a path segment consisting of the following series of links [+h], [+1], [+1], [-h].
   b) Else, the path segment consisting of the following series of links [+h], [+1], [+1], [-h].

In both cases, the faulty node is avoided and the node (d+2h) is reached. However the path length increases atleast by 2. In the above algorithm we use a recursive technique. So while following a path segment if any node is found faulty, the algorithm is applied at that node.

Results

The algorithm was implemented and the fault conditions simulated. We considered a network having 16 nodes. For this value of n, the optimal hop sizes were found to be 4, 6, 10 and 12 (refer [1]). We considered hop sizes of 4 , 5, 6 and 7 were also studied. For each value of hopsize, the number of packets generated in the network has been varied form 20 to 50 and in each case, the average delay for packet delivery has been calculated. This is done by calculating the time taken for each packet to reach the destination node and then summing these values. This total time divided by the total number of packets generated gives the average time delay. The results are tabulated in Table 1.

Table 1. Average delays for various hop sizes for varying number of packets (P)

Hopsize(h)	P = 20	P = 30	P =40	P = 50
4	(0.82,1.01,1.23)	(0.98,1.11,1.34)	(1.20,1.40,1.67)	(1.30,1.80,2.01)
5	(.0.85,0.89,1.10)	(1.10,1.17,1.32)	(1.15,1.60,1.80)	(1.60,2.10,2.34)
6	(1.05,1.15,1.30)	(1.10,1.25,1.45)	(1.17,1.38,1.59)	(1.31,1.49,1.8)
7	(1.10,1.21,1.41)	(1.20,1.37,1.56)	(1.40,1.51,1.72)	(1.60,1.75,2.06)

In the above table, 'P' indicates number of packets. Each cell has a 3-tuple which can be denoted as (D_w, D_s, D_d) where

D_w = Average delay when there are no faults

D_s = Average delay in the presence of a single fault

D_d = Average delay in the presence of double fault.

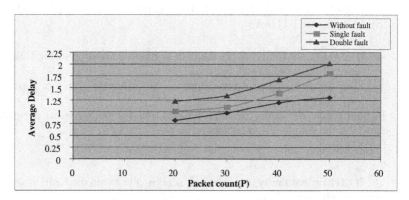

Fig. 1. Average Delay Vs P for h=16, h=4

The variation in average delay with increase in number of packets generated is shown in the above figures. Figures 1, 2, 3 and 4 show the variation in average delay for hopsizes of 4, 5, 6 and 7 respectively. In all the figures it can be seen that the av-

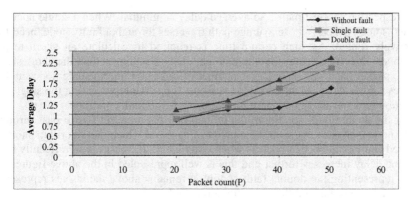

Fig. 2. Average Delay Vs P for n=16, h=5

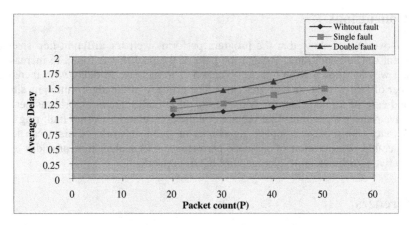

Fig. 3. Average Delay Vs P for n=16, h=6

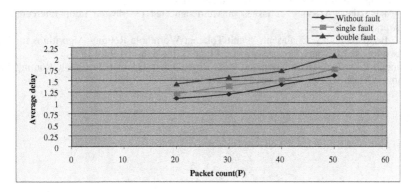

Fig. 4. Average Delay Vs P for n=16, h=7

erage delay for the no fault condition is significantly lesser. The delay increases as the number of faults increases. Furthermore, as the number of packets increases the average delay increases. When there are no faults in the network all packets go through their respective shortest paths. So average delay is minimal. When a single node fault occurs, some packets, whose average path traverses through a faulty node, need to be adaptively routed. As such certain time is required to calculate an alternate path. Moreover, in certain cases, the alternate path length is longer than the shortest path. So the packet has to traverse larger number of links and intermediate nodes and this induces further delay. Owing to these reasons, the curve representing the single fault condition remains above the curve representing the no fault condition.

For the double fault condition, the probability that a packet has to pass through a faulty node increases. As such the number of cases, in which the algorithm should be invoked and the number of packets whose path length increases is significantly higher and the delay increases further and this is well represented in the above figures. The curve representing the double fault condition remains above the curves representing the no fault condition and the curve for single fault.

4   Conclusions

The above results show that the program performs well for different hop sizes and different traffic conditions. Though the path of the packet was found to increase, no packet was lost nor was any packet blocked. The increase in delay with increase in number of faulty nodes is only marginal. The efficacy of the algorithm is its simplicity and ease of implementation. Most of the other fault tolerant algorithms deal with adaptive routing algorithms that require complex calculations to find fault rings, fault chains etc. Using these complex algorithms in small networks of sizes can lead to considerable deterioration of network performance. Our algorithm provides a good alternative to achieve fault tolerance in MCDL networks.

References

1. Ramesh Vasappanavara, Sasikiran Kandula, Nimmagadda Chalamaiah, "Delay performance simulation studies in MCDL networks".(under print)
2. N. Chalamaiah "A Study of Issues in Multiconnected Distributed Loop Interconnection Networks".
3. R.V. Boppana and S. Chalasani, "Fault-Tolerant Wormhole Routing Algorithms for Mesh Networks", IEEE Trans. Computers, vol. 44, no. 7, pp. 848-864, July 1995.
4. Seungjin Park, Jong-Hoon Youn and Bella Bose, "Fault-Tolerant Wormhole Routing Algorithms in Meshes in the Presence of Concave Faults".

Applications and Parallel Implementations of Metaheuristics in Network Design and Routing

Simone L. Martins, Celso C. Ribeiro, and Isabel Rosseti

Department of Computer Science, Universidade Federal Fluminense,
Rua Passo da Pátria 156, Niterói, RJ 24210-240, Brazil
{simone,celso,rosseti}@ic.uff.br

Abstract. Successful applications of metaheuristics in telecommunications and network design and routing are reviewed, illustrating the major role played by the use of these techniques in the solution of many optimization problems arising in these areas. The main issues involved in the parallelization of metaheuristics are discussed. The 2-path network design problem is used to illustrate the development of robust and efficient parallel cooperative implementations of metaheuristics. Computational results on Linux clusters are reported.

1 Motivation

Recent years have witnessed huge advances in computer technology and communication networks. New technologies like cellular mobile radio systems and optical fibers allow very fast connections. Many hard optimization problems in network design and routing are related with these new applications and technologies. They often involve the minimization of the costs involved in the design of networks or the optimization of their performance.

Metaheuristics such as genetic algorithms, ant colonies, and simulated annealing are time consuming methods that find very good solutions to hard optimization problems [10]. They offer a wide range of possibilities for effective parallel algorithms running in much smaller computation times, but requiring efficient implementations. Cung et al. [7] showed that parallel implementations of metaheuristics appear quite naturally as an effective approach to speedup the search for good solutions to optimization problems. They allow solving larger problems and finding better solutions with respect to their sequential counterparts. They also lead to more robust algorithms and this is often reported as the main advantage obtained with parallel implementations of metaheuristics: they are less-dependent on parameter tuning and their success is not limited to few or small classes of problems. However, developing and tuning efficient parallel implementations of metaheuristics require a thorough programming effort.

Efficient parallel implementations of metaheuristics and their applications in telecommunications and network design and routing are studied in this work. In the next section, we present an overview of the main issues on parallelization strategies of metaheuristics. Successful parallel implementations of metaheuristics in the above areas are reviewed in Section 3. In Section 4, we describe a typical network design problem and the general framework of a GRASP with

S. Manandhar et al. (Eds.): AACC 2004, LNCS 3285, pp. 205–213, 2004.
© Springer-Verlag Berlin Heidelberg 2004

path-relinking heuristic customized for the 2-path network design problem. A parallel cooperative implementation of the latter is described in Section 5. This approach can be extended to other network design and routing problems. Computational results obtained on a 32-processor Linux cluster are reported in Section 6, illustrating the effectiveness of the approach and the implementation issues involved. Concluding remarks are drawn in the last section.

2   Parallelization of Metaheuristics

The computation times associated with the exploration of the solution space may be very large. With the rapid increase in the number of parallel computers, powerful workstations, and fast communication networks, parallel implementations of metaheuristics appear quite naturally as an effective approach to speedup the search for approximate solutions. Besides the accelerations obtained, the parallelization also allows solving larger problems or finding better solutions.

Cung et al. [7] reviewed parallelization strategies, implementation issues, and applications of parallel metaheuristics. Parallel implementations of metaheuristics based on local search use several processors to concurrently generate or explore the neighborhood. Two approaches can be used: single-walk and multiple-walks. In the case of a single-walk parallelization, one unique trajectory is traversed in the neighborhood and the search for the best neighbor at each iteration is performed in parallel. A multiple-walk parallelization is characterized by the investigation in parallel of multiple trajectories, each of them by a different processor. A search thread is a process running in each processor traversing a walk in the neighborhood. These threads can be either independent (when they do not exchange any information among them) or cooperative (when the information collected along each trajectory is disseminated and used by other threads to improve or to speedup the search).

Efficient parallelizations of metaheuristics are often based on multiple-walk strategies. They can be implemented using independent or cooperative search threads. Independent parallelizations can be easily implemented. They lead to good speedups and robust implementations can be obtained by using different parameter settings in each processor. However, this model is quite poor and can be very easily simulated in sequential mode, by several successive executions with different initializations. The lack of cooperation between the search threads does not allow the use of the information collected by different processors.

The use of cooperative search threads demands more programming efforts and implementation skills. As the threads exchange information collected along each search trajectory, one expects not only to accelerate the convergence to the best solution but also to find better solutions than those found by independent strategies within the same computation times.

3   Parallel Metaheuristics in Network Design and Routing

The outbreak of new technologies in telecommunications and networks, together with the demand for more computer intensive applications, leads to huge developments and needs in network design and routing. The optimization problems involved require time consuming solution methods. As most of these problems are NP-hard and exact methods can only solve small problems, approximate algorithms based on metaheuristics play a very important role in their solution.

Applications of metaheuristics to problems in telecommunications abound in the literature. Due to the huge amount of work in this area in recent times, we attempt to give only a broad view of applications of metaheuristics.

Tabu search is often applied for finding approximate solutions to optimization problems in communications networks. Noronha and Ribeiro [11] developed a tabu search approach to routing and wavelength assignment in all-optical networks. Their algorithm combines the computation of alternative routes for the light-paths with the solution of a partition coloring problem. The computational experiments showed that it outperforms the best known heuristic for the problem. Castelino and Stephens [6] developed a surrogate constraint tabu thresholding algorithm for a frequency assignment problem minimizing interference. Xu et al. [20] employed tabu search for designing a least-cost telecommunications network where the alternate routing paths can be changed dynamically from hour to hour. The aim is to determine the optimal link capacities and the routing plan for each hour to minimize total trunk cost, subject to the grade-of-service constraint which requires that the fraction of calls blocked in each hour for each node pair should be less than a pre-specified number.

Genetic algorithms are also often used in network applications. Armony et al. [3] implemented a genetic algorithm for solving the stacked ring design problem, in which one searches for a topology defining to which self healing rings a node should be connected and how traffic should be routed on the rings. The aim is to optimize the trade-offs between the cost of equipments to implement the rings and the cost of exchanging traffic among rings. Poon et al. [12] described the GenOSys tool developed to optimize the design of secondary and distribution networks used on typical copper access network cabling to connect customers. Its objective is to determine the best locations for distribution points and to identify geographically advantageous tree-structured sub-networks to aggregate cables from customers. The tool allows the user to enter data about the network and provides information which can be used for ducting and cabling using the hybrid genetic algorithm. A practical problem on a network of 240 nodes was solved in less than 30 minutes on a Pentium 200 MHz.

Randall et al. [14] showed results obtained by a simulated annealing algorithm developed to find paths in a network which minimize the cost of transporting origin-destination flows subject to specified link, node capacity, node degree, and chain hop-limit constraints. Wittner et al. [19] developed a swarm algorithm to find a path of resources from a client terminal to a service provider, such that all resources in the path conform with constraints and preferences of a request profile specified by the user. Given a network composed of users, terminals, and services that have individual profiles containing quality of service parameters, the objective is to search for resource paths for each peer-to-peer communication.

Although all these solution approaches found very good solutions for the corresponding problems, their computation times are often very large. Several authors have shown that the parallelization of metaheuristics may lead to significant speedups, much smaller computation times, and more robust implementations [7]. Some examples are illustrated below.

GRASP and genetic algorithms are very amenable to efficient parallel implementations. Resende and Ribeiro [15] proposed a family of heuristics for the private virtual circuit routing problem. The GRASP with path-relinking variant similar to that reported in Section 4 was able to significantly improve on these simple heuristics, at the expense of additional computation time. GRASP with path-relinking has been shown to be efficiently implemented in parallel with linear speedups. Canuto et al. [5] developed a parallel GRASP heuristic for the prize-collecting Steiner tree problem. Given an undirected graph with prizes associated with its nodes and weights associated with its edges, this problem consists of finding a subtree of this graph minimizing the sum of the weights of its edges plus the prizes of the nodes not spanned. They proposed a multi-start local search algorithm. Path-relinking is used to improve the solutions found by local search. Their results show that the local search with perturbations approach found optimal solutions on nearly all of the instances tested, in much smaller computation times than an exact branch-and-cut algorithm that is able to handle only small problems. An independent parallelization obtained important speedups. Once again, the parallelization of the GRASP heuristic developed by Prais and Ribeiro [13] for the problem of traffic assignment in TDMA communication satellites led to linear speedups in [2].

Buriol at al. [4] presented a hybrid genetic algorithm for solving the OSPF weight setting problem, combining a genetic algorithm with a local search procedure applied to improve the solutions obtained by crossover. Experimental results showed that the hybrid heuristic found better solutions and led to a more robust implementation than the best known heuristic in the literature. Preliminary parallelization results have shown almost linear speedups. Watanabe et al. [18] proposed a new type of parallel genetic algorithm model for multi-objective optimization problems. It was applied to solve an antenna arrangement problem in mobile communications. The new proposed algorithm showed a very good performance when compared to other methods.

4 The 2-Path Network Design Problem

Let $G = (V, E)$ be a connected graph, where V is the set of nodes and E is the set of edges. A k-path between nodes $s, t \in V$ is a sequence of at most k edges connecting them. Given a non-negative weight function $w : E \to R_+$ associated with the edges of G and a set D of pairs of origin-destination nodes, the *2-path network design problem* (2PNDP) consists of finding a minimum weighted subset of edges $E' \subseteq E$ containing a 2-path between every origin-destination pair.

Applications of 2PNDP can be found in the design of communications networks, in which paths with few edges are sought to enforce high reliability and small delays. 2PNDP was shown to be NP-hard by Dahl and Johannessen [8].

GRASP (*Greedy Randomized Adaptive Search Procedure*) [16] is a multi-start metaheuristic. In each iteration, the construction phase builds a feasible solution, whose neighborhood is investigated until a local minimum is found during the local search phase. The best locally optimal solution is kept as the result.

Path-relinking is an intensification strategy originally proposed by Glover [9]. Resende and Ribeiro [16] reviewed advances and applications of GRASP using path-relinking to incorporate a memory-based intensification phase. This strategy strongly improves solution quality and reduces computation times with respect to memoryless implementations, see e.g. [1, 5, 15].

The pseudo-code in Figure 1 illustrates the main blocks of a sequential GRASP procedure for minimization, incorporating an additional path-relinking intensification phase. Max_Iterations iterations are performed and Pool is a set of elite solutions found along the search, while $f(x)$ denotes the cost of a solution x. The customization of the greedy randomized construction (step 3), local search (step 4), and path-relinking (step 7) phases to the 2-path network design problem are described in detail in [17].

---

procedure GRASP+PR;
1 Set $f^* \leftarrow \infty$ and Pool $\leftarrow \emptyset$;
2 **for** $k = 1, \ldots,$ MaxIterations **do**;
3   Construct a solution x using a greedy randomized algorithm;
4   Find y by applying local search to x;
5   **if** y satisfies the membership conditions **then** send y to Pool;
6   Randomly select a solution $z \in$ Pool;
7   Obtain w^1 by applying path-relinking from y to z and w^2 by applying
          path-relinking from z to y ;
8   **if** any w^1 and w^2 satisfy the membership conditions **then** send each to Pool;
9   **if** $f(w^1) < f^*$ **then do**; $x^* \leftarrow w^1$; $f^* \leftarrow f(w^1)$; **end**;
10   **if** $f(w^2) < f^*$ **then do**; $x^* \leftarrow w^2$; $f^* \leftarrow f(w^2)$; **end**;
11 **end**;
12 **return** x^*;
end GRASP+PR;

Fig. 1. Pseudo-code of the sequential GRASP with path-relinking heuristic.

5   Cooperative Parallel Implementation

Typical parallelizations of GRASP correspond to multiple-walk independent-thread strategies, based on the distribution of the iterations over the processors [7]. The iterations may be evenly distributed over the processors or according with their demands, to improve load balancing. The processors perform MaxIterations$/p$ iterations each, where p is the number of processors and MaxIterations the total number of iterations. Each processor has a copy of algorithm GRASP+PR, a copy of the data, and its own pool of elite solutions. One of the processors acts as the master, reading and distributing the problem data, generating the seeds which will be used by the pseudo-random number generators at each processor, distributing the iterations, and collecting the best solution found by each processor.

In the case of a parallel cooperative strategy, the master handles a centralized pool of elite solutions, collecting and distributing them upon request. The $p-1$ slaves exchange the elite solutions found along their search trajectories. In the proposed implementation for 2PNDP, each slave may send up to three different solutions to the master at each iteration: the solution y obtained by local search (step 5), and the solutions w^1 and w^2 obtained by path-relinking (step 7).

Aiex et al. [1] showed experimentally that the solution times for finding a target solution value with a GRASP heuristic fit a two-parameter exponential distribution. The same result still holds when GRASP is implemented in conjunction with a path-relinking procedure. In consequence, GRASP with path-relinking can be implemented in parallel with linear speedups.

6   Computational Results

The parallel cooperative GRASP with path-relinking heuristic described in Section 5 was implemented in C, using version egcs-2.91.66 of the gcc compiler and the MPI LAM 6.3.2 implementation. Computational experiments have been performed on a cluster of 32 Pentium II 400MHz processors with 32 Mbytes of RAM memory each, running under the Red Hat 6.2 implementation of Linux. Processors are connected by a 10 Mbits/s IBM 8274 switch.

The performance of the parallel implementation is quite uniform over all problem instances. The results illustrated in this section concern an instance with 100 nodes, 4950 edges, and 1000 origin-destination pairs. We use the methodology proposed in [1] to assess experimentally the behavior of randomized algorithms. This approach is based on plots showing empirical distributions of the random variable *time to target solution value*. To plot the empirical distribution, we fix a solution target value and run each algorithm 200 times, recording the running time when a solution with cost at least as good as the target value is found. For each algorithm, we associate with the i-th sorted running time t_i a probability $p_i = (i - \frac{1}{2})/200$ and plot the points $z_i = (t_i, p_i)$, for $i = 1, \ldots, 200$.

Results obtained for both the independent and the cooperative parallel implementations on the above instance with the target value set at 683 are reported in Figure 2. The parallel cooperative implementation is already faster than the independent one for eight processors. For fewer processors the independent implementation is naturally faster, since it employs all p processors in the search (while only $p-1$ slave processors take part effectively in the computations performed by the cooperative implementation).

When the number of processors increases, the number of messages sent by the processors becomes very high. As a consequence, the memory of the master may not be able to handle all buffered information and the system often crashes. To avoid this difficulty by significantly reducing the number of messages sent to the master, three different strategies were investigated:

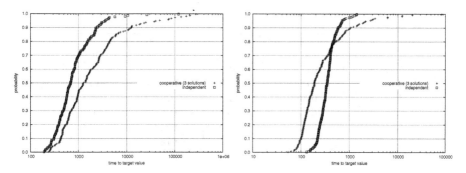

Fig. 2. Cooperative and independent parallelizations on two and eight processors.

(1) Each send operation is broken in two parts in steps 5 and 8 of algorithm GRASP+PR. First, the slave sends only the cost of the solution to the master. If this solution is better than the worst solution in the pool, then the full solution is sent. The number of messages increases, but most of them will be very small ones with light memory requirements.

(2) Step 5 of algorithm GRASP+PR is not performed and only the best solution among y, w^1, and w^2 is sent to the pool in step 8.

(3) A distributed implementation, in which each slave handles its own pool of elite solutions. Every time a processor finds a new elite solution, the latter is broadcast to the others.

Comparative results for these three strategies on the same problem instance are plotted in Figure 3. The first strategy outperformed all others.

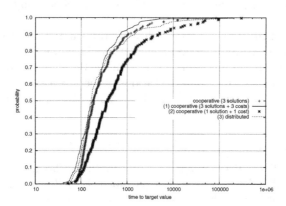

Fig. 3. Implementations of cooperative strategies on eight processors.

Table 1 shows the average computation times and the best solutions found over ten runs of each strategy for MaxIterations = 3200 iterations. There is a clear degradation in solution quality for the independent strategy when the number of processors increases. As fewer iterations are performed by each

Table 1. Average times and best solutions over ten runs.

processors	independent		cooperative	
	best value	avg. time (s)	best value	avg. time (s)
1	673	1310.1	—	—
2	676	686.8	676	1380.9
4	680	332.7	673	464.1
8	687	164.1	676	200.9
16	692	81.7	674	97.5
32	702	41.3	678	74.6

processor, the pool of elite solutions gets poorer with the increase in the number of processors. Since the processors do not communicate, the overall solution quality is worse. In the case of the cooperative strategy, the information shared by the processors guarantees the high quality of the solutions in the pool. The cooperative implementation is more robust. Very good solutions are obtained with no degradation in quality and with a large speedup of 17.6 for 32 processors.

7   Concluding Remarks

Recent years have witnessed large advances in computer technology and communication networks. Metaheuristics are powerful tools for finding high-quality solutions to optimization problems involved in network design and routing. Although these solution approaches are able to find very good solutions, their computation times are often very large. Parallel cooperative implementations may lead to significant speedups, smaller computation times, and more robust algorithms. However, they demand more programming efforts and implementation skills.

We described the 2-path network design problem and a GRASP with path-relinking heuristic for its approximate solution. They are used to illustrate the strategies and programming skills involved in the development of robust and efficient parallel cooperative implementations of metaheuristics. Conclusive computational results with speedups of 17.6 on a 32-processor cluster were reported.

References

1. R.M. Aiex, M.G.C. Resende, and C.C. Ribeiro. Probability distribution of solution time in GRASP: An experimental investigation. *J. of Heuristics*, 8:343–373, 2002.
2. A.C. Alvim and C.C. Ribeiro. Load balancing for the parallelization of the GRASP metaheuristic. In *Proceedings of the X Brazilian Symposium on Computer Architecture*, pages 279–282, Búzios, 1998.
3. M. Armony, J.C. Klincewicz, H. Luss, and M.B. Rosenwein. Design of stacked self-healing rings using a genetic algorithm. *Journal of Heuristics*, 6:85–105, 2000.
4. L.S. Buriol, M.G.C. Resende, C.C. Ribeiro, and M. Thorup. A hybrid genetic algorithm for the weight setting problem in OSPF/IS-IS routing. Technical report, Internet and Network Systems Research Center, AT&T Labs Research, 2003.

5. S.A. Canuto, M.G.C. Resende, and C.C. Ribeiro. Local search with perturbations for the prize-collecting Steiner tree problem in graphs. *Networks*, 38:50–58, 2001.
6. D. Castelino and N. Stephens. A surrogate constraint tabu thresholding implementation for the frequency assignment problem. *Annals of Operations Research*, 86:259–270, 1999.
7. V.-D. Cung, S.L. Martins, C.C. Ribeiro, and C. Roucairol. Strategies for the parallel implementation of metaheuristics. In C.C. Ribeiro and P. Hansen, editors, *Essays and Surveys in Metaheuristics*, pages 263–308. Kluwer, 2002.
8. G. Dahl and B. Johannessen. The 2-path network design problem. *Networks*, 43:190–199, 2004.
9. F. Glover. Tabu search and adaptive memory programing – Advances, applications and challenges. In R.S. Barr, R.V. Helgason, and J.L. Kennington, editors, *Interfaces in Computer Science and Operations Research*, pages 1–75. Kluwer, 1996.
10. F. Glover and G. Kochenberger. *Handbook of Metaheuristics*. Kluwer, 2003.
11. T.F. Noronha and C.C. Ribeiro. Routing and wavelength assignment by partition coloring. *European Journal of Operational Research*, to appear.
12. K.F. Poon, A. Conway, G. Wardrop, and J. Mellis. Successful application of genetic algorithms to network design and planning. *BT Technol. J.*, 18:32–41, 2000.
13. M. Prais and C.C. Ribeiro. Reactive GRASP: An application to a matrix decomposition problem in TDMA traffic assignment. *INFORMS Journal on Computing*, 12:164–176, 2000.
14. M. Randall, G. McMahon, and S. Sugden. A simulated annealing approach to communication network design. *J. of Combinatorial Optimization*, 6:55–65, 2002.
15. M.G.C. Resende and C.C. Ribeiro. A GRASP with path-relinking for private virtual circuit routing. *Networks*, 41:104–114, 2003.
16. M.G.C. Resende and C.C. Ribeiro. GRASP and path-relinking: Recent advances and applications. In T. Ibaraki, K. Nonobe, and M. Yagiura, editors, *Metaheuristics: Progress as Real Problem Solvers*. Kluwer, to appear.
17. C.C. Ribeiro and I. Rosseti. A parallel GRASP for the 2-path network design problem. *Lecture Notes in Computer Science*, 2004:922–926, 2002.
18. S. Watanabe, T. Hiroyasu, and M. Miki. Parallel evolutionary multi-criterion optimization for mobile telecommunication networks optimization. In *Proceedings of the EUROGEN 2001 Conference*, pages 167–172, Athens, 2001.
19. O. Wittner, P.E. Heegaard, and B. Helvik. Scalable distributed discovery of resource paths in telecommunication networks using cooperative ant-like agents. In *Proceedings of the 2003 Congress on Evolutionary Computation*, Canberra, 2003.
20. J. Xu, S. Y. Chiu, and F. Glover. Tabu search for dynamic routing communications network design. *Telecommunications Systems*, 8:55–77, 1997.

Comparison of Integrated Micro
and Macro Mobility Protocols

D. Saraswady, V. Sai Prithiv, and S. Shanmugavel

Telematics Lab, Department of ECE, Anna University
Chennai – 600 025, India
dsaraswady@hotmail.com, prith_vijay@yahoo.com,
ssvel@annauniv.edu

Abstract. In this paper, we evaluated and compared the UDP and TCP performance analysis of integration of Hierarchical Mobile IP protocol and Mobile IP
protocol with an integration of Cellular IP and Mobile IP protocols. The performance of integration of micro and macro mobility protocols are compared
using factors such as UDP packet loss and TCP throughput that occur due to
handoff are presented. We aim to provide a lightweight efficient solution suitable for local access to mobile stations in limited size cell systems with possible
high internal handoff rates. The simulation results are presented using the network simulator ns2. It is observed from the results that the integration of cellular IP with Mobile IP protocol gives better performance when compared to the
integration of Mobile IP with Hierarchical Mobile IP protocol.

1 Introduction

This paper utilizes the Mobile Ipv4 protocol as the mechanism for providing mobility
in a multi-access environment. For managing mobility on the level of the global
Internet, Mobile IP offers a practical solution. However, frequent handoffs inside a
relatively small geographic area tend to generate a remarkable amount of signaling
overhead due to required control messages between a mobile host and Home Agent
(HA). Additionally, the need for obtaining a new Care-of-Address (CoA) and notify-
ing it to a possibly distant home agent results in latency and disruption to user traffic
during every handoff. Smooth, fast and transparent handoffs are impossible to do with
the present basic Mobile IP. If a large number of mobile hosts quickly migrate between foreign networks, Mobile IP will turn out to be a weakly scalable solution for
mobility management [1], [2].

A number of micromobility protocols have been discussed in the IETF Mobile IP
working group. Micromobility protocols are designed for environment where mobile
hosts change their point of attachment to the network so frequently. Micromobility
protocols aim to handle local movement (e.g., within a domain) of mobile hosts without interaction with the Mobile IP enabled Internet. This has the benefit of reducing
delay and packet loss during handoff and eliminating registration between Mobile
Hosts (MH) and possibly distant home agents when mobile host remain inside their
local coverage areas. Eliminating registration in this manner reduces signaling load
experienced by the core network in support of mobility as the numbers of wireless
users grow so will signaling overhead associated with mobility management. Mobile
IP supports registration but not paging. To minimize signaling overhead and optimize
mobility management performance micromobility protocols support paging.

S. Manandhar et al. (Eds.): AACC 2004, LNCS 3285, pp. 214–221, 2004.
© Springer-Verlag Berlin Heidelberg 2004

In recent years, there has been much interest in developing efficient IP-based micromobility management schemes to handle mode mobility within a domain in next-generation wireless networks. Such a schemes are essential to achieve seamless integration of cellular network with existing IP-based data networks, popularly known as the Internet. In recent literature, several solutions have been proposed to support mobility in future wireless IP networks [3-5]. One of the challenges to keep connection with the Internet as the mobile user is roaming is to provide multiple real time services while achieving a high QoS support. Although the Mobile IP protocol is suited for macromobility as it is, it fails to support micromobility efficiently [6]. Mobile IP requires the mobile host to register with the home agent and the Correspondent Host (CH) when it changes its point of attachment in the Internet. Mobile IP supports registration but not paging. Therefore, this causes Mobile IP to incur long delay in the registration process, and add signaling traffic to the backbone network when the home agent and correspondent host are far away from the mobile host.

In this paper, we proposed new network architecture as show in Fig.1.This network architecture uses the standard Internet for the core network. The Mobile IP (MIP) is used as an interdomain mobility protocol for macromobility management; while Cellular IP and Hierarchical Mobile IP is employed for intra subnet mobility as support to the micromobility and paging management. In this paper, we present a performance comparison of integration of Mobile IP and Hierarchical Mobile IP (HMIP) protocols with integration of Mobile IP and Cellular IP protocols. We use UDP and TCP probing traffic between the corresponding host and mobile hosts, and count the number of packet lost during handoff, the number of packet loss as a function of speed and handoff latency during handoff is measured. The network simulator (ns2.1b7a) is used to evaluate the performance of the proposed architecture. The results show the best performance is achieved in integration of Mobile IP and Cellular IP protocols it provides significant improvement in handover performance, UDP packet loss and TCP throughput when compared to integration of Mobile IP and Hierarchical Mobile IP protocols.

2   Mobile IP

The starting point for the design of an IP-based micromobility management protocol is with Mobile IP, an Internet Engineering Task Force (IETF) proposed standard [1]. Indeed, this work is being looked at within the IETF Mobile IP and seamless mobility working groups. Mobile IP provides a network layer solution to node mobility across IP networks. While roaming, a mobile node (MN) maintains two IP addresses, a permanent home address used in all transport layer connections, and a topologically correct care-of address that reflects the current point of attachment. The care-of address is obtained through either a foreign agent (FA) or an auto-configuration process. While home the MN uses its permanent home address. A location register on the home subnet, referred to as a home agent (HA), maintains a mobility binding that maps the MN home address to a care-of address. The HA acts as proxy on the home subnet, attracting packets addressed to the MN and employing tunneling to redirect packets to the MN care-of address. MNs send registration requests to inform the HA of any change in care-of address or to renew a mobility binding. Mobile IP provides an elegant solution for node mobility when the MN moves infrequently, precisely addressing the problem space for which it was developed. When applying Mobile IP to wireless or cellular environments, it has been shown to introduce significant latency simply because handoffs occur frequently and registration messages may travel large distances before packet redirection occurs. Thus, there is a need for a specific micromobility protocol that interworks with mobile IP for a complete IP-based mobility management mechanism.

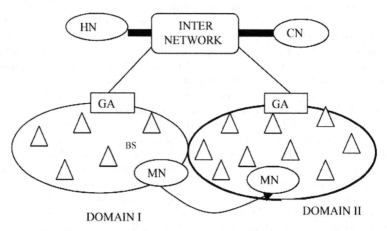

Fig. 1. Macro and Micromobility Protocols Integrated Architecture

3   Micromobility Protocols

The primary role of micromobility protocol is to ensure that packets arriving from the Internet and addressed to the mobile hosts are forwarded to the appropriate wireless access point in an efficient manner. Existing proposals for micromobility can be broadly classified into two types: routing-based and tunnel-based schemes.

3.1   Hierarchical Mobile IP

The Hierarchical Mobile IP protocol [5] from Ericsson and Nokia employs a hierarchy of Foreign Agents (FAs) to locally handle Mobile IP registration. In this protocol, the mobile host sends Mobile IP registration message (with appropriate extension) to update their respective location information. Registration messages establish tunnels between neighboring FAs along the path from the mobile host to a gateway FA (GFA). Packets addressed to the mobile host travel in this network of tunnels, which can be viewed as separate routing network overlay on top of IP. The use of tunnel makes it possible to employ the protocols in an IP network that carries non-mobile traffic as well. Typically one level of hierarchy is considered where all FAs are connected to the GFA. In this case, direct tunnel connects the GFA to FAs that are located at access points. Paging extensions for Hierarchical Mobile IP [7] allow idle mobile nodes to operate in a power saving mode while located within a paging area. The location of mobile host is known by Home Agents (HAs) and is represented by paging areas. After receiving a packet addressed to a mobile host located in a foreign network, the HA tunnels the packet to the paging FA, which then pages the mobile host to reestablish a path toward the current point of attachment. The paging system uses specific communication time slots in a paging area.

3.2 Cellular IP

The Cellular IP proposal [4] adopts a similar approach to mobility management based on a rooted domain, but uses a different signaling technique. Instead of sending and processing explicit message, the nodes have an ability to learn the source IP address of uplink data packet and map them to the corresponding downlink interfaces. The uplink path (i.e., the direction toward the domain root), or gateway, is inferred by each access point/access router within the domain using the beacon packets periodically transmitted by the gateway. All the packets generated by the mobile hosts are forwarded toward the gateway using this uplink path. In addition, to refresh its forwarding cache entries, a host may explicitly transmit uplink route update packets. Two handoff schemes are supported. Hard handoff allows some packet loss while being efficient in the amount of signaling overhead and latency. Semi-soft handoff aims to minimize the transient packet loss, while exploiting the capability of a mobile to receive packet from both old and new Access Points (APs). Similar to the Hawaii protocol, the forwarding cache of the gateway contains entries for all active mobiles in the domain.

4   Simulation Model

In this section, we present the simulation model and the performance comparison of integrated Mobile IP and Hierarchical Mobile IP protocols with integrated Mobile IP and Cellular IP protocols with respect to the handoff latency, the number of UDP packet lost and TCP throughput during handoff. The simulation network topology of integration of Mobile IP and Cellular IP protocols and integration of Mobile IP and HMIP are shown in Fig.2 and Fig.3 respectively. The simulation study presented in this paper uses the CIMS [8], which represent a micromobility extension of the ns-2 network simulator based on version 2.1b6[9]. The simulation models are briefly described in the following:

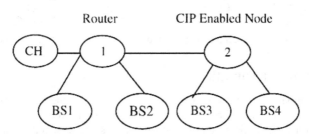

Fig. 2. Simulation Model for Integration of Mobile IP and Cellular IP

In integration of Mobile IP and Cellular IP topology, the node 1 acts as a router and node 2 acts as CIP enabled node, where as all the base station (BS_1–BS_4) act as mobility unaware routers as show in Fig.2. In integration of Mobile IP and Hierarchical Mobile IP topology, the node 8 acts as a router and node 9 and 10 acts as gateway Foreign Agent (GFA), node 0 and 1acts as foreign agents (FA) FA1 and FA_2 respectively and from BS_1 to BS_4 act as a base station (BS) as shown in Fig.3. Here each wired communication is modeled as 10MB/s duplex link with 2ms delay. Mobile host connects to the base station using ns-2 carrier sense multiple access with collision avoidance wireless link model with 2ms delay. Where as each base station operate on a different frequency band. Simulation results are obtained using a single mobile host, continuously moving between base stations at a speed that could be varied. Such a movement pattern ensures that mobile host always goes through the maximum overlapping region between the two-radio cells. In the simulation scenarios the overlap was set to 30m. Nodes are modeled without constraints on switching capacity or message processing speed. During such a simulation, MH has to perform three handover to move from BS_1 to BS_4 as shown in Figs.2 and Fig.3

The simulation network accommodates UDP and TCP traffic. UDP probing traffic is directed from Correspondent Host (CH) to Mobile host, with a packet interarrival time of 10ms and a packet size of 210 bytes. In all simulation a TCP source agent is attached to the CH and a TCP sink is attached at the MH. The MH is initially positioned near the BS_1. The MH starts to move towards the BS_4, 4 seconds after the simulation starts. This is to enable the establishment of TCP communication and allowing it to stabilize, meaning, TCP is transferring data with a full window. The TCP Tahoe implementation is used with a packet size of 1460 bytes, which follows a 'go back-n model using accumulative positive acknowledgement with slow start, congestion avoidance and fast retransmission' model, was chosen as the default TCP flavor. A FTP session between the MN and the CH is started 1 second after the simulation has started. The bulk FTP data traffic flow is from the CH to the MN.

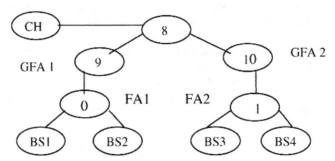

Fig. 3. Simulation Model for Integration of Mobile IP and Hierarchical mobile IP

5   Performance Evaluations

We first present simulation results for the UDP packet loss due to the basic handoff in integration of Mobile IP with Hierarchical Mobile IP protocols and integration of Mobile IP with cellular IP protocols. To obtain these results, the mobile node is allowed to move between base stations. During simulation, a MH travels periodically between neighboring access point with a constant speed of 20m/s and the UDP probing traffics transmitted between the CH and MH.

5.1   UDP and TCP Performance Due to Handoff

The simulation result for UDP and TCP download during handoff is plotted in Fig.4 and Fig.5. It shows the comparison of number of UDP packet loss and TCP throughput in integration of Mobile IP and HMIP protocols and integration of Mobile IP and Cellular IP. It is clear from the Fig.4 and Fig.5, the number of packet loss is increases with increasing handoff frequency and TCP throughput decreases with increasing handoff frequency respectively for both integration of Mobile IP with Cellular IP and Mobile IP with HMIP protocols but the number of packet loss is low in integration of Mobile IP and Cellular IP protocols architecture when compared to the integration of Mobile IP and HMIP protocols. This is because of the low handoff latency in cellular IP micromobility protocol.

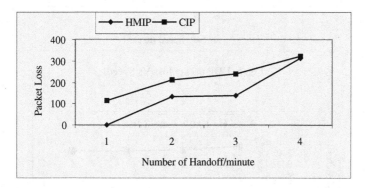

Fig. 4. UDP packet loss Vs Handoff

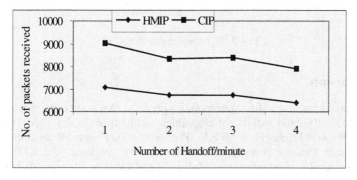

Fig. 5. TCP throughput Vs Handoff

5.2 UDP and TCP Performance with Variable Mobile Speed

In this case, the simulation results are obtained using a single mobile host, continuously moving between base stations with variable speed and UDP packet loss and TCP throughput performance is plotted in Fig.6 and Fig.7 for both integration of Mobile IP with Cellular IP and Mobile IP with HMIP protocols. It is observed from Fig.6 that as the speed of MH increases, the frequency of handoff gets increased and as a result the UDP packet loss also gets increased it is further observed that the UDP packet loss is low in integration of Mobile IP and Cellular IP when compared to integration of Mobile IP and HMIP. This is due to low handoff latency in Cellular IP. From Fig.7 it is observed that as the speed of MH increases the TCP throughput gets decreased.

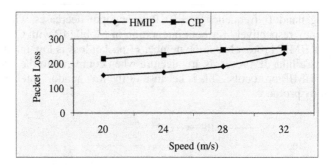

Fig. 6. UDP packet loss Vs Speed

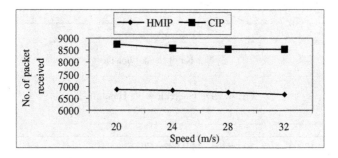

Fig. 7. TCP throughput Vs Speed

6 Conclusion

There is a need for a specific micromobility protocol that interworks with mobile IP for a complete IP-based mobility management mechanism. In this paper, integration of Mobile IP with Hierarchical Mobile IP micromobility protocol and integration of Mobile IP with Cellular IP micromobility protocol is proposed. The UDP and TCP performance results of integration of Mobile IP and Cellular IP protocols is presented and it is compared with the integration of Mobile IP and HMIP protocols. The results shows that the integration of cellular IP with Mobile IP protocols gives better performance when compared to the integration of Mobile IP with Hierarchical Mobile IP protocols.

References

1. C.Perkins: IP Mobility Support for pv4, IETF, RFC3344, Aug.2002.
2. A. Helmy: A multicast-based protocol for IP mobility support, in ACM SIGCOMM 2nd Int. Workshop Networked Group Comm., NGC, Nov.2000, pp. 49-58.
3. Ramachandran Ramjee,et al.: HAWAII: A Domain –Based Approach for Supporting Mobility in Wide-Area Wireless Networks, IEEE/ACM Transactions on networking, vol.10. No.3, June (2002).
4. A.T. Campbell, et al.: Design Implementation and Evaluation of Cellular IP, IEEE Personal Commun., Aug. (2000) 42-49.

5. Claude Castelluecia and Ludovie Bellier: A Hierarchical Mobility management Frame work for the Internet, Proceedings of the IEEE International Workshop on Mobile Multimedia Communication, Sans Deigo, November (1999)
6. A.T.Campbell and J.Gomez Castellanos: IP Micromobility protocols, ACMSIGMO-BILEMobile Comp. Commun. Rev., (2001).
7. E.Gustafsson, A.Jonsson, and C.Perkins: Mobile IP Regional Registration, Internet draft, draft-ietf-mobileip-reg-tunnel-06.txt, Mar. (2002).
8. Micro mobility home page, http://comet columbia.edu/micromobility.
9. ns2 home page, http://www.isi.edu/nsnam/ns

Genetic Algorithm Based Optimization for Location Update and Paging in Mobile Networks

Aniruddha Chandra and Kausik Mal

ETCE Department,
Jadavpur University,
Kolkata – 700032, WB, India
aniruddha_c@rediffmail.com, kausik_mal@yahoo.com

Abstract. When a call to a Mobile Terminal (MT) arrives, the network must locate the microcell where the MT is currently residing. The tracking problem is handled by two operations – Location Updating and Terminal Paging. The total cost per call is the sum of the cost for these two operations. It is difficult to optimize the total cost by classical calculus based techniques, as the expressions become very complex to handle. In this paper the total cost is optimized by finding the optimum distance threshold, value of the optimum distance required for a location update. Genetic Algorithm is proposed for optimization. Hexagonal cell structure and Shortest Distance First (SDF) algorithm are assumed for modeling. Effects of parameters - call to mobility ratio, maximum paging delay, cost ratio of location update to paging on optimized cost value are studied. The optimum cost per call is found to decrease for higher call to mobility ratio and also for larger paging delay. As the cost ratio of location update to paging increases the optimum cost increases. However the cost is found to be relatively less influenced by the statistical distribution of cell residence time.

1 Introduction

The most cultivated areas in telecommunication world is the wireless communication network offering enormous and ever growing interest among the researchers from various industries, research laboratories and universities. The major prospect of wireless network is that it need not have permanent wired line connections between free to move mobile terminals (MT) to centralized system overseeing and controlling the network in contrast to fixed or static wired line network. In a heterogeneous network which is nothing but the collaboration of various networks, a MT is free to move across several other networks for which it is not registered. But the most challenging aspect here in this type of network is the mobility management process. Unlike static network, some information overheads are needed for the centralized coordinator to keep track of the mobile terminals at any instant for the purpose of paging and also to provide some kind of authentication when required. These information overheads are stored in two types of database known as Home Location Register (HLR) and Visitor Location Register (VLR) incorporated within the network subsystem. The central component of the network subsystem is the Mobile services Switching Center (MSC). It acts like a normal switching node of the PSTN or ISDN, and in conjunction with HLR and VLR it provides all the functionality needed to handle a mobile subscriber, such as registration, authentication, location updating, handovers, and call routing to a roaming subscriber.

Accessing HLR database all the time is not effective when cost comes under consideration. To avoid this, VLR database is used as a temporary storage of selective

S. Manandhar et al. (Eds.): AACC 2004, LNCS 3285, pp. 222–231, 2004.
© Springer-Verlag Berlin Heidelberg 2004

information for each MT under the control of that MSC. But this network topology is an intelligent mobility management paradigm consisting of two individual processes called the location update (LU) and terminal paging (TP) process. In general location update can be done in three ways: Distance-based [2,3], Time-based [2, 4], and Movement-based [1, 2, 5]. In case of time-based LU, each MT updates its location after certain interval of time. In case of distance-based and movement-based location update, MT transmits an update signal whenever it crosses a certain distance in terms of number of cells or number of cell boundary crossing respectively. Numerical results show that distance based LU [2] requires lower cost than the other two methods. Again, distance-based location update depends on the size of the cell, whereas movement-based does not depend on the size of the cell thus reducing a constraint.

Terminal paging also causes a significant contribution to the total cost. Whenever a terminal searching request arrives to a MSC it then pages the cells within the current Location Area (LA) of the destined MT. The most simple and currently existing method of searching is the blanket paging [6, 7] in which all the cells within the desired LA are paged simultaneously in a single delay. But it causes the use of scarce network resources like radio bandwidth, power in a large quantity. Enormous power is wasted in paging redundant cells in this way. To reduce redundant paging cost various selective paging strategies have already been proposed. In selective paging strategy using shortest distance first (SDF) [1] algorithm, the total cellular coverage area under each LA is subdivided into several number of concentric rings depending upon the number of allotted polling delays. It uses several polling delays to search the mobile terminal instead of using a single delay to page the whole LA as in the case of blanket paging. Each delay is used to page one or more rings together depending upon the number of allowable polling delays. In this algorithm the rings having shorter distance from the center cell of the LA are paged first or in other words rings are paged sequentially starting from centre ring to the ring along the boundary of the LA using the allotted polling delays until the destined MT is found. The results of this paging algorithm show a drastic improvement in paging cost compared to blanket paging.

In this paper we have optimized the total cost (including both location update and terminal paging). The total cost decreases with distance threshold (d) for low values of "d", but for high values it again start to increase. So we can find an optimal cost value by finding the optimal "d" value. Classical calculus based optimization techniques (such as relaxation) are not suitable as the differentiation yields rather complex and interdependent equations. We propose a genetic search algorithm to find the optimal "d". It has certain advantages [8, 9, 10]. First, the algorithm may not always provide the best solution, but gives a range to work with. Second, the cost function is heavily dependent on various parameters which are user dependent. If the best solution is not acceptable for any such constraint violation, it can provide other solutions from the solution space. Third, as the search space increases with wider coverage area, the efficiency of the algorithm increases, whereas other techniques may become cumbersome to an extent that it is beyond the computing power of handheld devices or impossible to calculate optimum value in real-time applications.

2 System Description

Whenever the MT moves a certain distance away from initial position, where it received the previous call, location is updated. The minimum distance required for a location update is called Distance Threshold. After location update, paging is done. The total mobile coverage area is divided into several subareas. During paging one subarea is searched at a time. The number of subareas depends upon maximum allowable paging delay. The two costs are described separately. The total cost incorporates both the location update cost and paging cost.

2.1 Location Update Cost

We consider a movement based location update scheme. Location is not updated for each cell-boundary crossing. It is updated after "d" number of crossings. Here, "d" is called the location update movement threshold.

Suppose, when a call arrives, the user has crossed "j" cell-boundaries, with respect to his/her previous position, or, where he/she received the previous call. As location is updated per "d" crossings, we assign another variable "i" that denotes, the number of actual location updates. If user stays at his/her previous cell and crosses no boundaries then both "j" and "i" are 0. No location update is required, so cost is 0. We can exclude this case. Now the maximum number of location updates may be ∞, as user may traverse ∞ cell-boundaries. So "i" ranges between 1 to ∞.

If location update cost for one location is "U", then average or expected location updating cost

$$C_U = U \sum_{i=1}^{\infty} i.f(i) \text{ per call arrival} \tag{1}$$

where, f(i) denotes the probability of i number of location updates. Obviously $\sum_{i=1}^{\infty} f(i) = 1$. Now f(i) depends on the distribution of cell residence time, or, how much time user spends in a particular cell.

We start with α(K), which gives the probability of crossing "K" cell-boundaries between two calls [1]. When "K" ranges between 0 to "d-1", no location update is necessary, as location is updated only after "d" boundary crossings. Now for d < K < 2d – 1, only 1 location update is necessary. Whenever K = 2d, two location update is performed. So, the probability of 1 location update, f(1) is equal to the sum of probabilities, that "d" or, "d+1" or, ... "2d-1" boundaries are crossed.

$$\text{Mathematically, } f(1) = \sum_{K=d}^{2d-1} \alpha(K) \tag{2}$$

$$\text{And in general, } f(i) = \sum_{K=i.d}^{(i+1).d-1} \alpha(K) \tag{3}$$

Putting the value of f(i) in the previous equation and changing the variable "K" to "j" we get,

$$C_U = U \sum_{i=1}^{\infty} i \sum_{j=i.d}^{(i+1).d-1} \alpha(j) \text{ per call arrival.} \tag{4}$$

2.2 Paging Cost

SDF Algorithm is used for terminal paging. In widely used blanket paging scheme the total mobile coverage area is searched at a time. In SDF the total coverage area is separated into subareas. Each subarea constitutes some rings of neighbours as illustrated in figure 1.

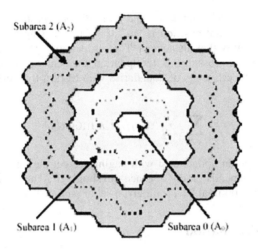

Subarea 2 (A₂)

Subarea 1 (A₁)   Subarea 0 (A₀)

Fig. 1. Subareas and corresponding rings of neighbours

While searching for the MT, searching starts from the centre cell and each subarea is searched at a time. Let the MT be in subarea "j". So we have to search up to "j" th subarea. If "V" be the searching cost for unit cell then average or, expected cost for paging is,

$$C_V = V \sum_{j=0}^{l-1} \rho_j w_j \text{ per call arrival.} \qquad (5)$$

where "ρ_j" is the probability that MT is in subarea "j" and "w_j" is the total number of cells counted from centre cell to the last ring of subarea "j". Upper limit of the summation is set to "l-1" and "l" is the number of partitions of the total coverage area. Here l = min (n , d) , n=maximum allowable paging delay.

We start with "w_j". $w_j = \sum_{k=0}^{j} N(A_k)$ where N(A$_k$) is the number of cells in subarea "k". Now N(A$_k$) can be found out by summation of cells in individual rings which are contained in the subarea $N(A_k) = \sum_{r_i \in A_j} g(i)$ The number of cells in a ring = g(i) = 6i. So ultimately,

$$w_j = \sum_{k=0}^{j} \sum_{r_i \in A_j} 6i \qquad (6)$$

For the calculation of the average probability that MT is in "j" th subarea we define, $\rho_j = \sum\limits_{r_i \in A_j} \pi_i$. The average probability that MT is in "i" th ring,

$\pi_i = \sum\limits_{k=0}^{\infty} \alpha(k)\beta(i, k \bmod d)$ and ring "i" or "r_i" belongs to subarea "j" (A_j). $\alpha(k)$ is probability of crossing "k" boundaries and β(m , n) is the probability that the distance between current and initial position is "m" after "n" crossings [1, 3]. Hence, β(i , k mod d) is the probability that distance is "i" after location update. Location is updated at every "d" number of crossings. After updation, the centre cell shifts. So the residue or, k mod d gives the crossings of boundaries with respect to latest centre cell. Combining them all,

$$\rho_j = \sum\limits_{r_i \in A_j} \sum\limits_{k=0}^{\infty} \alpha(k)\beta(i, k \bmod d) \tag{7}$$

After adding location update cost with paging we get the total cost. Both location update and paging depends on the distance threshold "d". The total cost is to be optimized by finding the optimal "d", for a given set of parameters.

3   Problem Formulation

According to the system description we formulate the problem mathematically in terms of several parameters. Our objective function "C_T" giving the total cost per call arrival, is defined as

$$C_T = C_U + C_V \tag{8}$$

where C_U is location update cost per call and C_V is the paging cost per call. The important parameters which significantly influence the cost per call are,

a) Maximum allowable paging delay (n)
b) Call to mobility ratio (λ_c/λ_m) [1]
c) Gamma (γ) = (Var. λ_m^2)$^{-1}$, where Var and $1/\lambda_m$ are variance and mean of statistical
    distribution of cell residence time [1]
d) Ratio of location update cost to paging cost U:V

Finally the total cost per call is to be optimized by finding the optimal distance threshold "d" for a given set of above parameters. The optimal value of the distance threshold is determined with the help of Genetic Algorithm.

4   Genetic Algorithm

A Genetic algorithm is mainly a probabilistic search algorithm based on the principles and concept of natural selection and evolution. At each generation it maintains a population of individuals where each individual is a coded form of a possible solution of the problem at hand and called chromosome. Each chromosome is evaluated by a function known as fitness function, which is usually the cost function or the objective function of the corresponding optimization problem. Next, new population is generated from the present one through selection, crossover and mutation operations. Purpose of selection mechanism is to select more fit individuals (parents) for crossover and mutation. Crossover causes the exchange of Genetic materials between the parents to form offsprings, whereas mutation incorporates new Genetic material in the offspring. The basic Algorithm is represented through the following flow chart [8, 9].

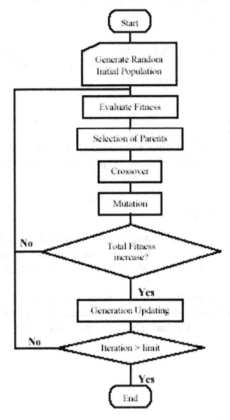

Fig. 2. Flow Chart of Genetic Algorithm

Implementations of above-mentioned components for the proposed Genetic algorithm are as follows [10].

Chromosome Representation
Binary encoding is used. Chromosome is a string of distance threshold value (d) converted to its binary form.

Initial Population
Initial population is generated by selecting d values as positive random numbers and less than 15. Population size is chosen as 8.

Fitness Function
As it is a minimizing problem the inverse of objective function, scaled properly, may suffice.

Selection Operation

Fitness value of each chromosome is directly proportional to the probability of selection of the corresponding solution set. Roulette wheel based selection procedure is adopted here. For low CMR values there is little probability that one string will have a big fitness and others having negligible fitness. So we didn't use rank selection. Steady state selection is also discarded, as it is slow. Elitism is preserved by making crossover probability < 100%.

Crossover Operation

We have used standard simple single point crossover for our purpose. For implementation we have used crossover probability of 75%, i.e., almost 2 chromosomes remain unchanged in every single iteration.

Mutation Operation

For binary encoding scheme the mutations are performed in the form of bit interchanging. The probability of mutation is set to 1%.

A new solution set obtained through crossover and mutation is accepted only if its total fitness value is better than that of the previous generation. Otherwise, the new solution is rejected.

5   Results and Discussions

The total cost per call arrival depends on various parameters. These parameters include update cost "U", paging cost "V", location update movement threshold "d", maximum paging delay "n" and statistical properties of call arrival and mobility – call to mobility ratio (CMR).

For low "d", location update cost dominates. But as "d" is increased above some optimal value "d*", the number of cells to be paged increases drastically. So paging cost dominates. Optimal cost value "C_T^{*}", corresponding to "d*" is found for a given set of parameters.

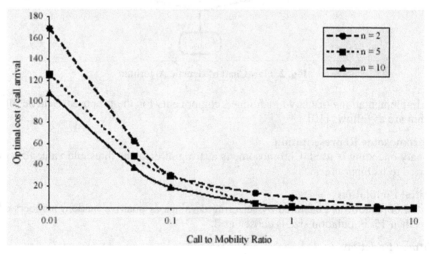

Fig. 3. Optimal cost per call arrival versus CMR for different paging delays. $\gamma = 1$ and Location Update cost to Paging cost ratio U:V = 10:1

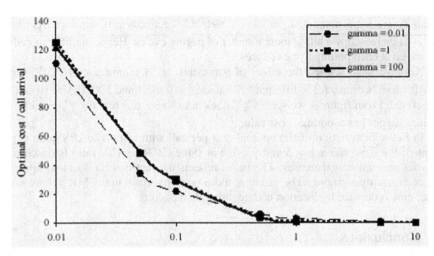

Fig. 4. Optimal cost per call arrival versus CMR for different gamma values. Paging delay n = 5 and Location Update cost to Paging cost ratio U:V = 10:1

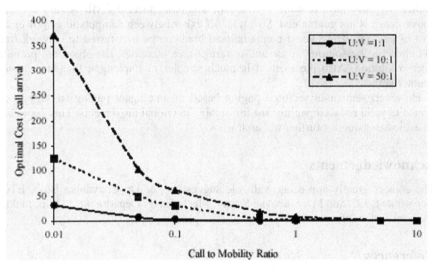

Fig. 5. Optimal cost per call arrival versus CMR for different Location Update cost (U) to Paging Cost (V) ratio. Paging delay n = 5 and γ = 1

CMR solely depends on users and therefore can serve as a measurement parameter of optimal cost for different practical networks. As CMR increases, optimal cost "C_T^*" decreases exponentially. This is because for high CMR, calls arrive before location is updated and only paging cost is considered. We have used a log scale for CMR so that change of "C_T^*" at low CMR is emphasized. CMR range considered in the paper is from 0.01 to 10.

For studying the effect of paging delay "n", optimized cost "C_T^*" versus CMR curve is drawn for 3 different "n" values, n = 2, 5 and 10. We fix U:V = 10 and γ = 1.

From figure 3 it is noted that, for same CMR, "C_T^*" reduces as n increases. As paging delay is increased, we allow more number of paging cycles. Hence, number of cells to be paged at each polling cycle reduces.

Next we have studied the effect of parameter "γ". Optimized cost "C_T^*" versus CMR curve is drawn for 3 different "γ" values, $\gamma = 0.01$, 1 and 100. U:V = 10 and n = 5 is fixed. From figure 4 we see, "C_T^*" does not change much with "γ". For low "γ" values we get lower optimal cost value.

In figure 5, variation of the optimal cost per call with respect to U:V ratio is presented. We have taken, n = 5 and $\gamma = 1$. For same CMR, as U:V ratio is raised from 1to 50, optimal cost increases. The result reflects the fact that the location update is more costly than paging. The effect is more pronounced at low CMR values where total cost is decided by location update rather than paging.

6 Conclusions

In this paper we have presented a method for location management that offers optimal cost. The calculation of cost function is rather tedious. As computing power of MT is limited, we may have to work with a little solution space. If CMR is very low then convergence is not guaranteed. So a tradeoff exists between computational power and cost of tracking. However if computational load can be transferred to network from MT then, as the solution space and coverage area increases, the algorithm provides finer resolution. Also the method is much simpler to implement than its classical counterparts.

However, sequential sectored paging based on intelligent paging strategy is expected to yield reduced paging cost for highly directional movements. That could be a possible extension for further research work.

Acknowledgements

The authors greatly appreciate valuable suggestions of Dr. Chayanika Bose, ETCE Department, J.U. and Mr. Shibayan Sarkar, Mech. Engg. Department, J.U. for making the final draft of the paper.

References

1. Akyildiz I. F., Ho J. S. M. and Lin Y. B. Movement-Based Location Update and Selective Paging for PCS Networks. *IEEE Transactions on Networking*, 4, 4 (August 1996), 629-638.
2. Bar-Noy A., Kessler I. and Sidi M. Mobile users: To update or not to update?. *ACM-Baltzer Journal Wireless Networks*, 1, 2 (July 1995), 175–195.
3. Ho J. S. M. and Akyildiz I. Mobile User Location Update and Paging under Delay Constraints. *ACM-Baltzer Journal of Wireless Networks*, 1, 4 (December 1995), 413–425.
4. Rose C. Minimizing the average cost of paging and registration: A timer-based method. *ACM-Baltzer Journal Wireless Networks*, 2, 2 (June 1996), 109–116.
5. Li J., Kameda H. and Li K. Optimal dynamic mobility management for PCS networks. *IEEE/ACM Tranactions on Networking*, 8 (June 2000), 319–327.
6. Lee H. and Sun J. Mobile Location Tracking by Optimal Paging Zone Partitioning. *In IEEE ICUPC'97*, 1 (October 1997), 168–172.

7. Xie H., Tabbane S. and Goodman D. Dynamic Location Area Management and Performance Analysis. *In IEEE VTC'92*, (May 1992), 536–539.
8. Goldberg D.E. *Genetic algorithms - in search, optimization and machine learning*, Pearson Education, Asia, 2002.
9. Naskar M. K., Mukherjee B., Majumder J. N. and Sarkar S. K. A Genetic Approach for Design Protection in WDM Optical Networks. In *Proceedings of Photonics-2002*, December 2002.
10. Chandra A., Pal P. and Naskar M. K. A Comparative Study of Lagrangian and Genetic Approach for Optimal Capacity Assignment in Computer Networks. *Submitted for publication*, 2003.

Global Backfilling Scheduling in Multiclusters

Jianhui Yue

Software College, The Sichuan University, Chengdu, China, 610065
yjh21cn@21cn.com

Abstract. There exist a centralized scheduler structure and a distributed scheduler structure at multiclusters scheduler. The current centralized scheduler
structure requires exact knowledge of scheduling activities about geographically distributed clusters. However, such timely and frequent information dissertation can not be supported by existed network infrastructure. In order to
make the centralized scheduler structure realistic, this paper investigates the
global scheduler at muliclusters without timely and frequently information distribution. This global scheduler is based on the backfilling scheduling policy
and the global scheduler tries to find holes at clusters for queued jobs at other
cluster. This global backfilling scheduling policy is evaluated by using real
workload trace driven simulation. The simulation results show that proposed
policy consistently outperforms the independent site execution.

1 Introduction

A grid is a collection of resources (computational devices, networks, online instru-
ments, storage archives, etc.) that can be used as an ensemble. Grids provide a great
potential of capabilities that can be brought to high-performance and resource-
intensive applications. In the existed or on-going gird projects, a gird is compromised
by a set of geographically distributed clusters. Such a grid environment is refereed by
the multiclusters environment [1,2]. Effective scheduling job in grid is important in
bringing more satisfactions to users, for the gird system is regarded as the user-centric
system. However, the task of job scheduling is much complicated in multicluster
because of clusters with different scheduling activities.

The local jobs p transparent execution at remote cluster is the greatest difference
between the job scheduling in the multicluster environment and the job scheduling in
cluster environment. Such remote execution is called grid job sharing. In the multiclusers environment, the job scheduling is comprised by local job scheduling and grid
shared scheduling. The local job scheduling can use traditional job scheduling policies such as the FCFS, SJF and backfilling [3,4]. Because the backfilling scheduling
policy is widely adopted at clusters [5], it is the local job scheduling policy in this
study. The grid scheduling structure can be mainly grouped into two kinds [6]. One is
the centralized scheduling and the other is distributed scheduling. The centralized
scheduler structure requires exact knowledge of scheduling activities, such as jobs
arrivals and jobs terminations inside geographically distributed clusters. However,
such timely and frequently information dissertation can not be supported by existed
network infrastructure. In order to make the centralized scheduler structure realistic,
this paper investigates the global scheduler at muliclusters without timely and frequently information distribution.

Since the local scheduling policy is backfilling, the global scheduler is also discussed at context of backfilling. Under the backfilling, the scheduler backfill jobs into

S. Manandhar et al. (Eds.): AACC 2004, LNCS 3285, pp. 232–239, 2004.
© Springer-Verlag Berlin Heidelberg 2004

holes in order to improve the resource utilization rate and reduce the job waiting time. In the multiclusters, the global scheduler can globally backfill jobs into remote clusters. Such global backfilling can further reduce the jobs waiting time. In this global scheduling, the timely and frequent information dissertation is not needed. A set of simulation experiments is conducted by using trace data from Parallel Job Archives [7]. The results show that the proposed global backfilling scheduling policy consistently outperforms the independent site execution.

The organization is as follows. Section 2 introduces the related works of parallel job scheduling in multiclusers environment. Section 3 addresses the global backfilling scheduling without timely and frequent information exchanges. Section 4 gives the performance analysis, and finally Section 5 is the conclusion.

2 Related Works

Srinivasan et al. [8] studied the effect of various backfilling schemes on different priority policies. Their results show that the conservative backfilling policy provides reservations to all jobs, hence limits the backfilling opportunities; on the other hand, the aggressive backfilling policy (EASY) enhances backfilling opportunities, so make the wide jobs difficult to get backfilled. At same time, jobs are grouped into four categories: SN (Short Narrow) jobs, SW (Short Wide) jobs, LN (Long Narrow) jobs and LW (Long Wide) jobs. Such finer categorization of jobs affects the overall slowdown.

Hamscher et al. [6] discussed the typical scheduling structures that occur in computational grids. There are centralized scheduling and hierarchical scheduling structure. In this paper, the hierarchical scheduling is regarded as distributed scheduling. Its simulation result indicates that the backfilling scheduling is better at hierarchical scheduling .So the backfilling scheduling is used in this study. Ernemann et al. [9] studied the influence of the partitioning of resource in a grid on the quality of the schedule. Its simulation results show that configurations with equal sized machines provide significant better scheduling results than machine configurations that are not balanced. In this paper, each cluster is same size. Ernemann et al.[10] addressed the benefit of sharing jobs between the independent clusters in grid environment and the discussed parallel multi-site job execution on different sites. In the case of multi-site job execution, a larger job can be fragmented into smaller sub-jobs and they are concurrently executed at different sites. In this study, the shared job is not fragmented. The structures of grid scheduler on the above researches are centralized scheduling.

Bucur et al [1,2] address the simultaneous allocation of processors to single jobs in different clusters. In the above two research, the structures of grid scheduler are centralized.

In this centralized scheduler, the global scheduler should have exact knowledge of scheduling activities inside each cluster geographically distributed at grid. For example, the global scheduler is notified with jobs arrivals and jobs terminations. Such timely and frequently information exchanges can be supported at current network infrastructure. This paper proposes a global schedule scheme without such timely and frequently information exchanges. At same time, fragmented jobs, namely shared jobs, are determined by the synthesized workload trace. So they also did not consider how to select a shared job. However, this paper will discuss the selection of shared job from local job queue.

Subramani et al [11,12] proposed distributed scheduling algorithms that use multiple simultaneous requests at different sites. In these studies, the local gird scheduler transmits each job to k least loaded sites and all the local jobs are regarded as potential shared job. However, the scheduling policy at this paper only selects some jobs to be shared jobs which can be backfilled into holes at other cluster. So the global backfilling scheduling policy proposed at this paper is complemented to it.

3 Proposed Scheduling Strategy

In the centralized scheduler structure, the global scheduler need have exact information about scheduling events across geographically distributed clusters at gird. Collecting each scheduling event originated from the individual cluster essentially is a issue of monitoring grid. Such directly monitoring is impossible at current network infrastructure [16]. In the grid monitoring projects, the living information can not be directly obtained and the grid information predication techniques are proposed [16]. So current centralized global schedulers with help of exact and timely grid information can not be employed in a real world.

In order to avoid frequent collecting information of each cluster, each cluster does not send every scheduling event to the global scheduler. Each cluster sends a snapshot of its own scheduling information, which includes resource utilization profile, running jobs profile and waiting jobs queue profile at fixed interval. These snapshots of scheduling information do not contain much data and do not consume network bandwidth. Additionally, such information distribution does not incur more overhead to the global scheduler, because the frequency of this information dissertation is slower than the current centralized global scheduler does. At other hand, such scheduling information is approximation of current cluster information and is a special variant of information predication. So it is a feasible information distribution scheme.

After collecting snapshots of all clusters scheduling information, the global scheduler computes the global jobs migration plan. Because the each cluster adopts backfilling policy to schedule local jobs, so the snapshots of scheduling information are related to backfilling policy. In order to make a good global jobs migration plan, the computation should work as the local backfilling policy. This computation is called global backfilling. Its aim is to backfill local jobs into holes at remote clusters.

In the each cluster, waiting jobs can not be started, because there is no hole in the local cluster for them. However, there exist holes for the some waiting jobs at other clusters. So the global scheduling finds holes at other clusters for the waiting jobs. After finding holes, the global scheduler migrates these jobs at remote cluster to execute. This paper proposes two methods to find holes to migration local jobs. One is the fixed order migration, referred as FO migration, the other is round robin migration, referred as RR migration. In the FO migration, the scheduler traverses waiting queues at a fixed order to find holes for these queued jobs and matches jobs with holes other clusters, which are traversed at fixed order too. The FO migration is illustrated at Figure 1. In the RR migration, jobs at one waiting queue are matched with holes at other cluster at round robin order. The RR migration is showed at Figure 2.

In the Figure1 and Figure 2 , the canBkf( ) judges whether the current cluster exists hole for the job with help of the snapshots of cluster information. Additionally, the job with great data size spends much time to be transferred and such a migration blocks other migrating jobs with smaller data size, thus degrading the scheduling quality. So the job with great data size should not be migrated.

```
global_scheduler_fixed_order ( ){
  1 compute the cluster order: cluster[] and wait-
    ing queue order : queue[].
    2 for(i=0;i<MAX;i++){// order of cluster
  for ( j=0;j < MAX ; j ++){ // order of queue
      if ( i == j) skip ;
      for(k=0;k<MAX;k++ ){
      job=queue[j][k];
      if ( job size is too great ) skip;
      if( canBkf( queue[j],cluster[i] )
      plan to migrate job from j to i ;
      }
    }
  }
  3 send migration plan to source cluster
}
```

Fig. 1. FO Migration

```
global_scheduler_RR ( ){
  1 compute the cluster order: cluster[] and
    waiting queue order : queue[].
    2 for(i=0,j=cluster[0];i<MAX;i++){
    // order of queues
      for(k=0;k<MAX;k++ ){ // for the job
      job=queue [k];
      if ( job is local to cluster[j] ) skip;
      if ( job size is too great ) skip;
      if( canBkf( queue[j],cluster[i] ){
      plan to migrate job from j to i ;
      j=j++%MAX;
      }
    }
  }
  3 send migration plan to source cluster
}
```

Fig. 2. RR Migration

4 Performance Analysis

4.1 Trace Workload

Since there is no available real gird systems workload, the CTC workload traces [11] are used in this investigation. The collection of workload traces is available from Feitelson's archive [7]. The CTC trace is from the 430-node Cornell Theory Center. In order to provide the real workload trace data to the different cluster, the original CTC workload trace data is divided into 5 partitions. Each partition contains continuous job logs at the original workload trace and they presents the nearly a one month set of jobs. Such division does not only maintain the variance of workload in the original workload with time but also represent the workload differences among clusters, which is a fact that resource sharing among grid systems.

4.2 Simulation Environments

The above distributed parallel job scheduling policies are implemented in an event-driven simulator. In this simulator, there are five same size clusters with capacity of the 430 nodes, which is same with the CTC environment. These clusters are refereed as CTC0, CTC1, ... , CTC4 respectively. The above partitions of parallel job trace data are used as input into the different clusters respectively and the simulator generates arrival and termination events. When an arrival or termination event occurs, the simulator executes the scheduling policies. When receiving the new job, the local scheduler entity checks the system resource state. If a new job can be started, it is sent to the allocated processor entities and the system resource state is updated. Otherwise, it is enqueued into the waiting queue. The processor entity sends the job termination event to the scheduler entity after the job's duration. When receiving the completed job, the local scheduler entity updates the system resource state and computes the completed job's bound slowdown and backfills jobs in waiting queue according to backfill policy.

At fixed interval, all the clusters send snapshot of the current scheduling information to the global scheduler. After receiving such information, the global scheduler finds holes for the queued jobs and computes job migration plan, which is send to clusters. On arrival of a migration plan, the home cluster scheduler transmits migrated jobs to one remote cluster over network entity. After receiving a migrated job, the cluster scheduler try to start it .If it fails, the job is placed into shared queue. When receiving a completed job event, the scheduler first schedules shared jobs queued at shared queue and then examine the local waiting queue.

In order to simulate the jobs migration at network, the network entity is added at the simulator. For the simplicity, the network topology is all-to-all connection and all connection path width is 10Mb/s [11]. The original CTC trace data does not contain information about the size of job data, which includes input data and job program. This paper believes that the size of job data is job duration 300 /Mb [13].

To evaluate the system performance, the bound slowdown [15] and waiting time are used. The bound slowdown is defined as:

$$\text{bound slowdown} = (\text{wait time} + \text{Max}(\text{running time}, 10)) / \text{Max}(\text{running time}, 10) \qquad (1)$$

Such metrics are a user centric. The reason to use these metrics is that the grid system also user centric one.

4.3 Comparison Global Backfilling Policy with Independent Execution

This subsection discusses the global backfilling and independent execution. The independent execution is that there is no job migration among clusters under the backfilling scheduling policy. In the global backfilling, the interval of information dissertation is 30 minutes. The Figure 3 shows job waiting time changes of global backfilling against the independent execution. The waiting time of jobs at each cluster is reduced. For example, the waiting time of jobs at CTC4 cluster under global backfilling is reduced to nearly 1/25 of independent execution and average waiting time of jobs under global backfilling at all clusters is reduced to nearly 1/10 of independent execution. This waiting time of jobs reduced so much is because that the migrated jobs are backfilled to other cluster to be executed and thus the waiting time of migrated jobs is reduced. The figure 4 shows changes of bounded slowdown of global backfilling against the independent execution. The slowdowns of all clusters under global back-

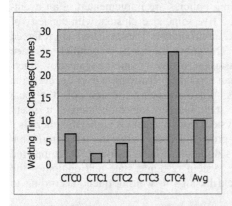
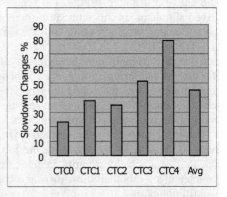
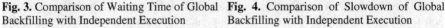

Fig. 3. Comparison of Waiting Time of Global Backfilling with Independent Execution

Fig. 4. Comparison of Slowdown of Global Backfilling with Independent Execution

filling policy are reduced compared with the independent execution. For example, slowdown of cluster CTC4 under global backfilling is reduced by 79.1% and the average slowdown of clusters under global backfilling is reduced by 45.2%. This reduction of slowdown is the result of global backfilling. In the global backfilling, the migrated jobs are executed earlier than they are executed at local cluster. So the slow-down under global backfilling policy is greatly reduced.

4.4 Comparison FO Migration with RR Migration and Independent Execution

This subsection compares the load balancing among clusters under FO migration with RR migration and independent execution. In order to evaluate the load balancing, the standard deviation of utilization rates among all clusters is introduced. The Figure 5 depicts standard deviations of utilization rate at individual cluster under different policies. In the Figure 5, the standard deviation of utilization rate under the independent execution is greatest, which reflects the difference of jobs configurations at different clusters. The standard deviations of utilization rate under both RR migration and FO migration are smaller than the independent execution. Such reduction shows the workloads among clusters under global backfilling are more balanced than the independent. This is because that the jobs migration among the global backfilling. In the both RR migration and FO migration, cluster with the least utilization rate is firstly to provide holes for jobs at other clusters. At same time, queue at cluster with great utilization rate is the last one to be selected. So the load balancing is obtained at global backfilling policy.

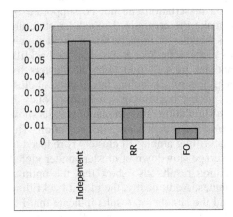
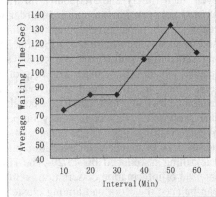

Fig. 5. Standard Deviations of Utilization Rate at Individual Cluster under Different Policies

Fig. 6. Average Waiting Time under Different Information Distribution Intervals

Additionally, the standard deviation of utilization rate under FO migration is smaller than the RR migration. So the workloads at different clusters are more evenly distributed under the FO migration than the RR migration. This is because that under the FO migration the jobs firstly fill holes at cluster with least weight, while under RR migration jobs are backfilled at holes at clusters according round robin order.

4.5 Comparison of Waiting Time
Under Different Information Distribution Intervals

Under the global backfilling policy, the snapshots of scheduling information, which includes resource utilization profile, running jobs profile and waiting jobs queue profile, at different clusters are sent to the global scheduler at a interval. In order to evaluate the scheduling qualities under different intervals, this subsection compares average waiting time among clusters at different intervals.

The following intervals of exchange information are tested: 10 minutes, 20 minutes, 30 minutes, 40 minutes, 50 minutes and 60 minutes. The Figure 6 describes average waiting time under different information distribution Intervals under FO migration. In the Figure 6, the average waiting time increase with value of interval increasing. This is because that with value of interval increasing the times to find holes at remote clusters for waiting jobs are reduced and thus many jobs potentially backfilled into remote cluster lose many backfilling chances. In the Figure 6, the waiting time at the interval of 20 minutes is nearly same as waiting time at the interval of 30 minutes. However, when the interval is 40 minutes, the waiting time is 25 minutes longer than the waiting time at interval 30 minutes. So the information distribution interval of 30 minutes is a optimal one.

5 Conclusion

There exist a centralized scheduler structure and a distributed scheduler structure at multiclusters scheduler. The current centralized scheduler structure requires exact knowledge of scheduling activities about geographically distributed clusters. However, such timely and frequently information dissertation can not be supported by existed network infrastructure. In order to make the centralized scheduler structure realistic, this paper investigates the global scheduler at muliclusters without timely and frequently information distribution. This global scheduler is based on the backfilling scheduling policy and the global scheduler tries to find holes at clusters for queued jobs at other cluster with help of snapshots of scheduling information at clusters, which are dissertated at interval. This global backfilling scheduling policy is evaluated by using real workload trace driven simulation. The simulation results show that proposed policy consistently outperforms the independent site execution. The average waiting time of jobs under global backfilling among all clusters is reduced to nearly 1/10 of independent execution and average slowdown of clusters under global backfilling is reduced by 45.2%.The simulation results also show that the optimal interval of information dissertation is 30 minutes. Additionally, the global backfilling can balance the workload among clusters and the simulation results indicate that FO migration can more effectively balance workload among clusters than RR migration.

References

1. A. Bucur and D. Epema. "Local versus Global Queues with Processor Co-Allocation in Multicluster Systems" ,In D. Feitelson,L. Rudolph, and U. Schwiegelshohn, editors, 8th Workshop on Job Scheduling Strategies for Parallel Processing, volume 2537 of LNCS, pages 184–204. Springer-Verlag, 2002.
2. A. Bucur and D. Epema," The Performance of Processor Co-Allocation in Multicluster Systems", In Proceedings of the CC-GRID 2003, 2003

3. D. Lifka. The ANL/IBM SP scheduling system. In *JSSPP*, 1995
4. J. Skovira, W. Chan, H. Zhou, and D. Lifka. "The easy-loadleveler API project". In *JSSPP*, 1996
5. O. Arndt, B. Freisleben, T. Kielmann, and F. Thilo. "A comparative study of online scheduling algorithms for networks of workstations". *Cluster Computing*, 3(2):95–112, 2000.
6. V. Hamscher, U. Schwiegelshohn, A.Streit, and R. Yahyapour, "Evaluation of Job-Scheduling Strategies for Grid Computing", In *Proc. Grid '00*, pages 191–202, 2000.
7. D. G. Feitelson. Parallel Workload Archive
   http://www.cs.huji.ac.il/labs/parallel/workload/logs.html.
8. S.Srinivasan,R.Kettinuthu,V.Subramani and P.Sadayappan, "Characterization of Backfilling Strategies for Parallel Job Scheduling". In Proceedings of 2002 Intl.Workshops on Parallel Processing,2002.
9. C. Ernemann, V.Hamscher,A.Streit, and R.Yahhyapour, "On Effects of Machine Configurations on Parallel Job Scheduling in Computational Grids", In Proceedings of International Conference on Architecture of Computing Systems,(ARCS 2002),pages 169-176,2002
10. C. Ernemann, V.Hamscher, U.Schwiegelshohn, R. Yahyapour, A. Streit,"On Advantages of Grid Computing for Parallel Job Scheduling", In Proceedings of the CC-GRID 2002,pages 39-46,2002
11. V. Subramani, R. Kettimuthu, S.Srinivasan and P. Sadayappan,"Distributed Job Scheduling on Computational Grids using Multiple Simultaneous Requests," *Proc. of 11-th IEEE Symposium on High Performance Distributed Computing (HPDC 2002)*, 2002.
12. V. Subramani, R. Kettimuthu, S.Srinivasan and P. Sadayappan,"Scheduling of Parallel Jobs in a Heterogeneous Multi-Site Environment" ,In Proceeding of 9th Workshop on Job Scheduling Strategies for Parallel Processing,(JSSPP2003) pages 87-104, 2003
13. Kavitha Ranganathan , Ian Foster, "Simulation Studies of Computation and Data Scheduling Algorithms for Data Grids", *Journal of Grid Computing* 1, Pages 53–62, 2003.
14. B.G Lawson,E.Smirni,and D. Puiu , "Self-adpating backfilling scheduling for parallel Systems",In International Conference on Parallel Processing, 2002.
15. A. W. Mu'alem and D. G. "Feitelson. Utilization, predictability,workloads, and user runtime estimates in scheduling the IBM sp2 with backfilling", In *IEEE Transactions on Parallel and Distributed Computing*, volume 12, 2001.
16. Wolski, R., Spring, N. and Hayes, J., "The Network Weather Service: A Distributed Resource Performance Forecasting Service for Metacomputing", *Journal of Future Generation Computing Systems* (1998) 757-768.

Computation of Ternary Covering Arrays Using a Grid

Jose Torres-Jimenez[2], Carlos De Alfonso[1], and Vicente Hernández[1]

[1] DSIC Universidad Politecnica de Valencia
Camino de Vera S/N
Valencia, Espanã
{vhernand,calfonso}@dsic.upv.es

[2] ITESM Campus Cuernavaca, Computer Science Department
Av. Paseo de la Reforma 182-A, Lomas de Cuernavaca
62589 Temixco Morelos, Mexico
Tel. +34-96-3877356, Fax +34-96-3877359
jtj@itesm.mx

Abstract. Grid technology emerged (mainly) in response to the need of making efficient use of underutilized computer resources, and the availability of many commercial and freeware grid management software is making a reality the dream of having huge distributed grid computing at reasonable costs. In this paper a brief introduction to the concept of grid computing is presented, and in order to evidence the usefulness of the grid computing approach, it was applied to compute instances of a hard NP-Complete problem, namely ternary covering arrays (CA) computation, using a mutation selection algorithm that ran using InnerGRID over a UPV's computer cluster.

Topics: Cluster and Grid Computing.

1   Introduction

The main ingredients of this paper are grid computing, and covering arrays (CA). Grid computing [11] offers the opportunity of tackling hard problems using underutilized computer resources at no extra costs. CA are very useful for hardware and software testing [1], and data compression [2]. A covering array(CA) $CA(N; t, k, v)$ is an $N \times k$ array on v symbols s.t. every $N \times t$ subarray contains all ordered subsets from v symbols of size t at least once.

In this paper is reported the use of grid computing, over a computer cluster, for calculate $CA(N; 2, k, 3)$ (ternary CA), using a a mutation-selection algorithm. The rest of the paper is organized as follows: firstly, a brief introduction to grid computing is presented, indicating also the features of the grid environment used at Universidad Politecnica de Valencia (UPV); secondly, a brief state of the art about CA is presented, highlighting the ternary case; thirdly, details of the simple mutation-selection algorithm for computing ternary CA is presented; fourthly the results obtained are presented; and finally conclusions are stated.

S. Manandhar et al. (Eds.): AACC 2004, LNCS 3285, pp. 240–246, 2004.

2   Grid Computing at UPV

Advances in networking have enabled the introduction and development of distributed computing paradigms [11]. Applying them, developers divide their tasks into independent and smaller tasks which are placed into independent address spaces. Networking has also fostered the interchange of information and the creation of virtual communities [12].

Scientific virtual communities, leaning on distributed computing, created the modern Virtual Organization (VO) concept. Scientific virtual communities need a vast amount of computing power for simulation. VO permits sharing distinct kind of resources (such as computation, storage, etc.), further than information interchange [13]. Grid technology appeared for allowing resource sharing in scientific developments in an organized way [14], providing a framework for efficient and balanced use of underused computer resources.

Shared resources in a grid environment are from different nature. i.e., computing power, sharing idle cpu cycles by executing third party's applications; storage, share main or secondary storage devices; sharing communications applications may obtain high bandwidth by using disjoint networks; special devices which organizations cannot afford buying several units, etc.

In order to create the grid infrastructure, some kind of middleware is needed. There are some well-known projects in grid middleware, such as the open source Globus Toolkit [16] or Unicore [17]. Recently private enterprises have noticed advantages on using grid technology and have developed their own developments, such as InnerGRID [15] or Avaki Data Grid [18].

InnerGRID is a set of tools which allow constructing and managing a grid environment formed by heterogeneous computers. One of its main applications is to distribute computer intensive jobs for taking advantage of unused cpu cycles, for speeding up calculations. InnerGRID considers a task to be ran on a multi-dimensional space defined by its parameters. It also assumes that the task can be subdivided into smaller tasks called microtasks whose results can be combination at a low cost for providing the full task results. This paradigm is suitable for parametric scientific simulation problems.

InnerGRID architecture consists of a server and agents which connect to it, reporting their state and available resources. The server monitors the state of the agents and assigns subtask executions to them. Once a task is assigned to be run, the agent downloads the needed files and performs the execution. When execution is finalized, the agent uploads the results to the server for being able to be retrieved by users. The server takes care of missing executions for reassigning resources for being carried out. The InnerGRID architecture can be seen in figure 1.

At UPV, the InnerGRID is currently installed over an IBM cluster with 64 Pentium Xeon biprocessor at 2.4 GHz, with 2.5 GB RAM per node, this installation was used to ran all the microtasks needed for ternary CA computation using a mutation-selection algorithm.

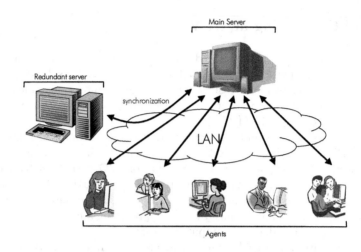

Fig. 1. Server Agent Interaction Under InnerGRID architecture

3   CA State of the Art

A covering array(CA) $CA(N; t, k, v)$ is an $N \times k$ array on v symbols s.t. every $N \times t$ sub array contains all ordered subsets from v symbols of size t at least once. In order to be more useful a CA must satisfy the condition that the value of N must be a minimum, for example $CA(v^2; 2, 3, v)$ is optimal, see for instance the optimal $CA(4; 2, 3, 2) = \{\{000\}, \{110\}, \{101\}, \{011\}\}$. Optimal CA are known only for limited cases, and the only case that is totally solved is $CA(N; 2, k, 2)$ [3]. An algorithm for computing optimal $CA(N; 2, k, 2)$ (assuming that the v values are 0 and 1) is:

1. Fill the first row of the CA with zeros.
2. Construct the $\binom{N-1}{\lceil \frac{N}{2} \rceil}$ combinations composed of $\lceil \frac{N}{2} \rceil$ ones and $(N - 1 - \lceil \frac{N}{2} \rceil)$ zeros and set these combinations as the columns for the remaining CA $N - 1$ rows.

For $v = p^x$ (p is prime and integer $x \geq 1$) optimal CA are known only for $k \leq v + 1$, and in general optimal CA computation is an NP-Complete problem [10]. For this reason many heuristic approaches (simulated annealing, genetic algorithms and tabu search) have been used for compute CA . For large k and $v = 2$ [3] the optimal $CA(N; 2, k, 2)$ satisfies $N \approx \log(k) + \frac{1}{2} \log(\log(k))$, and for large k and $v > 2$ the optimal $CA(N; 2, k, v)$ [9] satisfies the condition that $N \approx \frac{v}{2} \log(k)$.

The computation of optimal $CA(N; 2, k, 3)$ is still an open problem, even many related works were reported [2] [4] [7]. In the table 1 appear the best bounds reported in [4], the N column indicates the number of rows of the ternary CA, and the k column indicates the CA columns range for the indicated N value. It is remarkable that the CA for $2 \leq k \leq 7$ were demonstrated to be optimal [3].

Table 1. Reported maximum number of columns(k) for which optimal ternary CA for a fixed number of rows N

N	k
9	$2 \leq k \leq 4$
11	$k = 5$
12	$6 \leq k \leq 7$
13	$8 \leq k \leq 9$
14	$k = 10$
15	$10 \leq k \leq 16$
18	$17 \leq k \leq 24$
19	$25 \leq k \leq 27$
20	$28 \leq k \leq 36$
21	$37 \leq k \leq 48$
22	$49 \leq k \leq 50$

Table 2. Reported maximum number of columns(k) for which optimal ternary CA for a fixed number of rows N

N	k
9	$k = 4$
10	$k = 5$
11	$k = 5$
12	$7 \leq k \leq 14$
13	$9 \leq k \leq 18$
14	$10 \leq k \leq 20$
15	$16 \leq k \leq 32$
16	$16 \leq k \leq 32$
17	$16 \leq k \leq 32$
18	$24 \leq k \leq 48$
19	$27 \leq k \leq 54$
20	$36 \leq k \leq 72$
21	$48 \leq k \leq 96$
22	$50 \leq k \leq 100$

4 Mutation-Selection Algorithm

In order to present the mutation algorithm used, a brief description of blind searching algorithms is given first. Assuming that $f(x)$ is an objective function and x belongs to definite and bounded realm, the search space is the set of values that can take the variable x. A trial is an evaluation of $f(x)$ for a specific value, for instance $f(x = x_0)$. A blind searching algorithm tries to find a value x^*, s.t. $f(x = x*)$ be an optimum. Mutation-selection algorithms belongs to the class of blind searching algorithm.

A simple mutation-selection algorithm, uses one point of the search space (called *parent-point*) to generate multiple points (called *children-points*) using a mutation operator, next the selection of the best point of the set of *children-points* is done, and the cycle is repeated until a certain termination criterion is met. The pseudocode of the used mutation-selection algorithm is:

```
Mutation-Selection Algorithm One Parent m Children
     parent = random potential solution
     REPEAT
          FOR i=1 TO m
               child_i =mutate(parent)
          END FOR
          parent=best(set of children)
     UNTIL termination criteria is met
     RETURN parent
End Algorithm
```

Contextualizing the mutation-selection algorithm for ternary CA computation, we have the next points:

- A potential solution is an array of size $N \times k$ s.t. a specific array value is taken from the set $\{0, 1, 2\}$, in this way the total search space is 3^{Nk}. The search space was reduced assuming that a column may have a balance among the three alphabet symbols, then the reduced search space is approximately $\left(\left\lceil \frac{N!}{(\lceil \frac{N}{3} \rceil!)^3} \right\rceil_k \right)$. For instance if $N = 12$, and $k = 7$, the original search space is $3^{Nk} \approx 1.2 \times 10^{40}$, and the reduced search space is $\left(\left\lceil \frac{N!}{(\lceil \frac{N}{3} \rceil!)^3} \right\rceil_k \right) \approx 1.2 \times 10^{28}$

- The children cardinality was set to 10 (this value gives good results during the algorithm configuration).
- Even there are many options for the mutation operator, the exchanging of two different symbols within one column was selected, given that, the change introduced is smooth.
- The operator called **best** (see the mutation-selection pseudocode) searches for the element that has less missing pairs.
- The termination criteria (for a specific set of N and k) occurs when the number of missing pairs is zero or when a maximum of 100000 iterations was reached.

The microtasks that were ran over the grid receive as parameters the N (over the range 9 and 22), and the k value according the values of table 2 (the lower value for k was taken from the upper bound of table 1, and the upper bound is fixed to the double of this value, except for $2 \leq k \leq 7$ where optimallity was demonstrated [3]).

5   Results

Thanks to the grid technology applied, it was possible to improve or to equal the bounds previously reported. In table 3 a summary of the results is presented. Through the analysis of the best k found values, it can be seen that for $N = 3i$ ($i = 3, 4, ...$), the relationship among N and k can be stated as: for every three more rows (N value) the number of columns is doubled (k value), i.e. $k = 2^{\frac{N-3}{3}}$ for $N \geq 9$, see last column in table 3. Only for illustrative purposes, we give in table 5 and 4, the covering arrays computed for $(N = 12, k = 7)$, and $(N = 18, k = 30)$ respectively.

6   Conclusions

In this paper Grid technology was applied to solve a hard NP combinatorial problem, namely ternary covering array computation using a simple mutation-selection algorithm. Thanks to the features of grid computing (managed using InnerGRID and a UPV's cluster), it was possible to reproduce and improve the best bounds reported. Thanks to the gained experience, it is believed that Grid computing is suitable to solve hard combinatorial problems (like the one

Table 3. Reported maximum number of columns(k) for which optimal ternary CA for a fixed number of rows N

N	k	Best k Found	$k = 2^{\frac{N-3}{3}}$
9	$k = 4$	$k = 4$	$k = 4$
10	$k = 5$	$k = 4$	
11	$k = 5$	$k = 5$	
12	$7 \leq k \leq 14$	$k = 7$	$k = 8$
13	$9 \leq k \leq 18$	$k = 9$	
14	$10 \leq k \leq 20$	$k = 10$	
15	$16 \leq k \leq 32$	$k = 20$	$k = 16$
16	$16 \leq k \leq 32$	$k = 20$	
17	$16 \leq k \leq 32$	$k = 24$	
18	$24 \leq k \leq 48$	$k = 30$	$k = 32$
19	$27 \leq k \leq 54$	$k = 32$	
20	$36 \leq k \leq 72$	$k = 41$	
21	$48 \leq k \leq 96$	$k = 64$	$k = 64$
22	$50 \leq k \leq 100$	$k = 73$	

Table 4. Ternary CA for $N = 18$ and $k = 30$

```
0 0 0 0 0 0 0 0 0 0 0 0 0 0 0 0 0 0 0 0 0 0 0 0 0 0 0 0 0 0
0 0 0 0 0 0 0 0 0 0 0 0 0 0 0 0 0 0 1 1 1 1 1 1 1 1 1 1 1 1
0 0 0 0 0 0 0 0 1 1 1 1 1 1 1 1 1 1 0 1 1 1 2 2 2 2 2 2 2 2
0 0 0 0 1 1 1 1 0 0 0 0 1 1 2 2 2 2 2 2 2 2 2 0 1 1 1 2 2 2
0 1 1 1 1 0 1 1 1 0 1 1 2 2 2 0 0 1 2 0 0 2 2 1 0 1 2 1 1 2
0 2 2 2 2 2 2 2 2 2 0 0 0 0 1 1 1 1 2 0 2 0 0 1 2 0 2 2 2 1
1 0 1 1 1 0 1 1 2 2 2 1 2 2 2 0 0 1 0 0 2 2 0 1 2 0 1 1 2 1
1 1 0 1 1 1 1 2 2 1 2 1 0 1 1 2 0 2 1 0 0 0 2 2 1 0 2 0 1 1
1 1 1 0 1 2 2 1 2 2 2 1 2 0 2 2 1 1 0 2 1 0 0 1 1 0 0 0 2 2
1 1 1 1 2 1 2 0 1 0 0 1 1 0 1 1 1 1 1 2 1 2 2 0 0 2 2 1 0 0
1 1 1 0 1 2 2 1 2 2 1 2 0 2 2 1 1 0 2 1 0 0 1 1 0 0 0 0 2 2
1 1 1 1 2 2 0 2 1 1 1 2 0 2 2 1 1 0 2 1 0 0 1 1 0 0 0 0 2 2
1 2 2 2 0 2 1 0 0 2 2 1 1 1 0 2 1 1 2 2 0 2 2 0 1 0 2 0 1 1
2 0 2 2 2 2 2 2 0 0 1 2 1 1 1 0 0 1 2 2 2 0 1 2 2 0 1 0 0 1
2 1 2 2 0 0 2 2 2 1 0 0 1 2 2 2 2 1 0 2 0 0 2 2 2 1 1 1 1 0
2 2 0 2 2 2 2 1 1 2 0 2 2 2 1 0 2 2 0 0 1 1 2 1 1 0 2 2 0 0
2 2 1 2 1 1 0 0 2 0 2 2 2 2 2 2 1 2 1 1 1 1 0 0 2 1 0 0 0 2
2 2 2 0 2 0 1 2 1 1 2 2 2 0 2 1 0 2 2 1 1 0 1 1 0 2 1 2 0 2
2 2 2 1 1 1 0 1 1 2 1 1 0 0 0 2 2 0 1 1 2 2 1 2 2 2 2 0 2 0
```

Table 5. Ternary CA for $N = 12$ and $k = 7$

```
0 0 0 0 0 0 0
0 0 0 1 1 1 1
0 1 1 0 1 2 2
0 2 2 2 2 0 1
1 0 1 1 2 0 2
1 1 0 2 2 2 0
1 1 2 0 0 1 1
1 2 1 2 1 1 0
2 0 2 2 0 2 2
2 1 2 1 1 0 0
2 2 0 0 2 1 2
2 2 1 1 0 2 1
```

illustrated in this paper). As future works we are planning the generation of tables for ternary covering arrays for larger number of rows (i.e. $N > 22$) and in this way validate the empirical rule that $k = 2^{\frac{N-3}{3}}$ for $N \geq 9$.

References

1. D. M. Cohen, S. R. Dalal, M. L. Freeman, and G. C. Patton, *The AETG system: an approach to testing software based on combinatorial design*, IEEE Trans. Software Engineering 23:437-444, 1997.
2. B. Stevens, *Transversal covers and packings*, PhD thesis, University of Toronto, 1998.
3. N. J. A. Sloane, *Covering arrays and intersecting codes*, Journal of combinatorial designs, 1(1):51-63, 1993.
4. B. Stevens and E. Mendelsohn, *New recursive methods for transversal covers*, Journal of combinatorial designs, 7(3):185-203, 1999.
5. L. Yu and K. C. Tai, *In-parameter-order: a test generation strategy for pairwise testing*, In Proceedings Third IEEE International High-Assurance Systems Engineering Symposium, 1998, pp. 254-261
6. T. Yu-Wen and W. S. Aldiwan, *Automating test case generation for the new generation mission software system*, In Proceedings IEEE Aerospace Conference, 2000, pp. 431-437.
7. P. R. J. Östergard, *Construction of mixed covering codes*, Technical report, digital systems laboratory, Helsinki University of Technology, 1991.
8. M. B. Cohen, P. B. Gibbons, W. B. Mugridge, and C. J. Colbourn, *Constructing test suites for interaction testing*, Proceedings. of 25th International Conference on Software Engineering, 2003, pp. 38-48
9. L. Gargano, J. Korner, and U. Vaccaro, *Capacities: from information theory to extremal set theory*, Journal of Combinatory Theory Ser. A, 68(2):296-316, 1994.
10. G. Seroussi and N. H. Bshouty, *Vector sets for exhaustive testing of logical circuits*, IEEE Trans. Information Theory 34 (1988), pp. 513-522.
11. Berstis V., *Fundamentals of Grid Computing*, IBM Redbooks Paper, 2002.
12. Waldo J., Wyant G., Wollrath A., and Kendall S., *A note on Distributed computing*, Sun Microsystems Laboratories, Inc., November 1994.
13. Foster I., Kesselman C., and Tuecke S., *The Anatomy of the Grid: Enabling Scalable Virtual Organizations*
14. Foster I., Kesselman C., Nick J., and Tuecke S., *The Physiology of the Grid: An Open Grid Services Architecture for Distributed Systems Integration*, 2002
15. *InnerGRID User Manual*, GridSystems S.A., 2003.
16. Sandholm T., and Gawor J., *Globus toolkit 3 core - a grid service container framework*, http://www.globus.org, 2003
17. The Unicore Forum. http://www.unicore.org, 2003
18. Avaki page: http://www.avaki.com

Impact of Algorithm Design
in Implementing Real-Time Active Control Systems

M.A. Hossain[1], M.O. Tokhi[2], and K.P. Dahal[1]

[1] Department of Computing, School of Informatics
The University of Bradford, Bradford, BD7 1DP, UK
[2] Department of Automatic Control & Systems Engineering
The University of Sheffield, Sheffield S1 3JD, UK
m.a.hossain1@bradford.ac.uk

Abstract. This paper presents an investigation into the impact of algorithm design for real-time active control systems. An active vibration control (AVC) algorithm for flexible beam systems is employed to demonstrate the critical design impact for real-time control applications. The AVC algorithm is analyzed, designed in various forms and implemented to explore the impact. Finally, a comparative real-time computing performance of the algorithms is presented and discussed to demonstrate the merits of different design mechanisms through a set of experiments.

1 Introduction

Although computer architectures incorporate fast processing hardware resources, high performance real-time implementation of an algorithm requires an efficient design and software coding of the algorithm so as to exploit special features of the hardware and avoid associated problems of the architecture. This paper presents an investigation into the analysis and design mechanisms that will lead to reduction in execution time in implementing real-time control algorithms. Active vibration control (AVC) of a simulated flexible beam based on finite difference (FD) method is considered to demonstrate the effectiveness of the proposed methods.

In practice, more than one algorithm exists for solving a specific problem. Depending on its formulation, each can be evaluated numerically in different ways. As computer arithmetic is of finite accuracy, different results can evolve, depending on the algorithm used and the way it is evaluated. On the other hand, the same computing domain could offer different performances due to variation in the algorithm design and in turn, source code implementation. The choice of the best algorithm for a given problem and for a specific computer is a difficult task and depends on many factors, for instance, data and control dependencies of the algorithm, regularity and granularity of the algorithm and architectural features of the computing domain [1], [2].

The ideal performance of a computer system demands a perfect match between machine capability and program behaviour. Program performance is the turnaround time, which includes, disk and memory accesses, input and output activities, compilation time, operating system overhead, and CPU time. In order to shorten the turnaround time, one can reduce all these time factors. Minimising the run-time memory

S. Manandhar et al. (Eds.): AACC 2004, LNCS 3285, pp. 247–254, 2004.

management, efficient partitioning and mapping of the program for concurrent system, and selecting an efficient compiler for specific computational demands, could enhance the performance. Compilers have a significant impact on the performance of the system. This means that some high-level languages have advantages in certain computational domains, and some have advantages in other domains. The compiler itself is critical to the performance of the system as the mechanism and efficiency of taking a high-level description of the application and transforming it into a hardware dependent implementation differs from compiler to compiler [3, 4, 5].

This paper addresses the issue of algorithm analysis, design and software coding for real-time control in a generic manner. A number of design methodologies are proposed for the real-time implementation of a complex control algorithm. The proposed methodologies are exemplified and demonstrated with simulation algorithm of an AVC system for a flexible beam. Finally, a comparative performance assessment of the proposed design mechanisms is presented and discussed through a set of experimental investigations.

2   Active Vibration Control Algorithm

Consider a cantilever beam system with a force $U(x,t)$ applied at a distance x from its fixed (clamped) end at time t. This will result in a deflection $y(x,t)$ of the beam from its stationary position at the point where the force has been applied. In this manner, the governing dynamic equation of the beam is given by

$$\mu^2 \frac{\partial^4 y(x,t)}{\partial x^4} + \frac{\partial^2 y(x,t)}{\partial t^2} = \frac{1}{m} U(x,t) \tag{1}$$

where, μ is a beam constant and m is the mass of the beam. Discretising the beam in time and length using the central FD methods, a discrete approximation to equation (1) can be obtained as [6]:

$$Y_{k+1} = -Y_{k-1} - \lambda^2 S Y_k + \frac{(\Delta t)^2}{m} U(x,t) \tag{2}$$

where, $\lambda^2 = \left[(\Delta t)^2/(\Delta x)^4\right]\mu^2$ with Δt and Δx representing the step sizes in time and along the beam respectively, S is a pentadiagonal matrix (the so called stiffness matrix of the beam), Y_i $(i = k+1, k, k-1)$ is an $(n-1)\times 1$ matrix representing the deflection of end of sections 1 to n of the beam at time step i (beam divided into $n-1$ sections). Equation (2) is the required relation for the simulation algorithm that can be implemented on a computing domain easily.

A schematic diagram of an AVC structure is shown in Figure 1. A detection sensor detects the unwanted (primary) disturbance. This is processed by a controller to generate a canceling (secondary, control) signal so that to achieve cancellation at the observation point. The objective in Figure 1 is to achieve total (optimum) vibration suppression at the observation point. Synthesizing the controller on the basis of this objective yields [7]

$$C = \left[1 - \frac{Q_1}{Q_0}\right]^{-1} \qquad (3)$$

where, Q_0 and Q_1 represent the equivalent transfer functions of the system (with input at the detector and output at the observer) when the secondary source is *off* and *on* respectively.

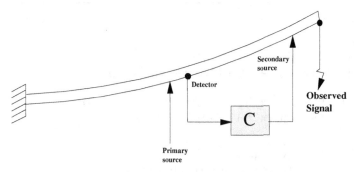

Fig. 1. Active vibration control structure

To investigate the nature and real-time processing requirements of the AVC algorithm, it is divided into two parts, namely control and identification. The control part is tightly coupled with the simulation algorithm, and both will be described in an integral manner as the control algorithm. The simulation algorithm will also be explored as a distinct algorithm. Both of these algorithms are predominately matrix based. The identification algorithm consists of parameter estimation of the models Q_0 and Q_1 and calculation of the required controller parameters according to equation (3). However, the nature of identification algorithm is completely different as compared with the simulation and control algorithms [8]. Thus, for reasons of consistency only the simulation and control algorithms are considered in this investigation.

3 Algorithm Analysis and Design

3.1 Flexible Beam Simulation Algorithm

The flexible beam simulation algorithm forms a major part of the control algorithm. Thus, of the two algorithms, the simulation algorithm has higher impact due to data dependency on real-time AVC. To demonstrate the real-time implementation impact, the simulation algorithm is designed in seven different methods [9, 10]. Three of these are considered here to explore real-time AVC. These are briefly described below.

Simulation Algorithm–1: Shifting of data array. The 'Simulation Algorithm–1' incorporates design suggestions made by Hossain, 1995 [8], is listed in Figure 2. It is noted that complex matrix calculations are performed within an array of three elements each representing information about the beam position at different instants of time. Subsequent to calculations, the memory pointer is shifted to the previous pointer in respect of time before the next iteration. This technique of shifting the pointer does not contribute to the calculation efforts and is thus a program overhead. Other algorithms were deployed to address this issue at further levels of investigation.

```
Loop {
//Step 1
  y0[2]=-y0[0]-lamsq*(a*y0[1]-4*y1[1]+y2[1]);
  y1[2]=-y1[0]-lamsq*(-4*y0[1]+b*y1[1]-4*y2[1]+y3[1]);
          :
  y18[2]=-y18[0]-lamsq*(y16[1]-4*y17[1]+c*y18[1]-2*y19[1]);
  y19[2]=-y19[0]-lamsq*(2*y17[1]-4*y18[1]+d*y19[1]);

//Step 2
  // Shifting memory locations
  y0[0]=y0[1]; y0[1]=y0[2]; y1[0]=y1[1]; y1[1]=y1[2];
          :
  y18[0]=y18[1]; y18[1]=y18[2];  y19[0]=y19[1]; y19[1]=y19[2];
}
```

Fig. 2. Design outline of 'Simulation Algorithm–1'

Simulation Algorithm–2: Array rotation. The 'Simulation Algorithm–2' incorporates design suggestions made by Hossain et al, 2000 [9]. A listing of the algorithm is given in Figure 3. In this case, each loop calculates three sets of data. Instead of shifting the data of the memory pointer (that contains results) at the end of each loop, the most current data is directly recalculated and written into the memory pointer that contains the older set of data. Therefore, re-ordering of array in the 'Simulation Algorithm–1' is replaced by recalculation. The main objective of the design effort is to achieve better performance by reducing the dynamic memory allocation and, in turn, memory pointer shift operation. Thus, instead of using a single code block and data-shifting portion, as in 'Simulation Algorithm–1', to calculate the deflection, three code blocks, are used with the modified approach in 'Simulation Algorithm–2'. Note that in 'Simulation Algorithm–2', the overhead of 'Simulation Algorithm–1' due to memory pointer shift operation is eliminated and every line of code is directed towards the simulation effort.

Simulation Algorithm–3: Two-element array rotation. The 'Simulation Algorithm–3' is listed in Figure 4. This makes use of the fact that access to the oldest time segment is only necessary during re-calculation of the same longitudinal beam segment. Hence, it can directly be overwritten with the new value. The 'Simulation Algorithm–3' is optimized for the particular discrete mathematical approximation of the governing physical formula, exploiting the previously observed features.

```
Loop {
//Step 1
  y0[2]=-y0[0]-lamsq*(a*y0[1]-4*y1[1]+y2[1]);
  y1[2]=-y1[0]-lamsq*(-4*y0[1]+b*y1[1]-4*y2[1]+y3[1]);
       :
  y18[2]=-y18[0]-lamsq*(y16[1]-4*y17[1]+c*y18[1]-2*y19[1]);
  y19[2]=-y19[0]-lamsq*(2*y17[1]-4*y18[1]+d*y19[1]);
//Step 2
  y0[0]=-y0[1]-lamsq*(a*y0[2]-4*y1[2]+y2[2]);
  y1[0]=-y1[1]-lamsq*(-4*y0[2]+b*y1[2]-4*y2[2]+y3[2]);
       :
  y18[0]=-y18[1]-lamsq*(y16[2]-4*y17[2]+c*y18[2]-2*y19[2]);
  y19[0]=-y19[1]-lamsq*(2*y17[2]-4*y18[2]+d*y19[2]);
//Step 3
  y0[1]=-y0[2]-lamsq*(a*y0[0]-4*y1[0]+y2[0]);
  y1[1]=-y1[2]-lamsq*(-4*y0[0]+b*y1[0]-4*y2[0]+y3[0]);
       :
  y18[1]=-y18[2]-lamsq*(y16[0]-4*y17[0]+c*y18[0]-2*y19[0]);
  y19[1]=-y19[2]-lamsq*(2*y17[0]-4*y18[0]+d*y19[0]);
}
```

Fig. 3. Design outline of 'Simulation Algorithm–2'

```
Loop {
  // Step 1
  y0[0]=-y0[0]-lamsq*(a*y0[1]-4*y1[1]+y2[1]);
  y1[0]=-y1[0]-lamsq*(-4*y0[1]+b*y1[1]-4*y2[1]+y3[1]);
       :
  y18[0]=-y18[0]-lamsq*(y16[1]-4*y17[1]+c*y18[1]-2*y19[1]);
  y19[0]=-y19[0]-lamsq*(2*y17[1]-4*y18[1]+d*y19[1]);
  // Step 2
  y0[1]=-y0[1]-lamsq*(a*y0[0]-4*y1[0]+y2[0]);
  y1[1]=-y1[1]-lamsq*(-4*y0[0]+b*y1[0]-4*y2[0]+y3[0]);
       :
  y18[1]=-y18[1]-lamsq*(y16[0]-4*y17[0]+c*y18[0]-2*y19[0]);
  y19[1]=-y19[1]-lamsq*(2*y17[0]-4*y18[0]+d*y19[0]);
}
```

Fig. 4. Design outline of 'Simulation Algorithm–3'

3.2 AVC Algorithm

As mentioned earlier, the AVC algorithm consists of the beam simulation algorithm and control algorithm. For simplicity the control algorithm in equation (3) can be rewritten as a difference equation as in Figure 5 [8], where b0, ..., b4 and a0, ..., a3 represent controller parameters. The arrays y12 and yc denote input and controller output, respectively. It is noted that the control algorithm shown in Figure 5 has similar design and computational complexity as one of the beam segment described and discussed in 'Simulation Algorithm-1'. Thus, the control algorithm can also be rewritten for recalculation in a similar manner as discussed in 'Simulation Algorithm-2' and 'Simulation Algorithm-3'.

```
yc[n]=b0*y12[n] + b1*y12[n-1] + b2*y12[n-2] + b3*y12[n-3]+ b4*y12[n-4]-(a0*yc[n-
1]+a1*yc[n-2] +a2*yc[n-3] +a3*yc[n-4]);
//Shift data array
   y12[n-4]=y12[n-3] ; y12[n-3]=y12[n-2] ; y12[n-2]=y12[n-1] ; y12[n-1]=y12[n] ;
   yc[n-4]=yc[n-3] ; yc[n-3]=yc[n-2] ; yc[n-2]=yc[n-1] ; yc[n-1]=yc[n] ;
```

Fig. 5. Design outline of the control algorithm (data array shifting method)

4   Implementation and Results

The AVC algorithms based on three different methods of the simulation and corresponding similar design of the control algorithms were implemented with similar specification [7], with 0.3ms sampling time. It is worth mentioning that the AVC Algorithm-1 was implemented combining the 'Simulation Algorithm-1' and the data array shift method of control algorithm as shown in Figure 5. The AVC Algorithm-2 implemented in combination of the 'Simulation Algorithm-2' and similar recalculation method of control algorithm. Finally, AVC Algorithm-3 was implemented combining the 'Simulation Algorithm-3' and similar recalculation method of control algorithm. For reasons of consistency, a fixed number of iterations (250,000) were considered in implementing all the algorithms. Therefore, the execution time should be 75 sec in implementing each algorithm to achieve real-time performance.

Figure 6 depicts a comparative performance of the AVC Algorithm–1 and Algorithm–2 for 20 to 200 beam segments. It is noted that the execution time for both algorithms increases almost linearly with the increment of the number of segments. It is also noted that Algorithm-2 performed better throughout except for 100 segments.

Figure 7 shows a comparative real-time performance of implementing Algorithm-2 and Algorithm-3. It is observed that Algorithm-3 performs better throughout except for smaller number of segments. It is also noted that the performance variation of Algorithm-3 as compared to Algorithm-2 was not linear and performed best when the number segments was 80. This is further demonstrated in Table 1, which shows the performance ratio of Algorithm-2 and Algorithm-3 relative to Algorithm-1. It is observed that the transition towards weaker performance occurred in AVC Algorithm–3 halfway between the transitions of Algorithm–1 and Algorithm–2. In spite of being outperformed by Algorithm–1 in a narrow band of around 100 segments, Algorithm–3 offered the best performance overall. Thus, the design mechanism employed in Algorithm–3 can offer potential advantages in real-time control applications.

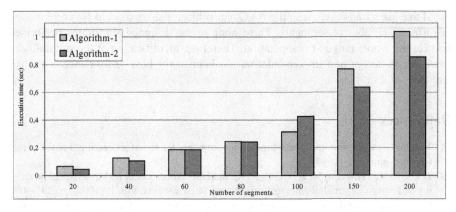

Fig. 6. Performance comparison of Algorithm–1 and Algorithm–2

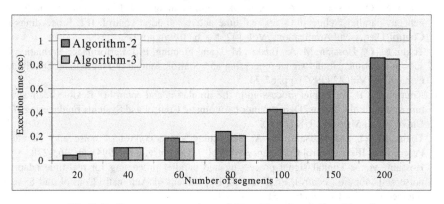

Fig. 7. Performance comparison of Algorithm–2 and Algorithm–3

Table 1. Performance ratio of Algorithm–2 (A2) and Algorithm–3 (A3) as compared to Algorithm–1 (A1)

Segments	20	40	60	80	100	150	200
A2/A1	0.67	0.83	1.0	1.4	1.6	0.83	0.83
A3/A1	0.83	0.83	0.83	0.83	1.3	0.83	0.82

5   Conclusion

An investigation into algorithm analysis, design, software coding and implementation so as to reduce the execution time and, in turn, enhance the real-time performance, has been presented within the framework of real-time implementation of active vibration control algorithms. A number of approaches have been proposed and demonstrated experimentally with the AVC algorithm of a flexible beam system. It has been observed that all three algorithms have achieved real-time performance. Although, execution time and in turn, performance of the algorithm varies with different approaches. Designs leading to large instructions cause non-linear transitions at certain stages where internal built-in instruction cache is unable to handle the load. It is also noted that such transitions with the AVC algorithm considered occur for computation of different number of segments. Thus, none of the designed algorithms performed best for the whole range of computation. Therefore, identification of the suitability of source code design and implementation mechanism for best performance is a challenge.

References

1. Thoeni, U. A: Programming real-time multicomputers for signal processing, Prentice-Hall, Hertfordshire, UK (1994).
2. Tokhi, M. O., Hossain, M. A: CISC, RISC and DSP processors in real-time signal processing and control, Journal of Microprocessors and Microsystems, Vol. 19(1995), pp.291-300.
3. Bader, G. and Gehrke, E: On the performance of transputer networks for solving linear systems of equation, Parallel Computing, 1991, Vol. 17 (1991), pp. 1397-1407.
4. Tokhi, M. O., Hossain, M. A., Baxter, M. J. and Fleming, P. J: Heterogeneous and homogeneous parallel architectures for real-time active vibration control, IEE Proceedings-D: Control Theory and Applications, Vol. 142, No. 6 (1995), pp. 1-8.
5. Tokhi, M. O., Hossain, M. A., Baxter, M. J. and Fleming, P. J: Performance evaluation issues in real-time parallel signal processing and control, Journal of Parallel and Distributed Computing, Vol. 42 (1997), pp. 67-74.
6. Kourmoulis, P. K: Parallel processing in the simulation and control of flexible beam structure system, PhD. Thesis, Department of Automatic Control and Systems Engineering, The University of Sheffield, UK (1990).
7. Tokhi, M. O. and Hossain, M. A: Self-tuning active control of noise and vibration, Proceedings IEE - Control Conference-94, Vol. 1, Coventry, UK (1994), pp. 263-278.
8. Hossain, M. A: Digital signal processing and parallel processing for real-time adaptive noise and vibration control, Ph.D. thesis, Department of Automatic Control and System Engineering, The University of Sheffield, UK (1995).
9. Hossain, M. A., Kabir, U. and Tokhi, M. O: Impact of data dependencies for real-time high performance computing, Journal of Microprocessors and Microsystems, Vol. 26, No. 6 (2002), pp. 253 – 261.
10. Tokhi, M. O., Hossain, M. A. and Shaheed, M. H: Parallel Computing for Real-time Signal Processing and Control, Springer Verlag, ISBN: 1-85233-599-8, (2003).

An Efficient Technique for Dynamic Slicing
of Concurrent Java Programs

D.P. Mohapatra, Rajib Mall, and Rajeev Kumar

Department of Computer Science and Engineering
Indian Institute of Technology Kharagpur
Kharagpur, WB 721 302, India
{durga,rajib,rkumar}@cse.iitkgp.ernet.in

Abstract. Program slice has many applications such as program debugging, testing, maintenance and complexity measurement. We propose a new dynamic program slicing technique for concurrent Java programs that is more efficient than the related algorithms. We introduce the notion of *Concurrent Program Dependence Graph* (CPDG). Our algorithm uses CPDG as the intermediate representation and is based on marking and unmarking the edges in the CPDG as and when the dependencies arise and cease during run-time. Our approach eliminates the use of trace files and is more efficient than the existing algorithms.

1 Introduction

The concept of a program slice was introduced by Weiser [1]. A static backward program slice consists of those parts of a program that affect the value of a variable selected at some program point of interest. The variable along with the program point of interest is referred to as a slicing criterion. More formally, a slicing criterion $< s, V >$ specifies a location (statement s) and a set of variables (V).

The program slices introduced by Wesier [1] are now called *static slices*. A static slice is valid for all possible input values. Therefore conservative assumptions are made, which often lead to relatively larger slices. To overcome this difficulty, Korel and Laski introduced the concept of *dynamic program slicing*. A dynamic program slice contains only those statements that actually affect the value of a variable at a program point for a given execution. Therefore, dynamic slices are usually smaller than static slices and have been found to be useful in debugging, testing and maintenance etc.

Object-oriented programming languages present new challenges which are not encountered in traditional program slicing. To slice an object-oriented program, features such as classes, dynamic binding, inheritance, and polymorphism need to be considered carefully. Larson and Harrold were the first to consider these aspects in their work [2].

Many of the real life object-oriented programs are concurrent which run on different machines connected to a network. It is usually accepted that understanding and debugging of concurrent object-oriented programs are much harder compared to those of sequential programs. The non-deterministic nature of concurrent programs, the lack of global states, unsynchronized interactions among processes, multiple threads of control and a dynamically varying number of processes are some reasons for this difficulty.

S. Manandhar et al. (Eds.): AACC 2004, LNCS 3285, pp. 255–262, 2004.

An increasing number of resources are being spent in debugging, testing and maintaining these products. Slicing techniques promise to come in handy at this point. However research attempts in the program slicing area have focussed attention largely on sequential programs. But research reports dealing with slicing of concurrent object-oriented programs are scarce in literature [3].

Efficiency is especially an important concern for slicing concurrent object-oriented programs, since their size is often large. With this motivation, in this paper we propose a new dynamic slicing algorithm for computing slices of concurrent Java programs. Only the concurrency issues in Java are of concern, many sequential Object-Oriented features are not discussed in this paper. We have named our algorithm *edge-marking dynamic slicing* (EMDS) algorithm.

The rest of the paper is organized as follows. In section 2, we present some basic concepts, definitions and the intermediate program representation: *concurrent program dependence graph* (CPDG). In section 3, we discuss our edge-marking dynamic slicing (EMDS) algorithm. In section 4, we briefly describe the implementation of our algorithm. In section 5, we compare our algorithm with related algorithms. Section 6 concludes the paper.

2   Basic Concepts and Definitions

We introduce a few definitions that would be used in our algorithm. In the following definitions we use the terms statement, node and vertex interchangeably. We also describe about the intermediate representation.

Definition 1. *Precise Dynamic Slice.* A dynamic slice is said to be *precise* if it includes only those statements that actually affect the value of a variable at a program point for the given execution.

Definition 2. *Def(var).* Let *var* be a variable in a class in the program P. A node *x* is said to be a *Def(var)* node if *x* represents a definition statement that defines the variable *var*.

In Fig. 2, nodes 2, 9 and 17 are the Def(a2) nodes.

Definition 3. *Use(var) node.* Let *var* be a variable in a class in the program P. A node *x* is said to be a *Use(var)* node iff it uses the variable *var*.

In Fig. 2, the node 4 is a Use(a3) node and nodes 2, 6 and 12 are Use(a2) nodes.

Definition 4. *RecentDef(var).* For each variable *var*, *RecentDef(var)* represents the node (the label number of the statement) corresponding to the most recent definition of the variable *var*.

Definition 5. *Concurrent Control Flow Graph (CCFG).* A *concurrent control flow graph* (CCFG) *G* of a program *P* is a directed graph *(N, E, Start, Stop)*, where each node *n* ∈ *N* represents a statement of the program *P*, while each edge *e* ∈ *E* represents potential control transfer among the nodes. Nodes *Start* and *Stop* are unique nodes representing entry and exit of the program *P* respectively. There is a directed edge from node *a* to node *b* if control may flow from node *a* to node *b*.

Definition 6. *Post dominance.* Let x and y be two nodes in a CCFG. Node y *post dominates* node x *iff* every directed path from x to *stop* passes through y.

Definition 7. *Control Dependence.* Let G be a *CCFG* and x be a *test (predicate node)*. A node y is said to be *control dependent* on a node x *iff* there exists a directed path Q from x to y such that

- y *post dominates* every node $z \neq x$ in Q.
- y does not *post dominate* x.

Definition 8. *Data Dependence.* Let G be a *CCFG*. Let x be a *Def(var)* node and y be a *Use(var)* node. The node y is said to be *data dependent* on node x *iff* there exists a directed path Q from x to y such that there is no intervening *Def(var)* node in Q.

Definition 9. *Synchronization Dependence.* A statement y in one thread is *synchronization dependent* on a statement x in another thread if the start or termination of the execution of x directly determines the start or termination of the execution of y through an inter thread synchronization.

Let y be a *wait()* node in thread t_1 and x be the corresponding *notify()* node in thread t_2. Then the node y is said to be *synchronization dependent* on node x.
For example, in Fig. 2, node 5 in Thread1 is *synchronization dependent* on node 10 in Thread2.

Definition 10. *Communication Dependence.* Informally, a statement y in one thread is *communication dependent* on statement x in another thread if the value of a variable defined at x is directly used at y through inter thread communication.

Let x be a *Def(var)* node in thread t_1 and y be a *Use(var)* node in thread t_2. Then the node y is said to be *communication dependent* on node x. For example, in Fig. 2, node 6 in Thread1 is *communication dependent* on nodes 9 and 13 in Thread2.

Definition 11. *Concurrent Program Dependence Graph (CPDG).* A concurrent program dependence graph (CPDG) G_C of a concurrent object-oriented program P is a directed graph (N_C, E_C) where each node $n \in N_C$ represents a statement in P. For x, y $\in N_C$, $(y,x) \in E_C$ *iff* one of the following holds:

- y is *control dependent* on x. Such an edge is called a *control dependence edge*.
- y is *data dependent* on x. Such an edge is called a *data dependence edge*.
- y is *synchronization dependent* on x. Such an edge is called a *synchronization dependence edge*.
- y is *communication dependent* on x. Such an edge is called a *communication dependence edge*.

2.1   Construction of the CPDG

A CPDG of a concurrent Java program captures the program dependencies that can be determined statically as well as the dependencies that may exist at run-time. The dependencies which dynamically arise at run-time are data dependencies, synchronization dependencies and communication dependencies. We will use different types of edges defined in Definition 11 to represent the different types of dependencies. We use *synchronization dependence* edge to capture dependence relationships between different threads due to inter-thread synchronization. We use *communication dependence edge* to capture dependence relationships between different threads due to inter-thread communication. A CPDG can contain the following types of nodes: (i) *definition (assignment)* (ii) *use* (iii) *predicate* (iv) *notify* (v) *wait*. Also, to represent different dependencies that can exist in a concurrent program, a CPDG may contain the following types of edges: (i) *control dependence edge* (ii) *data dependence edge* (iii) *synchronization dependence edge* and (iv) *communication dependence edge*. We have already defined these different types of edges earlier. Fig. 2 shows the CPDG for the program segment in Fig. 1.

3   EMDS Algorithm

We now provide a brief overview of our dynamic slicing algorithm. Before execution of a concurrent object-oriented program P, its CCFG and CPDG are constructed statically. During execution of the program P, we mark an edge when its associated dependence exists, and unmark when its associated dependence ceases to exist. We consider all the control dependence edges, data dependence edges, synchronization edges and communication edges for marking and unmarking.

Let *Dynamic_Slice (u, var)* with respect to the slicing criterion $< u, var >$ denotes the dynamic slice with respect to the most recent execution of the node u. Let $(u, x_1), \ldots, (u, x_k)$ be all the *marked* outgoing dependence edges of u in the updated CPDG after an execution of the statement u. Then, it is clear that the dynamic slice with respect to the present execution of the node u, for the variable *var* is given by :
Dynamic_Slice(u, var) $= \{x_1, x_2, \ldots, x_k\} \cup Dynamic\_Slice(x_1, var) \cup$
$Dynamic\_Slice(x_2, var) \cup \ldots \cup Dynamic\_Slice(x_k, var)$.

Let $var\_1, var\_2, \ldots, var\_k$ be all the variables used or defined at statement u. Then, we define the dynamic slice of the whole statement u as :
   dyn_slice(u) $= Dynamic\_Slice(u, var\_1) \cup Dynamic\_Slice(u, var\_2)$
$\cup \ldots \cup Dynamic\_Slice(u, var\_k)$.

Our slicing algorithm operates in three main stages:

- Constructing the concurrent program dependence graph statically
- Managing the CPDG at run-time
- Computing the dynamic slice

In the first stage the CCFG is constructed from a static analysis of the source code. Also, in this stage using the CCFG the static CPDG is constructed. The stage 2 of the algorithm executes at run-time and is responsible for maintaining the CPDG as the execution proceeds. The maintenance of the CPDG at run-time involves marking and unmarking the different edges. The stage 3 is responsible for computing the dynamic slice. Once a slicing criterion is specified, the dynamic slicing algorithm computes the dynamic slice with respect to any given slicing criterion by looking up the corresponding *Dynamic_Slice* computed during run time.

```
// In this example, SyncObject is a class, in which there are two synchron
   methods Swait( ) and Snotify( ). Swait( ) invokes a wait( ) method and
   Snotify( ) invokes a notify method . CompObject is a class which provide
   a method mul(CompObject, CompObject). If a1.mul(a2, a3) is invoked t
   a1 = a2 * a3. The detail codes are not listed here.
   class Thread1 extends Thread {
           private SyncObject  O;
           private CompObject  C;
           void Thread1(SyncObject O, CompObject a1,
                           CompObject a2, CompObject a3);

           {
             this.O=O;
             this.a1= a1;
             this.a2= a2;
             this.a3= a3;
           }
1          public void run( ) {
2              a2.mul(a1, a2); // a2= a1 * a2
3              O.Snotify( );
4              a1.mul(a1, a3); // a1= a1 * a3
5              O.Swait( );
6              a3.mul(a2, a2); // a3= a2*a2
           }
       }
   class Thread2 extends Thread {
           private SyncObject  O;
           private CompObject  C;
           void Thread1(SyncObject O, CompObject a1,
                           CompObject a2, CompObject a3);

           {
             this.O=O;
             this.a1= a1;
             this.a2= a2;
             this.a3= a3;
           }
7          public void run( ) {
8              O.Swait( );
9              a2.mul(a1, a1); // a2 = a1 * a1
10             O.Snotify( );
11         if (a1 = a2)
12                 a3 . mul(a2, a1); // a3 = a2 * a1
           else
13                 a2. mul(a1, a1); // a2 = a1 * a1


           }

       }
14 class example {
15    public static void main(mstring[ ] argm) {
               CompObject a1, a2, a3;

               SyncObject o1;

               o1.reset( ); // reset ( ) is a function for initializing Syr
16             a1 = new  CompObject(Integer.parseInt( argm[0] );
17             a2 = new  CompObject(Integer.parseInt( argm[1] );
18             a3 = new  CompObject(Integer.parseInt( argm[2] );

19         Thread1 t1 = new  Thread ( o1, a1, a2, a3);
20         Thread2 t2 = new Thread (o1, a1, a2, a3);

21             t1.start( );
22             t2.start( );
           }
       }
```

Fig. 1. An Example Program

Working of the EMDS Algorithm: We illustrate the working of the algorithm with the help of an example. Consider the Java program of Fig. 1. The updated CPDG of the program is obtained after applying stage 2 of the EMDS algorithm and is shown in Fig. 3. We are interested in computing the dynamic slice for the slicing criterion $< 6, a3 >$. For the input data *argm[0]=1, argm[1]=1 and argm[2]=2*, we explain how our algorithm computes the slice. We first unmark all the edges of the CPDG and

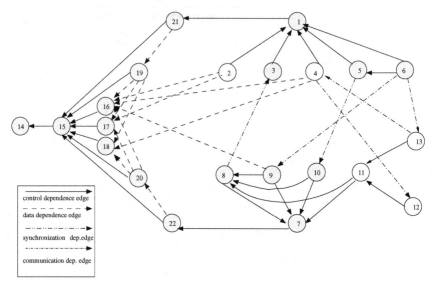

Fig. 2. The CPDG of Fig. 1

set $Dynamic\_Slice(u, var) = \phi$ for every node u of the CPDG. The figure shows all the *control dependence edges* as marked. The algorithm has marked the *synchronization dependence edges* (5, 10) and (8, 3) as *synchronization dependency* exists between statements 5 and 10, and statements 8 and 3. For the given input values, statement 6 is *communication dependent* on statement 9. So, the algorithm marked the *communication dependence edge* (6, 9). All the marked edges in Fig. 3 are shown in bold lines.

Now we shall find the backward dynamic slice computed with respect to the slicing criterion $< a3, 6 >$. According to our edge marking algorithm, the dynamic slice at statement 6, is given by the expression Dynamic_Slice(6, a3) = $\{1, 5, 9\} \cup$ dyn_slice(1) $\cup$ dyn_slice(5) $\cup$ dyn_slice(9). Evaluating the expression in a recursive manner, we get the final dynamic slice at statement 6. The statements included in the dynamic slice are shown as shaded vertices in Fig. 3. Although statement 12 can be reached from statement 6, it can not be included in the slice. Our algorithm successfully eliminates statement 12 from the resulting slice. Also, our algorithm does not include statement 2 in the resulting slice. But by using the approach of Zhao [3], the statements 2 and 12, both would have been included in the slice which is clearly imprecise. So, our algorithm computes precise dynamic slices.

3.1 Complexity Analysis

Space complexity. The space complexity of the EMDS algorithm is $O(n^2)$, where n is the number of executable statements in the program.

Time complexity. The worst case time complexity of our algorithm is $O(mn)$, where *m* is an upper bound on the number of variables used at any statement.

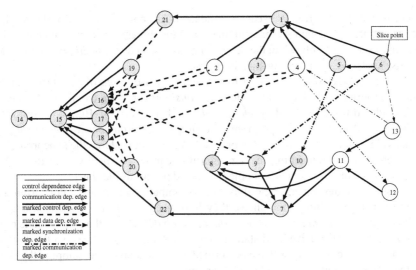

Fig. 3. The updated CPDG of Fig. 1

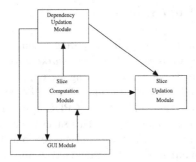

Fig. 4. Module Structure of the Slicer

4   Implementation

The *lexical analyzer* component has been implemented using *lex*. The *semantic analyzer* component has been implemented using *yacc*. The following are the major modules which implement our slicing tool. The module structure is shown in Fig. 4.

- Dependency Updation Module
- Slice Computation Module
- Slice Updation Module
- GUI Module

5   Comparison with Related Works

Zhao computed the static slice of a concurrent object-oriented program based on the *multi-threaded dependence graph* (MDG) [3]. He did not take into account that dependences between concurrently executed statements are not transitive. So, the resulting slice is not precise. Again, he has not addressed the dynamic aspects. Since our algorithm marks an edge only when the dependence exists, so this *transitivity* problem does not arise at all. So, the resulting slice is precise.

Krinke introduced an algorithm to get more precise slices of concurrent object-oriented programs [4]. She had handled the *transitivity* problem carefully. But she has not considered the concept of *synchronization* in her algorithm. But, synchronization is widely used in concurrent programs and in some environment it is necessary. So, krinke's algorithm can not be used in practice. We have considered the synchronization dependence in our algorithm. So, our algorithm can be practically used to compute dynamic slices of most concurrent object-oriented programs like Java.

Chen and Xu developed a new algorithm to compute static slices of concurrent Java programs [5]. To compute the slices, they have used *concurrent control flow graph* (CCFG) and *concurrent program dependence graph* (CPDG) as the intermediate representations. Since they have used static analysis to compute the slices, so the resulting slices are not precise. But, we have performed dynamic analysis to compute the slices. So, the slices computed by our algorithm are precise.

6   Discussion and Conclusions

We have proposed a new algorithm for computing dynamic slices of concurrent java programs. We have named this algorithm *edge-marking dynamic slicing* (EMDS) algorithm. It is based on marking and unmarking the edges of the CPDG as and when the dependences arise and cease at run-time. The EMDS algorithm does not require any new nodes to be created and added to the CPDG at run time nor does it require to maintain any execution trace in a trace file. This saves the expensive node creation and file I/O steps. Further, once a slicing command is given, our algorithm produces results through a mere table-lookup and avoids on-demand slicing computation. Although we have presented our slicing technique using Java examples, the technique can easily be adapted to other object-oriented languages such as C++. We are now extending this approach to compute the dynamic slice of object-oriented programs running parally in several distributed computers.

References

1. Weiser, M.: Programmers use slices when debugging. Communications of the ACM **25** (1982) 446–452
2. Larson, L.D., Harrold, M.J.: Slicing object-oriented software. In: Proceedings of the 18th International Conference on Software Engineering, German (1996)
3. Zhao, J.: Slicing concurrent java programs. In: Proceedings of the 7th IEEE International Workshop on Program Comprehension. (1999)
4. Krinke, J.: Static slicing of threaded programs. ACM SIGPLAN Notices **33** (1998) 35–42
5. Chen, Z., Xu, B.: Slicing concurrent java programs. ACM SIGPLAN Notices **36** (2001) 41–47

A Simple Delay Testable Synthesis
of Symmetric Functions

Hafizur Rahaman[1] and Debesh K. Das[2]

[1] Information Technology Dept., Bengal Engineering College (Deemed University),
Howrah-7111 03, India
rahaman_h@hotmail.com
[2] Computer Sc. & Engg. Dept., Jadavpur University, Calcutta -700 032, India
debeshd@hotmail.com

Abstract. This paper presents a new technique for implementing totally symmetric Boolean functions. First, a simple universal cellular module that admits a recursive structure is designed for synthesizing unate symmetric functions. General symmetric functions are then realized following a unate decomposition method. This design guarantees complete and robust path delay testability. Experimental results on several symmetric functions reveal that the hardware cost of the proposed design is low, and the number of paths in the circuit is reduced significantly compared to those in earlier designs. Results on circuit area and delay for a few benchmark circuits are also reported.

1 Introduction

The testable synthesis of symmetric Boolean functions is a classical problem in switching theory and received lot of interest in the past [1-4, 7]. The symmetric functions find application to reliable data encryption and Internet security [5]. We propose a new approach to synthesizing totally symmetric functions. We first redesign a well-known cellular logic array known as *digital summation threshold logic* (DSTL) array reported earlier in [6]. Such an array can be used directly for synthesizing unate symmetric functions. Non-unate symmetric functions can then be synthesized by the method proposed in [3]. The DSTL array [6] is not completely delay testable. But our design to synthesize any symmetric function provides 100% robust path-delay fault testability and reduces hardware cost drastically compared to other existing designs [2, 3]. Our technique ensures path-delay fault testability for some benchmark circuits [table 2] realizing symmetric functions, which are not originally path-delay testable and yields lesser area and delay compared to those of the original implementations.

2 Preliminaries

A *vertex (minterm)* is a product of variables in which every variable appears once. The *weight w* of a vertex v is the number of uncomplemented variables that appear in v. A Boolean function is called *unate*, if each variable appears either in complemented or uncomplemented form (but not both) in its minimum sum-of-products (s-o-p) expression. A switching function $f(x_1, x_2, ..., x_n)$ of n variables is called *totally symmetric*

S. Manandhar et al. (Eds.): AACC 2004, LNCS 3285, pp. 263–270, 2004.

with respect to variables $(x_1, x_2,..., x_n)$, if it is invariant under any permutation of the variables [4]. Total symmetry can be specified by a set of integers (called a-numbers) $A = (a_i, .., a_j,..., a_k)$, where $A \subseteq \{0, 1, 2,..., n\}$; all the vertices with weight $w \in A$ will appear as true minterms in the function. Henceforth, by a symmetric function, we would mean a function with total symmetry. An n-variable symmetric function is denoted as $S^n(a_i,..., a_j, .., a_k)$. A symmetric function is called *consecutive*, if the set A consists of only consecutive integers $(a_l, a_{l+1},..., a_r)$. Such a consecutive symmetric function is expressed by $S^n(a_l - a_r)$ where $l < r$. For n variables, we can construct $2^{n+1}-2$ different symmetric functions (excluding constant functions 0 and 1). A totally symmetric function $S^n(A)$ can be expressed uniquely as a union of maximal consecutive symmetric functions, such that $S^n(A) = S^n(A_1) + S^n(A_2) +...+S^n(A_m)$, such that m is minimum and $\forall i, j, 1 \le i, j \le m, A_i \cap A_j = \emptyset$, whenever $i \ne j$.

Example 1. The symmetric function $S^{12}(1,2,5,6,7,9,10)$ can be expressed as $S^{12}(1-2) + S^{12}(5-7) + S^{12}(9-10)$, where $S^{12}(1-2)$, $S^{12}(5-7)$ and $S^{12}(9-10)$ are maximal consecutive symmetric functions. A function is called *unate symmetric* if it is both unate and symmetric.

A unate symmetric function is always consecutive and can be expressed as $S^n(a_l-a_r)$, where either $a_l = 0$ or $a_r = n$. If it is positive unate, then it must be either $S^n(n)$ or any of the following $(n-1)$ functions: $S^n(1-n)$, $S^n(2-n)$, $S^n(3-n),....., S^n((n-1) - n)$. We express $S^n(n)$ as $u_n(n)$, and $S^n(a_l-a_r)$ as $u_l(n)$ for $1 \le l \le (n-1)$.

Theorem 1 [3]. A consecutive symmetric function $S^n(a_l-a_r)$, $a_l \ne a_r$, $l < r$, can be expressed as a composition of two unate and consecutive symmetric functions:

$$S^n(a_l-a_r) = S^n(a_l-a_n) \ \overline{S^n(a_{r+1}-a_n)} \qquad (1)$$

3   Synthesis of Unate Symmetric Function: Earlier Works

Unate symmetric functions can be synthesized by a DSTL array [6], which is not delay testable. To achieve path-delay fault testability, the above design is modified in [8]. A synthesis technique for implementing symmetric functions was proposed in [9] by redesigning the DSTL array so as to reduce the hardware cost and delay. However, the procedure does not guarantee robust testability of all path-delay faults. All the design procedures reported earlier [6, 8, 9] use a structure called *Module(n)* that has n inputs lines $x_1, x_2, x_3, ..., x_n$, and n output functions $u_1(n), u_2(n), u_3(n),....., u_n(n)$ [Fig. 1]. Each output u_i, implements a unate symmetric function as described below (where Σ denotes Boolean OR operation):

$u_1(n) = S^n(1, 2, 3,...., n) = \Sigma x_i$ for $i = 1$ to n;

$u_2(n) = S^n(2, 3, 4....., n) = \Sigma \ x_i x_j$,   for $i, j = 1$ to n;

$u_3(n) = S^n(3, 4,..., n) = \Sigma \ x_i x_j x_k$,   for $i, j, k = 1$ to n;

… … … … … … … … …

$u_n(n) = S^n(n) = x_1 x_2......x_{n-1} x_n$.

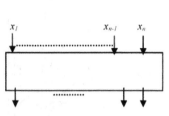

Fig. 1. Module(n)

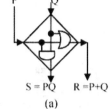

$S = PQ$ $R = P+Q$

(a)

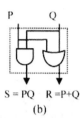

$S = PQ$ $R = P+Q$

(b)

Fig. 2. (a) DSTL cell (b) Proposed AND-OR cell

4 Proposed Technique

4.1 Synthesis of Unate Symmetric Functions

We first describe a new and simple design of Module(n), which is similar to DSTL array [6] in functionality, but more compact and simple in structure. The Module(n) uses an iterative arrangement of cells, where each cell consists of a 2-input AND gate and a 2-input OR gate, similar to that used in DSTL array described in [6]. For ease of representation, we redraw the cell of Fig. 2a in Fig. 2b. For n = 4, it is shown in Fig. 3, that the new design [Fig. 3b] needs fewer cells and has less delay compared to the DSTL array [Fig. 3a].

4.1.1 Design of Module (n) for $n=2^k$
The Module(n) consists of three stages.

First-stage: It consists of (log n) levels. Each level consists of (n/2) cells in parallel. The interconnections between the levels is analogous to shuffle-exchange network connections. The output lines of this stage are numbered from 0 to (n-1), where the line with number 0 [(n-1)] realizes u_1 [u_n]. The first stage for n = 4 [8] is shown in Fig. 4a [4b].

Second-stage: The 2nd stage of Module(n) for n= 2^k [Fig.5] has (k-1) parts [k > 1]. The ith part is Module(M_i) where $M_i=\binom{k}{i}$. The inputs to i^{th} part are fed by the out-puts of 1st stage which have 1's in i number of bits in the binary representation of the output line number. The 2nd stage of Module (16) has 3 parts: - Module (4), Module (6), Module(4) [Fig.6]. As binary representations of decimal numbers 1, 2, 4, 8 contain only single 1 in their patterns, the output lines of 1st stage corresponding to these numbers feed the 1st part of 2nd stage. Similarly, the output lines with numbers 3,5,6, 9, 10, 12 [7, 11, 13,14] of 1st stage feed the inputs to the 2nd [3rd] part of 2nd stage.

Third-stage: The 3rd stage of Module(n) for n= 2^k consists of a cascade of cells. For k ≤ 2 (i.e., n ≤ 4) the 3rd stage does not exist. For n = 4, Module(4) does not contain any 3rd stage. Thus the complete design for Module(4) is shown in Fig. 3b. The 3rd stage for n=8[16] is shown in Fig.7a [Fig.7b].

4.1.2 Design of Module (n) for $n < 2^k$
In this case, we first design the Module(2^k) and set (2^k-n) variables to logic 0 and remove the affected logic gates in Module(2^k) to realize Module(n). Module(3) is

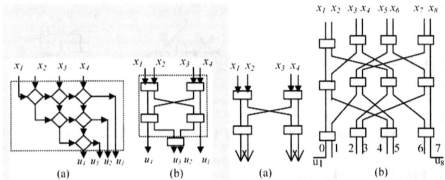

Fig. 3. 4-variable (a) DSTL array, (b) proposed array

Fig. 4. First stage of Module(n) for (a) n=4 (b) n=8

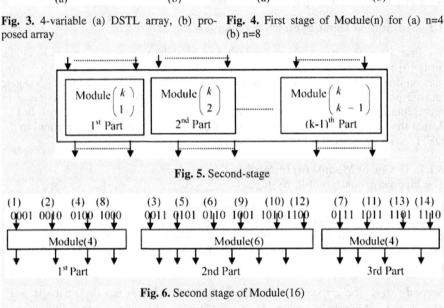

Fig. 5. Second-stage

Fig. 6. Second stage of Module(16)

obtained [Fig.8], by removing one variable and some gates from Module(4) of Fig.3b. As Module(8) [Fig.9] contains Module(3) in 2nd stage, we can now obtain the circuit for Module(8) by using Module(3) of Fig. 8.

4.1.3 Hardware Cost, Delay and Delay Testability

Hardware Cost and Delay: Let C(n) denote the number of 2-input cells. For n ≤ 16, C(n) ≤ n.log n + 2C(n/2) = $O(nlog^2n)$. Assuming unit gate delay through a 2-input gate, for n = 2^k, in Module(n), the min. delay is $\lceil log(n) \rceil$ and the max. delay is $(n - 1)$.

Delay Testability: Considering any single output $u_i(n)$ among the output functions $u_1(n)$, $u_2(n)$, $u_3(n)$,....., $u_n(n)$, if we consider the sub-circuit from input lines to the output line realizing $u_i(n)$, this sub-circuit is unate and irredundant. It is well known that any single-output unate and irredundant circuit is delay testable. This leads to the following Theorem.

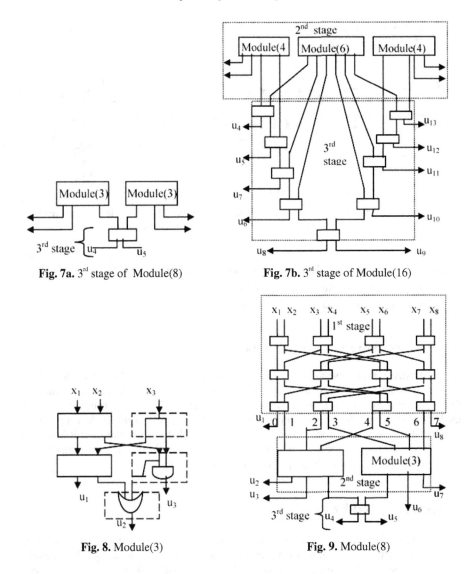

Fig. 7a. 3rd stage of Module(8)

Fig. 7b. 3rd stage of Module(16)

Fig. 8. Module(3)

Fig. 9. Module(8)

Theorem 2. The proposed design provides 100% path delay fault testability.

Proof: Follows from the above discussion.

5 Synthesis of General Symmetric Functions

5.1 Consecutive Symmetric Functions

To synthesize a consecutive symmetric function that is not unate, we use the result stated in Theorem 1[3] that $S^n(a_1\text{-}a_r)=S^n(a_1\text{-}a_r)=S^n(a_1\text{-}n)\ \overline{S^n}(a_{r+1}\text{-}n)= u_l(n)\cdot \overline{u}_{r+1}(n)$. The unate functions $u_l(n)$ and $u_{r+1}(n)$ are produced by *Module(n)* [Fig. 10a.].

Example 8. $S^6(3, 4)$ is realized as $S^6(3, 4) = S^6(3-6)$. $\overline{S^6}(5-6) = u_3(3)$. $\overline{u_5}(5)$. The circuit is shown in Fig. 10b.

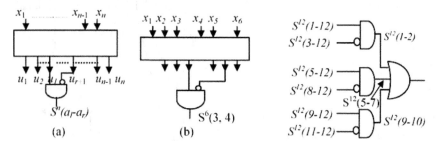

Fig. 10. Realization of (a) $S^n(a_l - a_r)$ (b) $S^n(3, 4)$ **Fig. 11.** Testable circuit realizing $S^{12}(1, 2, 5, 6, 7, 9, 10)$

Theorem 3. The above implementation of any consecutive symmetric function $S^n(a_l - a_r)$, $(a_l \neq a_r)$, is robustly path-delay testable.

Proof: Follows from Theorem 2 and the results in [3].

5.2 Nonconsecutive Symmetric Functions

To synthesize a nonconsecutive symmetric function for 100% robust path-delay testability, it is first expressed as a union of several maximal consecutive symmetric functions, and then each of the constituent consecutive symmetric functions is realized by combining the appropriate outputs of *Module(n)*, via unate decomposition. Finally, they are OR-ed together. It is shown in [3] that the overall circuit based on such decomposition is robustly path-delay fault testable. Synthesis of a nonconsecutive symmetric function of Example 1 is shown in Fig. 11.

6 Experimental Results

We compare the hardware cost and delay of *Module(n)* with earlier designs [6, 9] in Table 1. Both the parameters are favorably reduced in the new design. For general consecutive symmetric functions, table 3 shows that our method reduces the circuit cost significantly compared to those in [2, 3]. While the earlier methods use a fixed number of logic levels, for instance, at most 4 [2], or at most 5 [3], our method reduces the logic significantly at the cost of increasing the number of levels. However, the number of paths, and in turn, testing time in this design reduces drastically compared to that in [2, 3]. Table 2 depicts results on some benchmark circuits realizing symmetric functions. These circuits are not path-delay testable. Moreover, except *9sym* no other circuit has two-level delay testable realization. This technique ensures path-delay fault testability for all these circuits and yields lesser area and (max) delay compared to those of the original implementations. We have used the SIS tool [10] and mcnc.genlib library to estimate area for comparison.

Table 1. Cost and delay for realizing unate symmetric functions

n	# cells			delay					
	As in [6]	As in [9]	Proposed Method	As in [6]		As in [9]		Proposed Method	
				Min.	Max.	Min.	Max.	Min.	Max
2	1	1	1	2	3	1	1	1	1
3	3	3	3	3	5	2	3	2	3
4	6	5	5	4	7	2	3	2	3
5	10	9	9	5	9	3	5	3	7
6	15	12	12	6	11	3	5	3	7
7	21	16	16	7	13	3	7	3	7
8	28	19	19	8	15	3	7	4	7
9	36	29	26	9	17	4	10	4	12
10	45	32	31	10	19	4	10	4	12
11	55	43	39	11	21	4	12	4	12
12	66	47	42	12	23	4	12	4	13
13	78	54	49	13	25	4	13	4	13
14	91	58	54	14	27	4	13	4	13
15	105	71	59	15	29	4	15	4	13
16	120	75	63	16	31	4	15	4	13

Table 2. Comparison of area and delay on Benchmark Circuits

Benchmark Circuits	#inputs	#outputs	area		delay	
			Original circuit	Proposed Technique	Original circuit	Proposed Technique
sym9	9	1	202	89	13	12
sym10	10	1	159	127	15	13
rd53	5	3	50	52	11	8
rd73	7	3	93	88	11	9
rd84	8	4	228	114	15	9

Table 3. Cost of general symmetric functions

Functions $S^n(a_1-a_r)$	Number of gate inputs			Number of paths		
	As in [2]	As in [3]	Proposed Method	As in [2]	As in [3]	Proposed Method
$S^5(1,2)$	47	32	38	35	23	18
$S^6(1,2)$	83	56	50	50	41	34
$S^7(2,3)$	219	138	66	66	102	85
$S^8(2,3)$	394	228	78	78	176	64
$S^9(2,3)$	662	381	106	106	576	99
$S^{10}(3,4)$	1832	1009	126	1620	805	216
$S^{10}(4,5)$	2354	1296	126	2100	1034	316
$S^{11}(3,4)$	3137	1675	158	2805	1365	266
$S^{12}(4,5)$	8318	4330	170	7524	3548	464
$S^{13}(4,5)$	14445	7430	198	13156	6184	544
$S^{14}(5,6)$	37039	18596	218	34034	15540	804
$S^{15}(5-9)$	50052	24671	238	45045	21085	2559
$S^{15}(5,6)$	65067	32312	238	60060	27354	1170

7 Conclusions

This paper presents a simple technique for synthesizing symmetric Boolean functions with 100% path-delay fault testability. Module(n) is universal and cost-effective. Multiple symmetric functions of n variables can be synthesized by using *Module(n)* and some additional logic. The number of paths in the circuit is reduced significantly compared to earlier designs, and hence time needed for delay test generation and test application is likely to reduce proportionately. Further, because of the unateness and regular nature of Module(n), the test sequence for detecting all path-delay faults can be easily determined.

References

1. Dietmeyer, D.L.: Generating minimal covers of symmetric function. IEEE TCAD, vol. 12, no. 5, pp. 710-713, May 1993.
2. W. Ke, W., Menon, P.R,: Delay-testable implementations of symmetric functions. IEEE TCAD, vol. 14, pp. 772-775, 1995.
3. Chakraborty, S., Das, S., Das, D.K., Bhattacharya, B.B.: Synthesis of symmetric functions for path-delay fault testability. IEEE TCAD, vol. 19, pp. 1076-1081, September 2000.
4. Kohavi, Z.: Switching and Finite Automata Theory. New York: McGraw-Hill, 1977.
5. Yang, Y.X., Guo, B.: Further enumerating Boolean functions of cryptographic significance. J. Cryptology, vol. 8, no. 3, pp. 115-122, 1995.
6. Hurst, S. L.: Digital summation threshold logic gates: a new circuit element. IEE Proc., vol. 120, no. 11, pp. 1301-1307, 1973.
7. Ja'Ja', J., Wu, S.-M.: A new approach to realize partially symmetric functions. Tech. Rep. SRC TR 86-54, Dept. EE, University of Maryland, 1986.
8. Rahaman,H., Das,D.K., Bhattacharya.B.B.: A simple delay-testable design of digital summation threshold logic (DSTL) array. Proc. of the 5th International Workshop on Boolean Problems, Freiberg, Germany, pp.189-194, 2002.
9. Rahaman,H., Das,D.K., Bhattacharya.B.B.: A new synthesis of symmetric functions. Proc. of ASP-DAC/VLSI Design, pp. 160-165, January 2002.
10. Sentovich, E.M., Singh, K.J., Lavagno, L., Moon, C., Murgai, R.R., Saldhana, A., Savoj, H., Stephan, P.R., Brayton, R.K., Sangiovanni-Vincentelli, A.L.: SIS: a sequential system for sequential circuit synthesis. Technical Report UCB/ERL m92/41. Electronic Research Laboratory, University of California, Berkley, CA 94720, May 1992.

VOBA – A Voice Based Newsgroup

U.B. Desai, N. Balachander, P. Dinakar, and V. Madhavan

HP – IITM R&D Lab, Indian Institute of Technology, Madras
ubdesai@ee.iitb.ac.in
{balchand,dinakarp}@tenet.res.in
madhavan_vasudevan@hotmail.com

Abstract. In order for a newsgroup to be of use to all people irrespective of their literacy levels, a Voice Based News Group (VOBA) has been developed. This paper presents VOBA, an online discussion group designed for use in rural communities. Recognizing the fact that large segments of the population in developing countries have low literacy levels, VOBA provides voice based inputs and outputs. The user while navigating through the web pages is assisted by voice messages. The voice interfaces have been provided for various Indian vernacular languages.

1 Introduction

In its 1999 Human Development Report, the United Nations Development Programme stated "Knowledge is the new asset: more than half of the GDP in the major OECD countries is now knowledge-based"[1]. The rapid growth of Internet technology in countries like India has unleashed myriad sources of knowledge like Internet kiosks, Video Conferencing facilities, Virtual Universities, Online tutorials etc. These technologies are slowly making inroads into rural India. Still, these technologies come with a hidden caveat that the end user should be literate. The solution is to make all applications easily usable by people of all levels regardless of their capabilities. VOBA is an initiative in this direction.

Internet allows the creation of interest groups that go beyond geographic barriers. For an Internet based discussion forum, it is imperative that the user should be literate, for he/she has to type messages in English or any other language. To overcome this shortcoming, a Voice Based Newsgroup has been designed for use in rural areas. Recognizing the fact that large segments of the rural population have low levels of literacy, VOBA uses iconic interfaces and vocal assistance to convey information effectively. Since all messages posted in VOBA are going to be voice messages, the issue of font support plays no role. Moreover VOBA provides vernacular voice interfaces to remove language dependency.

Users can start discussions by posting a voice based query, an issue or convey some information. Anyone who wishes to take part in the discussion can reply back using voice. Interfaces for various Indian languages are provided. The user can select the language that he prefers to record his messages. The buttons provided in VOBA have a special purpose; they provide vocal assistance i.e. when the user moves the mouse over buttons, a voice message explains the purpose of the button. Some sample newsgroups

S. Manandhar et al. (Eds.): AACC 2004, LNCS 3285, pp. 271–278, 2004.

like "Health care", "Agriculture", "Wireless", "Science" etc. have been provided. Nevertheless new groups can be added.

In any newsgroup, whenever a user wants to post a message, he needs to subscribe to the group. This is usually done by a "user name" and a "password". A voice-based identification scheme is used i.e. while posting the very first message the user records a "pass phrase" thrice. This could be his name or some specific word. Subsequently whenever he wants to post a new message he utters his pass phrase and is identified by VOBA.

2   Related Work

The major stumbling block to widespread use of computers in rural areas is the low level of literacy that often exists. Many examples that have overcome this barrier can be found in the literacy research community. One such example is "Community Knowledge Sharing"[2], an asynchronous discussion system that has been evaluated in an agricultural community in the Dominican Republic. It concludes that low literate users prefer fully iconic interfaces. But messages can be typed as well as recorded. Also the system uses a fingerprint based authentication system. Community Board is another system[3], which presents a voice-based integrated view of discussion, participants, topics and time.

3   Description of VOBA

VOBA allows people to navigate through a bulletin board consisting of messages and discussions; listen to the messages posted and post new voice messages to the group. The website consists of various groups like "Health care", "Science", "Agriculture", "Cinema" (Figure 1) etc. Groups can be easily added or deleted. The user can move easily between groups and listen to all the messages posted.

VOBA has been guided by three main principles. (i) It is designed for people with different literacy levels. New technologies that target rural areas have to accommodate user-friendly interfaces and easy to use applications. (ii) In order to reach a wider range of audience VOBA uses different language interfaces. The user can also switch to different languages in between browsing. (iii) Using any computer application requires a little technical proficiency on the part of the user. In rural areas we cannot assume that the end-user will possess such technical skills. Hence VOBA has been designed to aid the user with iconic interfaces and voice messages.

3.1   Signing In

It is not mandatory for users to register with VOBA. They can navigate through the website and listen to all the messages posted. Only when they wish to post voice messages or reply to older messages, they need to sign in. This they can do by uttering their pass phrase.

Fig. 1. The index page of VOBA showing the list of groups, vernacular language interfaces etc.

3.2 Registration

If the user is not registered with the system, he has to register by giving a convenient user name and recording his pass phrase thrice to the system. Though verification doesn't require a user name, the user name has to be typed in order for other members to know who has posted which message. It is assumed that the kiosks will have a kiosk operator who can help the user in typing a user name. In future we plan to use a speech to text engine to get over the problem of typing in the user name.

3.3 Recording Messages

Messages are recorded using Java applets that are launched using Java Webstart (Figure 2) . The recording applet is completely iconic. There is a picture of a "teacher", which when clicked instructs the user on how to use the recording applet. The user can record a short subject that explains his message in brief. For a literate user, a subject text option is also given wherein he can type the subject of his message.

3.4 Icons Used

The first page of VOBA provides the user with a list of all the groups present in VOBA. One can see that the user need not know to read the names of the groups, though they are provided. Instead every group is symbolically represented with an image i.e. a Red Cross image to signify "Health care", an actress' image to mean "Cinema" and a picture

Fig. 2. The JAVA applet in which users can record their voice messages

of people working in a field to denote "Agriculture". An image of an instructor teaching on the black board symbolizes that by clicking on it one could learn how to use VOBA. Throughout the website a speaker image is embedded in every button. This suggests that when the user is going to move his mouse over it someone is going to speak and help him out. Even the "Record", "Play" and "Stop" buttons are two sided, one side giving an appropriate picture like a mike (it means one has to speak after clicking the button) and the other side giving a text description of the button (this is meant for the advanced user).

3.5   Speech Based Verification

Some of the governing criteria for the development of a speech based speaker verification have been: (i) very small training time, (ii) very short speech samples for verification, (iii) samples to be taken in a noisy realistic environment, (iv) variability of speech samples over time, (v) simplicity and (vi) robustness of the system. The block diagram of the system is shown in Figure 3. The system uses the speaker's voice and the pass-phrase to create a reference model for that speaker. The pass-phrase is an authentication key, known only to the user, which he utters to the system when being verified. The reference model is created using 3 training sequences. During verification the user utters his pass-phrase and features are extracted from the speech signal to be compared with the reference model. The claim will be accepted or rejected depending on the similarity of the utterance with the reference model.

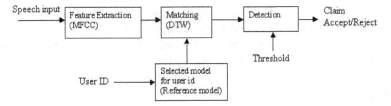

Fig. 3. The block diagram of the speech based verification system

Feature Extraction. The motivation for using Mel-Frequency Cepstral Coefficients (MFCC) for feature extraction is due to the fact that the auditory response of the human ear resolves frequencies non-linearly. The mapping from linear frequency to Mel-frequency is defined as

$$Mel(f) = 2595 log_{10}(1 + \frac{f}{700})$$

The speech signal is first pre-emphasized and then segmented into overlapping frames of 256 samples per frame. Then the magnitude spectrum of each frame is obtained. The frequency scale is then warped to Mel-frequency scale and coefficients are obtained from the cepstrum. While registering, the use utters his pass-phrase. From the uttered speech signal, the MFCC features are extracted and aligned in a time series to form a reference model. This is the training process.

Dynamic Time Warping. When a speaker wants access, his uttered pass-phrase is converted to a set of feature vectors (MFCC). The feature vectors of the speech submitted for verification and that of the reference model will, in general not be aligned. For the purpose of alignment we use dynamic time warping[5][4]. DTW normalizes the trial-trial timing variations of the utterances of the same text. Consider a test utterance 'A' represented as a sequence of feature vectors a_1, a_2, .., a_i, ... a_I and a reference model 'B' consisting of $b_1, b_2,$ .. $b_j, ..b_J$. Now a distance matrix D is obtained by placing the reference sequence on the y-axis and test sequence on the x-axis. The elements of the distance matrix D(i,j) are the distances between the vector a_i and b_j. The time warping between the test and reference sequence is done using a dynamic time warping algorithm, which gives a critical path called as 'warping path'. Warping path is the route taken when traveling from D(1,1) to D(I,J), while minimizing the accumulated path distance given by

$$d = \sum_{k=1}^{m} D(i(k), j(k))$$

where (i(k), j(k)) is the critical path obtained by time warping and m is the length of the path.

Given a reference and input signals, the DTW algorithm does a constrained, piecewise linear mapping of one (or both) time axis (es) to align the two signals while minimizing 'd'. At the end of time warping, the accumulated distance is the basis of match score. This method accounts for variation over time of parameters corresponding to the dynamic configuration of the articulators and the vocal tract.

The acceptance/rejection will be based on the value of 'd', which is a measure of proximity of the utterances to the reference model.

4   Results

The performance of the Voice Based verification system was tested using voice samples collected from a random group of 36 speakers. The recording was done with a sampling frequency of 16KHz and 16-bit precision in a real time office environment. During each recording, the speaker was allowed to utter the pass phrase with his natural accent without prior practice. The pass-phrase typically turns out to be the person's name (thus in our work the pass-phrase has very short interval – approximately 0.5 sec). From the speech samples collected at five different days and times, tests were conducted to analyze the performance of the system under variation of utterances of the pass-phrase from time to time. The reliability of the system was tested by voice samples obtained with a speaker uttering another user's pass-phrase.

The system was designed to provide high reliability and its performance was examined. Figure 4 shows the plot between the number of utterances used for training and the percentage accuracy, when the speech samples used for training and testing were recorded at the same time. It clearly shows the improvement in performance with increase in number of utterances used for training. When the number of utterances is 8 or above we get 100% accuracy. In all the remaining simulations a reference model based on 8 utterances of the pass-phrase is used.

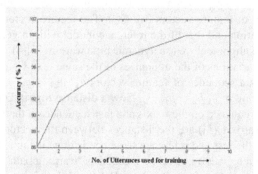

Fig. 4. No. of utterances used for training vs percentage accuracy

Figure 5 shows the results for speaker verification case. The user asks the kiosk operator to key in his user-id. Next he utters his pass-phrase in the microphone. This is then compared with only the reference model corresponding to the user-id. As seen from Figure 5, for speaker verification, 100% accuracy is obtained (using a threshold of 490).

Figure 6 depicts the result of our system in the speaker identification mode. Here the uttered pass-phrase is compared with the reference model of all speakers in the

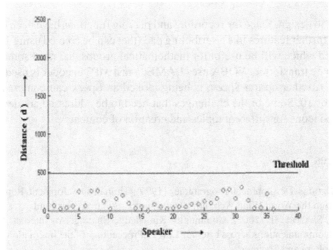

Fig. 5. Distance between the test utterance and reference model corresponding to each speaker

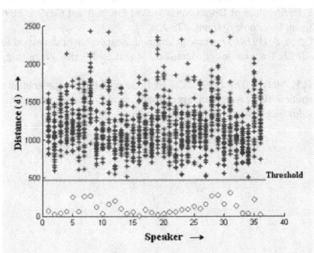

Fig. 6. The result of cross comparison of test utterances of each speaker with the reference model of every other speaker. The red 'o' represents auto comparison. The blue '*' represents the cross comparison

database. Such a system would obviate the need for a user-id. From Figure 6, one finds that with a threshold of 490, one gets 100% accuracy.

5 Conclusion

This paper has presented VOBA, an online voice based discussion group designed for use in rural areas. People with varying levels of literacy can use VOBA. Though VOBA has been lab tested and within a very short time it will be field-tested. As a future extension, one can add a voice-based search engine. It is to be noted that such engines are difficult to design. Since the recording and playing functions have been implemented using Java, further features like a scribbling pad (that can be created using Java) can also be integrated which will be useful for mathematical groups that need some equation or formulae to be transferred. VOBA uses LAME; a fast MP3 encoder is used to compress audio files. Another option Speex, is being looked at. Speex can compress WAV files by a factor of 10. Some of the challenges that need to be addressed are development of standardized icons for different topics and creation of content.

References

1. United Nations Development Programme. (1999). Human Development Report 1999. Retrieved from the World Wide Web: http://www.undp.org/hdro/report.html
2. Best, M., Shakeel, H. (2002). Community Knowledge Sharing: An Internet Application to Support Communications across Literacy Levels. Proceedings of the International Symposium on Technology and Society.
3. Matsubara, S., Ohguro, T., Hattori, F. (1998). Community Board: Social Meeting System able to Visualize the Structure of Discussions. Second International Conference on Knowledge-Based Intelligent Electronic Systems, 423-428.
4. Sakoe, H., Chiba, S. (1978). Dynamic programming algorithm optimization for spoken word recognition. IEEE Transactions on Acoustics, Speech and Signal Processing, Vol.ASSP-26, No.1.
5. Silverman, H.F., Morgan, D.P. (1990). The application of dynamic programming to connected speech recognition. IEEE Acoustics, Speech and Signal Processing magazine.
6. freshmeat.net/projects/lame

An ICT Based Framework
for Improving Rural Credit Delivery

S.S. Satchidananda and Srinath Srinivasa

Center for Banking and IT, Indian Institute of Information Technology,
26/C, Electronics City, Hosur Road, 560100 Bangalore, India
sssatchidananda@iiitb.ac.in

Abstract. There is an immediate need to step up the flow of credit to agricultural and other rural activities in India for improving rural productivity and economic welfare. In this context, we propose an ICT-based solution for improving the delivery of credit and other services to the rural areas through unbundling and outsourcing of the rural banking operations. The solution involves setting up of a *common infrastructure for rural data collection, information management and processing* and *sharing of the multi-service delivery channel* by banks and other service providers with a view to substantially reducing the transaction costs and improving the speed and quality of delivery.

Introduction

Despite India being an agricultural economy, and continuous efforts made by the authorities for the last fifty years, rural credit system is not able to meet the expected rural capital formation, employment generation and growth. The fact that the banking system has achieved most of the targets for priority sector advances other than the target of 18 percent of the total advance to agriculture and 12 percent for direct lending to agriculture highlight this problem. The recovery rates in agriculture lending being some of the lowest is also an indicator of the problems in this area. The Reserve Bank of India (RBI) has appointed a High Power Committee under the Chairmanship of V.S.Vyas in 2004 to examine the credit delivery system and to make recommendations for its improvement. In the recent past, the Reserve Bank had also to give directions to the banks to charge not more than 9 percent per annum interest on the small agricultural advances up to Rs.50, 000 despite the interest rates being free. These two developments clearly show that that there are certain inadequacies in the existing agricultural credit delivery system.

Agricultural credit delivery has been one of the most studied subjects in the country for over several decades by the government, bankers and academician. The study of the problems relating to agriculture in a formal way began with the establishment of an exclusive department for the purpose in RBI as far back as 1934 since the RBI Act required that RBI shall maintain expert staff to investigate and advice on the matters relating to rural credit. Beginning with the legendary All India Rural Credit Survey Committee Report in 1954, a large number of expert reports have examined and investigated the problems relating to the credit delivery for agriculture and rural area. Few of the important ones are National Agricultural Credit Review report 2000, and Expert Committee on Rural Credit Report 2002.

Rural credit has been a laboratory for various policies, initiatives, investigations and improvements since 1955. The first major strategy adopted for improving rural

S. Manandhar et al. (Eds.): AACC 2004, LNCS 3285, pp. 279–286, 2004.

credit delivery was the institutionalization of the credit delivering system with the cooperative as the primary channels.1971 brought in the multi-agency approach to the rural credit delivery with the induction of the commercial banks in to the scene. In 1979, specialized institutions called Regional Rural Banks and subsequently, another breed of institutions called Local Area Banks came on the scene. With the operationalisation of the Lead Bank Scheme, area approach to rural lending was formalized and attempts were made to match infrastructure development with bank credit flows for ensuring development of the rural areas. The Scheme sought to give a special supply-leading role to the banking system in rural development and also to ensure access of the rural population to bank credit through rural branch expansion. The latest initiative is the micro finance and the involvement of the self help groups wherein the banks are trying to involve other agencies for urgency of rural credit.

The National Agricultural Credit Review Committee Report documents the history, development and the status of the various important issues involved in rural credit delivery in India in detail. It is interesting to know from this comprehensive report that solutions have been advised and implemented for almost all the real as well as perceived problems in rural credit delivery and this area remains a problem defying a satisfactory solution. For example, some of the key concerns like the end-use of credit, infrastructure gaps, the high costs of lending have been attended and repeatedly. Despite that, the delivery of credit for agriculture and rural development remains unsatisfactory.

Technology-Based Solution for Rural Credit Delivery

Against this background, the key question to ask is whether an Information and Communication Technology (ICT)-based solution is possible to achieve desired results in credit delivery. There is evidence to suggest the scope for this in a recent field study conducted by bankers and the State Government in Orissa under the auspices of the State Level Bankers Committee [1], that identifies three major factors hampering rural credit delivery: knowledge-gap (ignorance), attitude gap and the lack of adequate processes and scoring models. All three impediments seem amenable to be addressed by the use of ICT. Realizing the urgency and the magnitudes of the problem, we propose a comprehensive and somewhat radical approach, which would require meticulous preparation and determined implementation.

The model provides for a low-cost technology platform for rural banking through a comprehensive, fully automated credit delivery system. The objectives sought to be accomplished through this model include the following:

- To improve the flow of rural credit for financing rural economic growth
- To lower transaction-costs of rural credit delivery by use of technology
- To enable the delivery of educational inputs and other documentation services in addition to credit
- To address the problem of the inadequacy of the data required for credit decision making such as potential for economic activities in the area of infrastructure, availability details of natural resources etc.

The model envisaged provides a low-cost technology platform for rural banking. The solution involves three elements:

1. Multi Service Delivery System (MSDS)
2. Integrated Multi-Entity Database System (IMDS)
3. Credit Monitoring

Multi-service delivery system (MSDS): The MSDS is a front-end delivery machine. It is a multipurpose ATM-like machine which can dispense not only the cash but also accept electronic requests for loan and repayment of loan, besides providing receipts and documents in printed form. It is possible to work out variants of this front-end machine. MSDS may provide all the cash point services, loaning and receiving of repayment and additionally other services like receipts or printout of data/ land records/ passbooks/ health services. Even booking of train tickets cinema tickets etc., is possible if the data centre is hooked to service providers.

Integrated multi-entity database system (IMDS): The IMDS is a data hub that is established for a cluster of villages and connected to the MSDS machines in each village. For connectivity, with falling cost of wireless and wire-line communications, a large number of options are opening up, thanks to technological advances. The IMDS handles the workflow and decision-making processes that guide actions of the MSDS machines. The IMDS is a *multi-entity* database, in that; it is a data center interfacing with multiple banks. The collection and feeding of the data to the IMDS would be an exercise of considerable magnitude in the first instance because all the data available in respect of every adult member in a village needs to be captured.

Credit monitoring: The third element in the solution is the credit monitoring by the banks. The centralized database could give access to the multiple banks through suitable linkages. The credit monitoring has to be done by an expert agency either in the bank or in any self-help group that is involved in financing. This function would involve mainly the verification of the end-use of funds, verification of the securities and updating the changes in regard to the borrower's profile happening in a dynamic context.

Data collection is a critical task and needs to be performed by trained people in a careful manner by building suitable cross-validations. For example, an important task is the verification of income given with reference to income from various assets held by the individuals as well as the expenditure of the family. Once such a comprehensive database is built even to a reasonable level of accuracy, it would provide a solid basis for not only a decision-making but also for a multitudinous welfare activity of the governments as well as for economic planning and poverty alleviation programmes.

Obviously an exercise of this kind, if it is to be completed with the required level efficiency and speed, authenticity and correctness; outsourcing it to an external agency appears to be the best option. However, adequate safeguards in terms of supervisory protection of the data and maintenance of integrity and purity of the data and for preventing the abuse of the data need to be established. In addition, the architecture of the IMDS is such that existing information Bhoomi land records database in Karnataka can be utilized by interfacing it with the IMDS.

Prima facie, based on interaction with several stake holders like banks, financial institutions, end-users, data-center operators and ICT companies, it appears that establishing and maintaining the IMDS and MSDS appears to a viable and even a profitable venture. Indicative costing for this activity is given in annexure. However, this model is to be tested and perfected and there is need for support during the pilot implementation.

Technology Issues and Overall Architecture

The overall architecture of the system is shown in Figure 1. End-users use the MSDS for most of their banking solutions. The MSDS is connected to the nearest IMDS. The IMDS itself is part of a grid, which is envisaged to eventually provide nation-wide connectivity. IMDS nodes may also query other databases like the Bhoomi land records, for their services.

The IMDS is the engine that powers all banking transactions made from any MSDS. It is an independently supported, reliable source of up-to-date data on all aspects affecting credit delivery. This includes transaction data in the form of user accounts. It also acts as a crucial information source for analytical activities and decision support systems.

Since a single IMDS database may not be scalable, the long-term strategy is to model the IMDS in the form of a grid, comprising of several data centers. Each such data center holds information about specific geographical areas. Once the system is completely deployed, it is expected to have one data center for every 2,00,000 people.

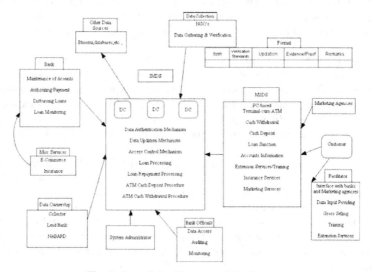

Fig. 1. Overall Architecture of the System

Architecture of the IMDS

Data Elements and Sources: Several factors affect credit delivery decisions in a rural context. Many of these factors differ from one geographic location to the other. In order to be able to factor these variations, the overall architecture of the IMDS should be modular in nature where data about specific aspects of the system can be added and removed without affecting the overall architecture or the application logic of the software using the IMDS.

The overall architecture of an IMDS node is schematically shown in Figure 2.

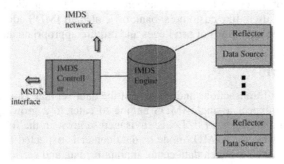

Fig. 2. Architecture of the IMDS

As shown in the figure, an IMDS node is driven by a core IMDS "engine" that contains business logic definitions for making decisions. This engine is fed by one or more data sources, each of which may optionally contain a "reflector" that specifies how data in the source should be read and interpreted. The reflectors can also contain some more statements of business logic that is integrated into the overall IMDS engine.

An illustrative list of mandatory data elements required by the IMDS engine is given in [2]. The overall architecture of the IMDS core engine is shown in Figure 3.

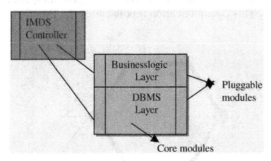

Fig. 3. Architecture of the IMDS engine

The IMDS core comprises of two layers – the database layer and the business logic layer. The database layer defines the mandatory and optional schematic structures that make up the database. The DBMS layer is managed by a database server like Oracle 10g [3], or IBM DB2 [4] enterprise edition.

The business logic layer defines relationships among different data elements in the context of several business processes. It also defines static and dynamic integrity constraints on business processes. Such integrity constraints define and govern the flow of business processes that use the database. It is likely for these rules to change over time. It is hence desirable to separate the rule system from the application program itself. This will obviate the need to rebuild the application program whenever there is a policy change.

The IMDS controller module is concerned with all aspects that govern the execution of the IMDS core itself. The IMDS controller is also governed by a rule set, which addresses the functioning of the IMDS core, rather than the business process. A prominent role of the controller is user authentication. IMDS applications are used by different kinds of users like customers, bank officials and IMDS administrators. Each of them enjoys separate kinds of privileges and require appropriate authentication.

The IMDS Grid

Given the nature of transactions and the size of the data-set that should be managed, it is impractical to expect a single IMDS engine to cater to a growing population of users. Hence, in the long term IMDS is envisaged to grow in the form of a grid with several IMDS nodes. Each IMDS node or data center is expected to serve a population of roughly 2,00,000. Each data center maintains data and carries out transactions pertinent to its geographical location.

The grid architecture is gaining popularity all over the world for managing extremely large databases. Grids similar to the proposed model are already in operation in several parts of the world serving specific data needs. Some examples include: The EU data grid project [5], The TeraGrid scientific database [6] and The Biomedical Informatics Research Network [7].

The overall architecture of the IMDS grid as shown in Figure 4, follows a "hub and spoke" model. A IMDS "hub" is a collection of IMDS machines connected by high bandwidth connection. The connectivity of such a hub – the number of machines that each machine in the hub is connected to – would be at least one-third of the number of machines that form the hub. Communication links across hubs are also required to be of high bandwidth. This communication link is called the IMDS "backbone" to which hubs connect.

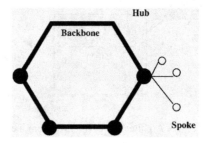

Fig. 4. The IMDS Grid

A "spoke" is a machine that connects to a hub using a lower bandwidth connection like a dial-up line. Machines at the end of a spoke would be usually much less powerful than the machines that form the hub. A spoke is assigned to connect to a hub and it can connect to any machine in the hub. This provides for multiple communication channels in case of failures of IMDS nodes or the communication lines.

The Multi-service Delivery System (MSDS)

The multi-service delivery system (MSDS) is the interface of the IMDS with end users. In its simplest implementation, the MSDS is an automated transaction machine

(ATM) augmented with a personal computer running software that provides the ATM with extra functionalities.

The MSDS could be a mobile unit mounted on a vehicle, in order to enable it to serve several villages for the same cost. The vehicle would dock at a specified place like the taluk office or the local post office in different villages at periodic intervals. Each MSDS would have at least two communication channels with which it can connect to the IMDS network. It would also have cash dispensers and cash collectors that can accept cash deposits of small denominations.

The main tasks of an MSDS unit include:

- Cash dispensation to the account holders through the ATM,
- On line cash remittance facility or issuing of DDs etc.
- Simple credit appraisal/dispensation, through networking and the PC connectivity
- Receiving of Cash to deposit and Loan accounts by the teller

The above activities require enumerating and maintaining of a data bank of all the residents of the group of villages. All the data captured will be warehoused in the IMDS attached to the MSDS. If required IMDS units may also query other units in the grid to provide required data elements.

Besides these services, the MSDS will have provisions for providing a host of banking and non-banking services. Banking services include opening of deposit accounts and transactions therein, various remittance facilities, issue of various authenticated documents like pass sheets, loan covenants, sanctions and disbursement advices and receipting of various transactions etc., The MSDS may also provide non-banking services such as information regarding the agricultural operations, training inputs to farmers and other e-government services and e-commerce services such as on-line reservation and booking of journey tickets, printing and issue of those and other documents of relevance to the rural people. In other words, it can be the hub of rural services delivery.

Conclusions

In order to achieve at least 8 percent overall economic growth in the country as targeted by the Planning Commission, it is essential to ensure sustained growth in agricultural sector. Increasing the adequate and timely flow of productive credit to this sector is a critical factor for improving investment growth and capital formation in this sector [8,9]. While there is an established multi-agency infrastructure for rural credit delivery comprising co-operatives, commercial banks and the micro finance agencies, the flow of credit still requires acceleration and qualitative improvement in delivery. In order to address this important issue, this paper proposes an ICT–based solution for improving the delivery of credit and other services of the rural areas. The solution proposes common infrastructure for the rural data collection and information management and processing and the sharing of the delivery channel by the banks with a view to substantially reducing the transaction costs and improving the speed and quality of delivery. The elements involved in the proposed solution are the establishment of a data hub for every village and ensuring its two way connectivity to a multi service delivery machine that provides banking, extension and other government services. The solution suggests the outsourcing of the data hub and the MSDS establishment and operations with required safeguards and robust structure.

References

1. District Managers (2004) "Feedback received from the District Managers of the National Bank for Agriculture and Rural development in Orissa State during an interaction"
2. S S Satchidananda, Srinath Srinivasa, Rajesh Jain, P S Kulkarni. Use of Information Technology for Improving Credit Delivery. IIITB Working Paper, WP 2004-01, Indian Institute of Information Technology, Bangalore, India, May 2004.
3. Oracle 10g Grids. http://www.oracle.com/database/
4. IBM DB2 Product Family. http://www-306.ibm.com/software/data/db2/
5. EU data grid project. http://eu-datagrid.web.cern.ch/eu-datagrid/
6. The TeraGrid Project. http://www.teragrid.org/
7. Biomedical informatics research network. http://www.nbirn.net/
8. State Level Bankers Committee (2004), "The Report of the Committee on Low Credit Offtake in Orissa", *Proceedings of the State Level Bankers Committee,* pp.19-21
9. Tomar J. S. (1997) "Managing Rural Banking in Banking Reforms in India", Tata McGraw-Hill, *Editors* Subramanian &T.K.Velayudham pp.409.

An Approach Towards a Decentralised Disaster Management Information Network

M. Scalem[1], S. Bandyopadhyay[1], and A.K. Sircar[2]

[1] Management Information Systems (MIS) Group, Indian Institute of Management Calcutta (IIM Calcutta), Joka, Diamond Harbor Road, Kolkata, 700 104 West Bengal, India
{scalem,somprakash}@iimcal.ac.in
[2] SPADE, Kolkata, 700 075 West Bengal, India
ashoks@cal3.vsnl.net.in

Abstract. The existing Disaster Management (DM) approaches are quite unstructured and are usually centralised in nature with the instructions following some sort of fixed hierarchy. This results in poor resource management and hence inefficiency. Since Disasters themselves are unstructured in scope and hence can't be managed centrally, there is a need for a user centric decentralised hierarchy independent approach wherein even the end user is empowered accordingly for quick and effective results. This working paper addresses the novel approach by underlining the need for a decentralised Information Network whose main objective is to match the available resources at any time with the needs, at the right time and to the right people. Our network uses concepts of multi mobile agents, mobile/AdHoc networking, real time operations, etc. The paper also presents a descriptive implementation setup of the network with the benefits accruing like efficient & effective resource management, real time networking, user centric and enabler decentralised operations, etc. Given the canvass and time-critical aspects of disasters, by this approach the level of success could be exponentially increased leading to an efficient, real time, and effective Disaster Management.

1 Introduction

A lot of research has been done on the traditional approach regarding technology viz., Management of Technology (MOT), Mobile Governance (mGov) [1], etc towards a new transversal and comprehensive vision of Technological Management [2]. There exists a set of active links between technology and the elements of management systems [3] and hence one can deduce that technology is impacted by and has an impact on all those functions, thereby underlining the importance of effective management of technology. One of the most important techno-management initiatives of the decade, Electronic Governance (eGov), has its inherent advantages and offers a new way forward helping connect citizens to the government [4]. However, one can argue about its success given that failing ratio is more than 60% [5, 6] and comparing with Baltius's ideal propositions [7]. Herein came our concept of 'Mobile Governance' (mGov) [1] facilitating the enhanced technologies incorporating new management

S. Manandhar et al. (Eds.): AACC 2004, LNCS 3285, pp. 287–295, 2004.

propositions including inherent aspects like effective real-time information sharing, transparency, security, implementation through wireless/mobile/AdHoc/Distributed networking schemas. The present paper presents an application of mGov by taking on the area of Disaster Management that has a high impact on general populace and economy incorporating Multi Mobile Agent Approach (MMAA), Networking, Wireless Topologies, etc. Mobile communications might be concluded to have a 'Physical Level' that signifies that at least one of the communication partner is mobile, and a 'Social Level' which purports to forcing a partner to quickly switch (urgency, priority, etc) between social contexts [8, 9, 10]. It is this paradox of capturing and catering to the populace correctly that forms both a challenge as also an aspiration in our context.

2   Disaster Management

In 2002 alone, as per the latest report [11], a total of as high a number as 608 million people were reported affected worldwide by disasters with the total amount of estimated damage inflicted by disasters during 2001 as high as US\$ 24 billion. Even after so much preparations, when comparing the decades 1983-1992 and 1993-2002, the number of people reported affected have risen by 54 per cent over the same period worldwide underlining the importance of the topic. Literally, the term "disaster management" (DM) encompasses the complete realm of disaster-related activities and can be defined [12] as "...a set of actions and processes designed to lessen disastrous effects either before, during and after a disaster." In our opinion, the critical success factor (CSF) for effective DM is that the level of approach should be a Grass-Root one rather than the typical haphazard/unstructured one that generally exists. We have incorporated this very approach in our DDMIN design, and have found out that the level of success could be exponentially increased this way. Our DMIN deals with the situations that occur prior to, during, and after the disaster and is facilitated with the electronic/IT/Mobile/Wireless components for effective and real-time solutions.

3   Strategic Frameworks

In this section we present relevant frameworks and our own model strategic framework:

Drabek Model: Drabek [13] proposed an approach through which it is possible to resolve disaster communications into four distinct levels of complexity that range from the individual to larger social and organizational system.

Thomas Model: Thomas [14] presented a categorical framework for disaster communications based on information flows, rather than functions or roles, and adopted a four-fold typology to examine technology issues and general communication problems:

- **Intra-organizational (Intra Org):** Communication within organizations
- **Inter-organizational (Inter Org):** Communication between organizations

- **Organizations-to-public (O to P):** Communication from organizations to the public
- **Public-to-organizations (P to O):** Communication from public to organizations

Proposed Strategic Model: Our strategic framework (refer Fig. 1) builds upon the Dedrick and Kraemer's [15] theoretical framework of an IT-led development and incorporates the distinct levels of communications complexity and Thomas's proposition of a concrete categorical framework for information flows. Our techno-management approach encompasses industrial policy, industry structure and environmental factors to showcase the relationship between IT and economic payoffs.

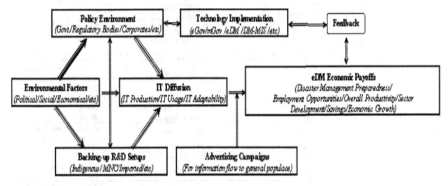

Fig. 1. Our Proposed Directional DM Strategic Framework

This model also takes into account the affects of IT in a heterogeneous atmosphere as compared to the homogeneous setups, viz., companies, firms, organizations, etc where the technology adaptability quotient, literacy levels etc are more or less static as against the former.

4 Decentralised DM Information Network (DDMIN)

Our research findings are reproduced below in a systematic manner:

For the purpose of modeling the structure, we had to research upon the existing hierarchy setups and found out that these are reflected similarly across the developing countries. The hierarchy structure of West Bengal state in India forms the backdrop for our prototyping purposes which consist of the following levels: District Level, Sub-Divisional Level, Block Level, Gram Panchayat Level and Booth/Volunteer Level. The information flow would have the following four sets of headers:

(a) To feed Information – UPDT
(b) To see Information – CHCK
(c) Instruct for info – INSTRCT
(d) To seek instructions – SEEK

We hereby propose the concept of 'Thematic Entities (T-E)' rather than the established entities to develop our model. Against our research and starting from the grass root level, the structure could be divided in the set of eight T-Es as follows:

Table 1. Information Interconnectivity Mapping

Sl. No.	Thematic Entity	Departments	Centers	Levels
1	WaTSaN	Health	▪ Primary Health Centre ▪ Sub Centre	. Block & Panchayat . Panchayat
		Public Health Engineering (PHE)	▪ PHE Deptt Centre	. Block
		Non Govt. Org. (NGO)	▪ NGO Units	. Block / Gram Samad/ Gram Panchayat
		Animal	▪ Veterinary Hospital ▪ Veterinary Centre	. Block . Gram Panchayat
2	HLTH	Human	▪ Primary Health Centre ▪ Sub Centre	. Block & Panchayat . Panchayat
		NGO	▪ NGO Units	. Block / Gram Samad/ Gram Panchayat
3	FD	Animal Resource	▪ Block Office ▪ Pranibandhu Office	. Block . Gram Panchayat
		Food Corporation	▪ FCI Office	. Sub Divisional
		Block Relief	▪ District Office ▪ Block Relief Office	. District . Block
		Panchayat Structure	▪ Panchayat Office	. Gram Panchayat
		NGO	▪ NGO Units	. Block / Gram Samad/ Gram Panchayat
4	RCUE/SHTR	Civil Defense	▪ CD Offices	. District & Block
		Block Relief	▪ District Office ▪ Block Relief Office	. District . Block
		Police Deptt	▪ Police Station	. Block
		NGO	▪ NGO Units	. Block / Gram Samad/ Gram Panchayat
		Block Deptt	▪ Block Office	. Block
5	EM	Panchayat Structure	▪ Panchayat Office	. Gram Panchayat
		Agriculture Deptt	▪ Agriculture Office	. Block & Gram Panchayat
		NGO	▪ NGO Units	. Block / Gram Samad/ Gram Panchayat
6	INFRA	Administration	▪ Block Relief Office	. Sub Division
		Telecom	▪ Central Office	. Central Gas
		Police Deptt	▪ Police Station	. Block
7	WRNG	Irrigation Deptt Police Deptt Public Works Deptt	▪ Block Office ▪ Police Station ▪ PWD Office	. Block . Block . Block
		State Electricity Board	▪ SEB office	. Block
		NGO	▪ NGO Units	. Block / Gram Samad/ Gram Panchayat
8	VPR	VPR Office	▪ Nodal Offices	. Block . Gram Samad . Gram Panchayat
		NGO	▪ NGO Units	. Block / Gram Samad/ Gram Panchayat

1. Water/Sanitation (WaTSaN)
2. Health (HLTH)
3. Food (FD)
4. Rescue/Shelter (RSCUE)
5. Emergency Materials (EM)
6. Infrastructure (INFRA)
7. Warnings (WRNG)
8. Volunteer Pool (VPR)

DDMIN has four distinct zones of working: Normal Stage [N], Pre-Disaster Stage [P], Disaster Stage [D] and the Post Disaster Stage [PO]. Each stage has 4-5 key information points that have been researched upon through country analysis and the relevant terrain/situations. The number of Stage Information Points depends upon the type of disaster, degree of disaster and the locality.

The entire information set could be depicted as [N P D PO] and the entire probable information points, for design purposes, could be calculated as follows:

$$I_p = E_n * T_e * Z_i * C_n$$

$$\dots \dots \dots \dots \dots \dots \dots \dots (1)$$

*Total Information points = [(Number of entities) * (Sub Themes of each entity) * (Number of zones) * (Critical information sets of each zone)]*

The figures (Fig 2 and 3) below showcase the concept.

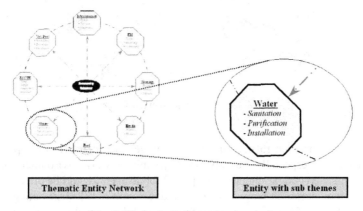

Fig. 2. Thematic Entity and its break-up

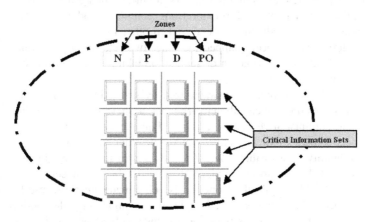

Fig. 3. DDMIN internal structure

Since the number is dependent of several factors like, type of disaster, geographic situations, environmental atmosphere, technology spread, etc, it is indeed a huge research problem whose address promises to contribute to the immense DM proportions worldwide. A depictive self-explanatory implementation set up is as shown in Fig 4 below for quick reference.

The proposed DDMIN utilizes the concept of Mobile Multi-Agent Systems. Broadly speaking, a mobile agent is an executing program that can migrate during the

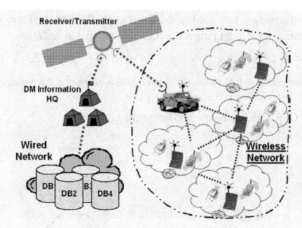

Fig. 4. Depictive Implementation setup

execution from machine to machine in a heterogeneous network atmosphere [16]. Mobile agents are especially attractive in a dynamic network environment involving partially connected computing elements [17]. Mobile agents could be effectively used for multifarious purposes ranging from adaptive routing [18], distributing topology information [19], offline messages transfer [20] and distributed information management [21]. One of the most important factors in our mobile agents' aided network is to collect all topology-related information from each node in ad hoc wireless network and distribute them periodically (as updates) to other nodes through mobile agents [22]. Once topology has been mapped the other two relevant aspects remain as Information retrieval and Information dissemination taking in the concepts of link stability, information aging, etc.

A centralized management is characterized by restricting important decisions to one or a few nodes on a given sub network wherein these special nodes become performance and administrative bottlenecks in a dynamic system [23]. A decentralized and fully peer-to-peer architecture like ours, on the other hand, offers potential advantages in scalability as also the scope. There is a growing interest in using mobile agents as part of the solution to implement more flexible and decentralized network architecture [24, 25]. While the front-end is being made simple to use for obvious reasons, the back end of the proposed application is highly complex with regards to the issues involved like complexity of the systems involved, networking issues, algorithms involved and the technology frontiers. The pilot implementation is under process and would involve a simulated run on a particular disaster. The system being developed is also benefiting by the author getting the SAARC fellowship towards visiting the countries where the DM systems are in place for extrapolation purposes. The benefits accruing by the DDMIN are immense, given the scenario where even a 10-20 % savings of the existing losses in life and equipment during a disaster could amount to huge monetary and human values. The user feedback so far has been very good. Please refer to Fig 5 for an example query on health inventory status.

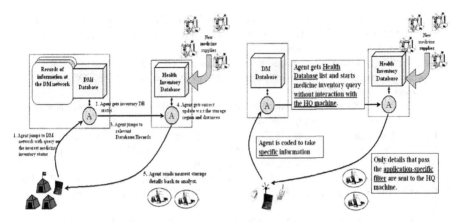

Fig. 5. Typical agent query system and an internal view of Agent-based query

DDMIN uses Flags/Emails/SMS for both off-line messaging and on-line instant messaging schemes [19].

5 Conclusions

In this working paper we extend the concept of mGov by taking an application in the context of Disaster Management. While we have incorporated the mobile technologies in the mGov and DMIN set-ups, the prime issues of interest still remains the Service Delivery, democracy, governance and law enforcement [26]. Application development is another aspect that has an immense scope for research. The applications as also the end product should be so developed so as to take into account the literacy levels, technology adaptability, ease of usage, effective GUI techniques, etc. Standards of technology and the effective bandwidth allocation are considered to be two of the most important aspects of wireless applications and their full potential [27] as also the security and authorisation policy matters.

References

1. Scalem M & Bandyopadhyay S (2002), "A Study of the Cross over between 'eGov' (Electronic Governance) and 'mGov' (Mobile Governance)", Proceedings of Annual Convention and Exhibition of IEEE Council - ACE-2003, IEEE Publications, pp: 275-279
2. Chanaron J J & Jolly D (1999), "Technological Management: Expanding the Perspective of MoT", 8th International Conference on 'The Management of Technology' - IAMOT, Cairo, Egypt, 15-17 March.
3. Open University Systems Group (1988), "Systems Behaviour", Third Edition, London: Paul Chapman Publishing
4. Heeks R (2001), "Understanding eGov for Development", Information Technology in Developing Countries, Vol. 11, No. 3
5. Matthews W (2002 a), 'Measuring e-gov", Federal Computer Week, April 8th

6. Matthews W (2002 b), "Study: E-Gov prone to falter", Federal Computer Week, May 6th
7. Balutis A P (1991), "Digital Government - When All is Said and done", Electronic Government Journal, Vol. 2, No. 6, November
8. Ling R (1997), "One can talk about common manners: The use of mobile telephones in inappropriate situations", Themes in mobile telephony, Final report of the COST 248 Home and Work Group, Haddon, L (ed.)
9. Ling R (2000), "We will be reached: The use of mobile telephony among Norwegian youth", Information Technology and people, Vol. 13, No. 2, pp: 102-120
10. Palen L, Salzman M & Youngs E (2001), "Going wireless: Behaviour & Practice of New Mo-bile Phone Users". Proceedings of the ACM Conference on Computer Sup-ported Cooperative Work (CSCW 2000), Philadelphia, pp: 201-210
11. World Disasters Report (2003), "World Disasters Report: Focus on reducing risk", Published by the International Federation of Red Cross and Red Crescent Societies, Jonathan Walter (ed.)
12. CEOS (2002), "Committee on Earth Observation Satellites Ad hoc Disaster Management Sup-port Group Report", Available online at:
    http://disaster.ceos.org/2001Ceos/reports_guide.html (Last accessed on May 10, 2004)
13. Drabek T (1985), "Emergent Structures", in Dynes, DeMarchi, and Pelanda (eds), Sociology of Disasters: The Contributions of Sociology to Disaster Research. Milano: Franco Angeli
14. Thomas B (1992), "Emergency Preparedness in Canada: A study of the command-and-control model and the emergence of alternative approaches", Doctoral Dissertation, McGill University, Montreal
15. Dedrick J & Kraemer K L (1998), "Asia's Computer Challenge: Threat or Opportunity for the United States and the World?" Oxford University Press
16. Brewington B, Gray R, Moizumi K, Kotz D, Cybenko G & Rus D (1999), "Mobile Agents in Distributed Information Retrieval", In: M. Klusch (ed.) Intelligent Information Agents, Chapter 12. Springer-Verlag
17. Gray R, Kotz D, Nog S & Cybenko G (1996), "Mobile agents for mobile computing", Technical Report PCS-TR96-285, Department of Computer Science, Dartmouth College, Hanover, May
18. Di Caro G & Dorigo M (1998), "Mobile agents for adaptive routing", In Proceedings of the 31st Hawaii International Conference on Systems, January
19. Minar N, Kramer K H & Maes P (1999), "Cooperating Mobile Agents for Dynamic Network Routing", In Alex Hayzeldon, editor, Software Agents for Future Communications Systems, Chapter 12, Springer-Verlag
20. Bandyopadhyay S & Paul K (1999), "Evaluating The Performance Of Mobile Agent Based Message Communication Among Mobile Hosts In Large Ad-Hoc Wireless Networks", Second ACM International Workshop on Modeling and Simulation of Wireless and Mobile Systems in conjunction with MOBICOM'99, Washington, USA
21. Dale J, "A Mobile Agent Architecture for Distributed Information Management", Thesis submitted for the degree of Doctor of Philosophy, Department of Electronics and Computer Science, University of Southampton
22. RoyChoudhury R, Bandyopadhyay S & Paul K (2000), "A Distributed Mechanism for Topology Discovery in Ad Hoc Wireless Networks Using Mobile Agents", Proceedings of the First annual workshop on Mobile AdHoc Networking & Computing (MOBIHOC 2000) in conjunction with IEEE/ACM Mobicom'00, Boston, Massachusetts, USA

23. Kramer K H, Minar N & Maes P (1999), "Tutorial: Mobile Software Agents for Dynamic Routing", Mobile Computing and Communications Review, Vol. 3, No. 2, ACM SIGMOBILE publications

24. Pham V A & Karmouch A (1998), "Mobile Software Agents: An Overview", IEEE Communication Magazine, July

25. Appeleby S & Steward S (1994), "Mobile software agents for control in Telecommunications networks", BT Technology Journal, Vol. 12, No. 2, pp: 104-113, April

26. De Maio A (2002), "Towards a wireless public sector", Gartner Research Report

27. Chang A & Kannan P K (2002), "Preparing for Wireless and Mobile Technologies in Government", Report for IBM Endowment for the Business of Government. Available online at: *http://www.businessofgovernment.org/pdfs/Chang_report.pdf* (Last accessed on May 10, 2004)

A Web-Based Examination System
in the Context of Bangladesh

Sanjoy Dey[1] and Sharif Mahmud[2]

[1] Department of Electrical and Electronics Engineering,
Bangladesh University of Engineering and Technology,
Dhaka-1000, Bangladesh
odhom@hotmail.com
[2] Dhaka University, Bangladesh
sharif_du@yahoo.com

Abstract. Bangladesh is standing at the threshold of IT explosion. IT has been the primary driving force for mass education evaluation in the western world. The education sector of Bangladesh is gradually entering into the IT arena. The World Wide Web (WWW) can play a vital role in distance education evaluation in Bangladesh where almost every schools & colleges have computers now. This paper presents a Web-Based Public Examination System (WBPES) which is based on client-server network. This exam system automatically carries out multiple-choice type examinations and processes the result. The presentation layer of this software system has developed using ASP (Active Server Pages) technology.

Keywords: Web-based examination, Apache, HTML, Oracle, N-Tier model.

1 Introduction

The multiple-choice examination is an integral part of the education system of Bangladesh. We have multiple-choice examination system from the primary level up to the Secondary School Certificate Exam. During this stage 50% of the total marks of the examinations are allocated to multiple-choice examinations. In Bangladesh the multiple-choice examination answer sheets are evaluated by computers but the exams are taken manually which is time consuming and less efficient. So the prospect of online multiple-choice examination system is quite bright in Bangladesh.

Some web-based examination systems have been developed for the same purpose such as WEBCT [1], ASSYST [2], PILOT [3] etc. In a recent work Zhenming et al [4] proposed a web based novel examination system using IIS (Internet Information Services) as the web server & Microsoft SQL Server as the Database engine. But the problem is that IIS is not a free-ware web server and Microsoft SQL Server has a slow response time that is not expected in such type of examination system. So we take a different approach using Apache as the web server and Oracle 8.0i as the database engine. We choose Apache [5] because Apache is more stable and more feature full than many other web servers. Although some commercial servers have claimed to surpass Apache's speed, we feel that it is better to have a mostly-fast free server than an extremely fast server that costs thousands of dollars.

S. Manandhar et al. (Eds.): AACC 2004, LNCS 3285, pp. 296–301, 2004.

Normally in web-based examination system objective type questions are provided and evaluated online. The questions may be of Yes/No type, multiple-choice/single-answer type, multiple-choice/ multiple-answer type. This developed examination system evaluates both multiple-choice/single-answer and multiple-choice/multiple-answer questions. This system uses ASP (Active server Pages), an enabling technology that brings together Web browsers, Web servers and Database systems to make applications that are easy to develop, access and deploy. Here structured analysis technique is used to analyze and develop the software system.

2   Need for Computerization

- As the existing examination taking system is a manual paper based system, it requires a large number of manpower to conduct the exam.
- To improve student satisfaction, there is a need to provide an interface to the student that should not only hold the exam paper but also show the questions and the associated right answers at the end of the exam.
- To reduce the result processing time.
- To provide a flexible interface to the students who are sitting for the exam from outside of the country.

3   Technology Used

Since the objective of the system is to implement a Web-Based Public Examination System on the Internet, we choose ASP to be the technology that can be taken to do all the functionality instance tasks [6] [7].Application logic is implemented using ASP Script and Oracle 8.0i [8] at the back end. We use Oracle 8.0i because it is the world's most popular database engine and it has the lowest response time. From the reference [9], we see that Oracle is the fastest Database engine. Active Server Pages (ASP) is a template for a web page that uses codes to generate an HTML document dynamically.

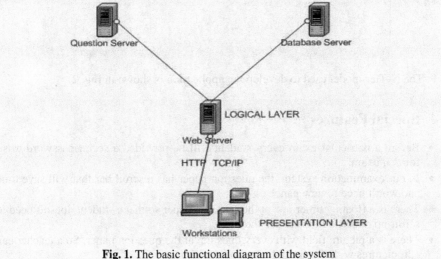

Fig. 1. The basic functional diagram of the system

ASPs are run in a server-side component. We use Apache as our web server. From reference [10], it is clear that Apache Web Server is one of the most popular Web Servers. Apache captures the client request and pipes it through a parsing engine like the ASP interpreter. This is achieved by setting the script mapping in Apache to direct all request for ASP pages to the ASP ISAPI DLL named asp.dll. Within the interpreter (asp.dll) examine the server side script sections. Non-script sections are simply piped back out to the client through to response. Script sections are extracted and passed to an instance of the appropriate scripting engine.

The basic functional diagram of the system is shown in Fig.1.

For the implementation of the system we first install the Apache on Windows 2000 platform according to the following addresses information http://httpd.apache.org/docs and http://httpd.apache.org/docs/install.htm. We can check the status of the Apache Web Server either startup or shutdown by typing the URL http://topbon or http://localhost or http://127.0.0.1 in the address bar. If the following page is showed then the Server is up successfully.

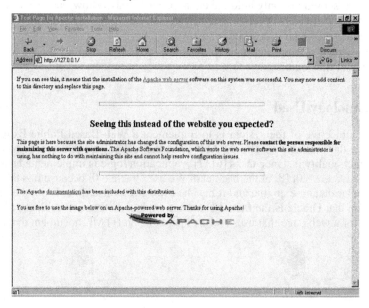

The N-Tier model used to develop the application is shown in Fig. 2.

4   Special Features

- Before a particular exam every student will be provided a secret password to sit for that exam.
- In our examination system, the question paper has a scroll bar that will save time and won't need review panel.
- There is a floating timer box at the question paper so that a student doesn't need to scroll-up or scroll down to see the time.
- There is a picture field with every question at the question paper. So a teacher can edit pictures with the normal text type questions.

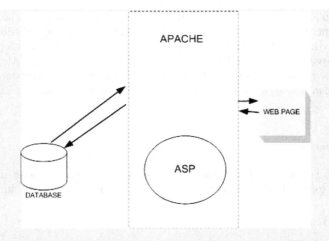

Fig. 2. The N-Tier architecture

- Results can be seen course wise or student ID wise that is we can see the results of all the students of a particular course and again can access the result of all the courses of a particular student.
- The correct answers will be loaded in the client machine as hidden fields with question paper as a result answer sheet will be evaluated in the client machine at a rapid speed.
- The database administrator can determine the time of the examinations.
- The database administrator can restrict the access of the student having any problems (violation of rules of the exam, dues, etc).
- Client side Cookies were set to avoid an examinee to open multiple browsers for login.
- Once the question paper is submitted, the students can't get back to the question paper.
- After submitting the question paper the examinee can see the possible answers along with the right answer(s) and the answer(s) given by him/her. At this page (s)he can also see the obtained number.

5   System Structure

The Web-Based Public Examination System (WBPES) can be divided into three stages: 1) Central Server Side 2) Web server 3) Remote Client Side.

5.1   Central Server Side

The Central Server Side is comprised of two servers. One is the question database server and other is the authentication server. The authentication server is used to manage the student registration number, student ID and the secret password that should be provided to the students just before the examination by examination control authority.

Then it grants the students' access to the question database server by checking these fields. On the other hand the question server is used for managing question database. There is a visual interface in the database server for the teachers to insert the questions, the possible answers and also the right answer number/numbers. Along with the questions the teacher will also fix the time limit for that particular examination. There is another database in the authentication server to contain the students' examination grading.

5.2 Web Server

The web server is used to contain the web pages. Web Server relays the question server data to the client computer. It also relays the client data to the authentication server.

5.3 Client Side

The client machines can communicate with the web server by using simple TCP/IP protocol. The client machines are provided with simple browsers like Internet Explorer 5.0, Netscape Navigator etc. When the students are provided the secret examination password, then they browse the authentication page and put their student ID, registration number and secret passwords in the specified fields. If those matches with the data reserved in the authentication database then they can get access to the question page. At the question page the students can view the timer along with the questions. After completing the examination the students press the submit button. Then the given answers are matched with the hidden right answers at the loaded question page and the grading is also performed at this page and it is directed to the authentication server. Then another page is showed to the students containing the probable answers, given answers along with the right answers. The grading of the students is also showed to the students at this page. An example of the question page is cited in Fig. 3.

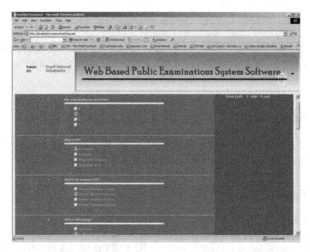

Fig. 3. Sample question page of WBPES

A sample of answer review page of WBPES is cited in Fig. 4.

Fig. 4. Sample of answer review page of WBPES

6 Conclusion

We have developed a smart Web Based Examination System especially for the public examinations. This Examination System has a bright prospect in Bangladesh because our Government has planned to extend the internet facilities even in the rural areas. So it will be possible for a village student to participate in a web-based public examination using this web-base examination system.

Acknowledgement

We wish to give thanks to Mr. Zularbine Kamal of IT Bangla Ltd, Dhaka, Bangladesh for his kind suggestions in some matters.

References

1. WebCT, "Web Courses Tolls", http://www.webCT.com
2. Jackson, D., Usher, M. "Grading student programs using ASSYST", In Proceedings of the 28th SIGCSE Technical Symposium (1997), pp. 335-339.
3. Stina, B., Michael T., Stephen G., Roberto T., "PILOT: An Interactive Tool for Learning and Grading", SIGCSEB: SIGCSE Bulletin, 2000.
4. Yuan Zhenming, Zhang Liang, Zhan Guohua, "A novel web-based online examination system for computer science education", 33rd ASEE/IEEE Frontiers in Education Conference,2003,Boulder,Co.
5. http://httpd.apache.org
6. Keith Morneau, Jill Datistick, "Active Server Pages".
7. Scott Mitchell, Games Apainson, "Sams Teach Yourself Active Server Pages 3.0 In 21 Days"
8. K.Lonely, "Oracle 8i The Complete Reference", Tata McGraw-Hill Publishing Company Limited, New Delhi, 2000.
9. http://www.eweek.com/slideshow/0, 3670, p=1&s=1590&a=23120&po=2&i=1, 00.asp
10. http://netcraft.com/survey.

Trust and Security Realization for Mobile Users in GSM Cellular Networks

Jesudoss Venkatraman[1], Vijay Raghavan[1], Debabrata Das[2], and Asoke K. Talukder[2]

[1] Lisle Technology Partners India Pvt Ltd., 45/3, Residency Cross Road,
Bangalore 560025, India
{Jesudoss,vijay}@ltp.soft.net
[2] Indian Institute of Information Technology, Bangalore, 26/C, Electronics City,
Hosur Road, Bangalore 560100, India
{ddas,asoke.talukder}@iiitb.ac.in

Abstract. In recent past SMS (Short Message Service) has become very popular data bearer in GSM networks. SMS, inherently being a messaging protocol, has always been point-to-point and in plaintext. For m-commerce transactions, SMS will be routed through public networks and some application servers of the merchant. Also, to protect itself against unknown roaming environments, SMS needs peer-to-peer object level security at the application level. This demands SMS to offer trustworthy model. The paper uses a novel philosophy to establish trust between users and services. We presented a model of trust and application level public key encryption of SMS with client authentication using JavaCard technology over GSM 03.48.

1 Introduction

Short message service (SMS) is the most popular data bearer/service within GSM (Global System for Mobile communications) today [1]. Some of the inherent strengths of SMS has made it very attractive bearer for content services [2].

SMS being a human readable messaging bearer, inherently is in plaintext. The architecture for point-to-point (P2P) message is different from that of person to machine (P2M). In a P2P message, the mobile originated (MO) message is sent to the service center (SC) (Figure 1a). The SC works as the switch for the message and forwards the same to the destination mobile station (MS) as a mobile terminated (MT) message. In case of a P2M message, the message is forwarded by the SC to a short message entity (SME) (Figure 1b). The SME forwards the same to the application or origin server for the content. In majority of cases the path between SME and the origin server will be through public networks like Internet [3]. Moreover, while roaming, the message will traverse through different networks. These networks may not provide homogeneous security infrastructure.

A survey [4] with decision-makers in Europe on their attitudes towards B2B (Business to Business) reveals that trust is an important element of concern. When endpoints of a transaction are within a deterministic framework, many of the envi-

S. Manandhar et al. (Eds.): AACC 2004, LNCS 3285, pp. 302–309, 2004.

ronmental parameters are constant. These relate to service, agent, user, network, location and context. Situation is completely different for a roaming 3GSM customer. In a 3GSM environment, these parameters are volatile.

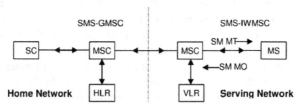

(a) Architecture for the short message transfer (point-to-point)

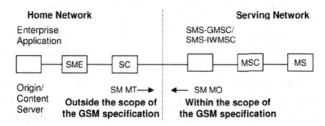

(b) Architecture for the short message as information bearer

Fig. 1. Basic architecture for SMS as data bearer

Let us consider some practical examples needed in trustworthy transaction:

– How can the buyer trust that the merchant will deliver what he is promising? How does a person trust a merchant whom he or she has never seen, met or heard before?
– A kid at home wants to order something from the net. Dad uses his credit card to complete the transaction and helps the kid buy his Christmas gift. Can this transaction be completed if dad is roaming in a different country?
– The sales manager will proceed for vacation for a week. He needs to delegate some access rights to some of his confidential files to another colleague so that some transactions can be completed while he is away. How can someone delegate or revoke rights while in vacation?
– Someone attempting to use his own roaming device for an electronic gambling facility from a place where gambling is a crime. How can a service make decisions based on the context of the user?

Security and trust concerns are major barriers for SMS to become a popular bearer for micro-payments and other transactions in business and m-commerce. In this paper the authors proposed some novel techniques of making electronic transactions trustworthy. The paper also address number of security concerns related to usage of SMS. Sections 2 and 3 talk about proposed security and trust infrastructure respectively. Section 4 presents philosophy and infrastructure for the realization of trustworthy network. Section 5 concludes with the views related to present studies on secured and trusted SMS network.

2 Security over SMS

When a user is roaming, SMS content passes through different networks and the Internet. This exposes the SMS content to various vulnerabilities and attacks. To protect these contents, network independent security infrastructure is recommended. We developed application within the SIM card (SmartCard) to offer peer-to-peer security understandable only by the service in the origin server and mobile phone. 3GPP has evolved the TS 03.48 [7] standard for secure packet through SMS. TS03.48 is designed to offer PKI (Public Key Infrastructure) for SMS. Within a PKI environment, a certification authority (CA) assigns a public-private key pair to the entity of a given distinguished name. PKI offers authentication; however, it does not give the confidence that this entity is trustworthy. PGP (pretty good privacy) introduced the concept of "Web of Trust" with a different certificate model. PGP uses public key encryption, but a formal third party CA is not involved. SPKI [5] though takes care of some components of trust. In mTrust, we implemented *truthfulness* with the help of all these technologies. In Internet commerce servers are authenticated, however, clients are not generally authenticated, because most of them do not have a unique identity. This becomes even more difficult when the device is mobile. As it is possible to identify a mobile phone uniquely independent of the network, in mTrust we authenticate both client and server.

3 Trust Infrastructure

It is perceived that low-quality information and fraud is on the raise in today's net-centric world. Not all the information and services on the Internet can be trusted. In any relationship, trust is the glue that holds two entities together. In social environment we first develop trust. Once trust is established, we enter into transactions. In electronic environment we need to develop the model of trust and secure transactions that are executed between trusted entities, i.e., before we enter into a transaction, we need to answer, how can I trust a seller or a buyer?

In a social framework trust is a combination of factors like, (i) truthfulness, (ii) competency, (iii) character/consistency, and (iv) context. Trust can be summarized through two simple questions:

1. Can I believe the service provider and make a judgment about the service?
2. Can I believe the service requester and allow him to access my resources?

We need to analyze and understand these socio psychological aspects of trust and then build digital trust for the digital society. Digital trust will help build a trustworthy computing environment. Trustworthy computing systems will be built with the combination of truthfulness, and a combination of 3C (consistency, competence, and context). Social attribute of truthfulness can map onto the authentication, non-repudiation, integrity, and confidentiality in the digital society. Context in the digital society can be determined from location, environmental, and device characteristics. Consistency and competence in the digital space can be built from knowledge built over time. Consistency and competence are temporal aspect of memory [6].

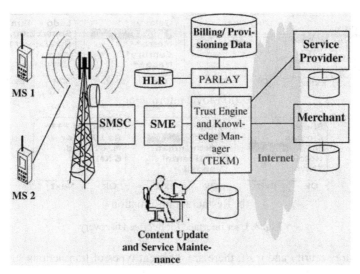

Fig. 2. mTrust architecture

4 Realization of Trustworthy and Secured SMS Communication

To allow trustworthy content service we built a framework called mTrust (mobile trust). The system is built with SmartCard technology in a GSM SIM card. The system is developed using Java 2.1 JavaCard technology. mTrust is a combination of trust realization using public key encryption and concepts proposed by PGP and SPKI (Simple PKI). mTrust offers trust based service discovery, commerce, approval, trust transitivity, and delegation of trust. It uses secure packet technology as recommended by 3GPP TS 03.48 to ensure interoperability. It uses standard Java Cryptography Architecture (JCA). The architecture of mTrust is depicted in figure 2. There will be a **Trust Engine and Knowledge Manager (TEKM)** connected to the SC (Service Center) through a SME (Short Message Entity or the SMS gateway). The trust manager will then be connected to different hosts and servers. These servers will be content servers, service provider's servers, merchant's server, bank server etc. The SMS messages transacted between two subscribers, between a subscriber and a server will be signed and secured through RSA public-key encryption algorithm. Connection between TEKM and the end servers (content, service provider or bank) will be through SSL (Secured Socket Layer), or TLS (Transport Layer Security). To ensure *truthfulness*, mTrust authenticates both server and client. This is achieved by exchanging the public keys (certificates) between the end points. mTrust uses concatenated SMS technology to transact messages greater than 140 octet.

Any user who wants to use the trust infrastructure needs to obtain a digital certificate. The management of the key and distribution of the certificate will depend upon the policy and business plan of the network operator. Before subscribers can use the public-key encryption, they also need to obtain and save the public key of the Root CA in the SIM card.

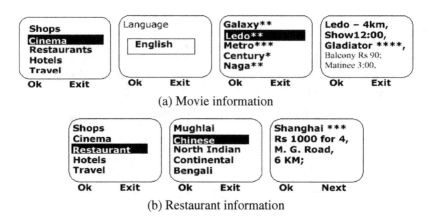

(a) Movie information

(b) Restaurant information

Fig. 3. User interface for Service Discovery

To ensure security and trust, there are different types of transactions supported in mTrust. These are:

1. **Service Discovery:** There is no built in trust between the user and the service provider. User does not have any idea about the service or the service provider. User uses knowledge available within TEKM to determine these properties to assess risk. Knowledge is derived from information collected from third party sources like media, surveys, credit rating agencies, community records etc. For example, when a new movie is released, the service provider will provide information like show name, casting, show timing, ticket availability. TEKM will add the rating of the cinema hall, art critics' rating. Also, if there was any recommendation about this service, same will be attached. Other rating details of the cinema hall like comfort of the theatre are also available as a part of knowledge (figure 3a). For restaurants, information like average cost for 4 people, distance, ratings are provided (figure 3b) as well.

2. **Context Information:** Local information is appended by the JavaCard applet with all transaction as available through 03.48 interface. This information is used to identify the location and context. Local information includes mobile country code (MCC), mobile network code (MNC), location area code (LAC) and cell ID (CID) of the current serving cell. It also contains the IMEI (International Mobile Equipment Identity) of the ME; the current date, time and time zone; the Timing Advance (TA); and some other information. MCC, MNC, LAC, CID, and TA combined with a GIS (Geographical Information System) system is used to determine the ***context***. From location information and the GIS information, the distance of the place from the current place is calculated and displayed as a part of the response. Location information is also used for other trust needs. For example, in certain or countries gambling or some other types of services may be banned. To enforce such regulatory norms, location information is used. Also, TEKM can be configured to bar some types of services for certain users. As a part of trust on the service provider, a parent may like to bar access to some adult content for their children.

3. **Standard Transactions:** This transaction assumes that some level of trust has already been established between the user and service provider. For this type of transactions establishment of *truthfulness* is sufficient. *Truthfulness* in a transaction is achieved through PKI/RSA using 03.48 standard.

4. **Approval:** Approval has two parts, viz., *Approval request* and *Approved*. Approval request is between two users (P2P), whereas approved is P2M. For example, in a micro-payment situation, the user may not have sufficient balance in his or her credit. In such cases a trust transaction is required seeking approval from some other user who has sufficient credit or trustworthy. A case could be son requesting father for approval of Rupees 395.00 for purchase of a book. Unlike the standard transaction, approval request for a payment will be a transaction from a mobile user to another mobile user. The request will only be honored by the approver (person approving the request), if he or she has the public key of the approvee (person requesting the approval). The *Approved* transaction will be between the approver and the merchant. This is implemented through proactive SMS. Pre-requisite for approval is that the approvee's public key needs to be available in the approver's SIM card.

5. **Delegate:** A user delegates the rights to some other user. This transaction will be mainly between two users. However, delegate transaction can also be between a user and a service provider. The user of the mobile phone who is responsible for certain functions can delegate his or her rights to someone else. User will delegate certain rights to other users by giving the privileges to do certain transaction. Privilege information for the service provider will be different for difference services. This transaction contains the detail of the resource, type of delegation (permissible actions on the resource), and the time period for which this delegation token is valid. In mTrust proliferation of the delegation is not permitted. This means that the delegation token cannot be shared or passed on to someone else. This type of transaction can be revoked.

6. **Recommend:** The user makes a recommendation for some other user. This transaction will be between two users or between a user and a service. Recommend token does not have any specific action associated with it. Also, the recommend token does not have any time limit associate with it. Recommend token can be used and published in the trust manager for a user to see and make a judgment for trust. Also, a user can use recommend token to prove credentials for a transaction. Recommendation token can be revoked.

4.1   JavaCard Interfaces of mTrust

Public Key Maintenance
Public keys of those who involved in approval and delegation process is stored in a transparent elementary file (FID_MF:0x4F51). Trusted Key/Certificates shall be in 4FXX files according to GSM 11.11 standard.

Private Key Maintenance
In mTrust the facility of *truthfulness* is realized through 512bit RSA encryption algorithm. Private key is encrypted and stored in an elementary file of the SIM Card. The

private key is encrypted using a user password. Encrypted key is stored in a transparent elementary file. Trusted Key/Certificates is saved in 4FXX files according to GSM 11.11 standard. Key Information are stored in file 4F50. A hash of the private key is also stored in the SmartCard. This is used to validate the authenticity of the password.

Token Maintenance

The delegation token is stored in elementary files within the SmartCard. This is done in a Linear Fixed file with FileID 5560. The recommend toke is also stored in a linear fixed elementary file with FileID 5561.

SMS Message Formats

Different formats used for encryption of messages for mTrust are:

- Generic format of transactions used for mTrust between mobile station (SIM) to a Server (P2M) have the following generic format:
  <Transaction ID> <Prelude – Service provider ID, Local info, MSISDN, etc> <Message Authentication Code encrypted with sender's private key> <DES key encrypted with the public key of the receiver> <Message (payload) encrypted using DES with CBC mode)>

- Format for transactions for between mobile station to mobile station (P2P have the following generic format:
  <Transaction ID> <Prelude – Service provider ID, Local info, MSISDN, etc> <Message Authentication Code encrypted with sender's private key> <DES key encrypted with the public key of the sender> <Message (payload) encrypted using DES with CBC mode)>

In a P2M transaction, the message is enveloped with a key protected with the private key of the receiver to ensure confidentiality and non-repudiation. Whereas, for a P2P transaction (approve request, delegate), the message is enveloped with a key protected by the private key of the sender. Fro a high security transaction, same message is once again enveloped with the private key of the receiver. This is to ensure that the original message can be read by the receiver but cannot be changed. When this message is forwarded to a server (P2M) for further processing (approve,), it is enveloped with the private key of the receiver.

5 Conclusion

The mTrust is a novel framework developed by us. mTrust has been developed using JavaCard technology in the SmartCard. It implements security at the application level. It implements trust at the transaction level too. It uses user and service context to arrive at trust. It uses SMS as the vehicle for security and trust transactions in the GSM world. It implements knowledge based service discovery, approval, delegation, and recommendation. It uses the 03.48 standard specified by 3GPP for secure SMS. It uses PKI for security and authentication of endpoints. It offers trust through T3C (Truthfulness, Consistency, Competency, and Context). This is achieved through knowledge. Currently knowledge is acquired mainly through manual interface. In future knowledge will be acquired in automated fashion. mTrust implements trust in the digital society.

References

1. EUROPEAN TELECOMMUNICATION STANDARD: Digital cellular telecommunications system (Phase 2); Technical realization of the Short Message Service (SMS) Point-to-Point (PP) (GSM 03.40); ETS 300 536, Fourth edition, October 1996.
2. Rishi Pal, Asoke K. Talukder, Global Service Portability and Virtual Home Environment through Short Message Service (SMS) and GSM, Proceeding of International Conference on Computer Communication 2002.
3. Ashish Tara, Debmalya De, N. J. Damodaran, and Asoke K. Talukder, Information Assurance and Security needs in an ASP/MVNO Environment for Pervasive Content through SMS/GSM, Proceedings of International Conference on Communication and Broadband Networking, 2003
4. Trust issues in European b2b e-procurement, PriceWaterHouseCoopers Report, http://www.pwcglobal.com/extweb/ncsurvres.nsf/docid/1db37f6b35610f1580256a6b00534494
5. C. Ellison, B. Frantz, B. Lampson, R. Rivest, B. Thomas, T. Ylonen, SPKI Certificate Theory, RFC 2693
6. Colin English, Paddy Nixon, Sotirios Terzis, Andrew McGettrick and Helen Lowe, Security Models for Trusting Network Appliances.
7. 3GPP TS 03.48, Digital cellular telecommunications system (Phase 2+); Security mechanisms for SIM application toolkit; Stage 2, version 8.8.0, 1999)

A Software Agent Based Approach
for Fraud Detection in Network Crimes

Manas Ranjan Patra[1] and Bipin Bihari Jayasingh[2]

[1] Department of Computer Science, Berhampur University,
Berhampur 760 007, India
manasrpbu@yahoo.com
[2] Computer Forensics Division, GEQD, Directorate of Forensic Science,
Ramanthapur, Hyderabad 500 013
bbjayasingh9@rediffmail.com

Abstract. There has been continuous effort by organizations to secure their information resources maintained in computer network infrastructures against security threats arising out of network related frauds. This paper presents a software agent based approach to detect such frauds and provides a means to gather relevant information about the nature of fraud that can be used for forensic analysis. A distributed agent deploy architecture has been presented to observe, gather and record data that can be used in detecting frauds. The applicability of the approach has been demonstrated for a network fraud scenario caused by the Routing Information Protocol (RIP) attack.

1 Introduction

Crimes relating to computer networks, be it Intranet or Internet, such as hacking, network intrusions, defacing of websites, creation and malicious dissemination of computer viruses have become rampant. Because of the very devastating nature and impact of such crimes, the topic of network fraud detection has received a significant amount of attention from government as well as law-enforcement agencies. Some commonly occurring frauds due to intrusion are: *Denial of Service attack, SYN flooding, Smurfing, Spamming, ICMP attacks, IP Spoofing attacks, TCP sequence number attack, Routing information protocol (RIP) attacks etc.*

The Routing Information Protocol (RIP) is widely used for routing traffic in the global Internet and is an *Interior Gateway Protocol* (IGP), which means that it performs routing within a single autonomous system. Exterior gateway protocols, such as BGP, perform routing between different autonomous systems. RIP itself evolved as an Internet routing protocol and other protocol suite use modified versions of RIP. The latest enhancement to RIP is the RIP2 specification, which allows more information to be included in RIP packets and provides a simple authentication mechanism.

During normal operation of a network, packets are created and flow from one node to another through an interconnection of IP-capable nodes [1]. Each instance of the IP protocol maintains a directory, called the *routing table*, which is consulted while forwarding outgoing message packets. The Internet protocol, in this case would require a complete end-to-end link. But in reality, one needs to specify only the next node (i.e., host or router) as the packet has to hop through several intermediate nodes.

S. Manandhar et al. (Eds.): AACC 2004, LNCS 3285, pp. 310–316, 2004.

At each stage, a packet is examined by comparing its destination address in the header to the local routing table to see whether the destination network has been reached. The packet is enveloped in the local physical transport and is sent to the next node for further routing. This is referred to as *indirect routing* because the packet is not sent directly to its destination. Eventually, data packets arrive at the destination network and are delivered to the local device (i.e., host).

In this paper, we analyze how a hacker can gain control over the communication path between two hosts exchanging messages between them by modifying the routing table. This helps us in designing software agents that can effectively deal with such attacks. The rest of the paper is organized as follows: section 2 discusses the need for software agents in fraud detection; section 3 elaborates on the distributed agent deployment architecture; section 4 describes the forensic analysis of frauds; section 5 presents our design approach for building specialist agents to detect RIP attacks, and section 6 summarizes the work.

2   Software Agents for Fraud Detection

An effective way of handling frauds occurring in networked systems is to adopt a mechanism that guarantees secured transactions and at the same time provides all the flexibility needed while using the network resources. Agent technology [2] is being advocated as a suitable means to fulfill requirements of flexibility, adaptability, autonomy, and pro-activeness in such problem areas. This upcoming technology uses software artifacts called, *agents* that can operate on behalf of a human counter part as per the design specifications. A system of intelligent agents with specific capabilities can be deployed through out the network, which can collaborate with each other to maneuver a fraud detection task.

3   Distributed Agent Deployment Architecture

Here, we consider the issue of providing security to the information resources of a large organization that maintains and transacts business electronically over a network of computers, which is possibly connected to the Internet. Once the organizational network is accessible through the Internet it is vulnerable to all kinds of security threats. An intruder can adopt any means to gain access to the resources maintained digitally or even try to manipulate transactions taking place electronically over the net.

In order to provide a full proof security infrastructure one cannot afford to leave even a slightest amount of loophole in the system. With this requirement in mind we propose to develop a security infrastructure consisting of intelligent agents that are deployed through out the organizational network. Here, we improve upon the framework that we proposed in our earlier work [3], which lacks the flexibility that was intended to accomplish security-monitoring tasks. With the lesson learnt in our previous experiment, the present work proposes a completely distributed deployment of agents with a defined communication framework so that the agents collaborate with each other in a predetermined manner to fulfill their design objectives. Except the agents at the lowest level, all other agents can be completely distributed but with a hierarchical collaboration structure.

No single agent can effectively handle all types of security threats, which appear in different attack formats. Each attack has to be handled precisely by agents at the lowest level by capturing relevant information and analyzing them for ascertaining probable security threats. We term such agents as *specialist agents* as they perform certain predefined security monitoring functions at a host. One can think of having a number of specialist agents housed in the same host each taking the responsibility of dealing with a particular attack signature. The coordination among the specialist agents is achieved with the help of a specially designated agent called a *supervisor agent* associated with a host. There is only one supervisor agent per host. A set of hosts may form a cluster and a *cluster agent* can be deployed to overseer activities at the hosts constituting a cluster. Finally, at the highest level of the hierarchy a single *enterprise agent* may be deployed to have a global view of the security monitoring system. One may consider presence of many enterprise networks that share common interest but are independently administered. In such cases, the enterprise agents would like to exchange information with a view to detect security threats cutting across enterprise boundaries. In order to achieve fault tolerance as well as effectiveness, each agent type can be replicated and appropriate mechanism can be adopted for them to act in unison.

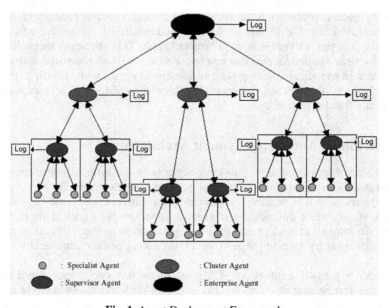

Fig. 1. Agent Deployment Framework

4   Forensic Analysis of Fraud

Log files are maintained with different agents that capture relevant data during the operation of a network system, such that their contents can be analyzed whenever required to establish an attack scenario. This component has been introduced in our architecture for the purpose of network forensic analysis and to help law enforcement agencies during investigation. Network forensics is *the scientific compilation, exami-nation, exploration and presentation of information held on or retrieved from com-puter networks in such a way that it can be used as potential legal evidence.* Cyber forensic experts or law enforcement investigators can collect and analyze evidence present in a computer network from the agent log. The *agent log* serves as a record keeping system for network intruders. The information's captured from the message packets are recorded in the agent log with a predefined format. Some of the relevant information that is stored in the agent log is, date and time of intrusion, intruder's IP address, and target IP address etc.

Providing secured intrusion detection system is also an important research agenda [4]. In order to address the security issue we try to protect the agent log from mali-cious manipulation even by the system administrator. An attempt to manipulate the agent log is treated as another intrusion. The attackers may try to delete the agent log from the server by using cloaking software or they may try to erase their trespassing activity from the agent log. Thus from security point of view, we maintain different *logs* with different agents so that in the event of any damage to a particular agent log, evidences can still be collected from the other agent logs. In the following section, we discuss on the *Routing Information Protocol* (RIP) attack and track an attack scenario to device a way to detect and protect a system from such attacks.

5   Routing Information Protocol (RIP) Attack

Here, we analyze the technique adopted during RIP attack and develop an algorithm that controls the behavior of the software agents during an attack.

5.1   Analysis of RIP Attack

Using a RIP (Routing Information Protocol) attack, it is possible to divert an entire communication link between two internal stations via the hacker [5]. To explain the process, let us focus on two hosts A and B of a network. A hacker X may simulate an internal station A and sends modified RIP packets to the second target station B and also to the gateways between X and B. The RIP packets inform B and the gateways not to send packets from B to A directly but to X. Thus, hacker X manages to receive the packets meant for A and can fiddle with the packet (looking for logins, passwords, and so on). Subsequently, X sends the packet to A by setting the source route option to X with an intention that all the packets emanating from A and targeted towards B would pass through X. Thus, hacker X gains control on the communication path be-tween A and B, and get an opportunity to monitor the packets exchanged between A and B.

RIP sends routing-update messages at regular intervals as and when the network topology changes. When a router receives a routing update that includes changes to an entry, it updates its routing table to reflect the new route. The metric value for the path is increased by one, and the sender is indicated as the next hop. RIP routers maintain only the best route (the route with the lowest metric value) to a destination. After updating its routing table, the router immediately begins transmitting routing updates to inform other network routers about the change. These updates are sent independent of the regularly scheduled updates that RIP routers send.

RIP prevents routing loops from continuing indefinitely by implementing a limit on the number of hops allowed in a path from the source to a destination. The maximum number of hops in a path is 15. If a router receives a routing update that contains a new or changed entry, and if increasing the metric value by one causes the metric to be infinity (that is, 16), the network destination is considered unreachable.

The routing information protocol (RIP) propagates route updates by major network numbers as a class full-routing protocol [6]. In version 2, RIP introduces routing advertisements to be aggregated outside the network class boundary. The RIP packet format is shown in figure 2; version 2 is shown in figure 3. The format fields are defined as follows:

Command: specifies whether the packet is a request or response to a request.
Version Number: identifies the current RIP version.
Address Family Identifier (AFI): indicates the protocol address being used:

1. IP (IPV4), 2. IP6 (IPV6), 3. NSAP, 4. HDLC (8-bit multidrop), 5. BBN 1822, 6. 802 (includes all 802 media), 7. E.163, 8 E.164 (SMDS, Frame Relay, ATM), 9. F.69 (Telex), 10. X.121 (X.25,Frame Relay), 11. IPX, 12. Appletalk, 13. Decnet IV, 14. Banyan Vines.

Route Tag: specifies whether the route is internal or external.
Entry Address: IP address for the entry.
Subnet Mask: Subnet mask for the entry.
Next Hop: IP address of next hop router.
Metric: Lists the number of hops to destination.

Command	Version number	Not used	AFI	Not used	Entry Address	Not used	Not used	Metric

Fig. 2. RIP format

Command	Version number	Not used	AFI	Route Tag	Entry Address	Subnet Mask	Next Hop	Metric

Fig. 3. RIP version 2 format

The hacker changes the routing table of the host he wishes to monitor so that all traffic on a network will pass through hacker's host [7]. That may be possible by sending a fake route advertisement message via the routing information protocol (RIP), declaring him as the default gateway. If successful, all traffic will be routed through his host. Ensure that hacker host has enabled both IP forwarding and the default gateway. All outbound traffic from the target host will pass through hacker's host onto the real network gateway. Hacker may not receive the return traffic, unless it has the ability to modify the routing table on the default gateway to reroute all return traffic back to him.

5.2 Detection Mechanism

Agents are built to detect and appropriately deal with a RIP attack. An agent maintains an *agent log* to capture relevant information which can be used for forensic analysis. As we know the RIP is encapsulated within the IP packet, in our proposed system AACF (section 2) an observer agent captures the message packet and sends the packet to the packet analyzer for analysis. The packet analyzer gets the field values from the packet header such as Source IP address (SIP), Command (COM) and Routing List (R_LIST) for further processing. As the SIP is the sender's IP address, and COM indicates whether the packet is a request or a response. The *request* option asks that a router sends all or a part of its routing table. The *response* option can be an unsolicited regular routing update or a reply to a request. Responses contain routing-table entries i.e. R_LIST.

If the field COM = "Request" then the router or host has to send the routing list to requested router and if the field COM = "Response" then the router or host receives updated routing list. For every "Response" that arrives, we make a database that contains SIP and R_LIST. Whenever a packet arrives with "Response" we check the SIP of packet with SIP of database. If the SIP does not match then add the packet into the database. If the SIP matches then compare R_LIST with the route list of packet. If the R_LIST does not match then send an *enquiry* message packet to that SIP as "is it an updated routing list (Y/N)". If the answer message packet is "N" then say "INTRUSION" and those nodes do not match with R_LIST send them to the agent log for detail analysis. If the answer message packet is "Y" then delete the previous R_LIST with routing list of packet. If the R_LIST matches then no need to change the routing list. However, for each " Request" message that arrives we need not check the SIP as it is only a request from a host/router. Whenever an intrusion is detected relevant information such as the date & time, source IP address etc. are maintained in an agent log for the forensic analysis.

5.2.1 Algorithm RIP_Attack

Each packet that is captured by the agent is analyzed by the Packet_analyzer function built into the agent software. The variable SIP refer to source IP address of the packet p. The variable COM refer to the command option of the packet p. The variable R_LIST refer to the routing list of the packet p. The variable ANSWER is Boolean type.

```
1. init ( )
   /* initialize   a   linked   list   with   the   node   structure
   <SIP,COM,R_LIST, LINK> that records all request for updating
   of RIP */
2. On receiving a packet p
   set SIPx = source_IP_addr(p)
   set COMx = command_option(p)
   set R_LISTx = routing_list(p)

     (a) if (COM = = "Response" then
             if  (SIPx = = SIP (node)) then
             /* compare SIPx with the SIP values of  each of the
             nodes in the list */
             if (R_LISTx != R_LIST(node)) then
             send message "Whether you updated routing list(Y/N)"
             to SIP (node)
             if (ANSWER == "N") then
                signal "INTRUSION"
```

```
Write  <Date  (  ),  Time  (  ),  SIPx,  unmatched
SIP(node)....> to Agent log.
   Send RST  to SIP (node)
   /* disable the connection */
   Exit
   endif
   if (ANSWER == "Y") then
   Replace R_LISTx with R_LIST (node)
   endif
endif

   else
insert_to_list (SIPx,COMx,R_LISTx)
      endif
endif

(b) if  (COM = = "Request") then
      No process
      endif
```

6 Conclusion

This paper analyzes a typical network fraud due to the routing information protocol (RIP) attack. Based on the detail analysis of the attack scenario a mechanism has been devised to build software agents that specialize on detecting and responding to such attacks. Besides dealing with the attack, the agents also keep track of all relevant information during an attack in an agent log, which can assist the forensic scientists for future analysis. Future extension of this work involves analysis of other frequently occurring network attacks and augmenting the software agents with additional capabilities to thwart such attacks.

References

1. Peterson, David M.: TCP/IP NETWORKING: A Guide to the IBM Environment, McGRAW International Editions (1995).
2. Bradshaw, J.M.: An introduction to software agents: J.M. Bradshaw (Ed.), Software Agents, AAA1 Press/MIT Press, Cambridge, MA, (1997) 3-46.
3. Jayasingh, B.B., Patra, M. R., Sastry, P. K.: An Agent based Architecture for Cyber Forensics, in proceedings of the5[th] International Conference on Information Technology (CIT 2002), Bhubaneswar, India, Dec. 21-24, (2002) 311-314.
4. Farmer W.M., Guttman, J.D., Swarup, V.: Security for mobile agents: issues and Requirements, in: Proceedings of the 19th National Information Systems Security Conference, vol. 2, National Institute of Standards and Technology, October (1996).
5. Othmar Kyas.: Internet Security: Risk Analysis, Strategies and Firewalls, International Thomson Computer Press, Copyright (1997).
6. Hack Attacks REAVEALED, A Complete Reference with custom security hacking toolkit, Wiley computer publishing (2001), USA.
7. Poulsen, Kevin L.: Hack Proofing your network: Internet Tradecraft (2000) Syngress publishing, inc. USA.

An Ontology for Network Security Attacks

Andrew Simmonds, Peter Sandilands, and Louis van Ekert

Faculty of IT, University of Technology Sydney, PO Box 123,
Broadway, NSW 2007, Australia
{simmonds,psandy,ekertl}@it.uts.edu.au

Abstract. We first consider network security services and then review threats, vulnerabilities and failure modes. This review is based on standard texts, using well-known concepts, categorizations, and methods, e.g. risk analysis using asset-based threat profiles and vulnerability profiles (attributes). The review is used to construct a framework which is then used to define an extensible ontology for network security attacks. We present a conceptualization of this ontology in figure 1.

Keywords: network, cyber, security, ontology, attack, threat, vulnerability, failure.

1 Introduction

This article was written as a result of the authors teaching a network security subject in the Faculty of IT, at the University of Technology Sydney. There are many concepts which need to be well understood by network security students and practitioners. To assist in this there have been several attempts to classify different aspects of the subject area. This article lists some of the common taxonomies, shows the relationship between them, and modifies or extends them where appropriate to make them consistent, and then defines an extensible ontology for network security based on this material. The article provides a framework to locate these taxonomies in the network security subject area. The aim of this article is thus to provide a new and improved understanding of the linkages between different components of a network security system.

In part 2 we consider security services; in part 3 we look at threats and system weaknesses; in part 4 we review failure modes – recognizing that perfect security is not achievable in practice; and finally in part 5 we define an ontology for network security attacks.

2 Security Services

There are two mnemonics commonly used to summarize services which a network security system should provide: 'CIA' and 'Triple A' (see tables 1 and 2). CIA provides a key to remember three important security services (Confidentiality, Integrity and Availability), but really another three services should be added (Authentication,

S. Manandhar et al. (Eds.): AACC 2004, LNCS 3285, pp. 317–323, 2004.

Access Control and Non-repudiation), see Stallings (2000), to make 'CIA+' (table 1). Integrity is sometimes used to refer to the ability to prevent all the outcomes outlined in table 3 (part 5: Outcome) below, but we will use it in a narrower sense to mean the ability to guard against message modification.

The 'Triple A' mnemonic is useful in that it makes clear the relationship between these three services: you cannot use the accounting service until you have been authorized, and you cannot be authorized until you have been authenticated.

Table 1. Security Services CIA+

CIA+
1.Confidentiality
2.Integrity
3.Availability
plus:
4.Authentication
4.1.of people (*something you know, have, are*)
4.2.of organizations
4.3.of applications
5.Access Control
6.Non-repudiation

Table 2. 'Triple A' Services

Triple A	
1.	Authentication
2.	Authorization
3.	Accounting

3 Know the Enemy and Know Yourself

Sun-Tzu states (400 – 320 BCE, translated Giles, 1910) "If you know the enemy and know yourself, you need not fear the result of a hundred battles". There is a clear need to understand different attacks and the people who would stage them.

Threat Profiles (table 3) considers individual threats. This table is from work on OCTAVE, by Wilson (2002), and Alberts and Dorofee. Each threat profile should be classified by its possible impact: low/medium/high. There are three phases to OCTAVE:

(i)   build asset-based Threat Profiles (from table 3), marked low/medium/high impact;

(ii)   identify vulnerabilities from Vulnerability Profiles (table 8);

(iii) develop a Security Strategy and Plan (based on a risk assessment from all the threat and vulnerability profiles).

The summation of the threat and vulnerability profiles will enable a risk assessment to be made, which together with other factors such as usability and cost determines the appropriate level of security for an organization. As there is no such thing as perfect security, there is always a trade-off, especially between (a) security and cost, and (b) security and usability.

In table 3 part 3, the term hacker is somewhat fluid: it is often used by the press to refer to someone who seeks to penetrate a computer system to steal or corrupt data, whereas people who call themselves hackers would reject that definition and use the term to describe someone who is enthusiastic and knowledgeable about computer systems. To avoid this confusion we use the term 'white hat' and 'black hat' (from the days of black and white cowboy films). Thus a 'white hat' hacker might be employed to test a system for flaws, whilst a 'black hat' hacker is synonymous with a cracker. A script kiddie is someone who uses already established and part automated techniques in attacking a system. Their expertise is less than a hacker, but still considerably more than a normal computer use. It would be unusual to have a 'white hat' script kiddie, so without a hat colour descriptor they are taken to be on the side of the black hats.

Table 4, which is an extension of a common classification scheme [e.g. Stallings (2000)], categorizes attacks in different ways and we then show examples of how to apply these categories to different types of threat in table 5. In table 4, some active attacks target the message - these are direct attacks on CIA. Other active attacks attempt to gain some level of control of the system. Once the system is compromised in this way then messages may be attacked, but this would be an indirect attack on CIA. The stages of an active attack to gain control of a system (table 6) are adapted from Cates (2003). Steps 1 – 3 are concerned with gaining access.

Table 3. Threat Profiles

1. Asset	2. Access	3. Actor		
1.Intangible	(attack on Access Control)	1. Script kiddie		
1.1.Trust	1.Physical	2. 'Black hat' hacker		
1.2.Reputation	1.1.internal	3. Cracker		
2.Information	– Trojan, bomb	4. Malevolent user		
2.1.Sensitivity	1.2.physical	5. Malevolent sys admin		
– unrestricted	2.Network			
– restricted	2.1.server			
– controlled	2.2.client			
2.2.Classification	2.3.man–in–middle			
– customer	3.Logical			
– business				
– employee	**4. Motive**	**5. Outcome**	**attack on**	
2.3.Access	1.Accidental	Interruption	Availability	
– internal employee	2.Deliberate:	Interception	Confidentiality	
– external employee	2.1.Fun	Modification	Integrity	
– business partners	2.2.Revenge	Fabrication	Authentication	
– customers	2.3.Gain			
– 3rd parties	– Direct			
	– Indirect			

Sun Tzu also emphasizes the need to understand your vulnerabilities and weaknesses. Table 8 showing Vulnerability Profiles (or attributes) is drawn from Knight (2000), the notes show which other tables expand the entry. The severity (table 7 - with 1 highest severity) is from the point of view of the computer being attacked, not from the point of view of the resulting outcome or damage to the organization. In table 10, based on the "Map of Vulnerability Types" of Knight (2000), the left side

Table 4. Attack Classification

1. Active attack
1.1   Direct attack on CIA
Spoofing (Masquerade)
Replay
Modification of message contents
DoS
1.2   Attack on control of system
Root access - see table 6
Blind attack
1.3   Active attack identifiers
1.3.1.   Program (complete or fragment)
1.3.2.   Replicates (Yes/No)
2. Passive attack
Release of message contents
Traffic Analysis

Table 5. Some active attack threat examples

Threat	Active attack	Program	Replicates
Bacteria	DoS	yes	yes
Worm	blind attack	yes	yes
Virus	blind attack	fragment	yes
Trojan horse	root access	yes	no
Logic bomb	root access	fragment	no

Table 6. Active attack steps to gain root access

1. Reconnaissance
2. Get a shell
3. Elevate access rights
4. Make a back door
5. Execute attack
6. Erase the trail

Table 7. Severity (influence on system)

1. admin access
2. read restricted files
3. regular user access
4. spoofing
5. non-detectability
6. DoS

Table 8. Vulnerability Profiles

Fault Taxonomy – see table 9 from Aslam, Krsul and Spafford (1996)
Severity – see table 7
Authentication – see table 1
Tactics – this is subsumed into table 3.2 (Access)
Vulnerability Map – see table 10
Consequence – this can be taken to be the same as table 3.5 (Outcome)

shows attacks and weaknesses of the security policy, whilst the right hand side shows technology vulnerabilities.

Table 9. Fault Taxonomy

1.Coding faults
1.1.Synchronization errors – race conditions
1.2.Condition validation errors – buffer overflows, etc.
2.Emergent faults
2.1.Configuration errors – incorrect permissions
2.2.Environment faults – different modules interact unexpectedly

Table 10. Vulnerability Map

Security Policy	Technology	Time scale
1.Social Engineering – attack on Security Policy, e.g.	**2.Logic error** – attack on technology (see also Table 9)	Short-term
– Information fishing	2.1.bugs	
– Trojan	2.2.OS/application vulnerabilities	
	2.3.Network Protocol Design	
3.Policy oversight – weakness of Security Policy	**4.Weakness** – of technology, e.g.	Long-term
3.1.poor planning	– Weak password system	
3.2.poor control, e.g. allowing weak passwords	– Old encryption standards	

4   Failure

Since there is no such thing as perfect security, we need to consider how a system will react to a successful attack. Indeed for Schneier (2002) the most critical part of a security system is not how well it works but how well it fails. He categorizes systems as either brittle or ductile. The point being that a strong but brittle security system that catastrophically fails is worse than a weaker but ductile system that degrades gradually (i.e. fails 'gracefully').

The number of faults that cause a system to fail can be (a) single, (b) dual, or (c) > 2 simultaneous failures ('baroque' faults). If a single event causes a system to fail then this (in table 9 Fault Taxonomy) is a coding fault. In a well designed system, more common causes of failure are dual faults or baroque faults (emergent faults in table 9).

To mitigate against failure, security systems should be small-scale, redundant and compartmentalized, and avoid a Single Point Of Failure (SPOF).

5   Network Security Attacks Ontology

This is a proposal to initiate the design of an ontology for network security attacks, it is meant to be extended. An ontology in this sense is an extensible specification of a vocabulary (McGuinness 2002), i.e. an attempt to define some realm of interest for network security. Together with the terms we have introduced in the previous tables (which become the classes in our ontology), we need properties to determine the relationship between the classes. In figure 1, the circles are the classes, with the number inside referring to the appropriate table (or sub-table), the arcs are the properties.

Figure 1 is meant to be used in conjunction with the tables presented in this paper. Thus the class 'Actor' with the annotation 3.3, means refer to table 3 part 3 for a breakdown of possible actors. The review and summarization of network security classifications in sections 2 and 3 thus forms the basis for the ontology presented here.

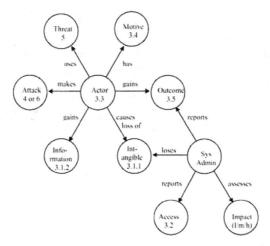

Fig. 1. Network Security conceptualization

The classes (and sub-classes) for this Network Security Attacks Ontology are: **Access**, **Actor** (Black hat hacker, Cracker, Malevolent user, Malevolent Systems Administrator, Script kiddie), **Attack** (Attack on control of system, DoS, Modification of message contents, Release of message contents, Replay, Spoofing, Traffic analysis), **Impact**, **Information**, **Intangible** (Reputation, Trust), **Motive** (Fun, Gain, Revenge), **Outcome** (Fabrication, Interception, Interruption, Modification), **Systems Administrator**, **Threat** (Bacteria, Logic bomb, Trojan horse, Virus, Worm).

The properties are: **assesses, causes loss of, gains, has, loses, makes, reports, uses**.

Some other security ontologies are an ontology for describing trust relationships for web services, see also Kagal et al (2003, 2004), Denker (2003); and an ontology describing the National Security Organization of the US. Both these ontologies can be found in the on-line list at DAML (DARPA Agent Markup Language).

6 Conclusion

We have presented a framework for network security based on proven concepts. From this review we present an ontology for network security attacks which shows the relationship between many of the standard classifications used, with the conceptualization drawn in figure 1. The conceptualization is linked to the tables reviewed and presented in this paper.

In addition we have consolidated the work done for analyzing system vulnerabilities, see table 8 which gives a starting point for drawing up vulnerability profiles, and for analyzing threat profiles, see table 3.

The next step, after getting feedback and refining this proposal, is to create a machine readable form of this ontology.

References

Alberts, Christopher and Dorofee, Audrey *OCTAVE Threat Profiles*. Carnegie Mellon Software Engineering Institute, Pittsburgh, PA 15213, USA. Available from http://www.cert.org/archive/pdf/OCTAVEthreatProfiles.pdf [accessed 12th April 2004].

Aslam; Krsul and Spafford (1996) *A Taxonomy of Security Faults*. Purdue University COAST Lab. Available from: http://www.cerias.purdue.edu/about/history/coast/coast-library.html [accessed 28th March 2004].

Cates, Sol (2003) *The Art of Hacking*. TRIPWIRE Security Industry Seminar, July 28th 2003. Available from: http://www.tripwire.com/events/archived_webcasts/ [accessed 28th March 2004].

DAML, list of ontologies from: http://www.daml.org/ontologies/keyword.html [accessed 19th August 2004].

Denker, Grit et al (2003) *Security for DAML Web Services: Annotation and Matchmaking*. Proceedings, Second International Semantic Web Conference , September 2003.

Kagal, Lalana; Finin, Tim; Joshi, Anupam (2003) *A Policy Based Approach to Security for the Semantic Web*. Proceedings, 2nd International Semantic Web Conference (ISWC2003), September 2003.

Kagal, Lalana et al (2004) *Authorization and Privacy for Semantic Web Services*. Proceedings, First International Semantic Web Services Symposium, AAAI 2004 Spring Symposium, March 2004.

Knight, Eric (2000) *Computer Vulnerabilities*. Available e.g. from: http://www.fi.upm.es/~flimon/compvuln_draft.pdf [accessed 28th March 2004].

McGuiness, Deborah (2002), Knowledge Systems Laboratory, Stanford University, *Ontologies come of age* from Fensel et al (ed.) *Spinning the Semantic Web: Bringing the World Wide Web to Its Full Potential*, MIT Press. Available from http://www.ksl.stanford.edu/people/dlm/papers/ontologies-come-of-age-mit-press-(with-citation).htm [accessed 6th June 2004].

Schneier, Bruce (2002) interviewed for the Atlantic Monthly by Mann, Charles (September 2002) *Homeland Insecurity*. Available from http://www.theatlantic.com/issues/2002/09/mann.htm [accessed 12th April 2004].

Stallings, William (2000) *Network Security Essentials: Applications and Standards*. New Jersey, Prentice-Hall Inc.

Sun Tzu (400 – 320 BC) *On the Art of War*. Translated by Lionel Giles (1910). Available from: http://www.kimsoft.com/polwar.htm [accessed 28th March 2004].

Wilson, Bill (2002) *The OCTAVE Methodology for Self-Directed Risk Assessment*. Carnegie Mellon Software Engineering Institute, Pittsburgh, PA 15213, USA. Available from http://www.fedcirc.gov/library/presentations/octave.pdf [accessed 12th April 2004].

Ensuring e-Security
Using a Private-Key Cryptographic System
Following Recursive Positional Modulo-2 Substitutions

Saurabh Dutta[1] and J.K. Mandal[2]

[1] Gomendra Multiple College, Birtamode, Jhapa, Nepal
saurabhdutta2003@yahoo.co.in
[2] Department of Computer Science and Application, University of North Bengal,
Darjeeling, West Bengal, India
jkmandal@sancharnet.in

Abstract. In this paper, a bit-level secret-key block cipher system is proposed which follows the principle of substitution. The decimal equivalent of the block under consideration is is evaluated and the modulo-2 operation is performed to check if the integral value is even or odd. Then the position of that integral value in the series of natural even or odd numbers is evaluated. The same process is repeated again with this positional value. This process is carried out recursively for a finite number of times, equal to the length of the source block. After each modulo-2 operation, 0 or 1 is pushed to the output stream in MSB-to-LSB direction depending on whether the integral value is even or odd, respectively. During decryption, bits in the target block are to be considered along LSB-to-MSB direction after which we get an integral value, the binary equivalent of which is the source block.

1 Introduction

The requirements of information security within an organization have undergone a major change in last the two decades. With the introduction of computers, the need of automated tools for protecting files and other information stored in the computer became evident. The need is even more acute for systems that can be accessed over a public telephone network, data network, or the Internet. The security of data being transmitted from source to destination over communication links via different nodes is the most important matter of concern. Someone can intercept message illegally during the process of transmission. Hence data security and communication privacy have become a fundamental requirement for such systems.

The proposed technique is a private key system with the following characteristics:

- Private Key System
- Bit-Level Implementation
- Asymmetric
- Block Cipher
- Substitution Technique
- Non-Boolean as Basic Operation
- No Alteration in Size

S. Manandhar et al. (Eds.): AACC 2004, LNCS 3285, pp. 324–332, 2004.

The proposed scheme has been presented in section 2. The implementation of the scheme on a sample plaintext is given in section 3. Section 4 shows the results of applying this technique on a set of files. One structure of the key is proposed in section 5. The analysis of the technique from different perspective is presented in section 6 and section 7 draws a conclusion.

2   The Scheme

Since the proposed technique is an asymmetric one, the schemes for encryption and decryption are being discussed separately along with relevant examples in sections 2.1 and 2.2.

2.1   The Encryption

A stream of bits is considered as the plaintext. The plaintext is divided into a finite number of blocks, each having a finite number of bits. The proposed technique is then applied for each of the blocks.

For each block $S = s_0 \, s_1 \, s_2 \, s_3 \, s_4 \, \ldots \, s_{L-1}$ of length L bits, the scheme, outlined in the pseudocode, is followed in a stepwise manner to generate the target block $T = t_0 \, t_1 \, t_2 \, t_3 \, t_4 \, \ldots \, t_{L-1}$ of the same length (L). Figure 1 is a pictorial representation of the approach of generating the target block corresponding to an 8-bit source block 01010101 using this technique.

Pseudo-code to generate a target block from a source block:

```
Evaluate: D_L, the decimal  equivalent,  corresponding  to  the
          source block S = s_0 s_1 s_2 s_3 s_4 … s_{L-1}
          Set: P = 0
          loop:
                evaluate: temp = remainder of D_{L-P} / 2
                if temp = 0
                        evaluate: D_{L-P-1} = D_{L-P} / 2
                        set: t_P = 0
                else
                If temp = 1
                        evaluate: D_{L-P-1} = (D_{L-P} + 1) / 2
                        set: t_P = 1
                        set: P = P + 1
                        If (P > (L - 1))
                        exit
          endloop
```

2.2   The Decryption

The encrypted message is to be converted into the corresponding stream of bits and then this stream is to be decomposed into a finite set of blocks, each consisting of a finite set of bits. During this process of decomposition, the way by which the source stream was decomposed during encryption is to be followed, so that corresponding to each block, the source block can be generated.

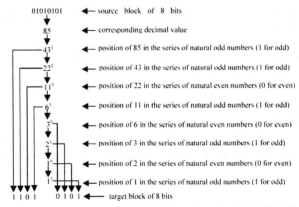

Fig. 1. Formation of target block for source block '01010101'

For each target block $T = t_0 \, t_1 \, t_2 \, t_3 \, t_4 \, \ldots \, t_{L-1}$ of length L bits, the technique is followed in a stepwise manner to generate the source block $S = s_0 \, s_1 \, s_2 \, s_3 \, s_4 \, \ldots \, s_{L-1}$ of the same length (L).

Pseudo-code to decrypt a target block:

```
Set: P = L - 1 and T = 1
loop:
      If t_p = 0
            evaluate: T = T^th even number in the series of
                         natural numbers
      else
      If t_p = 1
            evaluate: T = T^th odd number in the series of
                         natural numbers.
            set: P = P - 1
      If P < 0
            exit
endloop
evaluate: S = s_0 s_1 s_2 s_3 s_4 ... s_L-1, which is the binary
            equivalent of T
```

3 Implementation

Consider a plaintext (P) as: Local Area Network, the stream of bits corresponding to which is as follows:

S = 01001100/01101111/01100011/01100001/01101100/00100000/01000001/01110010/01100101/01100001/0010
0000/01001110/01100101/01110100/01110111/01101111/01110010/01101011.

As the technique is asymmetric one, the encryption and decryption are being discussed separately. Section 3.1 shows how the plaintext P is to be encrypted using this technique and section 3.2 describes the process of decryption.

3.1 The Process of Encryption

Decompose S into a set of 5 blocks, each of the first four being of size 32 bits and the last one being of 16 bits. During the process of decomposition, scan S along the MSB-to-LSB direction and extract required number of bits for different block. Proceeding in this way the following sub streams are generated:

S_1 = 010011000110111101100011011100001, S_2 = 01101100001000000100000101110010,
S_3 = 0110010101100001001000000001001110, S_4 = 0110010101110100011101110110111,
S_5 = 0111001001101011.

This way of decomposition is to be intimated as the key by the sender of the message to the receiver through a secret channel. More about this is discussed in section 5.

For the block S_1, corresponding to which the decimal value is $(1282368353)_{10}$, the process of encryption is as follows:

1282368353 $\rightarrow$ 641184177^1 $\rightarrow$ 320592089^1 $\rightarrow$ 160296045^1 $\rightarrow$ 80148023^1 $\rightarrow$ 40074012^1 $\rightarrow$ 20037006^0 $\rightarrow$ 100018503^0 $\rightarrow$ 5009252^1 $\rightarrow$ 2504626^0 $\rightarrow$ 1252313^0 $\rightarrow$ 626157^1 $\rightarrow$ 313079^1 $\rightarrow$ 156540^1 $\rightarrow$ 78720^0 $\rightarrow$ 39135^0 $\rightarrow$ 19568^1 $\rightarrow$ 9784^0 $\rightarrow$ 4892^0 $\rightarrow$ 2446^0 $\rightarrow$ 1223^0 $\rightarrow$ 612^1 $\rightarrow$ 306^0 $\rightarrow$ 153^0 $\rightarrow$ 77^1 $\rightarrow$ 39^1 $\rightarrow$ 20^1 $\rightarrow$ 10^0 $\rightarrow$ 5^0 $\rightarrow$ 3^1 $\rightarrow$ 2^1 $\rightarrow$ 1^0 $\rightarrow$ 1^1.

From this, the target block T_1 corresponding to S_1 is generated as: T_1 = 11111001001110010000100111001101.

Applying the similar processes, target blocks T_2, T_3, T_4 and T_5 corresponding to source blocks S_2, S_3, S_4 and S_5, respectively are generated as follows:

T_2=01110001011111011111101111001001, T_3=01001101111110110111100101011001,
T_4=10001001000100011101000101011001, T_5=1110100110110001.

Combining target blocks in the same sequence, the target stream of bits T is generated as follows:

T=11111001/00111001/00001001/11001101/01110001/01111101/11111011/11001001/010
01101/11111011/01111001/01011001/10001001/00010001/11010001/01011001/11101001/10
110001.

This stream (T) of bits, in the form of a stream of characters, is transmitted as the encrypted message (C), which will be •9°—q} √ ⌐M √yY►┬Y ⊖ ▌

3.2 The Process of Decryption

At the destination point, this encrypted message or the ciphertext C reaches and for the purpose of decryption the receiver has only the secret key. Now, by that secret key, the suggested format of which is discussed in section 5, the receiver gets the information on different block lengths. Using the secret key, all the blocks T_1, T_2, T_3, T_4 and T_5 are regenerated as follows:

T_1=11111001001110010000100111001101, T_2=01110001011111011111101111001001
T_3=01001101111110110111100101011001, T_4=10001001000100011101000101011001
T_5=1110100110110001.

Applying the process of decryption, the corresponding source blocks S_i are generated for all T_i, $1 \leq i \leq 5$.

As for example, for the target block T_1, the proceedings may be as follows:

"First odd number is 1, 1st even is 2, 2nd odd number is 3, 3rd odd number is 5, 5th even number is 10, 10th even number is 20, 20th odd number is 39, 39th odd number is 77, 77th odd number is 153, 153rd even number is 306, 306th even number is 612, 612th

odd number is 1223, 1223rd even number is 2446, 2446th even number is 4892, 4892nd even number is9784, 9784th even number is 19568, 19568th odd number is 39135, 39135th even number is 78720, 78720th even number is 156540, 156540th odd number is 313079, 313079th odd number is 626157, 626157th odd number is 1252313, 1252313th even number is 2504626, 2504626th even number is 5009252, 5009252nd odd number is 100018503, 100018503^{rd} even number is 20037006, 20037006th even number is 40074012, 40074012th odd number is 80148023, 80148023rd odd number is 160296045, 160296045^{th} odd number is 320592089, 320592089^{th} odd number is 641184177, and finally 641184177^{th} odd number is 1282368353, for which the corresponding 32-bit stream is S_1=01001100011011110110001101100001."

In this way all the source blocks of bits are regenerated and combining those blocks in the same sequence, the source stream of bits are obtained to get the source message or the plaintext.

4 Results

In this section results have been presented on the basis of the following factors:

- Computation of the encryption time, the decryption time, and the Pearsonian Chi Square value between the source and the encrypted files
- Performing the frequency distribution test
- Comparison with the RSA technique

Experimentations on the basis of these three factors are respectively shown in section 4.1, section 4.2, and section.4.3, respectively.

4.1 Result on Computing Encryption/Decryption Time and Chi Square Value

Sets of real-life .exe files are considered for the experimentation purpose. To ease the implementation, a unique block length has been considered. In this section all the results have been shown for block size of 16 bits. Table 1 shows the result for the .exe files.

Table 1. Results for .exe files in tabular form that shows the time of encryption, time for decryption and the Chi Square values of nine executable files

Source File	Encrypted files	Source Size	Encryption Time	Decryption Time	Chi Square Value
tlib.exe	a1.exe	37220	0.3297	0.2198	9.92
maker.exe	a2.exe	59398	0.6044	0.3846	17.09
unzip.exe	a3.exe	23044	0.2747	0.1648	13.95
rppo.exe	a4.exe	35425	0.3846	0.2747	9.92
prime.exe	a5.exe	37152	0.4945	0.3297	14.86
triangle.exe	a7.exe	36242	0.4396	0.2198	9.92
ping.exe	a8.exe	24576	0.2747	0.1648	17.39
netstat.exe	a9.exe	32768	0.3297	0.2198	17.39
clipbrd.exe	a10.exe	18432	0.2198	0.1648	9.92

4.2   Result on Frequency Distribution Tests

Representing the result of the frequency distribution test for all the files considered in section 4.1 being an impractical task, here in this section, for the representation purpose only one *.exe* file has been considered. In each case, the frequency distribution is pictorially represented for the source file and the encrypted file. Figure 2 shows the result, where blue lines indicate the occurrences of characters in the source file and red lines indicate the same in the corresponding encrypted file.

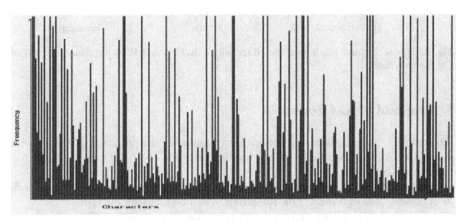

Fig. 2. A segment of frequency distribution for characters in tlib.exe and its encrypted file

4.3   Comparison with RSA Technique

For the purpose of comparing the performance of the proposed technique with the existing RSA system for a given set of ten *.cpp* files have been considered. Table 2 represents this report. The graphical comparison for files showing better results is shown in figure 3.

Table 2. Comparative results between RPMS technique and RSA technique for .cpp files for their Chi Square values and corresponding degree of freedom

Source file	Encrypted files using RPMS technique	Encrypted files using RSA technique	Chi Square value for RPMS technique	Chi Square value for RSA technique	Degrees of freedom
bricks.cpp	a1.cpp	cpp1.cpp	113381	200221	88
project.cpp	a2.cpp	cpp2.cpp	438133	197728	90
arith.cpp	a3.cpp	cpp3.cpp	143723	273982	77
start.cpp	a4.cpp	cpp4.cpp	297753	49242	88
chartcom.cpp	a5.cpp	cpp5.cpp	48929	105384	84
bitio.cpp	a6.cpp	cpp6.cpp	9101	52529	70
mainc.cpp	a7.cpp	cpp7.cpp	22485	4964	83
ttest.cpp	a8.cpp	cpp8.cpp	1794	3652	69
do.cpp	a9.cpp	cpp9.cpp	294607	655734	88
cal.cpp	a10.cpp	cpp10.cpp	143672	216498	77

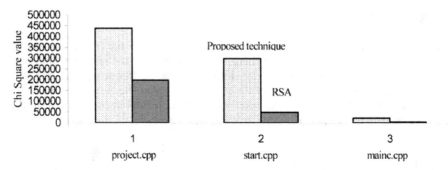

Fig. 3. Files with better result in proposed technique than existing RSA technique in terms of Chi Square values

5 Proposal of Key Format

For ensuring the successful encryption/decryption using the proposed technique with varying sizes of blocks, a 110-bit key format consisting of 11 different segments has been proposed in this section.

For the segment of the rank R, there can exist a maximum of $N = 2^{15-R}$ blocks, each of the unique size of $S = 2^{15-R}$ bits, R starting from 1 and moving till 11.

For different values of R, following segments are generated:

- Segment with R=1 formed with the first maximum 16384 blocks, each of size 16384 bits;
- Segment with R=2 formed with the first maximum 8192 blocks, each of size 8192 bits;
- Segment with R=3 formed with the next maximum 4096 blocks, each of size 4096 bits;
- Segment with R=4 formed with the next maximum 2048 blocks, each of size 2048 bits;
- Segment with R=5 formed with the next maximum 1024 blocks, each of size 1024 bits;
- Segment with R=6 formed with the next maximum 512 blocks, each of size 512 bits;
- Segment with R=7 formed with the next maximum 256 blocks, each of size 256 bits;
- Segment with R=8 formed with the next maximum 128 blocks, each of size 128 bits;
- Segment with R=9 formed with the next maximum 64 blocks, each of size 64 bits;
- Segment with R=10 formed with the next maximum 32 blocks, each of size 32 bits;
- Segment with R=11 formed with the next maximum 16 blocks, each of size 16 bits;

With such a structure, the key space becomes of 110 bits long and a file of the maximum size of around 44.74 MB can be encrypted using the proposed technique. Figure 4 presents this structure.

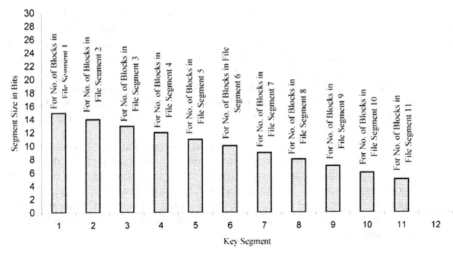

Fig. 4. 110-bit key format with 11 segments for RPMS Technique

6 Analysis

Analyzing all the results presented in section 4, following are the points obtained on the proposed technique:

- The encryption time and the decryption time vary linearly with the size of the source file.
- There exist not much difference between the encryption time and the decryption time for a file, establishing the fact that the computation complexity of each of the two processes is of not much difference.
- For non-text files, such as *.exe*, *.com*, *.dll*, and *.sys* files there is no relationship between the source file size and the Chi Square value.
- Chi Square values for text files, such as *.cpp* files are very high and vary linearly with the source file size.
- Out of the different categories of files considered here, Chi Square values for .CPP files are the highest.
- The frequency distribution test applied on the source file and the encrypted file shows that the characters are all well distributed.
- Chi Square values for this proposed technique and those for the RSA system highly compatible.

7 Conclusion

The proposed technique presented in this paper is a simple, easy-to-implement cryptographic system. The performance of the system increases with the varying block sizes because the length of the secret key increases reasonably enough, so that even the brute force may not estimate attack the secret key. If prior to the communication of the confidential message, a protocol is agreed by both the sender and the receiver regarding the maximum of block size as well as the maximum number of blocks, then accordingly a bit-level secret key, following a predefined format can be formed. It is seen that if the agreement on this possibility of varying block sizes is made, then the key of length of around 128 bits can easily be constructed. For the well accepted AES (Advanced Encryption Standard), the minimum key length is considered as 128 bits, for which it is calculated that for an as sophisticated computing device as to be able to do 10^6 encryptions per μs, it requires as impractical as 5.4×10^{18} years of average time for exhaustive key search.

The proposed technique may appears to produce a computationally non-breakable ciphertext. The result of the frequency distribution tests show the fact that the cipher characters are distributed wide enough. The fact that the source and the encrypted files are non-homogeneous is established by the Chi Square tests. It produces a highly competitive Chi Square value while comparing with the RSA system. From the angle of view of ensuring e-security or security in network, this system is supposed to be a highly appreciable system.

References

1. Dutta S., Mandal J. K., A Space-Efficient Universal Encoder for Secured Transmission, International Conference on Modelling and Simulation (MS' 2000-Egypt), Cairo, April 11-14, 2000.
2. Dutta S., Mandal J. K., A Universal Encryption Technique, Proceedings of the National Conference of Networking of Machines, Microprocessors, IT and HRD-Need of the Nation in the Next Millennium, Kalyani-741 235, Dist. Nadia, West Bengal, India, November 25-26,1999.
3. Dutta S., Mandal J. K., A Universal Bit-Level Encryption Technique, Proceedings of the 7th State Science and Technology Congress, Jadavpur University, West Bengal, India, February 28 - March 1, 2000.
4. Dutta S., Mandal J. K., Mal S., A Multiplexing Triangular Encryption Technique – A move towards enhancing security in E-Commerce, Proceedings of IT Conference (organized by Computer Association of Nepal), 26 and 27 January, 2002, BICC, Kathmandu,
5. Stallings, Williams, Cryptography and Network Security – Principal and Practices, Pearson Education
6. Bhattacharryya, D. K., Pandit, S. N., Nandi, S., A New Enciphering Scheme, Second International Workshop on Telematics, NERIST, India, May'97.
7. Reinhold, Arnold G., Diceware for Passphrase Generation and other Cryptographic Applications, downloaded from Internet at world.std.com/~reinhold/diceware.txt
8. Welsh, D. Codes and Cryptography, Oxford: Claredon Press, 1988.
9. Pieprzyk, Seberry J., "An Introduction to Computer Security", Australia: Prentice Hall of Australia, 1989.
10. Tanenbaum, A., "Computer Networks", Third Edition, Prentice Hall of India, 1999.

Author Index

Vol. 3251: H. Jin, Y. Pan, N. Xiao, J. Sun (Eds.), Grid and Cooperative Computing - GCC 2004. XXII, 1025 pages. 2004.

Vol. 3250: L.-J. (LJ) Zhang, M. Jeckle (Eds.), Web Services. X, 301 pages. 2004.

Vol. 3249: B. Buchberger, J.A. Campbell (Eds.), Artificial Intelligence and Symbolic Computation. X, 285 pages. 2004. (Subseries LNAI).

Vol. 3246: A. Apostolico, M. Melucci (Eds.), String Processing and Information Retrieval. XIV, 332 pages. 2004.

Vol. 3245: E. Suzuki, S. Arikawa (Eds.), Discovery Science. XIV, 430 pages. 2004. (Subseries LNAI).

Vol. 3244: S. Ben-David, J. Case, A. Maruoka (Eds.), Algorithmic Learning Theory. XIV, 505 pages. 2004. (Subseries LNAI).

Vol. 3243: S. Leonardi (Ed.), Algorithms and Models for the Web-Graph. VIII, 189 pages. 2004.

Vol. 3242: X. Yao, E. Burke, J.A. Lozano, J. Smith, J.J. Merelo-Guervós, J.A. Bullinaria, J. Rowe, P. Tiño, A. Kabán, H.-P. Schwefel (Eds.), Parallel Problem Solving from Nature - PPSN VIII. XX, 1185 pages. 2004.

Vol. 3241: D. Kranzlmüller, P. Kacsuk, J.J. Dongarra (Eds.), Recent Advances in Parallel Virtual Machine and Message Passing Interface. XIII, 452 pages. 2004.

Vol. 3240: I. Jonassen, J. Kim (Eds.), Algorithms in Bioinformatics. IX, 476 pages. 2004. (Subseries LNBI).

Vol. 3239: G. Nicosia, V. Cutello, P.J. Bentley, J. Timmis (Eds.), Artificial Immune Systems. XII; 444 pages. 2004.

Vol. 3238: S. Biundo, T. Frühwirth, G. Palm (Eds.), KI 2004: Advances in Artificial Intelligence. XI, 467 pages. 2004. (Subseries LNAI).

Vol. 3236: M. Núñez, Z. Maamar, F.L. Pelayo, K. Pousttchi, F. Rubio (Eds.), Applying Formal Methods: Testing, Performance, and M/E-Commerce. XI, 381 pages. 2004.

Vol. 3235: D. de Frutos-Escrig, M. Nunez (Eds.), Formal Techniques for Networked and Distributed Systems – FORTE 2004. X, 377 pages. 2004.

Vol. 3234: M.J. Egenhofer, C. Freksa, H.J. Miller (Eds.), Geographic Information Science. VIII, 345 pages. 2004.

Vol. 3232: R. Heery, L. Lyon (Eds.), Research and Advanced Technology for Digital Libraries. XV, 528 pages. 2004.

Vol. 3231: H.-A. Jacobsen (Ed.), Middleware 2004. XV, 514 pages. 2004.

Vol. 3230: J.L. Vicedo, P. Martínez-Barco, R. Muñoz, M. Saiz Noeda (Eds.), Advances in Natural Language Processing. XII, 488 pages. 2004. (Subseries LNAI).

Vol. 3229: J.J. Alferes, J. Leite (Eds.), Logics in Artificial Intelligence. XIV, 744 pages. 2004. (Subseries LNAI).

Vol. 3226: M. Bouzeghoub, C. Goble, V. Kashyap, S. Spaccapietra (Eds.), Semantics of a Networked World. XIII, 326 pages. 2004.

Vol. 3225: K. Zhang, Y. Zheng (Eds.), Information Security. XII, 442 pages. 2004.

Vol. 3224: E. Jonsson, A. Valdes, M. Almgren (Eds.), Recent Advances in Intrusion Detection. XII, 315 pages. 2004.

Vol. 3223: K. Slind, A. Bunker, G. Gopalakrishnan (Eds.), Theorem Proving in Higher Order Logics. VIII, 337 pages. 2004.

Vol. 3222: H. Jin, G.R. Gao, Z. Xu, H. Chen (Eds.), Network and Parallel Computing. XX, 694 pages. 2004.

Vol. 3221: S. Albers, T. Radzik (Eds.), Algorithms – ESA 2004. XVIII, 836 pages. 2004.

Vol. 3220: J.C. Lester, R.M. Vicari, F. Paraguaçu (Eds.), Intelligent Tutoring Systems. XXI, 920 pages. 2004.

Vol. 3219: M. Heisel, P. Liggesmeyer, S. Wittmann (Eds.), Computer Safety, Reliability, and Security. XI, 339 pages. 2004.

Vol. 3217: C. Barillot, D.R. Haynor, P. Hellier (Eds.), Medical Image Computing and Computer-Assisted Intervention – MICCAI 2004. XXXVIII, 1114 pages. 2004.

Vol. 3216: C. Barillot, D.R. Haynor, P. Hellier (Eds.), Medical Image Computing and Computer-Assisted Intervention – MICCAI 2004. XXXVIII, 930 pages. 2004.

Vol. 3215: M.G.. Negoita, R.J. Howlett, L.C. Jain (Eds.), Knowledge-Based Intelligent Information and Engineering Systems. LVII, 906 pages. 2004. (Subseries LNAI).

Vol. 3214: M.G.. Negoita, R.J. Howlett, L.C. Jain (Eds.), Knowledge-Based Intelligent Information and Engineering Systems. LVIII, 1302 pages. 2004. (Subseries LNAI).

Vol. 3213: M.G.. Negoita, R.J. Howlett, L.C. Jain (Eds.), Knowledge-Based Intelligent Information and Engineering Systems. LVIII, 1280 pages. 2004. (Subseries LNAI).

Vol. 3212: A. Campilho, M. Kamel (Eds.), Image Analysis and Recognition. XXIX, 862 pages. 2004.

Vol. 3211: A. Campilho, M. Kamel (Eds.), Image Analysis and Recognition. XXIX, 880 pages. 2004.

Vol. 3210: J. Marcinkowski, A. Tarlecki (Eds.), Computer Science Logic. XI, 520 pages. 2004.

Vol. 3209: B. Berendt, A. Hotho, D. Mladenic, M. van Someren, M. Spiliopoulou, G. Stumme (Eds.), Web Mining: From Web to Semantic Web. IX, 201 pages. 2004. (Subseries LNAI).

Vol. 3208: H.J. Ohlbach, S. Schaffert (Eds.), Principles and Practice of Semantic Web Reasoning. VII, 165 pages. 2004.

Vol. 3207: L.T. Yang, M. Guo, G.R. Gao, N.K. Jha (Eds.), Embedded and Ubiquitous Computing. XX, 1116 pages. 2004.

Vol. 3206: P. Sojka, I. Kopecek, K. Pala (Eds.), Text, Speech and Dialogue. XIII, 667 pages. 2004. (Subseries LNAI).

Vol. 3205: N. Davies, E. Mynatt, I. Siio (Eds.), UbiComp 2004: Ubiquitous Computing. XVI, 452 pages. 2004.

Vol. 3204: C.A. Peña Reyes, Coevolutionary Fuzzy Modeling. XIII, 129 pages. 2004.

Vol. 3203: J. Becker, M. Platzner, S. Vernalde (Eds.), Field Programmable Logic and Application. XXX, 1198 pages. 2004.

Vol. 3202: J.-F. Boulicaut, F. Esposito, F. Giannotti, D. Pedreschi (Eds.), Knowledge Discovery in Databases: PKDD 2004. XIX, 560 pages. 2004. (Subseries LNAI).

Vol. 3201: J.-F. Boulicaut, F. Esposito, F. Giannotti, D. Pedreschi (Eds.), Machine Learning: ECML 2004. XVIII, 580 pages. 2004. (Subseries LNAI).

Vol. 3251: H. Jin, Y. Pan, N. Xiao, J. Sun (Eds.), Grid and Cooperative Computing - GCC 2004. XXII, 1025 pages. 2004.

Vol. 3250: L.-J. (LJ) Zhang, M. Jeckle (Eds.), Web Services. X, 301 pages. 2004.

Vol. 3249: B. Buchberger, J.A. Campbell (Eds.), Artificial Intelligence and Symbolic Computation. X, 285 pages. 2004. (Subseries LNAI).

Vol. 3246: A. Apostolico, M. Melucci (Eds.), String Processing and Information Retrieval. XIV, 332 pages. 2004.

Vol. 3245: E. Suzuki, S. Arikawa (Eds.), Discovery Science. XIV, 430 pages. 2004. (Subseries LNAI).

Vol. 3244: S. Ben-David, J. Case, A. Maruoka (Eds.), Algorithmic Learning Theory. XIV, 505 pages. 2004. (Subseries LNAI).

Vol. 3243: S. Leonardi (Ed.), Algorithms and Models for the Web-Graph. VIII, 189 pages. 2004.

Vol. 3242: X. Yao, E. Burke, J.A. Lozano, J. Smith, J.J. Merelo-Guervós, J.A. Bullinaria, J. Rowe, P. Tiño, A. Kabán, H.-P. Schwefel (Eds.), Parallel Problem Solving from Nature - PPSN VIII. XX, 1185 pages. 2004.

Vol. 3241: D. Kranzlmüller, P. Kacsuk, J.J. Dongarra (Eds.), Recent Advances in Parallel Virtual Machine and Message Passing Interface. XIII, 452 pages. 2004.

Vol. 3240: I. Jonassen, J. Kim (Eds.), Algorithms in Bioinformatics. IX, 476 pages. 2004. (Subseries LNBI).

Vol. 3239: G. Nicosia, V. Cutello, P.J. Bentley, J. Timmis (Eds.), Artificial Immune Systems. XII, 444 pages. 2004.

Vol. 3238: S. Biundo, T. Frühwirth, G. Palm (Eds.), KI 2004: Advances in Artificial Intelligence. XI, 467 pages. 2004. (Subseries LNAI).

Vol. 3236: M. Núñez, Z. Maamar, F.L. Pelayo, K. Pousttchi, F. Rubio (Eds.), Applying Formal Methods: Testing, Performance, and M/E-Commerce. XI, 381 pages. 2004.

Vol. 3235: D. de Frutos-Escrig, M. Nunez (Eds.), Formal Techniques for Networked and Distributed Systems - FORTE 2004. X, 377 pages. 2004.

Vol. 3234: M.J. Egenhofer, C. Freksa, H.J. Miller (Eds.), Geographic Information Science. VIII, 345 pages. 2004.

Vol. 3232: R. Heery, L. Lyon (Eds.), Research and Advanced Technology for Digital Libraries. XV, 528 pages. 2004.

Vol. 3231: H.-A. Jacobsen (Ed.), Middleware 2004. XV, 514 pages. 2004.

Vol. 3230: J.L. Vicedo, P. Martínez-Barco, R. Muñoz, M. Saiz Noeda (Eds.), Advances in Natural Language Processing. XII, 488 pages. 2004. (Subseries LNAI).

Vol. 3229: J.J. Alferes, J. Leite (Eds.), Logics in Artificial Intelligence. XIV, 744 pages. 2004. (Subseries LNAI).

Vol. 3226: M. Bouzeghoub, C. Goble, V. Kashyap, S. Spaccapietra (Eds.), Semantics of a Networked World. XIII, 326 pages. 2004.

Vol. 3225: K. Zhang, Y. Zheng (Eds.), Information Security. XII, 442 pages. 2004.

Vol. 3224: E. Jonsson, A. Valdes, M. Almgren (Eds.), Recent Advances in Intrusion Detection. XII, 315 pages. 2004.

Vol. 3223: K. Slind, A. Bunker, G. Gopalakrishnan (Eds.), Theorem Proving in Higher Order Logics. VIII, 337 pages. 2004.

Vol. 3222: H. Jin, G.R. Gao, Z. Xu, H. Chen (Eds.), Network and Parallel Computing. XX, 694 pages. 2004.

Vol. 3221: S. Albers, T. Radzik (Eds.), Algorithms – ESA 2004. XVIII, 836 pages. 2004.

Vol. 3220: J.C. Lester, R.M. Vicari, F. Paraguaçu (Eds.), Intelligent Tutoring Systems. XXI, 920 pages. 2004.

Vol. 3219: M. Heisel, P. Liggesmeyer, S. Wittmann (Eds.), Computer Safety, Reliability, and Security. XI, 339 pages. 2004.

Vol. 3217: C. Barillot, D.R. Haynor, P. Hellier (Eds.), Medical Image Computing and Computer-Assisted Intervention – MICCAI 2004. XXXVIII, 1114 pages. 2004.

Vol. 3216: C. Barillot, D.R. Haynor, P. Hellier (Eds.), Medical Image Computing and Computer-Assisted Intervention – MICCAI 2004. XXXVIII, 930 pages. 2004.

Vol. 3215: M.G. Negoita, R.J. Howlett, L.C. Jain (Eds.), Knowledge-Based Intelligent Information and Engineering Systems. LVII, 906 pages. 2004. (Subseries LNAI).

Vol. 3214: M.G.. Negoita, R.J. Howlett, L.C. Jain (Eds.), Knowledge-Based Intelligent Information and Engineering Systems. LVIII, 1302 pages. 2004. (Subseries LNAI).

Vol. 3213: M.G.. Negoita, R.J. Howlett, L.C. Jain (Eds.), Knowledge-Based Intelligent Information and Engineering Systems. LVIII, 1280 pages. 2004. (Subseries LNAI).

Vol. 3212: A. Campilho, M. Kamel (Eds.), Image Analysis and Recognition. XXIX, 862 pages. 2004.

Vol. 3211: A. Campilho, M. Kamel (Eds.), Image Analysis and Recognition. XXIX, 880 pages. 2004.

Vol. 3210: J. Marcinkowski, A. Tarlecki (Eds.), Computer Science Logic. XI, 520 pages. 2004.

Vol. 3209: B. Berendt, A. Hotho, D. Mladenic, M. van Someren, M. Spiliopoulou, G. Stumme (Eds.), Web Mining: From Web to Semantic Web. IX, 201 pages. 2004. (Subseries LNAI).

Vol. 3208: H.J. Ohlbach, S. Schaffert (Eds.), Principles and Practice of Semantic Web Reasoning. VII, 165 pages. 2004.

Vol. 3207: L.T. Yang, M. Guo, G.R. Gao, N.K. Jha (Eds.), Embedded and Ubiquitous Computing. XX, 1116 pages. 2004.

Vol. 3206: P. Sojka, I. Kopecek, K. Pala (Eds.), Text, Speech and Dialogue. XIII, 667 pages. 2004. (Subseries LNAI).

Vol. 3205: N. Davies, E. Mynatt, I. Siio (Eds.), UbiComp 2004: Ubiquitous Computing. XVI, 452 pages. 2004.

Vol. 3204: C.A. Peña Reyes, Coevolutionary Fuzzy Modeling. XIII, 129 pages. 2004.

Vol. 3203: J. Becker, M. Platzner, S. Vernalde (Eds.), Field Programmable Logic and Application. XXX, 1198 pages. 2004.

Vol. 3202: J.-F. Boulicaut, F. Esposito, F. Giannotti, D. Pedreschi (Eds.), Knowledge Discovery in Databases: PKDD 2004. XIX, 560 pages. 2004. (Subseries LNAI).

Vol. 3201: J.-F. Boulicaut, F. Esposito, F. Giannotti, D. Pedreschi (Eds.), Machine Learning: ECML 2004. XVIII, 580 pages. 2004. (Subseries LNAI).